Economic Growth Amidst Social and Environmental Uncertainty

Oytun Meçik
Eskisehir Osmangazi University, Turkey

IGI Global
Scientific Publishing
Publishing Tomorrow's Research Today

Vice President of Editorial	Melissa Wagner
Director of Acquisitions	Mikaela Felty
Director of Book Development	Jocelynn Hessler
Production Manager	Mike Brehm
Cover Design	Jose Rosado

Published in the United States of America by
IGI Global Scientific Publishing
701 East Chocolate Avenue
Hershey, PA, 17033, USA
Tel: 717-533-8845 | Fax: 717-533-7115
Website: https://www.igi-global.com E-mail: cust@igi-global.com

Library of Congress Cataloging-in-Publication Data

Names: Meçik, Oytun editor
http://id.loc.gov/authorities/names/no2022045100
http://id.loc.gov/rwo/agents/no2022045100
Title: Economic growth amidst social and environmental uncertainty / edited by: Oytun Meçik.
Description: Hershey, PA : IGI Global Scientific Publishing, [2026] | Includes bibliographical references and index. | Summary: "This book explores the intricate relationship between economic inequality and the multifaceted crises shaping our world. It seeks to uncover how these crises interact with and exacerbate preexisting inequalities, while also examining how such disparities can, in turn, amplify the effects of crises"-- Provided by publisher.
Identifiers: LCCN 2025004351 (print) | LCCN 2025004352 (ebook) | ISBN 9798337315294 hardcover | ISBN 9798337315300 paperback | ISBN 9798337315317 ebook
Subjects: LCSH: Income distribution http://id.loc.gov/authorities/subjects/sh85064765 | Financial crises http://id.loc.gov/authorities/subjects/sh89002668 | Social change http://id.loc.gov/authorities/subjects/sh85123918
Classification: LCC HC79.I5 E225 2025 (print) | LCC HC79.I5 (ebook) | DDC 339.2--dc23/eng/20250530
LC record available at https://lccn.loc.gov/2025004351
LC ebook record available at https://lccn.loc.gov/2025004352

British Cataloguing in Publication Data
A Cataloguing in Publication record for this book is available from the British Library.

Editorial Advisory Board

Table of Contents

Detailed Table of Contents

This chapter examines the urgent need to combine scientifically defined environmental limits ('safe limits') with normative principles of justice ('just limits') to form a coherent governance model. Methodologically, the study combines a conceptual analysis of ethical, political science, and interdisciplinary justice models with an empirical case study analysis. Three contrasting country cases—Bangladesh, South Africa, and Germany—are selected according to the 'most different' principle and analyzed using quantitative indicators (e.g., emissions data, damage distribution) and qualitative interviews. The results show that without social support, safe limits deepen existing inequalities. Only through just limits—for example, through the fair allocation of CO_2 budgets, participatory decision-making processes, and targeted technology transfer—can ecological protection and social resilience be combined. On this basis, the article develops an integrative governance model that systematically anchors equity criteria.

The aim of this chapter is primarily to examine the balance between environmental pollution, global policy measures and regional inequalities and to explain alternative ways of achieving this balance. This chapter analyses the conflicts between the development needs and environmental obligations of developing countries in the realisation of sustainable development goals and the tendency of developed countries to avoid responsibility in climate policies. In addition, this chapter analyses the environmental impact of countries through indicators with various measurement criteria for the fair distribution of environmental damage. The difference in energy consumption of countries from past to present is analysed in terms of fossil fuel-based energy consumption per capita, carbon dioxide per capita, how countries use their environmental resources, biological capacity and ecological footprints, and the impact of heavy industries such as iron and steel, which cause intense carbon emissions, on global emissions.

It is stated that environmental pollution increases after countries use primary energy sources and as a result, global climate change is experienced. In order to prevent global climate change, it is important to reduce the use of energy sources that cause environmental pollution. Therefore, increasing the use of technology and renewable energy sources is seen as the most important factor in reducing environmental pollution. It is important for countries to increase their investments in technology and renewable energy sources. However, it should be noted that renewable energy sources can also lead to environmental pollution if not used effectively.

Environmental problems stand out as one of the biggest issues that countries have been focusing on recently. Along with deforestation, the destruction of the environment is happening more rapidly. In this study, the impact of deforestation on the EKC (Environmental Kuznets Curve) hypothesis is examined. This study employs PMG (Pooled Mean Group Estimation) analysis using data on deforestation, population, GDP, agricultural land, and gross production index number for the period between 2001 and 2022. When the results were estimated with the panel ARDL estimator PMG, a 1% increase in per capita income decreases deforestation by approximately 3.63%. A 1% increase in population increased deforestation by about 0.4% and a 1% increase in agricultural land decreased deforestation by about 0.09%. The study concluded that the EKC is valid for G20 countries.

This study investigates the complex interplay between economic inequalities and the intertwined social, political, and environmental crises within BRICS countries by empirically analyzing panel data from five nations to assess how women's income, political stability, and CO2 emissions influence wealth concentration among the top 10 percent, revealing through rigorous application of pooled OLS, random effects, and fixed effects models that environmental degradation measured by CO_2 emissions is the sole significant and robust predictor positively associated with increased wealth disparity, while social and political variables show no statistically significant effects, thereby underscoring the urgent need for integrated policy frameworks in BRICS that prioritize sustainable environmental reforms alongside inclusive socio-political strategies to effectively mitigate growing economic inequalities and promote equitable and sustainable development in these rapidly evolving economies.

This chapter explores BRICS+ as a transformative coalition aiming to reduce global economic inequality through South-South cooperation and financial innovation. Drawing on world-systems theory, it examines how instruments like the New Development Bank, the Contingent Reserve Arrangement, and de-dollarization strategies challenge the Western-dominated financial order. Empirical case studies from Brazil, South Africa, Ethiopia, Egypt, Nigeria, and India illustrate how BRICS+ projects support inclusive infrastructure, renewable energy, and digital finance. The analysis also addresses limitations, including elite capture, transparency gaps, and asymmetric power dynamics—particularly China's dominant role. While BRICS+ does not fully replace the Bretton Woods system, it offers a pragmatic framework for institutional multipolarity and developmental sovereignty. The chapter concludes that BRICS+ has the potential to restructure core-periphery relations if governance reforms strengthen its internal coherence and commitment to equitable development.

Preface

Economic inequality remains one of the most enduring and complex challenges of our time. While disparities in income, wealth, and opportunity have long defined the trajectory of societies, the convergence of multiple crises in recent decades has intensified their impacts. Financial downturns, social upheavals, political instability, and environmental degradation have not only disrupted economies but also deepened existing divisions, leaving vulnerable groups disproportionately affected. Against this backdrop of uncertainty, it becomes essential to examine how crises and inequalities interact, evolve, and shape the prospects for more equitable and resilient societies.

This book, *Economic Growth Amidst Social and Environmental Uncertainty*, was conceived to address this urgent need. It explores the intricate relationship between systemic inequalities and the crises that amplify them, while also asking how inequality itself may exacerbate the effects of crises. By doing so, the volume seeks to bridge critical gaps in scholarship and practice, moving beyond fragmented analyses toward a holistic understanding of these interwoven dynamics.

The chapters in this volume bring together an interdisciplinary group of scholars and practitioners from economics, sociology, political science, and environmental studies. Their contributions provide both theoretical and empirical insights, addressing questions such as: How do financial crises reshape the distribution of wealth and opportunity? In what ways do social upheavals, such as pandemics or mass migration, widen disparities in access to essential resources? How does political instability interact with inequality to produce cycles of unrest? And how do environmental crises, particularly climate change, disproportionately affect those already at the margins of society?

CHAPTER OVERVIEW

Chapter 1 sets the tone of the book by addressing the urgent nexus between climate change, environmental thresholds, and justice. By examining the concept of "safe limits" in conjunction with "just limits," the chapter demonstrates that ecological sustainability cannot be achieved without equity and social legitimacy. Drawing on cases from Bangladesh, South Africa, and Germany, the authors highlight how unequal burdens of climate adaptation and mitigation risk deepening global inequalities if left unaddressed. Through this interdisciplinary approach, the chapter offers an integrative governance model that places justice at the heart of climate policy, underscoring that fairness and resilience must be pursued together.

Chapter 2 turns to the global policy arena, interrogating the balance between industrial emissions, sustainable development, and regional inequalities. It critically assesses the conflicting priorities of developing nations striving for growth and developed nations reluctant to bear responsibility for climate action. Through a detailed analysis of energy consumption, ecological footprints, and emissions-intensive industries, the chapter illustrates how uneven environmental obligations perpetuate disparities between regions. It emphasizes the need for fairer global frameworks that reconcile development needs with ecological stewardship, pointing to more equitable pathways for sustainability.

Chapter 3 focuses on the role of technology and renewable energy in addressing climate change, positioning them as both critical tools and potential risks if mismanaged. The chapter argues that investments in renewable energy and technological innovation are indispensable for reducing reliance on polluting energy sources, yet it cautions that these solutions must be implemented responsibly to avoid unintended consequences. In doing so, it highlights the double-edged nature of technology in environmental governance, while making a strong case for coordinated global action to ensure renewable energy serves as a true driver of sustainable transformation.

Chapter 4 engages with the Environmental Kuznets Curve hypothesis through the lens of deforestation in G20 countries. By applying panel data and econometric analysis, the chapter reveals nuanced relationships between income growth, population pressures, agricultural expansion, and environmental degradation. The findings confirm the EKC hypothesis in the context of deforestation, suggesting that higher incomes may eventually reduce pressures on forests, though only under specific conditions. This contribution situates deforestation within broader debates on economic growth and environmental sustainability, providing valuable evidence for policymakers navigating trade-offs between prosperity and conservation.

Chapter 5 directs attention to the BRICS countries, examining how economic inequality interacts with social, political, and environmental crises. Using robust statistical models, the study finds that environmental degradation—measured through CO_2 emissions—emerges as the most consistent driver of widening inequality, while social and political variables appear less predictive. This chapter challenges conventional policy assumptions by emphasizing the central role of environmental sustainability in mitigating inequality. It calls for integrated policy frameworks that address environmental reform alongside inclusive economic and political strategies, making it a crucial intervention for emerging economies under strain.

Chapter 6 extends this discussion by analyzing BRICS+ as a potential catalyst for reducing global inequality through alternative governance and financial structures. Drawing on world-systems theory, the chapter explores how South-South cooperation, development banking, and de-dollarization could reshape the global financial order. Through diverse case studies, it demonstrates how BRICS+ initiatives can promote infrastructure development, renewable energy, and digital inclusion, while also acknowledging risks such as elite capture and asymmetric power dynamics. The chapter ultimately positions BRICS+ as a pragmatic yet imperfect framework for rebalancing international economic relations, underscoring its potential to foster more equitable development if internal reforms succeed.

Chapter 7 shifts focus to the micro-level, investigating how demographic factors shape financial risk tolerance among investors in Türkiye during the COVID-19 pandemic. By analyzing survey data from individual investors, the study uncovers significant differences based on age, experience, and investment periods, while finding little variation across other demographic categories. These findings not only enrich our understanding of financial behavior in times of crisis but also provide actionable insights for portfolio managers, policymakers, and institutions seeking to stabilize investment environments under conditions of uncertainty.

Chapter 8 explores patterns of innovation convergence across countries by analyzing the Global Innovation Index using the club convergence methodology. The chapter reveals that innovation trajectories are far from uniform, with countries clustering into distinct "innovation clubs" that reflect persistent heterogeneity in economic structures and technological capabilities. These findings highlight the structural divides that persist even among nations with similar income levels, underscoring that innovation-driven growth is neither evenly distributed nor universally accessible. By illuminating these disparities, the chapter contributes to a deeper understanding of how global innovation dynamics intersect with inequality.

Chapter 9 concludes the volume by examining the role of technology in corporate social responsibility (CSR) practices within India's banking sector. By comparing public, private, and foreign banks, the study highlights how digital tools can enhance CSR initiatives by improving transparency and extending economic inclusion, even amidst crisis conditions. At the same time, it cautions that digital divides and organizational constraints limit the full realization of these benefits. This chapter demonstrates the potential of technology-enabled CSR to promote sustainable growth, while calling for inclusive policies and collaborative frameworks that ensure such practices serve broader societal goals.

The strength of this book lies in its diversity of perspectives and cases. By presenting analyses from across regions and contexts, it uncovers universal patterns while also highlighting localized realities. This dual lens allows readers to identify both broad principles and context-specific solutions, offering lessons applicable to policymakers, institutions, and communities alike. A key emphasis of the book is intersectionality: the recognition that gender, race, ethnicity, and geography intersect to shape the lived experiences of inequality during crises. By foregrounding these dimensions, the volume enriches our collective understanding and calls for more inclusive approaches to policy and practice.

Importantly, the book is not limited to diagnosis but is equally committed to exploring solutions. The chapters identify opportunities for resilience, adaptation, and reform, showcasing innovative frameworks, successful interventions, and policy recommendations. They emphasize the necessity of rethinking governance systems, strengthening international cooperation, and leveraging technology responsibly, all while centering equity as a guiding principle.

This work is intended for a broad audience—scholars and students seeking comprehensive analyses, policymakers and international organizations aiming to design effective strategies, NGOs and advocacy groups working on social and environmental justice, and private sector leaders striving to align economic growth with inclusive development. It also serves as a resource for the informed public, providing evidence-based perspectives on some of the most pressing challenges of the twenty-first century.

As editor, my hope is that this volume will not only deepen our understanding of the intertwined crises of inequality but also inspire collaborative, forward-looking solutions. In an era marked by volatility and uncertainty, reimagining economic systems and governance structures is not simply desirable—it is imperative. I extend my gratitude to the contributors whose rigorous research and innovative insights form the heart of this book, and to the readers who will carry forward these conversations into practice.

Together, let us work toward a future where economic growth is not pursued at the expense of equity and resilience but instead serves as a foundation for inclusive, sustainable, and just societies.

Editor

Oytun Meçik
Eskişehir Osmangazi University, Turkey

Chapter 1
Justice and Climate Change:
An Interdisciplinary Perspective on Global Environmental Limits

Silvio Andrae
https://orcid.org/0000-0002-8586-7812
Independent Researcher, Germany

ABSTRACT

This chapter examines the urgent need to combine scientifically defined environmental limits ('safe limits') with normative principles of justice ('just limits') to form a coherent governance model. Methodologically, the study combines a conceptual analysis of ethical, political science, and interdisciplinary justice models with an empirical case study analysis. Three contrasting country cases—Bangladesh, South Africa, and Germany—are selected according to the 'most different' principle and analyzed using quantitative indicators (e.g., emissions data, damage distribution) and qualitative interviews. The results show that without social support, safe limits deepen existing inequalities. Only through just limits—for example, through the fair allocation of CO_2 budgets, participatory decision-making processes, and targeted technology transfer—can ecological protection and social resilience be combined. On this basis, the article develops an integrative governance model that systematically anchors equity criteria.

1. INTRODUCTION

Climate change is not a uniform phenomenon, but one that is starkly unequal in its origins. The lion's share of increased greenhouse gas emissions can be traced

DOI: 10.4018/979-8-3373-1529-4.ch001

back to the wealthiest ten percent of the world's population, who are responsible for two-thirds of global warming since 1990. This group, the wealthiest one percent, has contributed 26 times more to century heat waves than the global average. The emissions of the wealthiest 10% in China and the United States, which together account for nearly half of global carbon pollution, have led to a two- to threefold increase in heat extremes.

While the harmful effects of climate change are felt globally, they disproportionately affect the poor and less powerful. Achieving climate justice necessitates strategies that not only reduce emissions but also safeguard the most vulnerable populations from the impacts of climate change. However, it's crucial to note that all strategies to reduce emissions can inadvertently alter social, economic, political, and ecological processes, potentially leading to injustices in climate change mitigation.

In the public and scientific debate on climate change, the urgency of the climate crisis is increasingly coming to the fore. While scientific research in recent decades has impressively demonstrated that global warming is artificial and will have far-reaching consequences for ecosystems, extreme weather events, and sea level rise, it often remains unclear how the resulting burdens and opportunities can be distributed in a socially just manner (Otto, 2025). The tension between 'safe limits' and 'just limits' forms the core of our investigation. The central question is: How can global environmental limits be set and implemented without further exacerbating social imbalances? The urgency of this problem is underscored by the fact that it is precisely the most vulnerable population groups in poorer regions that suffer most from the consequences of the climate crisis. The wealthy and industrialized countries of the Global North bear the most significant historical responsibility for the climate crisis and continue to drive it forward today with their overwhelmingly high energy and resource consumption. A 2020 study concludes that the Global North, as a whole, is responsible for 92% of excess greenhouse gas emissions (those above 350 ppm), while the Global South is responsible for only 8%. Germany ranks fourth on the list of historical emissions despite having only about 1% of the world's population (84 million people) living there today.

Furthermore, resource consumption in the Global North is about four times higher than the safe per capita limit for the planet, while the Global South is well below its share of the budget. Not to mention that a large part of the natural resources used in the Global North have been appropriated and originate from the Global South (Hickel, 2020). Without explicit consideration of equity aspects, there is a risk not only of increasing global inequality but also of losing acceptance for necessary climate protection measures, which could jeopardize the achievement of international climate targets.

Nevertheless, it is worth noting that a significant number of citizens remain unaware of the issue of 'climate justice.' In a global survey of 5,627 adults in 11 countries across the Global North and South, most participants (66.2%) reported never having heard of climate justice (Ogunbode et al., 2024; similarly, Carman et al., 2025). Nevertheless, agreement with climate justice beliefs is widespread (e.g., recognition of the disproportionate impact of climate change on poor people and the fundamental role of capitalism and colonialism in the climate crisis).

1.1 Research Gaps

Despite intense theoretical debate on planetary boundaries (safe limits) and climate-just distribution (just limits), the empirical evidence base for their integrated political implementation has been remarkably limited to date—especially in the context of the Global South. Although numerous studies examine either ecological thresholds (e.g., national CO_2 budgets, water stress indicators) or aspects of social justice (e.g., access to energy, adaptation financing), there is a lack of systematic analyses that consider both dimensions as equally important and intricately interlinked. This interconnectedness is particularly relevant to policy implementation, i.e., the question of how global or national environmental goals are translated into concrete policies—whether in spatial planning, resource allocation, infrastructure development, or climate policy transfer systems. In the scientific literature, policy instruments such as climate funds, technology transfers, or emissions-based tax reforms are usually examined in isolation in terms of their ecological effectiveness or economic efficiency. However, there is little research into their distributional effects within specific governance contexts.

It is also worth noting that existing monitoring and evaluation systems are typically not designed to report on both environmental and equity metrics simultaneously. Although emissions inventories and SDG indicators exist, there is no systematic link between them, for example, in the form of equity-adjusted environmental indicators that show whether climate measures also strengthen the social resilience of disadvantaged groups. The current state of research presents an obstacle to the evidence-based assessment of climate policy and also promotes a political decoupling between environmental goals and social justice. An example of this development is the implementation of large-scale technology projects (e.g., hydropower, reforestation, carbon markets) in marginalized regions without participatory anchoring.

Against this backdrop, the study pursues two main objectives: First, to develop an integrative concept that combines scientific knowledge about planetary boundaries (PB) with normative principles of justice. The concept is rooted in the paradigm of socio-ecological transition theory (Biely & Chakori, 2025). Second, it aims to empirically examine the social upheavals that arise when safe limits are applied without the simultaneous implementation of just limits. It gives rise to four key questions:

1. How do safe limits and just limits differ, and how can they be integrated?
2. How can the equity aspects of global environmental assessments be improved through a framework for Earth system justice?
3. What empirical evidence exists for the unequal impact of climate change-related damage on different social groups?
4. What could a governance model look like that equally anchors ecological sustainability and social justice?

1.2 Methodological Approach

To answer these questions systematically, we combine two methodological approaches: First, we conduct an in-depth examination of existing justice and governance models (e.g., Rawls' difference principle, Sen's capability approach, and international climate law frameworks). To this end, we review the relevant literature and identify key normative criteria relevant to Just Limits. We also conduct empirical case study analysis. Based on globally available data sets on climate-related damage (e.g., EM-DAT, World Risk Index) and technological distribution models, we select three exemplary cases (extreme weather events in developing countries, technology transfer, financial compensation, and carbon outsourcing). Using quantitative evaluations (descriptive statistics, distribution indicators) and qualitative interviews with local actors, we identify disparities in the impact and effectiveness of existing climate programs.

The chapter is divided into eight sections: Section 2 provides the conceptual foundations for safe limits and climate justice. Section 3 discusses theoretical approaches from ethics, political science, and interdisciplinary models for linking environmental and justice issues. Section 4 presents the methodology of concept analysis, data sources, and case study selection. Section 5 summarizes safe and just limits, highlights measurement tools, and justice criteria, and identifies gaps in frameworks such as the UNFCCC and the Paris Agreement. Section 6 presents the three case studies and empirical findings on disparities in damage distribution and the effectiveness of established climate protection mechanisms. Section 7 develops an integrative governance model based on these findings, incorporating equity criteria, local needs orientation, and fair financing mechanisms. This model not only provides a roadmap for change but also empowers each individual to contribute to a more just and sustainable future. Section 8 draws conclusions, reflects on political resistance and opportunities, and identifies further research approaches.

2. BASIC TERMINOLOGY

2.1 Panetary Boundaries and Safe Limits

The theory of planetary boundaries (PB) was developed in the early 2000s by an interdisciplinary network of scientists led by Johan Rockström and Will Steffen (Rockström et al., 2009; Richardson et al., 2023; Steffen et al., 2015). It identifies nine key biophysical systems and processes—including global climate change, the nitrogen and phosphorus cycles, land use change, and the freshwater system—which, if exceeded, could cause the Earth to lose its stable Holocene equilibrium. The nine PBs represent the essential functions that are important for regulating the Earth system. In six cases, the safe operating space has already been exceeded (Rockström et al., 2024b). According to the latest research findings of the Earth Commission (Rockström et al., 2023), it is crucial to analyze ecological limits ('safe limits') and social minimum standards ('just limits') in an integrative approach. The study, published in the journal Nature, quantifies for the first time the safe and just boundaries for key biophysical systems, including climate, biodiversity, freshwater, and pollution. The analysis reveals that many of the examined boundaries have already been exceeded, indicating significant risks to the stability of the Earth system and the livelihoods of humanity. Particularly worrying is the fact that the integration of equity dimensions—such as minimizing existential damage to people worldwide—requires significantly stricter limits. Figure 1 illustrates this integrative concept: a safe and just corridor lies between ecological limits and social minimum standards. Exceeding the outer limits threatens ecological stability, while falling below the inner limits has serious social consequences. The study's findings emphasize that humanity is already outside many safe and just boundaries, and urgently needs just transformations to avoid irreversible tipping points and secure a stable planet for future generations in the long term.

Figure 1. Safe and just Earth boundaries

Figure 1: Safe and just Earth boundaries

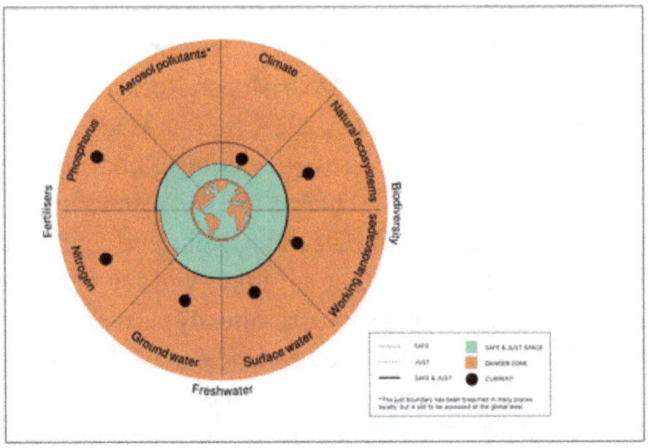

Source: Earth Commission

However, the PB concept has been used primarily so far to illustrate currently unsustainable environmental conditions. Vuuren et al. (2025) use the Integrated Model to Assess the Global Environment to simulate future developments (until 2050) for eight of the nine planetary boundaries under alternative scenarios with and without ambitious environmental measures. The results of the study suggest that with substantial political intervention, there is hope that all planetary boundaries except for the ozone layer can be preserved by 2050.

A 'safe limit' defines the threshold within each system beyond which there is a risk of triggering irreversible tipping points, such as the potentially catastrophic melting of the West Antarctic ice sheet or the collapse of the Amazon rainforest (Follingstad, 2023).

'This cause-and-effect injustice is widely acknowledged, yet a quantification of how emissions inequality translates into unequal accountability for the resulting global temperature levels and extreme climate events is missing. This translation should account for the individual warming contributions of emissions of non-CO_2 GHGs, such as methane (CH4), given their major role in recent warming.' (Schöngart et al., 2025, p.1)

These safe limits are determined using quantitative indicators. For example, in the case of climate change, the concentration of CO_2 in the atmosphere is used as a proxy; here, a critical value of 350 ppm (parts per million) is referenced. Exceeding this value increases the risk that natural feedback mechanisms, such as the release of methane from thawing permafrost soils, will reinforce themselves and lead to uncontrollable temperature rises. The gravity of the situation is similar in the area of biodiversity, where a loss of more than 10% of species is considered a critical threshold or tipping point, with potentially devastating consequences.

'Safe limits' serve as a scientific compass for environmental policy and sustainable economic activity, setting national CO_2 budgets, serving as a reference for emissions trading systems, and being incorporated into global climate models. However, they are not legally binding limits but rather guidelines: their effectiveness depends on how consistently policymakers and economic actors translate them into legislation, compliance mechanisms, and financial incentive systems. A key problem here is the international dimension. While some countries are reducing their emissions, others are continuing to increase them so that the global system as a whole is heading into dangerous territory.

2.2 Concepts of Climate Justice

'Climate justice' is a collective term for normative approaches that focus on the social, political, and ethical dimensions of climate change. At its core, it means that the consequences and costs of climate change interventions must not be borne solely by marginalized or poorer population groups. For scientists, students, and practitioners working at the intersection of climate change and social justice, a solid understanding of climate justice is crucial, as is a commitment to fair and inclusive solutions. In a recent publication, the concept of PB was expanded to include social indicators. It shows that societies do not perform well in this regard either (Rockström et al., 2023). The roots of this concept lie in the environmental justice movement of the 1980s and were later enriched by postcolonial and feminist theories (Sarang & Prabhakar, 2023).

Numerous authors have outlined central principles of justice. For example, John Rawls' difference principle stipulates that social and ecological inequalities should be tolerated only if they bring the most significant possible benefit to the worst-off individuals. This principle is important in the context of climate justice as it underscores the need to consider the most vulnerable populations when addressing climate change. Intersectional factors highly structure vulnerability to climate change. The impacts of climate-related extreme events, resource scarcity, or adaptation policies are not evenly distributed but overlap with social divisions such as gender, age, ethnicity, socioeconomic status, or indigenous identity (see Sections 6 and 8 for further details).

Rawls' difference principle, a structure-oriented distribution criterion, is a key concept in the realm of climate justice. It deems institutional rules fair if they systematically benefit those who are least advantaged. This principle can be applied with relative clarity to distribution issues in the climate regime, such as CO_2

budgeting, financing adaptation measures, and technology transfer. According to Amartya Sen, equality is not about resource possession, but about the ability to use them effectively (Sen, 1999). The capability approach, as he terms it, focuses on individual capabilities. In the context of climate justice, this approach has practical implications. It's not enough to provide financial resources and technologies. What's crucial is whether people can use them to secure their livelihoods, protect their health, or maintain their economic independence. This approach is relevant to climate justice as it highlights the importance of not just providing resources, but also ensuring that individuals have the capability to make use of these resources.

Rawls focuses on structural minimum standards, while Sen focuses on individual opportunities for action. Combining both approaches makes it possible to link fair, institutional allocation (Rawls) with real empowerment and resilience (Sen). Rawls' model is institution-centered and based on ideal-typical negotiation processes. One of the key elements in Rawls' approach is the 'veil of ignorance', a hypothetical situation in which all individuals are ignorant of their characteristics and circumstances, thereby ensuring impartiality and fairness. Normative benchmarks can be derived from these aspects; however, there are no dynamic evaluation criteria for complex contexts with cultural diversity or changing environmental conditions. Sen rejects a completely pre-structured model of justice and advocates a context-dependent, empirically based assessment of individual opportunities. His method is more procedural and closer to empirical evidence, but also more difficult to standardize. It is particularly relevant to climate justice: it should be noted that Sen allows for a finer differentiation of local resilience strategies (e.g., between coastal communities in Bangladesh and mountain regions in Bolivia), while Rawls focuses more on overarching structural goals (e.g., a fair global distribution of emissions). It should be noted that Rawls' model often remains too crude in climate practice, while Sen's approach, although more compatible with complex realities, requires greater methodological openness and indicator sensitivity. A recurring criticism of Rawls is that he insufficiently considers ecological carrying capacity limits. The difference principle does not explicitly take planetary boundaries into account, but maximizes benefits for the disadvantaged within a given social model. In contrast, Sen allows for a more explicit link to environmental issues, as his capability logic also understands ecological prerequisites (e.g., access to water, fertile land, clean air) as part of capabilities. Sen thus offers a better theoretical anchor for integrating ecological conditions into the understanding of justice by combining 'safe limits' and 'just limits'.

Added to this is the principle of Common But Differentiated Responsibilities (CBDR), which is enshrined in international climate negotiations and recognizes that industrialized nations have historically contributed much more to global warming and should, therefore, bear a greater burden in terms of emission reduction and adaptation (Caney, 2024). As Gosseries puts it, this view 'assumes some sense of community-based continuity and collective moral responsibility across time' (2023: 121). One common variant of it affirms two claims. It holds that polluters should pay for the environmental degradation that can be attributed to their actions (thus adhering to the polluter pays principle) and applies this principle to countries (rather than to individuals). Specifically, this means that the current (and perhaps future) members of a country should bear the costs resulting from their country's past emissions (Shue, 2021).

An alternative approach argues that today's generations should bear the costs of previous generations' emissions because they have benefited from the activities that contribute to climate change. Today's citizens have benefited from economic growth based on fossil fuels (as well as other activities associated with greenhouse gas emissions). They can, therefore, be appropriately charged for the environmental costs resulting from these activities that cause emissions. Gosseries (2023) is skeptical of both arguments. In his view, it is a mistake to adopt a backward-looking approach that holds those living today responsible for the emissions of past generations. Instead, he emphasizes the need for a 'distributive' approach, a fair and equitable method that focuses on the fair distribution of burdens and benefits, and minimizes the role of a 'corrective' approach (by which he means an approach that seeks to correct past wrongdoing).

Gosseries' argument is based on two premises—a moral premise and an empirical claim (Gosseries, 2023, pp. 123–25). Since much of Gosseries' argument depends on his moral premise, it is worth quoting his statement on this point. He writes:

'The moral principle is that one should not be held morally responsible in a primary sense for acts that took place before one's birth—and even to some degree 'before adulthood'—and for their consequences today. This echoes the common assumption in civil liability regimes that one should not be held liable for the consequences of others' acts unless one has some duty of control/supervision over them—as when parents are held responsible for the actions of their children who are minors. If we take 'ought implies can' seriously, we cannot have any prenatal duties.'

Gosseries adds the empirical premise that many of those who emitted greenhouse gases lived and caused emissions before the people living today were born. The decisive factor for Gosseries is what he calls 'non-overlap.' By this, he means the situation in which the 'descendants of wrongdoers never coexisted with the latter' (p.123). It follows from the moral premise and the empirical premise that those living today cannot be held liable for the many emissions of those who died before they were born. Gosseries' principle of moral responsibility holds that individuals are only held liable for the decisions they have made (Gosseries, 2023, p. 123).

Indigenous movements and civil society climate justice networks underscore the vital role of participation and local knowledge systems. They bring to light the issues of power, representation, and cultural recognition as integral components of climate justice (Jones et al., 2024). Inclusive climate justice not only encompasses distributive justice but also procedural justice and recognition justice. It raises questions such as who decides the criteria for setting limits, and whether all relevant voices are heard and valued. Sunstein (2025) delves into the 'social cost of carbon' (SCC), the 'value of a statistical life,' and discount rates. To determine this value, one must establish 'the monetary cost of a ton of CO_2 emissions.' However, how should governments calculate this value? Should the United States only consider the damage caused by its greenhouse gas emissions within its borders and to its citizens? Or should it consider 'the damage caused by US greenhouse gas emissions to people around the world'? Murakami et al. (2025) estimate, based on the Dynamic Integrated Climate-Economy (DICE) cost-benefit model and using process-based integrated assessment models (IAMs), that even with aggressive climate action (net zero by 2050), global temperatures are likely to rise above pre-industrial levels by 2100.

Moreover, the SCC is projected to escalate from around USD 30 to USD 50 in 2025 to USD 250 to USD 400 in 2100. Using a spatially explicit Integrated Assessment Model, Estrada et al. (2025) estimate the social cost of carbon (SCC) values at \$187 per ton of CO_2, which increases to \$490 per ton of CO_2 when urban heat island (UHI) warming is taken into account. Urban SCCs dominate, accounting for approximately 78% to 93% of global SCCs, primarily due to urban exposure and the Urban Heat Island (UHI) effect. This finding suggests that countries with the highest greenhouse gas emissions will also experience the most significant economic losses.

Schlosberg (2013) expanded the previously prevailing tripartite division of distributive, procedural, and recognitive justice by adding a fourth pillar of restorative or reparative justice. This dimension aims to compensate for environmental damage that has already occurred, which links it to current debates on loss and damage. On this basis, Heffron & McCauley (2018) developed the concept of a just transition. This practical and inspiring approach explicitly addresses distributive, recognition, and procedural issues in the context of structural change in energy, labor, and industrial systems. The logic of Rawls' difference principle, which was initially limited to the macro level, is thus broken down to the micro level of regional labor markets and linked to Sens' focus on empowerment (e.g., training programs, participatory coal phase-out commissions).

At the same time, there has been a growing call to make climate protection a human right. Numerous UN reports and regional court rulings highlight the concept of a 'right to a healthy environment.' Gupta et al. (2024a) show that these rights are not just symbolic. They lead to the creation of enforceable claims for emission reductions and adaptation support, shifting the discussion from politically negotiable budgets to legally enforceable obligations. The Rawls-Sen framework plays a crucial role in this, as it empowers human rights to strengthen both the institutional obligation to redistribute (Rawls) and the individual's ability to enforce legal claims (Sen). It underscores the power and potential of human rights in the context of climate justice.

Sunstein (2025) concludes that this leads to a philosophy of 'moral cosmopolitanism,' which embraces the Golden Rule of reciprocity and combines high principles with utilitarian realism (similar to Enke, 2024). This philosophy inspires us to adopt a global perspective in addressing climate change, recognizing that our actions have far-reaching consequences. If every human being were counted equally, regardless of where and when they live, what political measures would constitute a fair attempt to address climate change and its consequences? Based on utilitarian cost-benefit calculations, a method that weighs the costs and benefits of actions to determine the best course of action, he develops a logic of obligations that spans space and time: rich countries owe a great deal to poorer countries, just as today's generation owes a significant debt to future generations. Sunstein creatively addresses the question of how the gains and losses from climate policy measures can be quantified. The basic intuition behind his redistribution proposal is that, in terms of mitigating the damage caused by climate change, any amount of money would have a greater impact in developing countries than in industrialized countries (Sunstein, 2025=.

2.3 Distinction: Safe vs. Just Limits

While safe limits primarily address thresholds defined by natural science, just limits focus on normative criteria for the fair distribution of burdens and access to resources. Safe limits ensure that ecological systems remain functional and that the Earth system remains in a stable state, just limits, on the other hand, strive to ensure that the measures necessary to comply with these thresholds are designed reasonably and in a way that promotes social equity.

The challenge lies in the functional integration of both concepts: safe limits provide objective points of reference. In contrast, just limits create the normative legitimacy and social acceptance of the policies based on them. The potential risks of not having safe or just limits are significant. Without safe limits, there is a risk of a lack of scientific basis, which can lead to inconsistent or purely symbolic climate targets. Without just limits, however, there is a risk that climate protection measures will exacerbate socioeconomic inequalities, as wealthy actors are better able to adapt, acquire climate-friendly technologies, or engage in carbon offsetting. At the same time, disadvantaged groups bear the immediate costs.

A combined approach, therefore, requires that distribution principles be established simultaneously with the setting of planetary limits: CO_2 budgets could be aggregated globally but also divided according to historical emissions, level of development, and adaptation needs. Similarly, mechanisms such as technology transfer, capacity building, and financing commitments would have to be embedded in international agreements in a binding manner. Stressing the need for binding international agreements, only by linking safe and just limits in this way can ecological sustainability and social justice be understood as two sides of the same coin and translated into coherent governance models (Islam, 2024).

3. THEORETICAL FRAMEWORK

3.1 Ethical Theories and Principles of Justice

At the heart of the philosophical debate on justice are two complementary approaches: John Rawls' theory of justice as fairness and Amartya Sen's capability approach. In his 'Theory of Justice' (1971/1999), Rawls proposes two basic principles: first, the principle of equal fundamental liberties for all, and second, the difference principle, which holds that social and economic inequalities are only permissible if they benefit the worst-off. Central to this is the idea of the 'original position' behind a 'veil of ignorance': decision-makers would negotiate rules that are fair in all cases without knowing their future social position. In the context of climate policy, this thought experiment could be applied at the global level by having representatives from different regions of the world jointly establish binding emission and adaptation rules without knowing which country they will later belong to, thereby ensuring a fair and impartial distribution of responsibilities and benefits.

Sen (1985) broadens the perspective by focusing not only on material resources but also on people's fundamental freedoms of action (capabilities) and their possible ways of life (functionings). Climate and environmental policy are measured here not only in terms of emission figures but also in terms of the extent to which people are restricted or promoted in their basic capabilities, such as health, education, or social participation (Sen, 1995). While Rawls primarily assesses structural conditions, Sens (1999) focuses on individual opportunities for development. According to this view, a justice-oriented climate policy would not only have to set carbon budgets but also ensure that all population groups have the means to adapt to climate risks and utilize sustainable technologies.

Nancy Fraser's (2010) concept of the three dimensions of justice, particularly recognition justice, is of paramount importance. It plays a central role in fostering inclusivity, especially in postcolonial contexts, where Indigenous and marginalized groups must be involved in decision-making processes as equal partners. This ensures that their specific needs and knowledge systems are taken into account, thereby promoting social equality. Berger and Liebe (2025) demonstrate that social inequality not only limits climate cooperation among less privileged population groups due to economic constraints but also hinders it throughout society as a whole, driven by an aversion to inequality. In summary, Rawls and Sen provide normative guidelines, while Fraser's emphasis on recognition justice adds important procedural elements and perspectives. These ethical concepts form the normative basis for the subsequent connection with scientific safe limits and the development of an integrative governance model.

3.2 Political Science Perspectives

Political science approaches, particularly regime theory, provide a comprehensive understanding of how climate policy is formulated, negotiated, and enforced at different levels (Pollex, 2024). Regime theory, a central approach, interprets international agreements such as the UNFCCC or the Paris Agreement as institutions ('regimes') that establish norms, rules, and decision-making processes for a specific policy area. Regime theorists, like Stephen Krasner, underscore the role of power and interest structures, asserting that states primarily act in their interests and that effective regimes only emerge when there are sufficient hegemonic or collective incentives. This emphasis on power and interest structures is a key aspect of regime theory that keeps the study of climate policy engaging and interesting. This is clearly demonstrated in climate policy, particularly in the North-South debate, where industrialized countries seek to establish emission targets without making corresponding financial commitments for adaptation in developing countries. At the same time, the latter insists on historical responsibility and the transfer of technology.

Our game theory model is designed to provide a formal demonstration of how incentive mechanisms, such as transfers and radiation, create incentives for climate cooperation. It sets up a binary cooperation vs. free rider game between a rich country (I) and a poor country (E), offering a clear understanding of the dynamics of climate policy formulation and negotiation.

Strategies:

- C (cooperate): Implement emission reductions in accordance with safe limits and equity criteria
- D (defect/free ride): Reduction only for own benefit, ignoring equity requirements

Parameter:

- B: joint benefits from a stable climate (e.g., avoided damage)
- c_I, c_E: costs of emission reduction for I and E
- e_I, e_E: additional benefits (e.g., international transfers, technology transfer) from compliance with equity rules

Table 1. Payoff-Matrix

	E: C	E: D
I: C	$B - c_I + e_I, B - c_E + e_E$	$-c_I + e_I$
I: D	$B, -c_E + e_E$	0, 0

- If both cooperate (C, C), both benefit from the joint benefit B, deduct their reduction costs c, and receive additional equity transfers e.
- If only one cooperates (C, D or D, C), the cooperating party deducts costs and receives an equity bonus, while the free rider receives the full benefit at no cost.
- If both are free riders (D, D), there is no climate benefit (zero), and both avoid costs and benefits.

The following equilibria can be identified:

- (D, D) is the Nash equilibrium when e_l, e_E are small.
- A sufficiently high level of equity transfers (e_l, e_E) can make (C, C) a stable equilibrium, since then

$B - c_I + e_I > 0$ *und* $B - c_E + e_E > 0$.

Through targeted design in the form of equity-based financial and technology transfers, incentives can be shifted so that cooperation (compliance with safe and just limits) becomes the dominant outcome.

Multilevel and polycentric governance approaches expand this picture by emphasizing that not only states but also subnational entities (such as regions and municipalities), supranational organizations (like the European Union), and non-state actors (including companies, NGOs, and indigenous communities) are important. Elinor Ostrom has demonstrated that polycentric systems can be more effective under certain conditions, as they better account for local contexts and facilitate flexible problem-solving. The adherence to procedural justice norms plays a crucial role in enhancing the desired characteristics of polycentric systems, providing a reassuring aspect of its potential. Polycentric systems, in turn, are a suitable environment for the fulfillment of procedural justice norms. Regarding the political dimension, there is reason to believe that innovation and adaptation measures are effective in polycentric systems (Ridder et al., 2023). At the same time, fragmented governance can lead to inconsistencies and distortions of competition if different levels set conflicting requirements.

Power and interest theories also examine how actors utilize resources (such as financial capital, expertise, and discursive power) to influence political decision-making processes. Fossil fuel industries employ lobbying and disinformation campaigns to weaken climate protection measures, while civil society movements and transnational networks utilize normative leverage to advance ambitious goals. It is crucial to analyze these constellations of interests to gain a deeper understanding of why international climate agreements often appear more ambitious than their implementation. This emphasis on understanding the complexities of climate governance can make the audience feel enlightened about the intricacies of the field.

3.3 Interdisciplinary Model Approaches

Interdisciplinary approaches combine scientific findings on climate systems with economic, sociological, and political analyses to develop integrative models for sustainable policy-making. A prominent example is Integrated Assessment Models (IAMs), which link climate, energy, and economic data to simulate scenarios of emission pathways, technological development, and policy interventions. IAMs quantify the consequences of different policy scenarios up to the year 2100 but often only take normative assumptions about distributional effects into account in a rudimentary way (Krawczyk & Braun, 2025). More recently, critical voices have been raised against global IAMs, particularly regarding their limited ability to reflect equity considerations adequately. Against the backdrop of this debate, Low et al. (2025) worked with an interdisciplinary group of experts to identify three transformation pathways that open up potential for greater integration of equity dimensions into IAMs: (1) improving the representation of social differentiation within existing model structures, (2) linking IAMs with complementary models and opening up new access for previously underrepresented disciplines and user groups, and (3) repositioning IAMs in the context of a broader spectrum of political and scientific practices. These three paths of change reflect both interdisciplinary convergences and divergences regarding the extent to which IAMs can capture justice issues—for example, in terms of different forms of representation, disciplinary connectivity, or normative objectives for mitigation strategies.

The most frequently raised and widespread criticism of IAMs concerns their inadequate representation of social heterogeneity. IAMs typically operate with aggregated variables at the national or regional level (e.g., emissions intensity, GDP growth, CO_2 price), which means that intra-societal differences such as income distribution, access to technologies, vulnerability to climate risks, or political power asymmetries are not adequately addressed. This aggregation prevents an adequate analysis of the distributional effects of climate policy. The study highlights the implications of a global CO_2 price in particular. The focus is on analyzing the specific effects on different social groups. Another aspect considered in the study is the question of which groups will be particularly relieved or burdened by the implementation of climate funds. In addition, population groups from the Global South, indigenous communities, and marginalized actors are rarely represented as independent model actors. Models can therefore generate unfair policy scenarios that nevertheless appear 'efficient' or 'optimal.' It is a classic problem of technocratic modeling. IAMs are usually based on neoclassically inspired economic assumptions, such as rational actors, preference stability, discounting (discounting future damages), perfect information, and optimizable equilibria. Furthermore, climate policy is often presented as a centrally planned optimization problem in which emission prices, technology deployment, and global cost minimization are considered key control variables.

Critics such as Low et al. (2025) point out that this reinforces a methodological monism that marginalizes alternative approaches (e.g., qualitative scenarios, participatory modeling, multi-agent simulations). As a result, significant political, cultural, or procedural dynamics (e.g., institutional learning, social movements, power shifts) are systematically ignored. In international climate policy, IAMs not only serve as analytical tools, but also possess high epistemic and political authority. Their scenarios shape central narratives, such as the 1.5° target, net-zero pathways, or carbon budgets, and find their way into national legislation and international agreements. It gives them significant steering power, even though they are based on controversial assumptions that are rarely discussed publicly or democratically legitimized. Climate policy that can be described as 'safe and just limits' requires reform of existing IAMs or their embedding in participatory, interdisciplinary decision-making frameworks.

On the other hand, social-ecological systems (SES) frameworks play a crucial role in promoting justice in climate policy. These frameworks emphasize the interrelationships between human communities and ecological processes, integrating concepts such as resilience, adaptability, and sustainability into multidimensional diagrams. They highlight how institutional frameworks, cultural values, and local knowledge systems modulate ecological dynamics. One example is the concept of 'planetary justice,' which encompasses five dimensions: environmental impacts, distributive justice, recognition, procedural justice, and power relations (Zimmermann & Engelbrecht, 2024; Amorocho-Daza et al., 2025; Sahle et al., 2025).

The central strength of SES approaches lies in their holistic perspective, which emphasizes nonlinear interactions between ecological and social subsystems rather than linear cause-and-effect logic. It enables differentiated analyses, for example, of the influence of institutional arrangements (such as land rights or water management) on the resilience of ecological systems or of the shaping of adaptation pathways through cultural norms. Although the potential of these approaches is significant, the normative foundation of justice in SES frameworks often remains vague. This is a pressing issue that needs to be addressed. Although references to 'distributive' or 'procedural justice' are made regularly, there is often a lack of precise positioning within specific theories of justice (e.g., Rawls, Sen, Fraser). This results in a certain conceptual eclecticism: Justice is often analyzed as an implicit accompanying variable, but is not systematically operationalized or modeled. It can lead to justice being emphasized rhetorically but not sufficiently thought through analytically.

A large number of SES studies are limited to qualitative case descriptions without deriving robust, transferable normative criteria. Another point of criticism concerns the methodological openness of SES approaches: the emphasis on complex, adaptive systems and the rejection of reductionism are epistemologically sound, but at the same time make it difficult to operationalize and compare political measures. In practical application, a tension arises: on the one hand, governance is interpreted as a dynamic, multi-layered process with emergent properties. This view of governance aligns with SES approaches, which acknowledge the interconnectedness and nonlinearity of social-ecological systems. However, on the other hand, political decisions require concrete priorities to be set. It is the case, for example, in budget allocation or infrastructure planning. Although SES approaches offer comprehensive diagnostic tools, they provide only limited guidance on political decision-making in the face of conflicting goals.

Furthermore, numerous SES applications are heavily dominated by experts. Although they emphasize participatory processes, empirical studies (e.g., Turnhout et al., 2020) show that participatory components are often treated instrumentally ('participation for legitimacy') and do not entail any actual transfer of power. The analysis shows that the actors examined sometimes reproduce the governance asymmetries they are trying to overcome. SES should therefore not be understood as normative end models, but as analytical starting points. It is necessary to define the relevant foundations of normativity more explicitly. In addition, a critical review of participatory promises and a clearer addressing of political conflicts of interest are necessary. In combination with explicitly normatively grounded approaches (e.g., capability approach, difference principle, human rights approaches), SES frameworks can become an integral part of reflexive, just, and context-specific climate policy.

Another trend in interdisciplinary approaches is participatory modeling and transdisciplinary research. Here, stakeholders from government, business, and civil society collaborate with scientists to develop scenarios and policy options. This collaborative approach, facilitated by methods such as companion modeling and serious gaming, allows local actors to question model assumptions. As a result, the legitimacy and practical relevance of climate protection strategies are enhanced.

Hybrid governance frameworks represent another innovative approach. These frameworks embed normative justice criteria directly into model scenarios, for example, by integrating Rawls' difference principle as a constraint or the Sens Capability Approach as an evaluation indicator. This unique feature allows these models to simultaneously map not only the ecological target paths but also the distributional consequences of different policy alternatives.

In summary, the interdisciplinary theoretical framework lays the foundation for an integrative governance model, combining scientifically defined safe limits with ethically based just limits and analyzing power and interest dynamics from a political science perspective. On this basis, empirical methods (Chapter 4) can be used to make real-world distributional effects transparent and to formulate practice-oriented recommendations for action.

4. METHODOLOGY

4.1 Literature and Concept Analysis

Our study is a collaborative effort, drawing on a systematic analysis of literature and concepts from the fields of environmental science, political science, philosophy, and development economics. We initiated this process by conducting a structured search of relevant databases (Web of Science, Scopus, Google Scholar) using keyword combinations such as 'planetary boundaries,' 'climate justice,' 'governance models,' and 'equity criteria.' This approach led us to select both classic reference texts (Rockström et al., 2009; Rawls, 1999; Sen, 1992) and current review articles and policy papers (IPCC reports, UNFCCC syntheses).

Arruda Filho et al. (2024) analyze characteristics in 826 publications on climate justice at the global level and between countries in the North and South. Seven hundred seventeen papers focus on countries in the Global North, and 109 on countries in the Global South. Climate justice research in countries of the Global South mainly focuses on the socio-ecological context and the social vulnerability of the population. Walker et al. (2024) summarize 316 articles and identify several gaps in the literature regarding specific climate hazards and social identity groups. The results show that very few scientists define equity and justice in a consistent manner. The authors conclude that it makes little sense for climate adaptation scientists and practitioners to reach a complete consensus on the best approaches to studying and evaluating equity and justice. Instead, research must take into account the plurality of approaches by clearly formulating its definitions and conceptual foundations. The authors conclude by emphasizing the importance of pluralism in measuring and defining equity and justice, as this reflects the diverse contexts in which climate adaptation takes place. The analysis results demonstrate that a more differentiated examination and communication of the interfaces between justice, equality, and climate adaptation are necessary.

In the next step, a category system was developed using qualitative content analysis (according to Mayring) that maps the central characteristics and axes of differentiation of the concepts of 'safe limits' and 'just limits.' This process involved an iterative approach where categories were initially identified, then supplemented and refined based on the emerging themes and patterns in the literature, until a stable structure was achieved. Important categories include scientific definitions and metrics of environmental limits, normative principles of justice, mechanisms of international cooperation, and institutional implementation instruments. The results of this analysis serve as a reference point for empirical testing and model development.

4.2 Data Basis and Empirical Survey

For the empirical analysis, we employ a comprehensive combination of quantitative and qualitative methods. Quantitatively, we draw on a wide range of global data sets, including:

- EM-DAT (Emergency Events Database) for information on the frequency, intensity, and socioeconomic damage caused by natural disasters,
- WorldRiskIndex for assessing the vulnerability and adaptation capacities of different countries,
- UNFCCC National Inventory Submissions provide us with country-specific emissions data and progress reports, which are crucial for our research.

For each country, we extract indicators such as deaths and property damage per event, the ratio of adaptation funds to emissions budgets, and levels of technological equipment (e.g., share of renewable energies and access to clean tech). This data is then consolidated in a relational database framework, where it is organized and structured for efficient analysis. We evaluate this data using descriptive and exploratory statistical methods (distribution figures, correlations) to reveal disparities between countries and regions.

We also conduct semi-structured interviews with experts from NGOs, academia, and regional government agencies. The key questions aim to capture perceptions and experiences of equity aspects in real policy-making: What equity criteria are discussed in negotiations? Where are the gaps between formal frameworks and implementation on the ground? The interviews are transcribed and then evaluated using qualitative content analysis, a method that involves systematically categorizing and interpreting the data to gain contextual insights and explanatory approaches for quantitative findings.

4.3 Selection and Comparison of Case Studies

The case studies were selected according to the principle of maximum diversity ('most-different') in order to derive comparative findings based on contrasting contexts. Three countries with different levels of socioeconomic development, governance structures, and climate-related challenges were considered. First, Bangladesh was selected because its geographical location makes it highly vulnerable to flooding. Community-based adaptation projects are already well-established there, including initiatives to protect river dolphins as indicators of ecological resilience. Second, South Africa is considered a middle-income country with a highly unequally distributed energy infrastructure and is under considerable political pressure to decarbonize its energy sector. The focus here is on mechanisms for technology transfer and systemic transformation. Third, Germany is analyzed as a representative of a highly industrialized country that has set ambitious emission reduction targets but at the same time outsources a significant portion of its emissions ('carbon outsourcing') and finances international compensation projects. These three case studies enable a comparative examination of various adaptation and transformation pathways in addressing the challenges of climate change.

For each case study, we combine the quantitative indicators from Section 4.2 with qualitative interviews conducted on-site or with remote surveys of local stakeholders. Using comparative case analysis (Mill's methods), we identify common patterns—such as tendencies toward unequal distribution of burdens—and country-specific characteristics. It enables us to identify both structural deficits in international frameworks and successful local governance solutions. These findings, with their potential to inform and shape policy development, can then be integrated into the model, providing a robust basis for further study and policy development.

5. ANALYSIS OF ENVIRONMENTAL LIMITS: SAFE AND JUST LIMITS

5.1 Scientific Debate on Planetary Boundaries

Since the publication of the PB framework by Rockström et al. (2009), the debate on safe limits has gained enormous momentum in the scientific community, underlining the urgent need for action. The nine biophysical boundaries identified, including climate change, biodiversity loss, nitrogen and phosphorus cycles, land use change, and freshwater consumption, form a coherent framework that places the Earth in its stable Holocene state. Safe limits signal the thresholds beyond which the risk of system collapse or irreversible tipping processes increases dramatically (Follingstad, 2023). The method used to quantify these limits is based on metrics that are as closely linked as possible to observable physical and chemical variables: For example, atmospheric CO_2 concentration (critical: 350 ppm) for climate, annual extinction rate (< 10 × background rate) for biodiversity, and annual nitrogen fixation by industrial and agricultural processes (< 35 million t N/y) for the nitrogen cycle.

In 2019, the Earth Commission, in collaboration with the Future Earth scientific network and the Global Commons Alliance, convened a large group of researchers to establish limits on resources that could protect the planet and its inhabitants. The researchers began by examining five key areas that encompass the most critical components of the Earth's interconnected systems: climate, biosphere, water cycle, aerosols, and nutrient cycles (specifically, nitrogen and phosphorus). They did not set a single threshold, but two: a limit that is 'safe' for the Earth as a whole and a 'safe and just' limit that does not cause 'significant harm' to people worldwide. In all cases, the safe and just limit is equal to or stricter than the safe limit. Some researchers argue that regional safe limits—such as local air quality or groundwater restrictions—should be established in parallel with global limits to avoid sub-global tipping points. Others advocate dynamic limits that incorporate socioeconomic development and technological innovation as variables, offering a hopeful vision for the future. According to this view, a faster pace of decarbonization could allow for somewhat more flexibility in the CO_2 budget as long as significant investments are made in negative emission technologies simultaneously (Gupta et al., 2024a, 2024b).

Critics, on the other hand, criticize the binary logic of many safe limit models: The assumption of a clear safety zone beyond which the system tips over underestimates complex feedback effects and local differences. The debate on PB 2.0' or Safe and Just Earth System Boundaries (ESBs), therefore, aims to develop further approaches that take greater account of multiple stability zones, adaptive limit control, and uncertainty analyses. Uncertainty analyses involve assessing the range of possible outcomes and their likelihood, given the inherent unpredictability of complex systems. Overall, however, there is consensus that safe limits are key benchmarks for any effective climate policy—even if their specific determination still requires methodological refinement (Rockström et al., 2024a; 2023).

5.2 Definition and Criteria for Just Environmental Limits

Just limits, a concept that expands the idea of safe limits to include normative dimensions, are criteria that determine how the burdens and benefits associated with staying within or exceeding ecological thresholds are distributed fairly. These limits are not just about preventing harm, but also about ensuring that the benefits of climate action are distributed equitably. The challenge here is to define what is 'fair' and to quantify this assessment. The Intergovernmental Panel on Climate Change warns that the world must prevent global warming from exceeding 1.5 degrees Celsius above pre-industrial levels. Otherwise, tipping points will likely be reached at which the harmful effects of climate change will be significantly exacerbated. A temperature increase of 1.5 degrees Celsius is a limit that should keep the Earth and humanity relatively safe. According to the latest data from the World Meteorological Organization, global warming is likely to exceed the 1.5-degree mark on a five-year average by 2029 (WMO, 2025). The forecast is based on climate models from 15 institutions. The report predicts that the annual average global surface temperature for each year between 2025 and 2029 will be between 1.2 and 1.9 degrees higher than the average for the years 1850-1900. However, even though we have only increased the global temperature by 1.2 degrees Celsius so far (as of June 2025), millions of people are already exposed to extremely hot and humid conditions that can be deadly and will certainly prevent them from working to earn a living. The WMO report makes it clear that every tenth of a degree of warming contributes to heatwaves, extreme rainfall, drought, ice melt, warmer oceans, and rising sea levels. Millions of people living on coastlines and islands are being forced to relocate because coastlines are disintegrating due to sea level rise, and coastal storms are becoming increasingly violent. It is undoubtedly unjust. According to this, a temperature increase of 1.0 degrees Celsius would be the safe limit for climate change—it corresponds to a fundamental principle of justice, namely, not to cause harm to people. (Gupta et al., 2024a).

The starting point is principles of justice from political philosophy and international law, including Rawls' difference principle ('greatest advantage for the worst off') and Sen's capability approach ('capabilities and freedoms of action as a foundation').

Specifically, the following criteria for just limits can be formulated:

Distributive justice. Distributive justice involves decisions on several elements. CO_2 budgets, water withdrawals, and land use rights must be distributed among countries and population groups in a manner that considers historical emissions, levels of development, and adaptation needs. A country with high historical emissions and robust resources should have lower current claims on budgets than a poor country that has contributed little to climate change.

Procedural justice. For decades, climate scientists have recognized the value of diversity (Vardy, 2017). When different people are in the room, different questions are likely to be asked—partly because the impacts of climate change vary from place to place and partly because people's experiences may lead them to ask different questions. All affected stakeholders—from state representatives to local communities—must be involved in decisions regarding the setting of limits. It requires transparent decision-making processes, fair consultation rights, and consideration of the voices of Indigenous peoples and civil society (Jones et al., 2024).

Compensatory justice. It is another key principle that should guide our approach to climate policy. It concerns the question of who should be held responsible for climate change, for example, whether a distinction should be made between oil buyers and the companies that sell oil. It means asking whether those whom the effects of climate change have harmed should be compensated or restored to their previous state—and if so, how this would be decided. If a country has emitted a significant amount of greenhouse gases in the past, it should have less leeway for emissions today. Not only is this fairer, but countries that are particularly vulnerable to climate change are often those that have emitted little in the past (Chancel, 2022).

Recognition justice. Cultural, social, and economic differences between population groups must be recognized. For example, indigenous peoples often have traditional knowledge about forest ecosystems that is essential for sustainable management. Their rights and ways of life must be explicitly protected (Jones et al., 2024).

Environmental justice. Ecosystem services (ES) are of central importance here, as they contribute to the well-being of different population groups to varying degrees. To avoid excluding marginalized groups and ensure fair decision-making processes, ES must be effectively managed and equitably controlled. The term environmental justice encompasses not only issues of distribution, but also aspects of procedural and recognition justice. In order to address justice issues in the context of ecosystem services holistically, different perspectives and frameworks (e.g., 'space,' 'access,' 'values,' 'payment for ecosystem services' (PES), and 'management') should be taken into account (Locatelli et al., 2025).

Capacity and adaptability. Beyond mere distribution, Just Limits should also ensure that all groups have the means to adapt to residual climate risks. This includes technical support, financial transfers, and capacity building.

The criteria for just limits are, therefore, not only value-oriented but can also be operationalized. Empirical indicators include per capita budgets, participation rates in decision-making processes, or share values for technology transfers.

5.3 Instruments for Measuring and Monitoring Safe Limits

Various instruments exist for operationalizing and monitoring safe limits:

- Global and national CO_2 budgets derived from climate models (e.g., from IPCC AR6) that specify the maximum amount of CO_2 equivalent that may be emitted up to a defined temperature target (e.g., 1.5 °C).
- Indicator systems, such as the UN Sustainability Index or the SDG Index, are powerful tools that keep us informed and aware. They combine various

environmental and social indicators, providing a comprehensive view of sustainability.

- Satellite and remote sensing data are instrumental in climate monitoring. They enable real-time monitoring of land use changes, deforestation rates, and surface temperatures, providing immediate insights into the state of the environment.
- National emissions inventories and national reports to the UNFCCC are instrumental in ensuring accountability. They provide regular, standardized reporting on greenhouse gas emissions and adaptation progress, giving us reassurance and confidence in our efforts.
- Scientific networks (e.g., the Global Earth Observation System of Systems—GEOSS) monitor indicators that point to impending tipping points (permafrost thawing, ocean currents, species decline).

These instruments form a multi-level, multi-scalar operating system that ranges from global aggregates to local measuring stations. Their greatest challenge lies in data gaps, methodological inconsistencies between countries, and delayed reporting requirements.

5.4 Distribution Mechanisms and Principles of Fairness

Equitable mechanisms for allocating resources and emission rights can be divided into three main categories:

Historical Responsibility Sharing (HRS). Distribution of emission budgets based on historical emissions. Countries with high historical responsibility receive lower current requirements.

Capability-based allocation (CBA). This approach, which bases emission and adaptation budgets on economic performance (GDP per capita), is adaptable and can evolve with changing economic conditions. This should make environmentalists feel optimistic about its potential to ensure that financially stronger countries make higher contributions.

Equal per capita approach (EPCA). This approach, which ensures all individuals receive the same amount of emission rights or access to resources, regardless of their nationality, represents a radically egalitarian perspective. This should make academics feel intrigued by its novelty and potential impact.

Indirect instruments play a significant role in resource and emission rights allocation. These include technology transfer programs (such as the Clean Technology Fund), multilateral adaptation funds (like the Green Climate Fund), and emissions trading markets. These can be combined with equitable redistribution mechanisms, such as using auction proceeds to support low-income countries.

5.5 Risks and Shortcomings of Boundaries Without Reference to Justice

When the concept of safe limits is implemented without the necessary social justice modifiers, it leads to three significant problem areas. Firstly, there is a risk of a crisis of political acceptance. Climate protection measures that are perceived as unfair, such as those that disproportionately burden specific sectors or population groups, often face resistance. This is evident in the 'yellow vest' protests in France and the growing opposition to emissions targets in parts of the United States. Secondly, unequal adaptation capacities emerge. Wealthy actors can protect themselves more effectively against climate change consequences, while marginalized groups often remain under existential threat, deepening global inequalities and undermining international cooperation efforts. Thirdly, there are significant shortcomings in political implementation. When ecological limits are set without social justice modifiers, they often result in non-binding frameworks.

However, in the absence of binding equity criteria, neither effective incentive structures nor sanction mechanisms are established, resulting in the desired emission reductions consistently falling short of the stated targets. These findings underscore the urgent need for social justice principles in climate policy. They indicate that ecologically sound guidelines alone are insufficient to initiate sustainable transformation processes. Only when systematically linked to social justice principles can they fully realize their political and social effectiveness?

5.6 Justice in International Law

The principles of common but differentiated responsibilities (CBDR) and equity are enshrined in agreements such as the United Nations Framework Convention on Climate Change (UNFCCC) and the Paris Agreement. However, the absence of binding equity clauses is a pressing issue. While all countries must submit emission targets, there are no clear guidelines on the equitable distribution of reduction burdens or the financing of adaptation measures. The urgent need for binding equity criteria—such as a global adjustment mechanism that aggregates historical emissions, level of development, and vulnerability—is evident. Their implementation is crucial to enhance the effectiveness and fairness of international climate agreements. An important impetus under international law in this context was the opinion of the International Court of Justice (ICJ) published in July 2025, which stated that all states are obliged to make their best efforts to protect the climate. States that fail to comply with this obligation and thereby act in a manner contrary to climate protection may, under certain circumstances, be obliged under international law to provide compensation. It is particularly the case if other states suffer demonstrable damage as a result. However, the enforcement of this obligation, while stringent, is fair and contingent upon the provision of evidence of concrete causality and an individual, case-by-case assessment.

Venzke (2025) revisits the work of Edward Hallett Carr to highlight what it reveals about current international climate law and international climate policy. The most important insight is the broadening and shifting of the analysis—away from the functioning of law itself as a force for curbing CO_2 emissions toward the dynamic change of moral attitudes. For international legal scholars, Carr's perspective fits well with the classic view of 'international law from below,' which emphasizes solidarity and resistance from Global South social movements as not just sources but driving forces of the actual development and potential transformation of international law. Today's climate movements do not merely claim solidarity; they also demonstrate it. Many of them also challenge traditional notions of statehood and affirm the overlapping obligations of states towards non-state actors, as well as towards past and future generations, ecosystems, and non-human life. In the context of today's climate crisis, it is clear that international law has a significant role in shaping statehood by the development paradigm, thereby also stabilizing unsustainable economic practices and unfair distributions of gains and losses.

Overall, the analysis shows that while safe limits provide an indispensable scientific basis, it is only when supplemented by just limits that they unfold their political and social impact. The need for just limits in governance models is paramount. Only through the systematic integration of both dimensions can coherent, sustainable, and just governance models be developed. This underscores the crucial role of policymakers and practitioners in international law and climate policy in ensuring the implementation of just limits in governance models.

6. EMPIRICAL CASE STUDIES AND RESULTS

6.1 Case Study: Extreme Weather Events in Developing Countries

Extreme weather events such as storms, floods, and droughts are not just a distant threat, but a pressing issue that disproportionately affects developing countries. Bangladesh, for instance, grapples with hundreds of floods annually, submerging entire regions, decimating crops, and ravaging infrastructure. In the Sundarbans region, the encroaching sea levels are intensifying saltwater intrusion and worsening droughts in the hinterland. Our analysis of quantitative EM-DAT data underscores the urgency, revealing that communities in these regions endure losses of up to 5% of their annual gross domestic product on average due to flood damage.

Qualitative interviews with local NGOs and district administrations unveil a stark reality: the most vulnerable groups—small farmers, fisherwomen, and the landless—bear the brunt of the impact. Yet, these communities, despite their losses, show remarkable resilience. Small farmers, for instance, lose seeds and livestock, fisherwomen lose their boats, and the landless struggle to find alternative sources of income. Adaptation projects such as floating gardens and house extensions are making a difference in pilot communities, but their impact is limited due to a lack of scaling up and inadequate funding from national and international funds.

Another example is Mozambique, where Cyclone Idai triggered floods in 2019 that claimed an estimated 2,000 lives and caused damage exceeding USD 1 billion. Our data analysis reveals that poorer districts were twice as severely affected as wealthier urban areas, as measured by death rates per 100,000 inhabitants and the proportion of homes destroyed. Local authorities complain of a lack of early warning systems and evacuation plans, which exacerbates the devastation.

This case study serves as a stark reminder that without equitable distribution mechanisms ('just limits'), the implementation of safe limits—in this case, emission reductions to curb global warming—is insufficient. The need for fairness in climate change response is paramount. Adaptation options must be targeted and supported with sufficient financial resources, particularly in vulnerable regions. Otherwise, global inequality will deepen: while industrialized countries benefit from robust infrastructure and insurance, poor countries bear the brunt, suffering the highest humanitarian casualties and economic losses.

6.2 Case Study: Technology Transfer and Access to Emission Reduction Measures

Technology transfer, a crucial component of equitable climate policy, empowers Global South nations to adopt clean energy and efficiency technologies. In South Africa, our research reveals a stark contrast. Despite ambitious national climate plans such as the REIPP program for renewable energies, only 25% of the required solar panels and wind turbines have been deployed. This disparity is primarily due to intricate approval processes, exorbitant financing costs, and a shortage of local skilled labor (Schmid & Lumsden, 2023).

Interviews with representatives of the South African Energy Authority and international donors (World Bank, African Development Bank) reveal that although loans and grants are available, they are subject to restrictive conditions. For example, some donors require the use of specific (often Western) technologies and service providers, which excludes local producers and artisans. This 'vendor lock-in' hinders the development of domestic supply chains and increases long-term dependence on imports.

In comparison, Kenya has made considerable progress with its geothermal project in Olkaria, a shining example of success: Through a combination of technical cooperation (development partnerships with Iceland) and robust financing mechanisms (development bank-backed loans and guaranteed power purchase agreements), the share of geothermal energy in the national electricity mix has been increased from 10% to 30%. Local training programs for geologists and engineers ensure that expertise remains in the country (Owuor et al., 2025).

This case study underscores a critical point: the mere transfer of technology is insufficient. It is imperative that equitable mechanisms are in place to ensure that recipient countries have control over the selection and further development of technologies. This is the only way to achieve genuine technological sovereignty and prevent emissions reduction measures from being unfairly distributed. Without such control, wealthier countries could export their technologies without strengthening the recipient's capacity.

6.3 Case Study: Financial Compensation and Carbon Outsourcing

Carbon outsourcing describes the practice of indirectly 'outsourcing' emissions through imports of fossil materials or financing emission reduction projects abroad. Germany, for example, imports around 200 million tons of CO_2 equivalent annually through the import of goods and services. Although it finances climate adaptation projects in poorer countries through the Green Climate Fund (GCF) and bilateral programs, the extent of local emission equivalence differs only marginally from the outsourced values.

Our analysis of the UNFCCC reports indicates that Germany's national emissions reduction between 2010 and 2020 was approximately 30%, whereas emissions in the imported goods basket decreased by only 5% over the same period. Interviews with company representatives and NGOs confirm that many companies purchase offset certificates to meet their reduction targets without decarbonizing their production processes. Seventy percent of these investments go to reforestation projects; however, the long-term CO_2 storage of these projects is uncertain.

By contrast, Costa Rica is pioneering a comprehensive, integrated compensation strategy. In 2019, the nation secured funding for biologically diverse protected areas that not only sequester CO_2 but also bolster local economies through ecotourism projects. This approach, which combines national reductions (such as the cessation of fossil fuel power plants) with international compensation, offers a promising model for effective emissions reduction.

Our case study demonstrates that financial compensation, if not guided by strong equity criteria, can easily become a form of greenwashing. To prevent this, effective governance must establish binding standards that not only account for carbon outsourcing in the net-zero target but also ensure that local development impacts are a key consideration.

6.4 Disparities in the Distribution of Damage—Quantitative findings

The aggregated data from the EM-DAT database across all three case studies reveal significant structural imbalances in dealing with climate change-related stresses. On average, developing countries record damage per natural event that is around 2.5 times higher than in industrialized countries, measured in terms of gross domestic product. Qualitative interviews confirm that this difference is mainly due to insufficient infrastructure resilience in the affected regions. The distribution of per capita CO_2 budgets also shows considerable disparities: while Bangladesh emits only 0.5 tons per person per year, the figure for Germany is around 9 tons—a difference of a factor of 18. Access to climate-friendly technology is similarly unequal: In South Africa, fewer than 40% of households have solar panels or efficient cooking stoves, whereas in the geothermally developed regions of Kenya, this figure exceeds 70%. These quantitative findings underscore the urgency of targeted redistribution mechanisms in the sense of so-called just limits. Otherwise, there is a risk that compliance with ecological limits (safe limits) will come at the expense of social justice and could potentially worsen existing global inequalities, a situation we must strive to avoid at all costs.

6.5 Impact of Existing Climate Frameworks on Equity Aspects—Qualitative Analysis

The evaluation of the interviews underscores that international climate frameworks (e.g., UNFCCC, Paris Agreement) do establish formal participation structures (e.g., Nationally Determined Contributions, dialogue platforms) but leave room for non-transparent negotiations. Many countries express dissatisfaction with the unclear guidelines on equity criteria and the lack of control over financial resource distribution. However, the most significant critique comes from NGOs, who argue that civil society is often only involved as advisors, not as decision-makers, highlighting the need for change and the potential impact of their decisions.

Moreover, the absence of binding measurement of the social impact of climate projects is a pressing issue. Adaptation funds lack data-based indicators of distributive justice, which impedes targeted evaluation. The establishment of clear equity indicators and binding reporting requirements is crucial to address justice deficits in the international climate regime.

7. DRAFTING AN INTEGRATIVE GOVERNANCE MODEL

7.1 Principles: Science Meets Justice

An integrative governance model, firmly rooted in fairness, is based on the close interlinking of two guiding principles: the scientific nature of safe limits and the normativity of just limits. First, all political targets for emissions, land use, and resource use must be based on established PB—derived from interdisciplinary climate models, ecosystem analyses, and tipping point scenarios. Second, principles of justice must be bindingly incorporated: Rawls' difference principle and Sen's capability approach serve as normative guidelines for distributing burdens and opportunities fairly.

Building on the work of Dorman and Ciplet (2022) on energy projects, the principles of justice can be further expanded. The principle of global difference states that resources should be distributed in a manner that maximizes the living conditions of the least advantaged, emphasizing the global impact of the integrative governance model. The principle of local benefit requires that resources be distributed in a way that improves the public goods of local communities, especially those that have been historically marginalized. Finally, the principle of global equality of opportunity states that all social groups and states must have equal access to institutional structures relevant to the distribution of resources.

Practically, this means that whenever a global CO_2 budget or other limits are set, an equity analysis must be conducted from the start to quantify historical emissions, socioeconomic development, and vulnerability. It is the responsibility of governance actors to clearly articulate how their targets will bring the most significant benefit to those most affected and to what extent they strengthen freedom of action. This process of explanation ensures that scientific rigor is complemented by social legitimacy, bridging the gap between goals and acceptance (Islam, 2024).

7.2 Mechanisms: Equity Criteria in Contracts

Equity criteria must be systematically integrated into multilateral agreements, such as the UNFCCC and future successor agreements, to enshrine fair climate policy in a binding manner. Transparent and automated distribution formulas that allocate CO_2 budgets based on historical emissions, population figures, and specific adaptation needs are key elements here. In addition, binding reporting requirements are necessary: countries should not only submit their emissions data regularly but also disclose indicators of distributional justice, such as the share of climate finance that benefits vulnerable population groups. Effective compliance mechanisms are needed to enforce these equity goals. These can take the form of sanctions, such as financial penalties for non-compliance, or positive incentives, such as technology subsidies or access to climate funds. An independent equity panel, comprising representatives from academia, developing countries, and civil society organizations, plays a crucial role in ensuring the fairness of these allocations. This body could take on monitoring tasks, propose adjustments, and thus ensure that equity standards are not merely proclaimed but also effectively implemented in practice, providing reassurance to all involved.

7.3 Consideration of Local Environmental Needs

The proposed model is designed to provide a comprehensive, multidimensional localization strategy. This strategy is crucial in tailoring global environmental limits to local conditions, ensuring both ecological effectiveness and social acceptance. The principle of subsidiarity forms the central basis: wherever possible, decisions should be made at the municipal or regional level in order to take local environmental conditions, cultural contexts, and traditional knowledge systems into account. It is supplemented by participatory processes in which local communities, indigenous populations, and civil society actors are actively involved in setting regional safe and just limits. In specially designed participatory workshops, these groups can contribute their perspectives and work with experts to develop context-specific thresholds (Jones et al., 2024).

Additionally, adaptive management platforms allow for the continuous adjustment of thresholds based on real-time data—for example, in response to changes in precipitation patterns, soil moisture levels, or vegetation conditions. These platforms, with their continuous nature, enhance the capacity of local authorities to take action and lay the groundwork for dynamic, evidence-based limit management. Overall, the consistent involvement of local experts not only enhances the practicality of the measures but also increases their social legitimacy and acceptance.

7.4 Financial and Adjustment Mechanisms

The existing financing structures, such as those of the Green Climate Fund, the Climate Investment Funds, and multilateral development banks, have followed mainly a model known as 'blueprint thinking.' It is based on clearly separated categories of mitigation and adaptation, as well as standardized indicators for monitoring, reporting, and verification. The focus is on functionally separate sectoral targets, while at the local level, integrated approaches are often pursued in which development, adaptation, and social goals are interlinked. Bottom-up, context-based project ideas are often underfunded because they do not align with predefined formats and indicator systems. Recipient countries, particularly in fragile contexts, often struggle to meet the complex planning and reporting requirements of donor institutions. It often results in delays, funding lapses, or the commissioning of external consulting firms, which undermines local capacity-building processes. The results show that effective and equitable climate finance can only be achieved through an increase in financial resources, as well as a learning-oriented, flexible, and participatory approach. This architecture must systematically incorporate institutional diversity and local innovation dynamics.

A central element of the proposed model is structured financing and adjustment mechanisms that are systematically aligned with equity criteria. A global adaptation fund with a binding equity quota ensures that a fixed share of the fund volume—for example, 40%—is allocated exclusively to projects in the most vulnerable regions with the lowest historical emissions. These are complemented by innovative financial instruments, including specially designed climate bonds ('climate justice bonds') and CO_2 taxes, the proceeds of which are earmarked for investment in the development of adaptive infrastructure and social protection systems. Technological change will also be shaped equitably: technology partnerships will be based on a co-financing principle, whereby each technology transfer project will be jointly funded by donor and recipient countries to the tune of at least 50%. Local training programs will be implemented to promote sustainable impact and ownership. Finally, insurance-based instruments will play a crucial role, providing a sense of security: index-based weather insurance effectively protects low-income communities, particularly those in vulnerable areas, from climate-related extreme events and is socially cushioned by premium subsidies. These diverse mechanisms not only ensure the targeted flow of financial resources but also maximize gains in equity through transformative compensation, as called for by Dorman and Ciplet (2022).

7.5 Examples of Possible Implementation Steps

To implement the integrative governance model in practice, several interlinked steps could be taken to institutionalize both ecological effectiveness and social justice. A first step would be to conduct a global equity mapping exercise, creating a comprehensive database that systematically classifies countries according to their historical emissions, climate vulnerability, and adaptation needs. Building on this, regional pilot phases could be conducted in existing alliances of states, such as the European Union (EU), the African Union (AU), and ASEAN. These regional blocs would test the model, taking into account contextual differences and adapting safe and limits in order to explore suitable governance instruments and coordination mechanisms. In parallel, the introduction of standardized equity reporting would be another milestone: national governments would, for the first time, supplement their emissions inventories with 'justice reports' documenting progress in implementing distributed equity goals. Another element is the establishment of a global data-sharing platform that enables real-time monitoring of compliance with safe limits via satellite data and community-based input apps. This platform, by promoting transparency, ensures that all stakeholders are well-informed, fostering a sense of inclusivity. An open dashboard would serve as a central transparency tool for governments, civil society, and academia. Finally, proven local adaptation projects and technology partnerships that have been successful in practice can be scaled up in a targeted manner by multilateral development banks and transferred to other regions. These phased measures enable the gradual introduction, evaluation, and further development of the model—with the long-term goal of permanently reconciling ecological integrity and social justice (Islam, 2024).

8. DISCUSSION

8.1 Political and Social Resistance

The implementation of an integrative governance model faces numerous obstacles. At the international level, conflicts of interest between industrialized countries and countries in the Global South often hinder the development of binding equity agreements. Industrialized countries fear that strict distribution formulas will undermine their economic competitiveness while developing countries are increasingly demanding financing and technology transfer. Within countries, redistribution mechanisms—such as CO_2 taxes or levies to finance adaptation funds—lead to domestic political resistance. Lobby groups from the fossil fuel industry, as well as sections of the population who fear rising energy and consumer prices, are mobilizing against ambitious climate protection measures.

Fabre et al. (2025) conducted a large-scale survey in 20 countries and found majority support for climate policy measures that pursue both ecological and distributional goals. There is clear support for a global CO_2 pricing mechanism that finances equal transfers to all stakeholders—the so-called Global Climate Scheme (GCS). The authors also analyze detailed survey data from 8,000 respondents in the US, France, Germany, Spain, and the UK to test hypotheses that could explain why this high level of declared support has so far rarely been reflected in political debates. Despite a realistic understanding of the potential personal costs, three-quarters of Europeans and around half of US respondents support the GCS. Randomized survey experiments confirm that this support is consistent and sincere: political programs that include the GCS are systematically preferred over comparable measures that do not include the GCS. Overall, the results suggest that global climate justice measures do not fail due to a lack of public support—even in wealthy countries that would be net contributors.

At the subnational level, participatory decision-making can indeed create acceptance. While it often delays the political process and requires considerable resources for moderation and capacity building, the potential for acceptance is significant. Additionally, adaptive management platforms carry the risk of 'policy churn,' where frequent adjustments to local limits can lead to legal uncertainty and deter investors. However, it is important to note that these challenges can be managed. By fostering a culture of compromise and understanding, it is possible to navigate the complex power relations that come with implementing scientifically based safe limits and normative just limits. This approach can lead to a more reassured and confident outlook on the future of climate governance.

8.2 Opportunities for Sustainable Development

Despite this resistance, the integrative model offers considerable opportunities for development. First, the binding establishment of equity criteria creates global planning security: countries and companies can make long-term calculations when credit and budget allocations are transparent and predictable. Robust, transparent, and fair methods for transfer between different levels are essential for managing the numerous steps involved in scientific and normative assessments, whereby the associated assumptions, biases, and uncertainties must be clearly understood (Bai et al., 2024). Second, focusing on local needs and participatory processes not only strengthens trust in climate policy and promotes social cohesion, but also empowers marginalized groups who are actively involved in shaping policy and are no longer seen as passive recipients of prevention measures.

Third, targeted technology transfer and co-financing can build local value chains in developing countries, create new jobs, and strengthen technical capacities. This aspect of the integrative model should be particularly appealing to policymakers and stakeholders, as it shows that climate policy can also be a driver of economic growth. Models, such as the Kenyan geothermal project, show that integrated partnerships can achieve both environmental goals and accelerate socioeconomic development. Fourth, innovative financial instruments—such as climate justice bonds and index-based insurance—offer new sources of revenue for sustainable infrastructure and social safety nets. This shifts climate protection away from being a cost factor to becoming a driver of ecological and social innovation.

8.3 Limitations and Open Questions

Despite the potential, significant challenges in climate policy remain unresolved and require urgent attention. First, the data basis for equity indicators is incomplete in many countries, with missing or inconsistent statistics on vulnerable groups making it difficult to allocate budgets and financial resources precisely.

Second, there are no tried-and-tested approaches for uniformly recording and sanctioning carbon outsourcing in global accounting systems. Without clear methods for calculating imported emissions, loopholes will remain.

Third, scaling up participatory processes raises questions about resource requirements and timeframes: such processes are easier to implement in rich countries than in states with weak administrative structures. How can time-critical climate measures be reconciled with lengthy consultation processes? It should be noted that participation processes must not address 'the community' in general terms, but must specifically involve marginalized voices. It can be achieved, for example, through women's councils, indigenous committees, or age-appropriate formats. An 'intersectional perspective', which considers the interconnected nature of social categorizations such as race, class, and gender, contributes to analytical depth and prevents generalization of the principle of justice. It therefore constitutes an essential component of inclusive, resilient, and democratically legitimate climate policy, especially in regions where social strata overlap the most and environmental pressures are highest.

Fourth, it remains unclear how a global equity panel could be established legitimately and what legal force its recommendations would have; moreover, questions remain as to who would be represented in such a body and how accountability to affected communities—particularly in the Global South—would be ensured..

Ultimately, your work as climate policy researchers, policymakers, and environmental advocates is crucial. Further research is necessary to explore dynamic limits that account for technological innovation and socioeconomic developments while maintaining normative consistency. The question of how adaptive safe limits and just limits can be continuously integrated into governance processes is a central field of research for ensuring stable, equitable, and effective climate policy in the long term.

9. CONCLUSIONS AND OUTLOOK

9.1 Key Findings

This study has shown that effective climate policy cannot be based solely on scientific limits ('safe limits') but must also integrate normative criteria of justice ('just limits'). The starting point for these considerations is the research findings of Gupta et al. (2024a, 2024 b), who argue that, from a global perspective, the safe limit for the climate is 1.5 °C, and the safe and just limit is 1.0 °C.

First, empirical case studies confirm that more vulnerable and poorer population groups in developing countries suffer significantly more from climate risks—whether from flooding in Bangladesh, technological dependencies in South Africa, or inadequate compensation mechanisms in Germany. Second, quantitative analyses highlight the vast disparities: per capita CO_2 budgets differ by a factor of more than 10, and damage from extreme events relative to GDP is, on average, 2.5 times higher in poor countries than in industrialized countries. Third, the conceptual analysis reveals that Rawls' difference principle, Sen's capability approach, and Fraser's three-dimension model are not just complementary, but together provide a robust normative framework. This robustness should reassure and instill confidence in the audience. They make it possible to operationalize not only distributive justice but also procedural and recognition justice. Fourth, the proposed integrative governance model demonstrates how equity criteria can be anchored throughout the policy cycle—from budget allocation and reporting requirements to compliance mechanisms—without undermining the scientific rigor of safe limits.

Finally, the discussion shows that political and social resistance is to be expected but is not insurmountable. Participatory processes and adaptive platforms can foster acceptance, but they also require adequate resources and effective conflict management. However, the potential of innovative financial instruments such as climate justice bonds and index-based insurance to offer concrete levers to direct funds to where they yield the most significant gains in equity should inspire and motivate the audience. Overall, the results make it clear that ecological integrity and social justice are not opposites but are mutually dependent: without justice, sustainable climate protection remains politically unstable; without a scientific basis, it risks being ineffective (Otto, 2024).

9.2 Implications for Research and Policy

Several implications can be drawn from these findings. For scientific research, the further development of indicator systems is of central importance. The systematic collection of equity indicators in global datasets holds the potential to accurately measure distribution effects, offering a promising future for climate policy. This includes harmonizing national statistics on vulnerable groups, emissions balances in the import-export context, and access data on cleantech. Furthermore, integrated assessment models should, in the future, incorporate normative parameters, such as

Rawls' difference principle or capability measures, to evaluate scenarios not only from a climate perspective but also from an equity perspective.

Polycentrism, procedural justice, and innovation and adaptation policies possess specific characteristics that are well-suited to a complex environment characterized by positive uncertainty about the future and the involvement of multiple actors with diverse normative perspectives. Fundamental to this is John Rawls' concept of liberalism, in which everyone shows consideration for others based on mutually acceptable principles of reciprocity. Rawls, therefore, considers the idea of fair social cooperation in society to be essential. This results in a way of thinking that is altruistic, impartial, and polyphonic. It is based on social integrity and the assumption that people should benefit each other, leaving it up to others to decide whether they want to agree rather than overwhelming or controlling them. Together, they form a system that is flexible and adaptable over time. It is the particular strength of our conceptual system as a framework for climate policy, governance, and research (Ridder et al., 2023).

At the political level, we recommend gradually embedding equity formulas in multilateral agreements. Pilot projects in regional blocs (such as the EU, AU, and ASEAN) can serve as a blueprint before a global agreement is established. At the national level, governments should make 'justice reports' mandatory in their reporting to the UNFCCC to create transparency in the distribution of adaptation funds and technology transfers. Parallel investments in capacity building for participatory processes—moderation skills, digital platforms, and community outreach—are necessary to ensure procedural justice, reassuring all stakeholders about the fairness of the process, and adequately reflect local environmental needs.

Innovative financing mechanisms deserve special attention: climate justice bonds could be linked to sustainable index funds, while CO_2 fees could flow directly into a global adaptation fund with explicit equity quotas. Insurance models should protect people with low incomes against extreme weather events while creating incentives for risk reduction. At the technical level, joint development and financing programs for technology transfer should be promoted to strengthen local value creation, empowering local communities, and avoid vendor lock-in.

Finally, the international community must develop mechanisms for sanctions and rewards: compliance mechanisms that take into account both emissions and equity goals increase the binding nature of agreements and reduce the risk of symbolic politics.

9.3 Further Research Approaches

Three areas of research appear particularly promising: First, the development of dynamic, safe limits is of utmost importance. These limits integrate technological innovation and socioeconomic changes as control variables. Such flexible thresholds could be adapted to regional conditions while maintaining the same level of ambition for climate protection. Second, more in-depth studies are needed to calculate and control carbon outsourcing. Standardized methodologies for accounting for imported emissions globally would help close these loopholes. Third, research into effective participatory processes is urgently needed: What forms of moderation, digital tools, and institutional arrangements ensure short-term decision-making capacity while simultaneously including marginalized groups? Field experiments conducted in various political contexts could provide valuable insights here.

Additionally, transdisciplinary pilot projects in which scientists, politicians, business leaders, and representatives from civil society jointly test and evaluate integrative governance models are not just worthwhile, but hold immense potential. Such 'living labs' offer the opportunity to link theory and practice and establish adaptive learning loops—a necessary step toward a permanently fair and sustainable climate policy.

REFERENCES

Amorocho-Daza, H., Sušnik, J., van der Zaag, P., & Slinger, J. H. (2025). A model-based policy analysis framework for social-ecological systems: Integrating uncertainty and participation in system dynamics modelling. *Ecological Modelling*, *499*, 110943. DOI: 10.1016/j.ecolmodel.2024.110943

Arruda Filho, M. T. d., Torres, P. H. C., & Jacobi, P. R. (2024). A systematic review of the literature on climate justice: A comparison between the Global North and South. *Sustainability*, *16*, 9888. DOI: 10.3390/su16229888

Bai, X., Hasan, S., Andersen, L. S., Bjørn, A., Kilkiş, Ş., & Ospina, D. (2024). Translating Earth system boundaries for cities and businesses. *Nature Sustainability*, *7*, 108–119. DOI: 10.1038/s41893-023-01255-w

Berger, J., & Liebe, U. (2025). Effective climate action must address both social inequality and inequality aversion. *npj. Climate Action*, *4*(1), 1–6. DOI: 10.1038/s44168-025-00208-7

Biely, K., & Chakori, S. (2025). Sustainability transition theories: Perpetuating or breaking with the status quo. *Sustainable Development*, *33*(1), 52–68. DOI: 10.1002/sd.3101

Caney, S. (2024). Climate justice and the moral relevance of the past. *Journal of Practical Ethics*, *12*(1). Advance online publication. DOI: 10.3998/jpe.6269

Carman, J. P., Lu, D., Ballew, M., Low, J., Verner, M., & Rosenthal, S. A. (2025). Americans' support for climate justice. *Environmental Science & Policy*, *163*, 103976. DOI: 10.1016/j.envsci.2024.103976

Chancel, L. (2022). Global carbon inequality over 1990–2019. *Nature Sustainability*, *5*, 931–938. DOI: 10.1038/s41893-022-00955-z

de Ridder, K., Schultz, F. C., & Pies, I. (2023). Procedural climate justice: Conceptualizing a polycentric solution to a global problem. *Ecological Economics*, *214*, 107998. DOI: 10.1016/j.ecolecon.2023.107998

Dorman, D. R., & Ciplet, D. (2022). Sustainable energy for all? Assessing global distributive justice in the green climate fund's energy finance. *Global Environmental Politics*, *22*(1), 94–116. DOI: 10.1162/glep_a_00621

Enke, B. (2024). Moral boundaries. *Annual Review of Economics*, *16*, 133–157. DOI: 10.1146/annurev-economics-091223-093730

Estrada, F., Lupi, V., Botzen, W. J. W., & Tol, R. S. J. (2025). Urban and non-urban contributions to the social cost of carbon. *Nature Communications*, *16*, 4193. DOI: 10.1038/s41467-025-59466-y

Fabre, A., Douenne, T., & Mattauch, L. (2025). Majority support for global redistributive and climate policies. *Nature Human Behaviour*. Advance online publication. DOI: 10.1038/s41562-025-02175-9

Follingstad, G. (2023). Tipping points for a seminal new era of climate resilience and climate justice. *Journal of Climate Resilience and Justice*, *1*, 3–7. DOI: 10.1162/crcj_e_00011

Fraser, N. (2010). *Scales of justice: Reimagining political space in a globalizing world*. Columbia University Press.

Gosseries, A. (2023). *What is intergenerational justice?* Wiley.

Gupta, J., Bai, X., Liverman, D. M., Rockström, J., Qin, D., & Stewart-Koster, B. (2024a). A just world on a safe planet: A Lancet Planetary Health–Earth Commission report on Earth-system boundaries, translations, and transformations. *The Lancet Planetary Health Commission*, *8*, e813–e873. DOI: 10.1016/S2542-5196(24)00042-1

Gupta, J., Prodani, K., Bai, X., Gifford, L., Lenton, T. M., & Otto, I. (2024b). Earth system boundaries and Earth system justice: Sharing the ecospace. *Environmental Politics*, *33*(7), 1286–1305. DOI: 10.1080/09644016.2023.2234794

Hickel, J. (2020). Quantifying national responsibility for climate breakdown: An equality-based attribution approach for carbon dioxide emiss. ions in excess of the planetary boundary. *The Lancet. Planetary Health*, *4*(9), e399–e404.

International Court of Justice. (2025). Obligations of states in respect of climate change. July 23, 2025. https://www.icj-cij.org/sites/default/files/case-related/187/187-20250723-sum-01-00-en.pdf

Islam, M. S. (2024). Rethinking climate justice: Insights from environmental sociology. *Climate (Basel)*, *12*, 203. DOI: 10.3390/cli12120203

Jones, R., Reid, P., & Macmillan, A. (2024). An Indigenous climate justice policy analysis tool. *Climate Policy*, *24*(8), 1080–1095. DOI: 10.1080/14693062.2024.2362845

Krawczyk, F., & Braun, A. Ch. (2025). Models like heroes? Making Integrated Assessment Models (IAMs) ready for deep decarbonization and a socio-economic transformation. *Energy Research & Social Science*, *121*, 103959. DOI: 10.1016/j.erss.2025.103959

Locatelli, B., Benra, F., Geneletti, D., Loft, L., Loos, J., & Schröter, B. (2025). Framing the relationship between justice and ecosystem services: A systematic review. *Ecosystem Services*, *74*, 101755. DOI: 10.1016/j.ecoser.2025.101755

Low, S., Brutschin, E., Baum, C. M., & Sovacool, B. K. (2025). Expert perspectives on incorporating justice considerations into integrated assessment modelling. *npj. Climate (Basel)*, *4*, 10. DOI: 10.1038/s44168-025-00218-5

McCauley, D., & Heffron, R. (2018). Just transition: Integrating climate, energy and environmental justice. *Energy Policy*, *119*, 1–7. DOI: 10.1016/j.enpol.2018.04.014

Murakami, D., Shevchenko, P. V., Matsui, T., Arandjelović, A., & Myrvoll, T. A. (2025). Climate-economy projections under shared socioeconomic pathways and net-zero scenarios. *arXiv*. https://doi.org//arXiv.2504.11721DOI: 10.48550

Ogunbode, C. A., Doran, R., Ayanian, A. H., Park, J., Utsugi, A., & van den Broek, K. L. (2024). Climate justice beliefs related to climate action and policy support around the world. *Nature Climate Change*, *14*, 1144–1150. DOI: 10.1038/s41558-024-02168-y

Otto, F. (2024). The climate crisis is solvable, but human rights must trump profits. *Nature*, *630*, 551–553. DOI: 10.1038/d41586-024-01762-6

Otto, F. (2025). *Climate injustice: Why we need to fight global inequality to combat climate change*. Greystone.

Owuor, S., Wamukota, C., Klagge, B., Greiner, C., & Nyandega, I. (2025). Unintended socio-economic transformations associated with large-scale renewable energy projects: the case of Menengai Geothermal Project in Kenya. *Review of Regional Research*. https://doi.org/DOI: 10.1007/s10037-025-00240-4

Pollex, J. (2024). Climate justice and policy analysis: Still a reserved relationship. *npj. Climate Action*, *3*, 65. DOI: 10.1038/s44168-024-00146-w

Rawls, J. (1999). *Theory of justice*. Harvard University Press.

Richardson, K., Steffen, W., Lucht, W., Bendtsen, J., Cornell, S. E., & Donges, J. F.. (2023). Earth beyond six of nine planetary boundaries. *Science Advances*, *9*(37), eadh2458. Advance online publication. DOI: 10.1126/sciadv.adh24

Rockström, J., Donges, J. F., Fetzer, I., Martin, M. A., Wang-Erlandsson, L., & Richardson, K. (2024b). Planetary Boundaries guide humanity's future on Earth. *Nature Reviews. Earth & Environment*, *5*, 773–788. DOI: 10.1038/s43017-024-00597-z

Rockström, J., Gupta, J., Qin, D., Lade, S. L., Abrams, J. F., & Andersen, L. S.. (2023). Safe and just Earth system boundaries. *Nature*, *619*, 102–111. DOI: 10.1038/s41586-023-06083-8

Rockström, J., Kotzé, L., Milutinović, S., Biermann, F., Brovkin, V., & Donges, J.. (2024a). The planetary commons: A new paradigm for safeguarding Earth-regulating systems in the Anthropocene. *Proceedings of the National Academy of Sciences of the United States of America*, *121*(5), e2301531121. DOI: 10.1073/pnas.2301531121

Rockström, J., Steffen, W., Noone, K., Persson, A., Stuart, I. I. I., Chapin, F., Lambin, E., & Lenton, T. M.. (2009). Planetary boundaries: Exploring the safe operating space for humanity. *Ecology and Society*, *14*(2), 32. https://www.ecologyandsociety.org/vol14/iss2/art32/

Sahle, M., Lahoti, S. A., Lee, S. Y., Brundiers, K., van Riper, C. J., & Pohl, C.. (2025). Revisiting the sustainability science research agenda. *Sustainability Science*, *20*, 1–19. DOI: 10.1007/s11625-024-01586-3

Sarang, S., & Prabhakar, R. (2023). Capacity-Building for Successful Climate Justice Collaborations. *Journal of Climate Resilience and Justice*, *1*, 93–106. DOI: 10.1162/crcj_a_00008

Schlosberg, D. (2013). Theorising environmental justice: The expanding sphere of a discourse. *Environmental Politics*, *22*(1), 37–55. DOI: 10.1080/09644016.2013.755387

Schmid, N., & Lumsden, C. (2023). Sowing the seeds of change: Policy feedback and ratcheting up in South African energy policy. *Energy Policy*, *178*, 113597. DOI: 10.1016/j.enpol.2023.113597

Schöngart, S., Nicholls, Z., Hoffmann, R., Pelz, S., & Schleussner, C.-F. (2025). High-income groups disproportionately contribute to climate extremes worldwide. *Nature Climate Change*. Advance online publication. DOI: 10.1038/s41558-025-02325-x

Sen, A. (1985). *Commodities and capabilities*. Oxford University Press.

Sen, A. (1995). *Inequality reexamined*. Oxford University Press.

Sen, A. (1999). *Development as freedom*. Knopf.

Shue, H. (2021). *The pivotal generation: Why we have a moral responsibility to slow climate change right now*. Princeton University Press.

Steffen, W., Richardson, K., Rockström, J., Cornell, S. E., Fetzer, I., & Bennett, E. M.. (2015). Sustainability. Planetary boundaries: Guiding human development on a changing planet. *Science*, *347*(6223), 1259855. DOI: 10.1126/science.1259855

Sunstein, C. R. (2025). *Climate justice: What rich nations owe the world—and the future*. The MIT Press., DOI: 10.7551/mitpress/15431.001.0001

Turnhout, E., Metze, T., Wyborn, C., Klenk, N., & Louder, E. (2020). The politics of co-production: Participation, power, and transformation. *Current Opinion in Environmental Sustainability*, *42*, 15–21. DOI: 10.1016/j.cosust.2019.11.009

van Vuuren, D. P., Doelman, J. C., Schmidt Tagomori, I., Beusen, A. H. W., Cornell, S. E., & Röckstrom, J. (2025). Exploring pathways for world development within planetary boundaries. *Nature*, *641*, 910–916. DOI: 10.1038/s41586-025-08928-w

Vardy, M., Oppenheimer, M., Dubash, N. K., O'Reilly, J., & Jamieson, D. (2017). The Intergovernmental Panel on Climate Change: Challenges and opportunities. *Annual Review of Environment and Resources*, *42*, 55–75. DOI: 10.1146/annurev-environ-102016-061053

Venzke, I. (2025). Carr and the climate: Solidarity and sacrifice in international law. *London Review of International Law*, lraf004. https://doi.org/DOI: 10.1093/lril/lraf004

Walker, S. E., Smith, E. A., Bennett, N., Bannister, E., Narayana, A., & Nuckols, T. (2024). Defining and conceptualizing equity and justice in climate adaptation. *Global Environmental Change*, *87*, 102885. DOI: 10.1016/j.gloenvcha.2024.102885

World Meteorology Organization. (2025). (WMO) Global Annual to Decadal Climate Update 2025-2029. https://wmo.int/sites/default/files/2025-05/WMO_GADCU_2025-2029_Final.pdf

Zimmermann, B., & Engelbrecht, S. (2024). Transforming work towards social-ecological sustainability: A capability perspective. *Transfer: European Review of Labour and Research*. Advance online publication. DOI: 10.1177/10242589241281014

KEY TERMS AND DEFINITIONS

Climate justice: Climate justice is a powerful concept that links the physical facts of climate change with questions of global distributive justice and responsibility. It's about who causes climate change, who is most affected, and who has the means to cope with it. By calling for a differentiated burden-sharing, for example, through climate finance, emission rights, and adaptation assistance for the Global South, climate justice underscores the need for global cooperation and shared responsibility in addressing climate disparities.

Environmental limits ('safe limits') with normative principles of justice ('just limits'): 'Safe limits' refer to ecological limits within which the Earth system functions stably and human development remains possible in the long term. However, it's the concept of 'Just limits' that truly underscores the urgency and significance of environmental justice in policy. These normative principles of justice aim to ensure environmental impacts are not minimized at the expense of disadvantaged groups or regions. The transition from purely ecological security to ecological and social justice is a central concern of sustainable global policy.

Governance models: Governance models are crucial in managing complex systems such as the environment, markets, or technologies. In the context of climate change, they include multilateral agreements, national policies, and local participation formats. Effective climate governance, which requires transparency, accountability, and the integration of different actors and forms of knowledge, is essential for managing these complex systems and ensuring inclusive decision-making.

Planetary boundaries: The concept of planetary boundaries was developed to define the ecological limits of the Earth, beyond which the Earth system could become destabilized. It encompasses nine biophysical processes, including climate change, biodiversity loss, and nitrogen cycles. Compliance with these boundaries is intended to ensure a 'safe operating space' for humanity.

Principles of fairness: Principles of fairness are based on normative standards, such as equality, need, or the polluter-pays principle. The polluter-pays principle, for instance, holds that those who produce pollution should bear the costs of managing it to prevent damage to human health or the environment. These principles play a central role in the climate debate, for example, in the allocation of emission rights or adaptation measures. Fair policy-making means not only legal equality, but also sensitivity to historical inequalities and structural disadvantages.

Social inequality and distribution mechanisms: Social inequality refers to the unequal distribution of opportunities, resources, and power relations within and between societies. Distribution mechanisms—such as taxes, subsidies, or transfers—can either mitigate or exacerbate existing inequalities. In the context of ecological transformations, it is crucial how burdens (e.g., CO_2 pricing, which can increase the cost of living for some) and benefits (e.g., climate financing, which can support the development of renewable energy) are distributed fairly.

Chapter 2
Global Environmental Policy:
Industrial Emissions and Regional Inequalities Towards Equitable and Sustainable Development

Tuğba Koyuncu Çakmak
https://orcid.org/0000-0002-2721-1313
İstanbul Esenyurt University, Turkey

ABSTRACT

The aim of this chapter is primarily to examine the balance between environmental pollution, global policy measures and regional inequalities and to explain alternative ways of achieving this balance. This chapter analyses the conflicts between the development needs and environmental obligations of developing countries in the realisation of sustainable development goals and the tendency of developed countries to avoid responsibility in climate policies. In addition, this chapter analyses the environmental impact of countries through indicators with various measurement criteria for the fair distribution of environmental damage. The difference in energy consumption of countries from past to present is analysed in terms of fossil fuel-based energy consumption per capita, carbon dioxide per capita, how countries use their environmental resources, biological capacity and ecological footprints, and the impact of heavy industries such as iron and steel, which cause intense carbon emissions, on global emissions.

DOI: 10.4018/979-8-3373-1529-4.ch002

1. INTRODUCTION

Environmental pollution is a global problem that not only negatively affects the region or country where it occurs but also threatens the whole world by causing global warming and climate change problems. These problems are in parallel with the increase in greenhouse gas emissions due to increasing energy consumption, especially with industrialisation. Fossil fuel-based energy consumption and increasing emissions cause global temperature increase (Sadorsky, 2014). In addition, human health is adversely affected, and food insecurity is increasing due to climate change and environmental pollution (Naqvi, 2021). In addition to all these negativities, since environmental pollution is not only a threat to the region or country where it is located, but also a global problem affecting the whole world, attention is drawn to global environmental policy measures in combating environmental pollution, climate change and global warming.

Energy consumption, which has been the primary catalyst of global economic growth since the Industrial Revolution, is predominantly driven by the extensive utilisation of fossil fuels. It is evident that the European Union (EU) and other developed countries have historically based their industrialisation, and welfare increases on fossil energy resources, such as coal, oil and natural gas. While this energy model has facilitated economic growth in the short term, it has resulted in significant environmental concerns and elevated levels of carbon dioxide (CO2) in the atmosphere. The climate crisis that is currently being experienced is, to a significant extent, a consequence of the elevated levels of greenhouse gas emissions that have emerged during this historical process. The European Green Deal, a set of environmental policies developed by the European Union, aims to restructure international trade and production processes in line with carbon neutrality targets. The Carbon Border Adjustment Mechanism (CBAM), a component of these policies, entails the imposition of supplementary tax obligations, contingent on the carbon content of imported goods. Nevertheless, despite the fact that these regulations are presented as a significant step in the fight against climate change, they engender considerable economic pressures on developing countries. These countries, which have yet to complete their industrialisation process and are in the economic development stage, are still dependent on fossil fuels to meet their energy needs. Furthermore, these countries have not yet attained the level of technological development and innovation that would enable them to reduce costs. Consequently, the imposition of contemporary carbon emission limitation policies on developing countries by developed countries, which have historically been the primary emitters, appears to be an egregious injustice in the allocation of environmental burden. The development of these policies, which is characterised by a disregard of the historical responsibilities of developed countries, results in the exacerbation of environmental inequalities. From the perspective of environmental justice, the right to industrialisation and the sustainable development goals of developing countries are impeded by the current regulatory framework. Consequently, the formulation of global environmental policies should not be limited to the pursuit of emission reduction targets; it is imperative that these policies also embrace the principle of equitable burden sharing among nations. The realisation of equitable and sustainable development is predicated on the premise of global collaboration, wherein historical responsibilities are duly acknowledged, and effective mechanisms are instituted to address prevailing structural inequalities. It is evident that concrete measures, such as the provision of financial assistance, the facilitation of technology transfer, and the implementation of capacity-building programmes in developing countries, have the potential to expedite their transition to low-carbon production processes. In particular, strategies should be developed to reduce the environmental impacts of industrial sectors, and financial and technical support should be provided to developing countries in these processes.

Especially since the Industrial Revolution, the European Union (EU) and other developed countries have relied heavily on fossil fuels for their energy consumption. In this process, industrialisation based on the use of fossil fuels has led to major environmental degradation and a significant increase in CO2 emissions. The EU's Green Deal policy and border carbon regulations impose severe sanctions that limit the economic growth of developing countries. However, these countries still need energy to sustain their industrialisation and economic development. Developed countries, historically responsible for a large share of industrial emissions, are now imposing similar obligations on developing countries. This clearly demonstrates that the burden of environmental degradation is not fairly distributed. This leads to deepening environmental inequalities. A just and sustainable development is possible only if historical responsibilities and existing inequalities are taken into account. Global environmental policies should aim not only to reduce carbon emissions, but also to ensure fair burden sharing among countries. By focusing on the environmental impacts of industrial sectors and providing financial support mechanisms to developing countries, both environmental and economic sustainability can be achieved on a global scale.

This chapter focuses on the challenges of achieving a balance between regional inequalities and equitable sustainable development on the path to sustainable industrialisation and global environmental sustainability. The aim of this chapter is firstly to examine the trade-off between environmental pollution, global policy measures and regional inequalities and to explain alternative ways of achieving this trade-off. It also draws attention to the contradictions between the development needs and environmental protection objectives of developing countries and the difficulties of developed countries' reluctance to take responsibility for achieving equitable and sustainable development. Resource efficiency in industries is discussed, together with the improvement of energy efficiency through technological innovations. In addition, this chapter includes a detailed analysis of the environmental impact of countries through indicators with various measurement criteria for the fair distribution of environmental damage. How the energy consumption of countries differs from past to present will be evaluated by comparing fossil fuel-based energy consumption per capita, carbon dioxide and greenhouse gas emissions per capita, how countries use their environmental resources, biological capacity and ecological footprints, and the impact of heavy industries such as iron and steel, which cause intense carbon emissions, on global emissions. Finally, the various criteria developed in this chapter are thought to be a new method that can be used to ensure fair burden sharing among countries in global environmental policy measures.

2. ENVIRONMENTAL POLLUTION: THE ROLE OF CARBON EMISSIONS

Increasing carbon emissions more than needed triggers air pollution and environmental degradation. On the other hand, unstoppable increases in emissions bring along the problems of climate change and global warming. In addition to energy consumption resulting from the use of fossil fuels, the accumulation of greenhouse gas emissions (GHG) in the atmosphere increases and air pollution increases due to economic activities that lack environmental sensitivity. Carbon dioxide emissions are the most common greenhouse gas emissions into the atmosphere (Andreoni and Galmarini, 2012). The IPCC (2024) report shows that global warming triggered by greenhouse gas emissions is 1.5 °C above pre-industrial levels. This emphasises the urgency and importance of the necessary measures to combat climate change and environmental degradation (Koyuncu Çakmak, 2025).

Carbon emissions in the world have increased rapidly since the 1800s with the development of the Industrial Revolution. These carbon emissions into the atmosphere have been following a continuously increasing trend until today. Figure 1 shows the change in per capita carbon dioxide emissions in the world and some developed countries since 1750s. The increase in per capita carbon emissions has been experienced especially in the USA since 1900s. This increase is followed by Canada in second place, China, South Africa, European Union countries, England, India and Kenya.

Figure 1. Per capita CO2 emissions

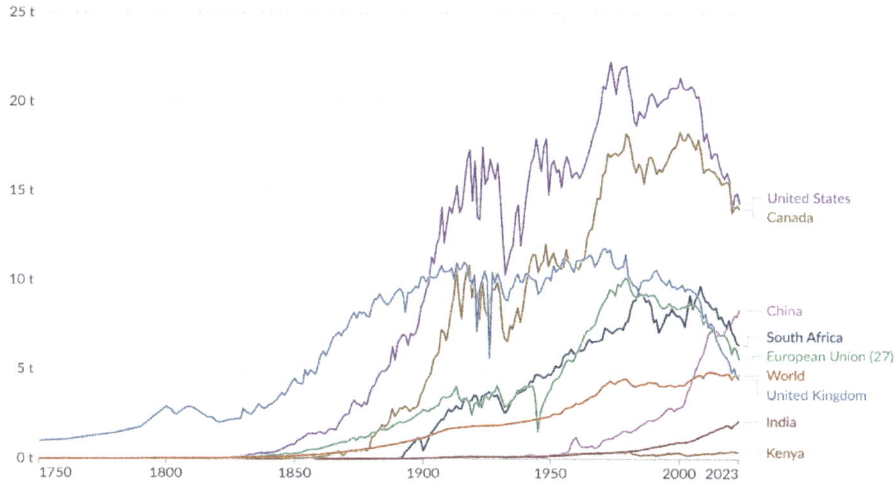

Data Source: *Our World in Data, 2025 (https://ourworldindata.org/)*

Figure 2 shows the carbon emissions from industry and the use of fossil fuels. China has been causing carbon emissions from fossil fuels and industrial production activities with a rapid acceleration in the 2000s. In 2023, China's annual carbon emissions from fossil fuels and industry are approximately 12 billion tonnes. China is followed by the USA with approximately 5 billion tonnes of carbon emissions per year and India with 3 billion tonnes.

Figure 2. Annual CO2 emissions from fossil fuels and industry

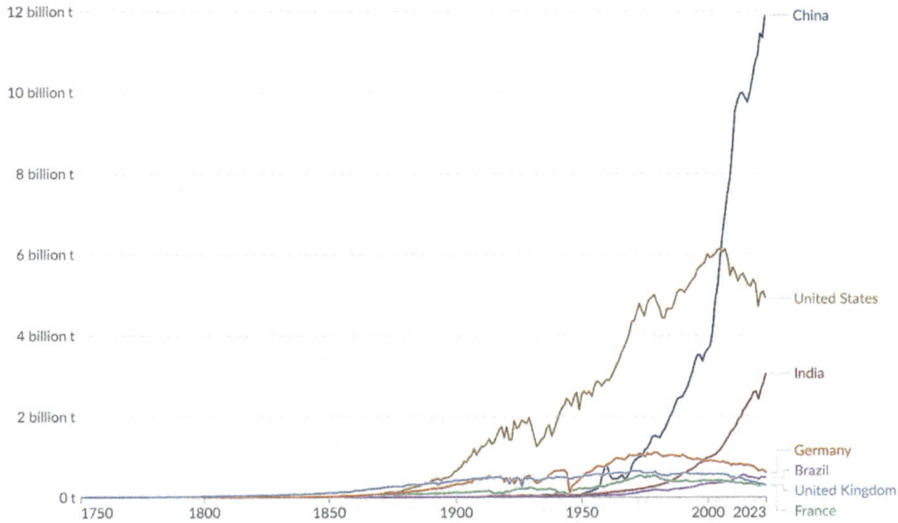

Data Source: *Our World in Data, 2025 (https://ourworldindata.org/)*

The negative effects of the increase in carbon emissions on climate change and air pollution have drawn attention to the industrial sector in environmental economics and sustainable development literature. In particular, the contribution of energy-intensive production activities on emissions has led researchers to the structure, causes and policy measures to reduce industrial emissions. Studies in the literature (such as; Chen et al.,2018; Gorus and Aslan, 2019; Jiang et al., 2019; Papiez et al., 2021) have shown that economic growth increases carbon emissions. While industrial production based on fossil fuel consumption triggers economic growth, it also causes an increase in carbon emissions. China, which provides significant economic growth in the world, is also a huge carbon emission producer (Dai et al.,2018).

In the year 2024, an examination was conducted on the relationship between green investment, institutional quality and CO2 emissions in G7 countries. The study concluded that CO2 emissions are the primary cause of greenhouse gas emissions. Işık et al. (2024) investigated the impact of renewable energy, climate policy uncertainty, industrial production and exports on carbon emissions in the USA. Empirical findings provide evidence that industrial production and exports have an increasing effect on carbon emissions. In view of the mounting uncertainties surrounding climate policies in advanced economies, particularly in the US, there is an increasing necessity for more detailed monitoring of the direct and indirect environmental impacts of trade.

Sohail, et al. (2021) conducted an empirical analysis of the relationship between clean energy use and air pollution in South Asian countries, utilising data from the period 1991-2019. The present study examined the role of institutional quality in determining this relationship through the cases of India, Pakistan and Nepal. The findings indicate that institutional quality exerts a statistically significant and positive influence on clean energy utilisation in India and Nepal, both in the short and long term. This finding indicates that the presence of a robust institutional framework is conducive to the adoption of renewable energy sources. However, the same study also finds that institutional quality has an increasing effect on environmental degradation in Pakistan and Nepal. This finding suggests that the effectiveness of institutional structures and their implementation patterns may vary across different countries. In a similar vein, Rahman and Alam (2022) analysed the effects of industrialisation, financial development, renewable and non-renewable energy consumption on environmental pollution using time series data for Australia for the period 1990-2020. The objective of the present study was to ascertain the impact of these economic and energy variables on carbon dioxide (CO2) emissions. Empirical evidence has demonstrated that the processes of industrialisation and the consumption of non-renewable energy sources have been found to result in a substantial increase in CO_2 emissions. Conversely, it has been determined that the consumption of renewable energy and the provision of financial support for development initiatives can contribute to environmental sustainability, as evidenced by a reduction in CO2 emissions. The findings indicate that the effective functioning of the financial system and the orientation towards clean energy have positive consequences on environmental quality. It has been demonstrated that both studies emphasise the complex interplay between institutional structures, energy policies and economic development in terms of environmental sustainability. Furthermore, the evidence indicates that not only are technological investments important for policymakers, but institutional reforms and financial infrastructure also play a critical role in the successful management of the energy transition.

Conversely, a paradox exists within the extant literature on environmental issues, wherein the pursuit of economic growth is seen to be in direct opposition to the mitigation of environmental degradation. Empirical studies demonstrate a positive correlation between increases in economic growth and environmental pollution. It can thus be concluded that an increase in economic growth is concomitant with an increase in environmental degradation. In this context, Ongan et al. (2023) investigated the question of whether there is a contradiction between economic growth and environmental pollution. The objective of this study is to ascertain the optimal level of government expenditure that would result in an increase or decrease in CO_2 emissions for the USA, Mexico and Canada. Empirical evidence from Mexico indicates that a maximum increase in real GDP per capita and a minimum reduction in CO2 emissions can be achieved through public expenditure of 26.4%. Should this threshold be exceeded, it is anticipated that both economic growth and emission levels will decline.

Taghvaee et al. (2022) conducted an examination of the relationship between environmental pollution, economic structure and economic complexity in OECD countries between 1971 and 2016. The present study comparatively analysed the effects of different economic sectors on environmental pollution and evaluated the role of economic structure and complexity on environmental sustainability. The empirical findings support the Environmental Kuznets Curve (EKC) hypothesis and draw attention to the fact that the transformation of the economic structure and sectoral composition is decisive in terms of environmental impacts in the socioeconomic development process. Furthermore, the results of sectoral analyses demonstrate that the service sector exhibits a higher polluting profile in terms of environmental impacts compared to other sectors. This provides a critical perspective on the common assumption that the service sector has a lower environmental impact compared to the traditional industrial and agricultural sectors. A further study was conducted by Koyuncu, Cakmak et al. (2024) that analysed environmental pollution in terms of sectors. In this study, the effect of sectoral employment on environmental degradation is analysed in terms of the Environmental Employment Curve (EEC). This study utilises data from China for the period 1990-2020, with the objective of conducting an analysis of the impact of employment in three primary sectors – industry, services and agriculture – on environmental pollution. The findings provide evidence that employment growth in the industrial and agricultural sectors is associated with increased carbon emissions and subsequent environmental degradation. Conversely, employment in the service sector has been demonstrated to exert a detrimental effect on environmental degradation. Furthermore, empirical evidence demonstrates a positive correlation between increases in energy consumption and increases in carbon emissions, while the utilisation of renewable energy is associated with a decrease in emissions. In consideration of the findings, it can be concluded that investments in green energy transformation do not result in a loss of employment.

3. ENVIRONMENTAL POLLUTION: THE ROLE OF ECOLOGICAL FOOTPRINT AND BIOLOGICAL CAPACITY

In a considerable number of studies in the relevant literature, environmental pollution is represented by carbon dioxide (CO2) emissions and greenhouse gas emissions. However, it must be noted that these variables are solely responsible for the generation of air pollution; consequently, they are inadequate in representing the totality of environmental pollution (Madaleno and Moutinho, 2018). Given the established link between deterioration in air quality and global warming, it can be concluded that the use of carbon dioxide and other greenhouse gas emissions as a variable representing environmental pollution is not necessarily erroneous. However, the concept of ecological footprint offers a more comprehensive definition of environmental pollution. The ecological footprint is defined as the data set pertaining to environmental pollution, including emissions, which serve to determine the extent of the burden placed on nature by the consumption habits and lifestyles of a particular country or community. To elaborate, the term ecological deficit signifies that a nation generates a level of consumption and waste that its extant natural resources are incapable of supporting. In this context, factors such as the intensity of industrial activities, high energy consumption, production processes based on fossil fuels and rapid urbanisation lead to an increase in the ecological footprint. This phenomenon, evident in both developed and developing countries, engenders local environmental challenges and concurrently contributes to multifaceted global environmental issues, including climate change, biodiversity loss, and environmental injustice.

The ecological footprint is comprised of the following components: the settlement area footprint, the carbon footprint, the agricultural area footprint, the fishing area footprint, the forest products footprint and the grazing area footprint. Consequently, the ecological footprint is a more appropriate metric for evaluating the environmental degradation caused by the production and consumption activities of a society or population in the context of climate change and global warming. The data presented in Figure 3 comparatively reveal the current situation between the ecological deficits and biological capacity reserves of countries. A thorough examination of the available data reveals that the ecological footprint of developed countries with a high level of industrialisation, as well as developing countries in the process of industrialisation, exceeds their biological capacity. This phenomenon indicates that the rate of consumption of natural resources in these countries exceeds the self-renewal capacity of their respective ecosystems.

Figure 3. Ecological deficit/reserve status by country in the world

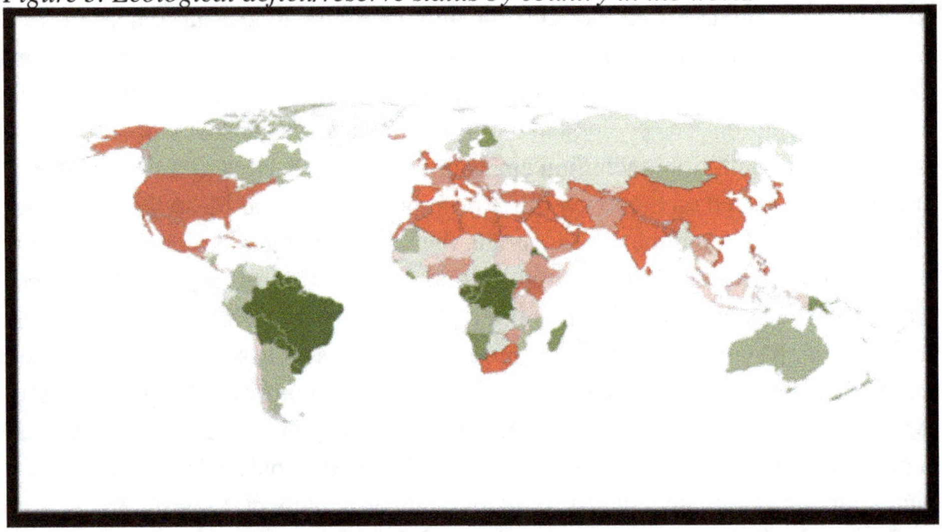

Data Source: *Global Footprint Network, 2025*

Recent empirical and theoretical studies in the environmental economics literature demonstrate that the ecological footprint is a more comprehensive and holistic indicator for measuring environmental degradation. A comparison of traditional environmental indicators with the ecological footprint reveals the latter to provide a more descriptive framework for the assessment of environmental sustainability. This is due to the fact that the ecological footprint combines various environmental impacts, including carbon emissions, biological capacity utilisation, land consumption and natural resource depletion, into a single scale. Caglar et al. (2022) conducted a study to ascertain the impact of economic growth, renewable energy, biocapacity and natural resources on ecological footprint. The present study analyses the effects in the US case for the period 1980-2017 within the framework of the Environmental Kuznets Curve hypothesis. Empirical findings support the hypothesis that economic growth and biocapacity increase environmental degradation, while increases in renewable energy consumption help to reduce environmental degradation. Murshed et al. (2021) conducted a study to examine the impact of economic activities on ecological footprints in four South Asian countries (Bangladesh, India, Pakistan and Sri Lanka) that demonstrate high levels of fossil fuel-based energy consumption. The empirical findings reveal that environmental regulations play important roles in directly and indirectly reducing ecological footprints in South Asian countries. Furthermore, it has been demonstrated that non-renewable energy consumption has a detrimental effect on ecological footprints, whilst the converse is true of renewable energy consumption. A further salient finding in this study is that environmental regulations serve to mitigate the deleterious effects of economic growth, non-renewable energy use and foreign direct investment inflows on the environment.

Cetin et al. (2025) investigated the relationship between technological innovation and environmental pollution using data from 1994-2018 for 10 OECD countries. The findings indicate that economic growth is positively correlated with an increase in ecological footprint, while technological innovation, renewable energy consumption and financial development are inversely associated with ecological footprint. Furthermore, the empirical results provide evidence of a bidirectional causal relationship between technological innovation and ecological footprint. Wang et al. (2025) conducted a comprehensive investigation into the economic efficiency, economic growth, separable energy, industrialisation and ecological footprint of OECD countries from 1995 to 2018. The empirical evidence indicates that the intensity of economic development and industrialisation exacerbates environmental degradation. Conversely, energy consumption plays a pivotal role in maintaining the ecological footprint and promoting economic growth. The present study demonstrates the environmental disadvantages of industrialisation in OECD countries. Tunio et al. (2025) investigated the relationship between renewable energy consumption, urbanisation, trade openness and economic development in 34 high-income European and Asian economies for the period 1970-2022. Empirical findings demonstrate that while economic development exerts an increasing effect on environmental degradation over time, it can also play a mitigating role in the short term. While the consumption of renewable energy is undoubtedly a significant factor in supporting economic growth, its impact on reducing the ecological footprint is time dependent. Conversely, urbanisation and trade openness have been identified as the primary long-term determinants of environmental degradation, underscoring the necessity for effective and targeted policy interventions in these domains. In the study examining the impact of nuclear energy production on CO2 emissions and ecological footprint in European Union member countries in the period 1990-2022, Soto et al. (2024) reveal that the adoption of nuclear energy by countries tends to affect CO2 emissions. However, this relationship is not direct; instead, it is more accurately modelled as a relationship from CO2 emissions to nuclear energy consumption according to the causality test. In addition, the ecological footprint variable does not show a causal relationship with nuclear energy consumption.

Sabir et al. (2019) conducted an investigation into the impact of economic globalisation and technological changes on environmental degradation in South Asian countries during the period 1975-2017. The investigation was conducted using the concept of ecological footprint. The empirical evidence indicates the presence of an inverted U-shaped relationship between globalisation, technological changes and environmental degradation. Furthermore, the findings indicate that foreign direct investment and trade openness exert a positive and significant influence on ecological footprint. Conversely, Pata (2021) analysed the impact of renewable energy production, globalisation and agricultural activities on ecological footprint and carbon dioxide emissions in BRIC countries (Brazil, Russia, India and China). Empirical findings reveal a long-term relationship between Brazil and China, and an increasing effect of globalisation on environmental pollution indicators. Renewable energy production has been demonstrated to have a substantial impact on reducing environmental pressures, particularly in China. In a similar vein, while the phenomenon of globalisation has been demonstrated to exert an increasing influence on carbon dioxide emissions in Brazil, the concurrent rise in renewable energy production has been shown to have a beneficial effect on environmental quality. The findings of the causality analysis demonstrate the existence of a bidirectional relationship between the agricultural sector and environmental degradation. However, a unidirectional causality from globalisation to both ecological footprint and carbon dioxide emissions has been demonstrated. Furthermore, a unidirectional causality from renewable energy production to ecological indicators is identified. The findings of this study indicate that globalisation dynamics and investments in renewable energy play a critical role in the formulation of sustainable development policies.

In the study conducted by Destek et al. (2018), the ecological footprint, a more comprehensive indicator of environmental sustainability, was utilised to analyse cross-sectional dependence between countries. Second generation panel data methods were employed in the analysis conducted using the panel data set for the European Union (EU) countries for the years 1980-2013. Empirical findings reveal a statistically significant U-shaped relationship between real per capita income and ecological footprint. This finding challenges the classical ECA assumption that economic growth has a counterbalancing effect on environmental degradation, with the level of environmental pressure increasing beyond a certain threshold. Conversely, the findings of the study reveal a direct U-curve relationship, rather than the inverted U-curve relationship that has been previously hypothesised. This new finding requires a revised interpretation in terms of environmental sustainability. Moreover, the present study also analysed the environmental impacts of energy use patterns and trade openness. The findings indicate that the utilisation of non-renewable energy sources is associated with an increase in environmental degradation; conversely, the adoption of renewable energy sources and a propensity for trade openness have been demonstrated to be inversely associated with environmental degradation. These findings imply that energy policies and foreign trade strategies of EU countries should be re-evaluated in terms of environmental sustainability.

In an empirical study conducted by Eregha et al. (2022), the effects of economic growth, energy consumption and environmental regulations on ecological footprint were analysed. The study focused on eleven fastest developing economies (the Next-11, N11). The research findings indicate that the environmental regulations implemented were not effective in reducing ecological degradation to the expected level. Conversely, economic growth, international trade volume and energy consumption have been demonstrated to exert a substantial increasing influence on ecological footprint. Country-by-country assessments indicate that energy consumption and economic growth are associated with environmental degradation across all N11 countries. These findings are consistent across all model estimations utilised, providing a robust evidence base for the analysis. In conclusion, the study proffers implications for policy makers in accordance with the findings, in conjunction with recommendations concerning the limitations of the analyses and the potential for future research.

4. ENVIRONMENTAL POLLUTION: THE ROLE OF EMISSIONS FROM INDUSTRIAL PRODUCTION AND MATERIAL CONSUMPTION

The interplay between population growth, economic development and technological advancement on a global scale has led to a consistent and incremental increase in energy demand. This is particularly evident in high energy-consuming sectors such as steel, chemicals, cement, automotive and textiles, where extreme temperatures ranging from 1500°C to 2000°C and substantial electrical energy are requisite in the process of transforming raw materials into final products. The utilisation of energy resources, which are predominantly reliant on fossil fuels, in this process gives rise to significant environmental concerns and is among the primary catalysts for global pollution.

In this framework, Sumaira and Siddique (2023) analysed the effects of industrialisation and fossil fuel-based energy use on environmental degradation in South Asian countries using panel data for the period 1984-2016. The findings of the study reveal that industrialisation and energy consumption are the determinants of the increase in environmental pollution and that there is a long-term cointegration relationship between these variables. Consequently, the necessity of developing technologies to increase energy efficiency in the industrial sector and implementing sustainable environmental policies is emphasised. Chen et al. (2021) investigated the impact of industrial activities and energy structure on environmental pollution by creating a panel data set for 30 provinces in China between 2000-2016. As a result of the empirical findings, they concluded that industrial activities increase environmental pollution. In the long run, they pointed out that increasing investments in research and development (R&D) activities, systematically improving energy efficiency in the industrial sector and reorganising the current structure of coal consumption in line with environmental sustainability goals can make significant contributions to significantly reducing emissions that cause air pollution. On the other hand, Rao and Yan (2020) analysed the industrial factors affecting economic growth in China. The empirical analyses in the study reveal that the main environmental factors that have a determinant effect on economic growth are industrial wastewater emissions, industrial waste gas emissions, and industrial smoke and dust emissions. Moreover, it is found that the interaction dynamics between industrial waste gas emissions and industrial wastewater emissions have a limiting effect on the economic growth process. These findings point to the necessity of addressing environmental management policies with a holistic and interactive approach in order to achieve sustainable development goals, taking into account the multidimensional effects of environmental pollution factors on economic performance.

Wang et al. (2021) conducted an investigation into the industrial and service sub-sectors between 1995 and 2009, with a view to examining the relationship between technological developments and environmental pollution in five developing countries: Brazil, Russia, India, China and Mexico. Empirical analyses indicate that the impact of technological developments on environmental pollution will decrease after developing countries reach a certain level of production and trade efficiency. The study by Alola et al. (2020) sought to examine the effects of domestic material consumption, per capita income level and renewable energy use in achieving environmental sustainability targets within the framework of 28 member countries of the European Union (EU-28). The findings of the analyses using the panel data set demonstrate that domestic material consumption has a detrimental effect on environmental quality. An escalation in material consumption, both in the short term and over an extended timeframe, exerts mounting pressure on environmental resources and jeopardises the attainment of sustainability objectives. This situation indicates that intensive utilisation of natural resources and resultant waste generation are contributing factors to environmental degradation. The study demonstrates that the effect of real income per capita varies depending on the time dimension. In the short term, it has been demonstrated that an increase in income has a detrimental effect on environmental quality, due to an increase in greenhouse gas emissions. This phenomenon signifies that escalating levels of production and consumption, consequent to economic growth, exert an increased pressure on the environment. In conclusion, the study by Alola et al. (2020) demonstrates that in order to achieve environmental sustainability targets in European Union member countries, policy makers should develop strategies according to the development levels of the countries. This is especially important in reducing domestic material consumption and promoting the use of renewable energy. Therefore, considering the environmental impacts of economic growth, investing in environmentally friendly technologies and adopting a green growth perspective will be important steps towards sustainable development.

The consumption of energy, the emission of carbon, and the subsequent environmental impact, vary significantly among developed, developing, and underdeveloped countries within the global economy. In particular, developed countries have been found to be responsible for a substantial proportion of environmental degradation, primarily due to their high levels of production and industrial activities. A study was conducted with G20 countries, which play a pivotal role in the global economy, accounting for over 80 per cent of worldwide energy consumption and responsible for the highest carbon emissions on the planet. The investigation focused on the impact of energy policies on environmental sustainability and social welfare. Kumar et al. (2021) conducted a study to examine the impact of energy consumption and environmental quality on welfare in G20 countries over the period from 2006 to 2019. The findings demonstrate that an increase in renewable energy consumption and a concomitant improvement in environmental quality, as evidenced by reduced carbon emissions, has a substantial impact on the level of welfare in G20 countries. Conversely, the consumption of non-renewable energy sources has been demonstrated to exert a detrimental effect on individuals' life satisfaction. Furthermore, the analyses indicated a bidirectional relationship between renewable energy consumption, non-renewable energy consumption and economic growth variables. This finding suggests that these variables interact with each other and affect each other dynamically.

5. DISCUSSION AND CONCLUSION

Environmental pollution is a global problem that affects not only the region or country where it occurs, but also the whole world through global warming and climate change. These problems are directly related to the increase in greenhouse gas emissions as a result of increasing energy consumption, especially with the industrialisation process. The use of energy based on fossil fuels is one of the main causes of global temperature increase; climate change has negative impacts on human health and increases food insecurity.

The global nature of environmental problems necessitates international cooperation and holistic environmental policies in combating these problems. Especially since the Industrial Revolution, the European Union (EU) and other developed countries have largely fueled their energy consumption with fossil fuels. In this process, developed countries have caused significant environmental degradation and an increase in CO_2 emissions. Today, these countries are developing policies to reduce carbon emissions; however, the economic costs of these targets are largely imposed on developing countries. This situation reveals that environmental burdens are not distributed fairly on the basis of historical responsibility.

Practices such as the EU's Green Deal policy and carbon regulations at the border are restrictive to the economic growth of developing countries and hinder the industrialisation and development processes of these countries. However, historically, most of the industrial emissions originate from developed countries. Nevertheless, developed countries impose similar environmental obligations on developing countries, which deepens environmental inequalities. In this framework, a fair and sustainable development approach requires taking into account historical responsibilities and existing structural inequalities. Global environmental policies should aim not only to reduce carbon emissions but also to ensure fair burden sharing among countries. In this context, both environmental and economic sustainability can be achieved by focusing on the environmental impacts of industrial sectors and providing financial support mechanisms to developing countries.

This chapter has discussed the challenges of striking a balance between addressing regional inequalities and equitable development in line with the goals of sustainable industrialisation and environmental sustainability. It also draws attention to the contradictions between the development needs of developing countries and environmental protection goals, and to the failure of developed countries to assume sufficient responsibility within the framework of historical responsibilities. In addition, in order to ensure a fair distribution of environmental damage, the environmental impact of countries is examined through various variables such as per capita CO2 emissions based on fossil fuel use, ecological footprint and biological capacity, industrial production and material consumption by country.

In the contemporary era, developed countries have implemented a series of environmental policies and regulations with the aim of combatting climate change. In this context, policies such as the European Green Deal and the Carbon Border Adjustment Mechanism (CBAM) aim to reduce carbon emissions on a global scale. However, the methods applied to achieve these targets have been shown to cause serious structural and economic problems, especially for developing countries. Developed countries are largely transferring the economic burden of contemporary climate policies to developing countries without adequately assuming their historical environmental responsibilities arising from the industrial-based development processes of the past.

In this context, although the historical and current responsibility for environmental degradation and CO2 emissions is concentrated in developed countries, the financial and structural burdens of the environmental measures taken are unfairly reflected on less developed and developing countries. The environmental crisis, which has resulted from the high-emission production and consumption practices of developed countries for many years, is now limiting the development potential of countries that have not yet completed the process of industrialisation, and which are therefore unable to meet the environmental standards and carbon regulations imposed by these countries.

In this framework, the objective of international environmental policies should not only be the reduction of current emissions, but also consideration of historical responsibilities. The introduction of additional obligations and costs, especially for industrialised countries that have previously caused high levels of environmental damage, is critical to ensure fair burden sharing. In this context, it is imperative to emphasise that in the design and implementation of environmental measures, each country or region should assume differentiated responsibilities according to the level of environmental damage it has caused in the historical process. In order to achieve this objective, it is necessary to develop a set of objective criteria that can be used to measure the environmental impact of countries. The indicators to be used in these calculations should include per capita carbon emissions, environmental degradation caused by industrial activities, biological capacity utilisation and ecological footprint.

In conclusion, the legitimacy and effectiveness of global environmental policies depend not only on technical arrangements for reducing emissions, but also on a fair and balanced approach based on historical responsibilities. In this context, the introduction of additional obligations in environmental regulations for industrialised countries is necessary both for the establishment of climate justice and for developing countries to achieve their sustainable development goals.

REFERENCES

Alola, A. A., Akadiri, S. S., & Usman, O. (2020). Domestic material consumption and greenhouse gas emissions in the EU-28 countries: Implications for environmental sustainability targets. *Sustainable Development, 29*(2), 388–397. DOI: 10.1002/sd.2154

Andreoni, V., & Galmarini, S. (2012). Decoupling economic growth from carbon dioxide emissions: A decomposition analysis of Italian energy consumption. *Energy, 44*(1), 682–691. DOI: 10.1016/j.energy.2012.05.024

Caglar, A. E., Yavuz, E., & Mert, M.. (2022). The ecological footprint facing asymmetric natural resources challenges: Evidence from the USA. *Environmental Science and Pollution Research International, 29*, 10521–10534. DOI: 10.1007/s11356-021-16406-9

Cetin, M., Ozturk, I., Sumerli Sarigul, S., Murshed, M., & Kilavuz, E. (2025). Nexus between technological innovation and environmental pollution in selected OECD countries. *Natural Resources Forum, 49*(1), 841–862. DOI: 10.1111/1477-8947.12458

Chen, J., Wang, P., Cui, L., Huang, S., & Song, M. (2018). Decomposition and decoupling analysis of CO2 emissions in OECD. *Applied Energy, 231*(1 December), 937-950. doi:DOI: 10.1016/j.apenergy.2018.09.179

Chen, L., Li, K., Chen, S., Wang, X., & Tang, L. (2021). Industrial activity, energy structure, and environmental pollution in China. *Energy Economics, 104*, 105633. DOI: 10.1016/j.eneco.2021.105633

Eregha, P. B., Nathaniel, S. P., & Vo, X. V. (2022). Economic growth, environmental regulations, energy use, and ecological footprint linkage in the Next-11 countries: Implications for environmental sustainability. *Energy & Environment, 34*(5), 1327–1347. DOI: 10.1177/0958305X221084293

Gorus, M. S., & Aslan, M. (2019). Impacts of economic indicators on environmental degradation: Evidence from MENA countries. *Renewable & Sustainable Energy Reviews, 103*(April), 259–268.

Işık, C.. (2024). Renewable energy, climate policy uncertainty, industrial production, domestic exports/re-exports, and CO2 emissions in the USA: A SVAR approach. *Gondwana Research, 127*, 556–164.

Jiang, J.-J., Ye, B., Zhou, N., & Zhang, X.-L. (2019). Decoupling analysis and environmental Kuznets curve modelling of provincial-level CO2 emissions and economic growth in China: A case study. *Journal of Cleaner Production, 212*(1 March), 1242-1255. doi:DOI: 10.1016/j.jclepro.2018.12.116

Koyuncu Çakmak, T. (2025). Green Industrial Policies and Sustainable Economy Approaches Ensuring Industrial Growth and Environmental Balance. In Meçik, O. (Ed.), *Macroeconomic Challenges to Structural Reform and Industrial Development* (pp. 447–462). IGI Global., DOI: 10.4018/979-8-3693-5508-4.ch017

Madaleno, M., & Moutinho, V. (2018). Effects decomposition: Separation of carbon emissions decoupling and decoupling effort in aggregated EU-15. *Environment, Development and Sustainability, 20,* 181–198. DOI: 10.1007/s10668-018-0238-4

Murshed, M., Rahman, M. A., & Alam, M. S.. (2021). The nexus between environmental regulations, economic growth, and environmental sustainability: Linking environmental patents to ecological footprint reduction in South Asia. *Environmental Science and Pollution Research International, 28,* 49967–49988. DOI: 10.1007/s11356-021-13381-z

Naqvi, A. (2021). Decoupling trends of emissions across EU regions and the role of environmental policies. *Journal of Cleaner Production, 323*(10 November), 129130. doi:DOI: 10.1016/j.jclepro.2021.129130

Ongan, S., Işık, C., & Amin, A.. (2023). Are economic growth and environmental pollution a dilemma? *Environmental Science and Pollution Research International, 30,* 49591–49604. DOI: 10.1007/s11356-023-25698-y

Pata, U. K. (2021). Linking renewable energy, globalization, agriculture, CO2 emissions and ecological footprint in BRIC countries: A sustainability perspective, *Renewable Energy,* Volume 173, 197-208, ISSN 0960-1481, DOI: <ALIGNMENT.qj></ALIGNMENT>10.1016/j.renene.2021.03.125

Rahman, M. M., & Alam, K. (2022). Impact of industrialization and non-renewable energy on environmental pollution in Australia: Do renewable energy and financial development play a mitigating role? *Renewable Energy, 195,* 203–213.

Rao, C., & Yan, B. (2020). Study on the interactive influence between economic growth and environmental pollution. *Environmental Science and Pollution Research International, 27,* 39442–39465. DOI: 10.1007/s11356-020-10017-6

Sabir, S., & Gorus, M. S. (2019). The impact of globalization on ecological footprint: Empirical evidence from the South Asian countries. *Environmental Science and Pollution Research International, 26,* 33387–33398. DOI: 10.1007/s11356-019-06458-3

Sadorsky, P. (2014). The effect of urbanization on CO2 emissions in emerging economies. *Energy Economics*, *41*(January), 147–153.

Sohail, M. T., Ullah, S., & Majeed, M. T.. (2021). The shadow economy in South Asia: Dynamic effects on clean energy consumption and environmental pollution. *Environmental Science and Pollution Research International*, *28*, 29265–29275. DOI: 10.1007/s11356-021-12690-7

Soto, G. H., & Martinez-Cobas, X. (2024). Nuclear energy generation's impact on the CO2 emissions and ecological footprint among European Union countries. *Science of The Total Environment*, Volume 945, 173844, ISSN 0048-9697, DOI: <ALIGNMENT.qj></ALIGNMENT>10.1016/j.scitotenv.2024.173844

Sumaira, , Siddique, H. M. A. (2023). Industrialization, energy consumption, and environmental pollution: Evidence from South Asia. *Environmental Science and Pollution Research International*, *30*(2), 4094–4102. DOI: 10.1007/s11356-022-22317-0

Taghvaee, V. M., Nodehi, M., & Saboori, B. (2022). Economic complexity and CO2 emissions in OECD countries: Sector-wise Environmental Kuznets Curve hypothesis. *Environmental Science and Pollution Research International*, *29*, 80860–80870. DOI: 10.1007/s11356-022-21491-5

Tunio, F. H., Nabi, A. A., Memon, R. U. R., Fraz, T. R., & Haluza, D. (2025). Sustainability in High-Income Countries: Urbanization, Renewables, and Ecological Footprints. *Energies*, *18*(7), 1599. DOI: 10.3390/en18071599

Wang, Q., Ge, Y., & Li, R. (2025). Does improving economic efficiency reduce ecological footprint? The role of financial development, renewable energy, and industrialization. *Energy & Environment*, *36*(2), 729–755. DOI: 10.1177/0958305X231183914

Wang, S., He, Y., & Song, M. (2021). Global value chains, technological progress, and environmental pollution: Inequality towards developing countries. *Journal of Environmental Management*, *277*, 110999. DOI: 10.1016/j.jenvman.2020.110999

KEY TERMS AND DEFINITIONS

Carbon emissions: The term refers to carbon-based gases released into the atmosphere, in particular carbon dioxide (CO_2) and carbon monoxide (CO).

Climate change: It is a term that refers to global warming and changes in the world's climate system.

Ecological footprint: It is an indicator that measures how much resources an individual, community, region or country consumes from nature to sustain its lifestyle and to what extent this consumption is compatible with nature's self-renewal capacity (biological capacity). In other words, it is the total amount of biologically productive land and water area required to produce the resources consumed by humans and to absorb the resulting wastes (especially carbon emissions).

Environmental pollution: It is a term that refers to the pollution of natural resources such as air, water, soil and the damage to ecosystems due to human activities.

Industrial growth: It is a term that refers to the growth and expansion of sectors of an economy such as manufacturing, mining, construction, energy production, more production capacity, application of new technologies, increase in labour force and increase in economic output.

Sustainable Growth: It is a term that refers to ensuring the sustainability of natural resources through the development of technology and innovation while ensuring economic growth.

Chapter 3
Effective Solutions to Global Climate Change Policies:
Increasing the Importance of Technology and Renewable Energy Sources

Hasan Umutlu
https://orcid.org/0000-0002-2604-3573
Duzce University, Turkey

Ayşenur Şakalak
https://orcid.org/0000-0002-8420-4718
Selcuk University, Turkey

ABSTRACT

It is stated that environmental pollution increases after countries use primary energy sources and as a result, global climate change is experienced. In order to prevent global climate change, it is important to reduce the use of energy sources that cause environmental pollution. Therefore, increasing the use of technology and renewable energy sources is seen as the most important factor in reducing environmental pollution. It is important for countries to increase their investments in technology and renewable energy sources. However, it should be noted that renewable energy sources can also lead to environmental pollution if not used effectively.

DOI: 10.4018/979-8-3373-1529-4.ch003

INTRODUCTION

The process of industrialization has led to a range of environmental challenges driven by multiple factors. Among these, increased mechanization, globalization, economic growth, rural-to-urban migration, and the resulting population growth have played significant roles. Additionally, the reliance on fossil fuels to meet both human needs and production demands has contributed substantially to environmental degradation. While the rise in carbon dioxide emissions is largely attributed to these factors, it is also driven by broader human activities. These developments are widely considered to be key contributors to global climate change. In response, the use of renewable energy sources—which are generally perceived to cause minimal or no harm to the environment—has emerged as a viable alternative. Nevertheless, the dominance of fossil fuels in certain regions has resulted in the political and economic dependence of countries lacking such resources. Consequently, investment in renewable energy has become a prominent topic in contemporary academic and policy discussions. Recent global events, such as the COVID-19 pandemic and the ongoing Ukraine-Russia conflict, have further intensified attention on this issue.

The availability of adequate water resources and favorable climatic conditions is crucial for human survival. In particular, the existence and well-being of living organisms are closely linked to the presence of specific chemical compositions in the atmosphere, even in precise proportions. Alterations in these chemical balances can trigger climate change, which, in turn, may affect numerous dimensions of human life, including food security, housing, and public safety. In this regard, it is essential for countries to formulate long-term strategies and implement projects aimed at mitigating the potential consequences of future climate change (Şen, 2022: 2–3). Moreover, climate change is not only driven by atmospheric shifts but also by anthropogenic factors, as previously discussed. Although the individual contribution to environmental degradation may appear negligible, the cumulative impact of human behavior remains significantly underestimated by many governments. Climate change continues to exert a global influence, affecting both developed and developing countries alike, while air pollution poses serious threats to public health and human life. The exploitation of nature as an inexhaustible resource has led to a decline in green spaces and a rapid increase in high-rise constructions, particularly skyscrapers (Demirbaş & Aydın, 2020: 164). However, a growing recognition of nature's vital role in sustaining human life has prompted the emergence of numerous policies and initiatives aimed at combating global climate change. Among these, the Paris Climate Agreement stands out as one of the most significant international efforts documented in the literature.

Dating back to 2016, the Paris Climate Agreement represents a significant international accord aimed at realizing a long-term technological vision in the fight against climate change. Under the framework of this agreement, numerous initiatives have been undertaken to enhance climate resilience and reduce greenhouse gas emissions. These initiatives aim to promote and facilitate the development and transfer of environmentally sound technologies. Furthermore, a dedicated technology framework has been established to guide the implementation of the Technology Mechanism. In the context of climate change, fostering, enabling, and accelerating innovation is regarded as essential for achieving long-term solutions, driving economic growth, and ensuring sustainable development. To fulfill this objective of the Paris Climate Agreement, it has been stipulated that a range of measures will be employed—including collaborative actions and financial assistance to developing countries—across various stages of the technology cycle (Paris Agreement, 2015).

Consequently, global developments and the environmental pollution resulting from the use of fossil fuels have prompted countries to shift towards the consumption of renewable energy sources. As emphasized in the Paris Climate Agreement—an international initiative aimed at addressing global climate change—particular attention has been given to the roles of technology and renewable energy in fostering sustainable solutions. Unlike fossil fuels, renewable energy sources represent a strategic advancement that can be harnessed by all countries, offering the potential to reduce reliance on foreign energy and enhance national energy independence. However, the initial installation and infrastructure costs associated with these resources can be significantly high. Moreover, if such environmentally friendly energy sources are not utilized efficiently and with appropriate oversight, they may still contribute to environmental degradation, albeit to a lesser extent than fossil fuels. Therefore, effective solutions to these challenges may include the formation of bilateral agreements between nations and the provision of financial or regulatory support to companies engaged in the development and deployment of renewable technologies.

Building on the aforementioned context, this study aims to evaluate the role of renewable energy sources within the broader framework of technological advancement, which is considered a critical component in addressing global climate change through solution proposals and policy development. Specifically, the research focuses on the effective role of technology—highlighted under a distinct provision in the Paris Climate Agreement—in mitigating the adverse impacts of climate change. Renewable energy sources are pivotal not only in reducing greenhouse gas emissions but also in enhancing the strategic importance of technological innovation. Accordingly, this study intends to examine global climate change, its associated effects, potential solutions, and relevant policy recommendations, while emphasizing the significance of technology and renewable energy in reducing the overall impact of environmental degradation. In this context, the study will first explore the progression and anticipated consequences of global climate change, followed by proposed solutions. It will then address the role of technological investments and renewable energy in mitigating environmental pollution. The analysis will also include a focus on various types of renewable energy—such as wind, solar, geothermal, hydroelectric, and biomass. Finally, the conclusion will provide a comprehensive assessment and outline key policy recommendations.

1. EVOLUTION OF GLOBAL CLIMATE CHANGE

Climate constitutes one of the most vital resources for fulfilling the basic survival needs of living organisms (Davarcıoğlu, 2018). Specifically, the existence of life on Earth depends on the availability of adequate water resources and favorable climatic conditions. These conditions are closely tied to the presence of specific chemical components in the atmosphere, which must remain within certain balanced proportions. Disruptions or imbalances in these components can pose serious threats to human life (Şen, 2022: 2). Both natural processes and anthropogenic activities have altered the chemical composition of the atmosphere, thereby triggering climatic changes. The scientific recognition of this phenomenon dates back to the work of chemist Svante A. Arrhenius, who first proposed that even minor fluctuations in atmospheric gas concentrations—particularly carbon dioxide—could lead to increases in global temperature. This insight laid the groundwork for understanding climate dynamics. However, systematic observational studies did not begin until 1958, when regular monitoring of atmospheric carbon dioxide levels was initiated (Kılıç, 2009: 21).

Climate change, which dates back to prehistoric times, was initially driven by natural phenomena such as tectonic activity and astronomical interactions with the sun. Over time, environmental indicators such as glacial melting, increased frequency of heatwaves, and rising sea levels have disrupted ecological systems (Türkeş, 2008: 26–27). Since the 19th century, however, the influence of human activities has become increasingly evident, contributing significantly alongside natural factors to the progression of climate change (Öztürk, 2002). Early signs of this transformation include fluctuations in the Earth's energy balance, temperature increases resulting from solar or volcanic activity, and global warming exacerbated by anthropogenic factors (IPCC, 2001: 7). In this context, the United Nations Framework Convention on Climate Change (UNFCCC) defines climate change as a phenomenon resulting not only from natural processes but also from direct or indirect human activities that alter the composition of the global atmosphere (UN, 1992: 3).

At this juncture, the Industrial Revolution is widely regarded as a pivotal turning point in human history. The transformation in production processes, the altered dynamics of supply and demand, and the rapid increase in population density led to the diversification of human needs and brought the issue of migration to the forefront. Rising living standards as a result of social mobility and the growing demand for industrial goods significantly contributed to various climate-related changes. During this period, the unsustainable exploitation of natural resources and the intensifying use of fossil fuels in production processes began to pose a serious threat to the atmosphere (Asan, 1995: 23; Kadıoğlu & Sonu, 2007). In particular, the rise in atmospheric energy, in parallel with the increase in average global temperatures, led to the more frequent occurrence of extreme weather events such as hurricanes and floods—bringing global climate crises into sharper focus (Koçak & Bozyurt, 2024). Consequently, greenhouse gas emissions resulting from human activity have been identified as the primary driver of climate change, which is now recognized as one of the most pressing environmental issues worldwide. These gases—comprising six key components as outlined in the Kyoto Protocol—not only threaten the planet's ecological balance but also pose a significant risk to the long-term survival of the human species (Yurduseven et al., 2024). This existential threat has, in turn, spurred a series of critical studies and international initiatives, as illustrated in Table 1.

Table 1. International Initiatives to Reduce Greenhouse Gas Emissions

Effective Date	Agreement	Countries Parties
1994	United Nations Conference on Environment and Development in Rio de Janeiro	Annex I: Eastern European and former Soviet countries and OECD member countries that have transitioned to market economies; Annex II: OECD countries
2005	Kyoto Protocol (KP)	191 countries and the European Union
2016	Paris Agreement	197 from the country party, 187 members

Source: Created by the author based on Beşballı's 2023 study

Furthermore, in order to address the challenges posed by climate change, the promotion of economic systems that support sustainable development was emphasized within the framework of the convention advocating for sustainable growth (IDCC, 2002). The Kyoto Protocol, which ranks as the second major international agreement, was adopted in 1997 and entered into force in 2005. This protocol, serving as a complement to the United Nations Framework Convention on Climate Change (UNFCCC), shares the same overarching objectives (Republic of Turkey Ministry of Energy and Natural Resources, 2025a). Subsequently, the Paris Agreement, which came into effect in 2016, represents a landmark accord encompassing the participation of all nations. This agreement envisages the provision of financial and technical resources to support underdeveloped and developing countries. Its primary objective is to limit the increase in global average temperature to 1.5°C above pre-industrial levels (Republic of Turkey Ministry of Energy and Natural Resources, 2025b). Although these international instruments differ in certain aspects, they fundamentally converge on the goal of reducing greenhouse gas emissions resulting from human activities (Beşballı, 2023: 516).

Figure 1. Greenhouse Gas Emissions

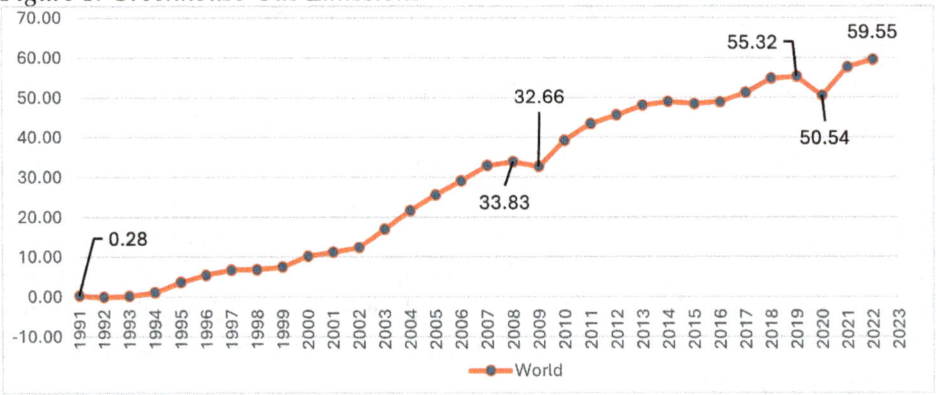

Source: World Development Indicators (2025)

Despite the implementation of numerous initiatives aimed at mitigating greenhouse gas emissions, concentrations of these gases—namely CO_2, CH_4, N_2O, HFCs, PFCs, and SF_6—continue to rise rapidly on a global scale, as illustrated in Graph 1 presenting worldwide data. For example, the emission level, recorded at 0.28 in 1991, peaked in 2022 with an increase of 59.27%. Although a temporary decline was observed during the global economic crises of 2008 and 2019, emission levels quickly rebounded. Specifically, in the years following these crises, 2009 and 2020, decreases of -1.17% and 4.78% were noted, respectively; however, these reductions were followed by sharp increases of 6.59% and 7.12% in subsequent periods. These trends suggest that current international efforts are insufficient to effectively address the escalating greenhouse gas emissions. Consequently, urgent and comprehensive action plans must be formulated and implemented to resolve this global crisis, which poses significant challenges for countries worldwide. Protecting endangered ecosystems and adopting robust mitigation measures are imperative for safeguarding both present and future generations.

Climate serves as a vital source of life not only for humans but for all living organisms. Consequently, it is imperative to prevent environmental pollution and other factors that may adversely impact climatic conditions. While climate change can arise from natural processes, it is increasingly recognized as being significantly influenced by anthropogenic activities. Therefore, various measures have been implemented to mitigate human-induced drivers of climate change. International negotiations and agreements, such as those conducted under the Kyoto Protocol and the Paris Climate Agreement, constitute key components of these global mitigation efforts.

2. POTENTIAL IMPACTS OF GLOBAL CLIMATE CHANGE

The alteration of atmospheric chemistry has led to numerous adverse natural and social consequences over time. Among these effects, foremost is the existential threat to future generations, manifesting as issues such as deteriorating air quality, diminished water resources, and increased prevalence of viral and bacterial diseases. Climate variability, which poses a significant threat to living organisms, also jeopardizes biodiversity, thereby undermining the natural resources available to future generations (Aydoğdu, 2024). Furthermore, rising sea levels have resulted in more frequent flooding and coastal inundation. The replacement of cold waves with extreme heat events has accelerated drought occurrences, while the destruction of forested areas has led to environmental degradation, including the loss of arable land. These changes adversely affect agricultural productivity, contributing to malnutrition and food insecurity. Economic hardships arising from resource scarcity and heightened climate-related anxiety provoke societal unrest and trigger migration waves. Such population movements generate a spectrum of economic and social challenges for both origin and destination regions. For instance, irregular urbanization associated with migration has been linked to increased incidence of stress disorders, psychological illnesses, and mental trauma within affected communities. Additionally, ethnic tensions emerging during this process exacerbate social conflicts, further escalating violence (Çetin et al., 2024; Baxtiyarovich & Vaxobovich, 2025). In this context, poverty exacerbated by climate change deepens existing social inequalities. Particularly vulnerable groups, despite contributing least to environmental degradation through carbon emissions, disproportionately bear the adverse impacts of climate change, thereby perpetuating social injustice (Murat & Şengül, 2024).

In addition to the aforementioned impacts, disruptions in employment processes are recognized as another consequence of global climate change. Health issues induced by climate change, including heat stress and exposure to extreme weather events, adversely affect labor productivity, thereby contributing to employment losses. Furthermore, environmental degradation that impairs the functions of certain occupational sectors exacerbates unemployment rates. The resulting decline in productivity not only precipitates crises in the labor market but also imposes broader economic challenges, such as increased income inequality and corruption (Murat & Şengül, 2024).

Furthermore, the increase in global food prices resulting from natural disasters exerts upward pressure on inflation rates and causes significant sector-specific economic challenges. According to projections by the European Central Bank and the Potsdam Institute for Climate Impact Research, inflation is expected to rise by 0.32% to 1.18% over the next decade in correlation with food price increases attributable to global warming (Başoğlu, 2014; Tanboğa, 2024). Additionally, the adverse impacts extend to the transportation sector, disrupting supply chains worldwide. Reduced water availability amid drought conditions hampers transit operations critical to global trade, while flooding events impair production processes, prolong delivery times, and incur substantial costs, including customer attrition (Tanboğa, 2024).

In summary, climate change, characterized by its complex and multifaceted nature, encompasses various risk elements that transcend socio-economic dimensions to include political and ecological disruptions. Although the severity of these effects varies across societies, climate change holds the potential to impact all individuals globally. Moreover, it exacerbates income inequality and intensifies the associated economic burdens. Consequently, climatic variability driven by diverse factors is regarded as an existential threat with the potential to destabilize the entire global ecosystem (Kahraman & Şenol, 2008: 367; Atvur et al., 2023: 50).

Policy inertia constitutes a significant challenge in addressing climate change. Following the adoption of the Paris Climate Agreement, there has been a notable increase in climate-related litigation aimed at ensuring that state regulations and actions align with obligations to combat global warming. Such lawsuits, which seek to compel states to enhance their climate actions, simultaneously constrain the authority of legal institutions and judges. To effectively respond to these demands, national courts have begun to engage with emerging legal concepts, reinterpret existing regulations, and exercise their powers with a focus on robust judicial review (Açımuz, 2022: 343).

The issue of free-riding in the context of global climate governance remains a critical concern. For instance, while the Clean Development Mechanism (CDM) may contribute to increased prices for natural resources, it also risks exacerbating their exploitation. Similarly, the Reducing Emissions from Deforestation and Forest Degradation (REDD) program is susceptible to free-riding problems (Ostrom, 2009).

Technological inadequacy is recognized as a major barrier to effectively combating climate change and environmental pollution. Consequently, the advancement and dissemination of technological innovations are imperative. A lack of appropriate technology undermines efforts to address environmental pollution effectively. In this regard, the development of modern irrigation systems alongside wind and solar energy technologies has been identified as particularly crucial for mitigating climate change and environmental degradation (Kızmaz, 2021: 450–451).

Carbon dioxide emissions and other environmental pollutants are dispersing globally throughout the atmosphere. Presently, most economic sectors—and increasingly more in the future—are subject to global competition, rendering international cooperation essential for effective environmental pollution reduction. Within this context, it is understood that broader implementation of policy and technological initiatives by companies and governments can create additional opportunities to accelerate the transition toward lowering carbon dioxide emissions. Such coordinated efforts may facilitate the more rapid identification and adoption of feasible solutions. When multiple countries endorse similar technologies and enact comparable support policies, key features of technological diffusion—such as scaling, cost reductions, and performance improvements—can be realized more extensively and swiftly. This dynamic is likely to strengthen the resistance of incumbent actors and intensify efforts to restructure the infrastructure and political frameworks necessary for deeper global decarbonization (Victor et al., 2019: 33).

Extensive research has been conducted on the interrelations among climate change, environmental pollution, economic growth, and economic policies. Notable topics include the impact of economic growth on carbon dioxide emissions, the costs associated with technological investments aimed at reducing pollution, and the quantification and taxation of the social costs of carbon emissions. From the perspective of economic growth, governments prioritize not only the expansion of their economies but also public health, environmental sustainability, and quality of life. Economic growth and climate change are intricately linked, as economic expansion drives the sources of carbon emissions, while climate change in turn affects economic performance in both the short and long term. Additionally, the implications of reducing carbon dioxide emissions on economic growth constitute a critical aspect of this relationship (Stern, 2007: 5).

Climate change is anticipated to yield diverse natural, social, and economic impacts. These include biodiversity loss, increased frequency of natural disasters, disruption of production processes, economic challenges resulting from resource depletion, migration flows, and psychological effects.

3. SOLUTION PROPOSALS FOR COMBATING THE GLOBAL CLIMATE CHANGE

As climate change has evolved into a global challenge over time, it has become imperative to act with the consciousness of preserving a livable environment for future generations. At this juncture, responsibility lies not only with policymakers but also with individuals and societies at large (Aydoğdu, 2024). Primarily, comprehensive research should be conducted to identify the root causes of the crisis. Social awareness can be enhanced through educational programs aimed at informing citizens' economic and political decision-making processes (Çakır, 2012). A key objective in this regard is the development and implementation of actionable plans to address global warming. Specifically, efforts to reduce carbon emissions should prioritize the phased elimination of fossil fuel energy use. Production processes based on alternative resources should be promoted by supporting technological development through research and development (R&D) initiatives. Investments in renewable energy sources—such as solar, wind, and hydroelectric power—should be intensified, alongside campaigns to raise public awareness. The European Union, actively engaged in this field, predominantly focuses its solutions on the energy sector, emphasizing the need to revise industrial policies to reduce greenhouse gas emissions (Reyhan & Reyhan, 2016). Accordingly, measures such as carbon taxation should be implemented to mitigate environmental harm caused by corporate activities. Additionally, infrastructure improvements aimed at increasing energy efficiency and rigorous emission monitoring systems are essential for combating global warming (Aydoğdu, 2024; Baxtiyarovich & Vaxobovich, 2025).

Furthermore, enforcement mechanisms must be strengthened to ensure that penalties are imposed for illegal environmental practices. Global impacts can be mitigated through financial and technological transfers to developing countries facilitated by international cooperation. Initiatives focused on the development and deployment of technologies that reduce greenhouse gas emissions should be prioritized. The advancement of environmentally sustainable practices across agriculture, industry, and the service sector should be actively encouraged (Aydoğdu, 2024). Production and consumption patterns must align with the ecological carrying capacity, with particular attention to the ecosystem's transport potential as a guiding principle (Çakır, 2012). Environmental legislation should be reviewed and strengthened to support green production processes, while integrated cooperation between the industrial sector and renewable energy investments must be promoted. Moreover, sanctions should be enforced against activities detrimental to the environment (Çetin et al., 2024: 225–226).

It is particularly crucial that the state, as the primary actor in this process, initiates cooperation and solidarity efforts both domestically and through international agreements. However, the management of potential climate change consequences should not be confined solely to greenhouse gas reduction action plans. For sustainable management, it is essential to address the social dimensions of change as well (Murat & Şengül, 2024). In this context, migration policies must be restructured to address the migratory pressures induced by climate change. Technological investments should target environmental issues that drive migration in source countries, and comprehensive, radical solutions should be implemented. The promotion of drought-resistant agricultural crops is necessary to mitigate water scarcity. Furthermore, media outlets should be closely monitored and effectively utilized to raise public awareness regarding this struggle (Çetin et al., 2024: 225–226).

In combating this global crisis, which poses a significant threat to human life, green policy initiatives must be launched to protect the foundational structure of ecosystems, accompanied by sustainable action plans on the international stage. Protective strategies aimed at vulnerable groups should be implemented to safeguard individuals' fundamental right to life. To ensure sustainability, adequate financial resources should be allocated to communities grappling with poverty. Climate policies should be designed to align and integrate with social protection systems, fostering resilience in addressing the crisis. Consequently, the process should be managed to minimize damage by enhancing the capacity to withstand periodic disruptions (Murat & Şengül, 2024).

Health sector infrastructure must be reinforced to address pandemics exacerbated by global warming. Resilient health system policies and sustainable practices are essential to combat life-threatening diseases (Baxtiyarovich & Vaxobovich, 2025). Additionally, irrigation techniques should be improved to mitigate water and food shortages, and projects such as underground dam construction should be implemented (Yaşar, 2023).

Nature should no longer be regarded as an inexhaustible resource serving solely human interests. Moreover, states must relinquish self-interested objectives such as profit maximization and unchecked economic growth. Therefore, states need to realign their priorities within the framework of sustainable development. In collaboration with other nations, climate policies must be developed with a transnational sense of responsibility toward the global environment, accompanied by stringent action plans (Kayan & Küçük, 2022: 522; Atvur, 2023: 54). Furthermore, the role of non-governmental organizations operating from local to global levels is increasingly significant in this challenging struggle, as they undertake various initiatives aimed at crisis management (Kahraman & Şenol, 2018: 367).

Numerous global conferences are convened to propose solutions to environmental pollution and climate change. One prominent example is the Conference of the Parties (COP) summit. Notably, the presidents of the United States and China have convened to discuss a range of issues, from transitioning away from primary energy sources to renewable energy, to climate change mitigation. This cooperation has the potential to stimulate technological innovation in both countries. The COP28 summit gathered nations to assess progress in these areas, aiming to review successful and unsuccessful practices, draw lessons from failures, and enhance risk management strategies. While COP28 underscored the critical role of renewable energy in achieving sustainable development goals (Jiang et al., 2024), COP29 emphasized hydrogen's potential as a cost-effective renewable energy source and highlighted its importance for meeting renewable energy targets by 2030. Saudi Arabia and China have initiated collaborative hydrogen investments, stressing hydrogen's role in industrial decarbonization. Nevertheless, both developed and developing countries have yet to make substantial advancements in this domain (Wei et al., 2025).

As demonstrated, although multiple factors contribute to the fight against climate change, this study focuses on the pivotal role of renewable energy resources aligned with technological investments, a cornerstone element of the Paris Agreement.

4. THE ROLE OF TECHNOLOGICAL DEVELOPMENTS IN PROPOSING SOLUTIONS TO CLIMATE CHANGE

Climate change, recognized as a global issue due to its occurrence, effects, and profound impact on life, necessitates international cooperation and concerted efforts regarding mitigation strategies. Technology plays a critical role in addressing climate change, one of the foremost challenges faced by humanity today. It is anticipated that environmental pollution caused by climate change and greenhouse gas emissions can be mitigated through the development and widespread adoption of clean technologies. In this regard, the integration of clean technologies within the manufacturing sector is vital for reducing environmental pollution and facilitating the technological transformation of industry (Dinçbaş, 2017: 289). Given the significance of technological innovation and development, achieving long-term reductions in environmental pollution is unlikely without numerous pioneering technological initiatives (Ostrom, 2009).

The industrialization process has foregrounded the adverse environmental impacts of energy policies reliant on fossil fuel technologies, with climate change emerging as a critical concern in the 21st century. Initially, the consequences of this change were perceived as marginal; however, recent evidence indicates more pronounced effects. Addressing environmental pollution and its fossil fuel-driven effects requires a paradigm shift in energy policy, emphasizing the transition from traditional to renewable energy technologies (Sevim, 2011: 3516–3521).

An examination of political, scientific, and technical efforts related to climate change and greenhouse gas emissions reveals the prominent role of industrialized nations. Scientific endeavors to substantiate climate change, investments in renewable energy technologies, and political initiatives such as international agreements aimed at reducing emissions have predominantly originated from the United States and European countries. Consequently, developed countries bear responsibility for slowing growth rates, decelerating industrialization, and allocating resources toward technological research (Duru, 2001: 1).

Under the auspices of the United Nations (UN), initiatives addressing climate change have gained momentum particularly in the post-Cold War era. The UN Framework Convention on Climate Change (UNFCCC) represents a milestone in this trajectory, aiming to curtail greenhouse gas accumulation while distinguishing obligations between developed and developing nations. The Kyoto Protocol and the Paris Climate Agreement further exemplify the UN's pivotal role in combating climate change (Öztürk & Öztürk, 2019: 538).

According to the Paris Agreement, technology is a fundamental element in climate change mitigation. Notably, eight articles across Chapters 10, 11, and 13 emphasize the importance of technology deployment, including the development and transfer of appropriate technologies, dissemination of existing technologies, and fostering international cooperation. These provisions foreground the interplay of economic growth, sustainable development, and technology to deliver comprehensive and long-term solutions (Köseoğlu & Erten, 2022: 1357).

The Climate Technology Center and Network (CTCN) and its stakeholders actively support the Paris Agreement's objectives, particularly by facilitating technology transfer to developing countries to reduce carbon dioxide emissions. CTCN enhances cooperation by connecting stakeholders and devising political, regulatory, and legal frameworks tailored to national needs. Leveraging global expertise from technology companies and institutions, CTCN collaborates with both public and private sectors to strengthen regional markets, mitigate investment risks, and develop national strategies. Its primary focus areas include the water-energy-food nexus, sustainable mobility, industry and business, energy systems, buildings, and infrastructure. The Global Environment Facility (GEF), CTCN's main financial partner, provides essential funding that reduces risks and catalyzes projects by attracting third-party capital (UN Climate Technology Centre & Network, 2025).

Efforts to reduce carbon emissions and environmental pollution also require region- and country-specific strategies. For instance, the European Green Deal outlines the European Union's vision to become a global leader in climate action by 2050 through a range of policies, legislative measures, and action plans. This initiative has gained renewed momentum following the COVID-19 pandemic (Teevan et al., 2021). China, similarly, has intensified investments in renewable energy—especially wind and solar power—to address global warming and environmental degradation. However, seasonal and regional variability affects the utilization of these resources (Li et al., 2024). Türkiye, as an energy-importing country with a reliance on foreign energy and environmental concerns, seeks to diversify its primary energy mix by expanding investments in renewable energy sources such as hydroelectric, wind, biomass, and solar energy. Türkiye also ranks among the top ten countries worldwide in geothermal potential, with increasing investments in this area (Yüksel & Kaygusuz, 2011: 4143).

Comprehensive economic and technological transformations are imperative to curtail greenhouse gas emissions, phase out coal-fired power plants and fossil fuels, develop renewable energy sources, and increase their share in primary energy supply. Following the Paris Agreement, numerous countries have intensified investments in wind power, battery technologies, solar energy, and other renewables, supported by climate finance and necessary technological transitions (Türkeş, 2022: 31–44).

The European Union Commission has pursued technological and renewable energy initiatives to reduce emissions. Among these efforts, the "White Paper: Energy for the Future – Renewable Energy Sources – Community Strategy and Action Plan" seeks to increase renewable energy consumption. The "Directive on Electricity

Generation from Renewable Energy Sources" aims to boost renewable electricity production (green electricity) within the EU. To facilitate market integration and commercialization of renewables, the EU has promoted standardization efforts, including standards for solar photovoltaic, wind turbines, solar thermal equipment, solid biomass, and biodiesel. The EU also encourages the transition to advanced clean solid fuel technologies to reduce emissions and develop cost-effective technologies (Türkeş & Kılıç, 2004: 8–15).

Climate change encompasses complex economic, political, social, and psychological dimensions. Consequently, multifaceted solutions are proposed to mitigate its impacts. A key strategy involves increasing investments in technology, as emphasized within the Paris Agreement framework. While technological engagement can be analyzed from various perspectives, the emphasis on renewable energy adoption is expected to reduce environmental pollution and diminish dependence on foreign energy. The following section will evaluate countries' orientations towards renewable energy sources.

5. THE USE OF RENEWABLE ENERGY RESOURCES IN COMBATING CLIMATE CHANGE

Recent studies concur that the primary drivers of global warming are the increasing global energy demand and the consequent rise in greenhouse gas emissions into the atmosphere. Elevated greenhouse gas concentrations cause significant ecosystem degradation and adversely affect both plant and animal species. Moreover, rising temperatures contribute to water scarcity, thereby disrupting agricultural and livestock activities. In this context, both developed and developing countries engage in international efforts to mitigate these impacts. Policy measures aimed at reducing environmental pollution include limiting greenhouse gas emissions, minimizing fossil fuel consumption, implementing pollution control strategies in the industrial sector, and promoting environmentally sensitive technologies alongside the expanded use of renewable energy sources. Should participating countries enact regulations that encourage the adoption of renewable energy and environmentally friendly technologies, the global adverse effects currently experienced can be substantially alleviated (Şanlı et al., 2017: 210).

A central objective of energy supply policies—critical for sustaining human life—is the mitigation of environmental pollution threats. Contemporary paradigms of development, energy consumption, and abundance have shifted toward approaches emphasizing technological advancement and optimized resource utilization for more economical energy supply. This shift underpins policies prioritizing a healthy environment, clean energy, energy diversification, and energy supply security. Such policies are foundational for addressing global warming and climate change impacts. Within renewable energy policy frameworks, enhancing economic competitiveness aligns with reducing environmental pollution through more effective and efficient energy use. Increasing the proportion of renewable energy in the energy mix contributes to sustainability, environmental protection, and reduced foreign energy dependency. Moreover, diversifying energy sources with options such as wind, geothermal, and solar energy mitigates risks associated with energy supply security (Güner & Turan, 2017: 48–54).

The continuous rise in energy demand driven by population growth and economic development necessitates policies that reduce dependence on fossil fuels and nuclear energy. Countries reliant on fossil fuel imports or lacking nuclear technology—as well as oil- and natural gas-rich nations with nuclear capabilities—are increasingly adopting renewable energy sources. Consequently, the share of renewables in energy production is anticipated to grow progressively. Nevertheless, challenges remain, including the intermittent nature of wind and solar energy due to weather dependency, limited accessibility of geothermal resources, constrained hydropower utilization, and suboptimal exploitation of biomass energy. Advances in energy technologies are expected to overcome these barriers. For instance, innovative projects aiming to develop wind-tracking aircraft instead of fixed wind turbines exemplify the potential for countries to transition away from fossil fuels and nuclear power, driven by economic and environmental considerations (Çıtak & Kılınç Pala, 2016: 85–86).

Enhancing effectiveness in combating climate change necessitates measures to ensure energy security, reduce energy waste, decrease energy intensity, and improve efficiency across the entire energy production, distribution, and consumption chain. In this regard, numerous global organizations actively advocate for the reduction of greenhouse gas and carbon emissions. Compared to fossil fuel-based energy sources, renewable energy technologies emit significantly lower carbon emissions. Among these, geothermal energy stands out for its minimal environmental impact. Accordingly, prioritizing renewable energy technologies and implementing programs to foster their development are of paramount importance (Çoban & Şahbaz Kılınç, 2016: 602–603).

Chart 2 illustrates the global share of renewable energy consumption relative to total final energy consumption. Between 1990 and 2017, fluctuations in this share were observed, followed by a consistent upward trend from 2017 onward. This trend reflects the positive outcomes of policy decisions and initiatives promoting renewable energy consumption. Investments by countries in renewable energy have contributed to an increase in its share, which now accounts for approximately 20% of total final energy consumption globally. Although significant progress remains necessary for further expansion of renewable energy resources worldwide, the current trajectory offers promising prospects for reducing environmental pollution and decreasing reliance on fossil fuel resources, which remain key contributors to global climate change.

Figure 2. Renewable Energy Consumption Ratio in World Final Energy Consumption

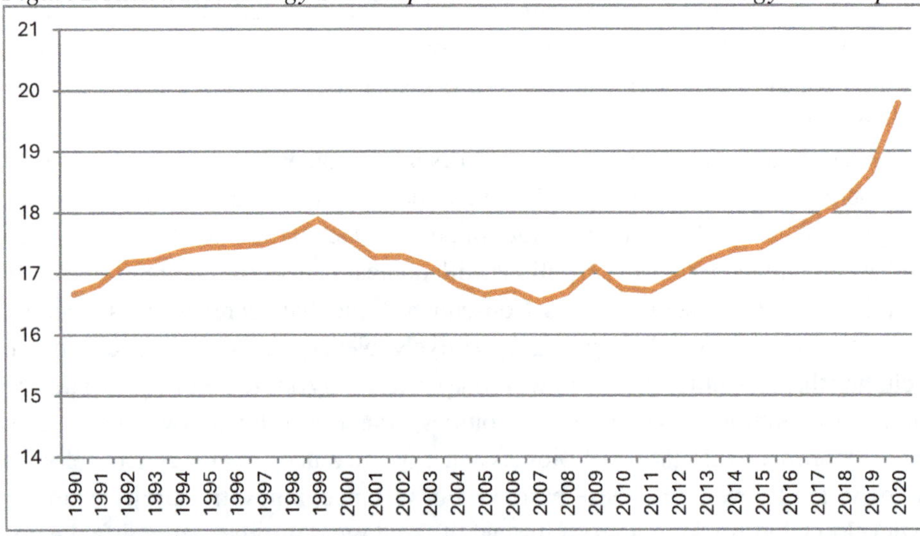

Source: World Bank (2025)

All countries bear responsibility for maintaining ecological balance and ensuring a sustainable future. However, this responsibility varies according to the development levels of the countries. Historically, developed countries have contributed more significantly to environmental pollution and, given their current economic status, are expected to assume a greater role in addressing these issues. As the primary contributors to global climate change, developed nations should take on enhanced responsibility and play a more active role in mitigation efforts. Specifically, concrete measures such as supporting renewable energy investments in developing and less developed countries, providing financial assistance, and facilitating technology transfer must be implemented more effectively. Failure to do so may hinder these countries' capacities to address climate change challenges (Sağır, 2025: 88).

Energy, indispensable for fulfilling fundamental human needs such as food production, water supply, lighting, heating, and transportation, has gained heightened importance since the Industrial Revolution. As a critical driver of economic growth, industrialization, and global competition, energy must be supplied sustainably within the global market. Historically, global energy consumption has heavily depended on traditional fossil fuels, which are geographically concentrated in specific regions. The finite availability of these energy resources and the conflicts arising from such scarcity pose significant challenges to energy supply security, prompting efforts to develop viable solutions. Furthermore, global warming, limited access to clean water resources, ecological imbalance, and greenhouse gas emissions derived from fossil fuels—alongside risks such as famine and migration—pose threats to the global energy market. In response, the utilization of renewable energy resources and the pursuit of sustainable development have gained increasing prominence worldwide. Many countries have adopted strategies aimed at reducing global warming and foreign energy dependency through increased demand for renewable energy sources (Dışkaya, 2017: 130).

Renewable energy resources are naturally replenished and inexhaustible resources, some of which can be converted through various methods for repeated use. The principal renewable energy sources include wind, solar, geothermal, hydroelectric, and biomass energy (Arı, 2023: 704).

Wind Energy

Wind energy, which is easily accessible worldwide and derived from wind power, originates from the uneven heating of the Earth's surface by solar radiation (Koç & Kaya, 2015: 43). This energy source has a history as long as human civilization, initially utilized in activities such as grain milling and maritime transportation. Over time, increasing social demands and technological advancements, such as the development of wind turbines, have enabled its use for electricity generation (Hayli, 2001).

Produced without relying on fossil fuels, wind energy offers multiple advantages and contributes to favorable environmental conditions. For instance, it mitigates air pollution by reducing emissions of greenhouse gases, such as carbon dioxide and nitrous oxide, which are key contributors to climate change. Additionally, wind turbines, which optimize the utilization of wind speed, reduce the consumption of scarce water resources compared to traditional energy generation methods (Saidur et al., 2011; Kaplan, 2015).

Developed in the early twentieth century, wind turbines gained increased importance with the rise in oil prices and have rapidly advanced alongside technological progress (Ackermann & Söder, 2002). Their significance is evident not only in developed countries but also in developing nations. For example, the installation of wind turbines in rural areas has fostered regional economic development by creating new employment opportunities (Saidur et al., 2011).

Nevertheless, the literature presents some criticisms regarding wind turbines, including potential threats to wildlife habitats, particularly birds, as well as noise pollution and environmental degradation (Leung & Yang, 2012). Concerns have also been raised about possible interference with radar and television signals caused by magnetic interactions, which might increase the risk of lightning strikes (Saidur et al., 2011). Moreover, wind energy installations are often criticized for their relatively large spatial requirements and potential visual incompatibility with natural landscapes (Hayli, 2001).

Despite these drawbacks, considering ongoing research and technological improvements, wind energy is expected to make a substantial contribution to sustainable environmental management and economic growth.

Solar Energy

Solar energy is one of the most significant global energy sources. Solar radiation constitutes a primary energy input influencing both atmospheric and terrestrial physical processes. The circulation of matter and energy on Earth is fundamentally driven by solar energy. In fact, wind, biomass energy, oceanic temperature gradients, and wave energy are all forms of solar energy in transformed states. Additionally, solar energy plays a crucial role in the water cycle and contributes to the formation of hydroelectric power. Fossil fuels can also be understood as stored solar energy accumulated in biomass over geological timescales. As the origin of numerous natural and renewable energy sources, solar energy can be directly harnessed for various applications, including electricity generation and heating (Varınca & Gönüllü, 2006: 270).

The International Energy Agency (IEA) has estimated that the amount of solar radiation reaching the Earth in ninety minutes has the potential to satisfy the world's annual energy demand. Although fossil fuels—widely recognized as key contributors to climate change—remain the predominant energy source globally, renewable energy systems, which have recently gained extensive adoption, represent the primary alternatives to reverse this trend. Initially limited to applications such as solar water heating, solar energy systems have increasingly contributed to electricity generation, particularly in countries offering incentives for clean energy. Currently, solar energy technologies possess the largest installed capacity among renewables, and their costs are declining more rapidly compared to other renewable energy sources (Özcan, 2013: 55).

Geothermal Energy

Geothermal energy constitutes a renewable source of thermal and electrical energy. Unlike other renewable sources, it is not dependent on weather conditions and can be supplied continuously. By reducing reliance on fossil fuels, geothermal energy contributes to the conservation of valuable chemical fossil resources and serves as an effective measure against global warming. Deep geothermal resources provide both electrical and thermal energy, offering a reliable, renewable, and sustainable energy solution for the future. Electricity generated from geothermal sources significantly contributes to the primary electricity supply and represents an alternative to large-scale fossil fuel power plants. Furthermore, geothermal energy can meet the heating demands of entire districts as well as individual buildings (Stober & Bucher, 2013: 5).

Geothermal energy is regarded as an important alternative energy source due to its low carbon dioxide emissions and renewable nature. Compared to other renewables such as wind and solar energy, geothermal energy holds a distinct advantage because of its uninterrupted availability. Depending on the temperature of the resource, geothermal energy can be utilized for electricity generation, treatment processes, and heating, allowing integrated use of high-temperature geothermal fluids across diverse applications. This resource incurs relatively low costs compared to fossil fuels, causes minimal environmental damage, and does not require highly advanced technology for its operation (Arslan et al., 2001: 21-27).

Geothermal energy consists of water, gases, and vapors heated by the Earth's core temperature, containing various chemicals and minerals at different depths beneath the surface. Its wide range of applications, independence from weather variability, high sustainability, and direct usability distinguish geothermal energy among renewable sources. Existing technologies enable the exploitation of geothermal energy where resources reach the Earth's surface or can be transported thereto. With further advancements in geothermal technology, it is projected that a significant portion of global energy demand will be met by geothermal energy in the future (Çıtak & Kılınç Pala, 2016: 85).

Hydroelectric Energy

Hydroelectric energy is a well-established technology and represents one of the cleanest available energy sources. It holds significant potential, particularly for developing countries, as it can supply a substantial portion of the electricity required to sustain industrial production and urban lighting. Micro-hydroelectric power plants are capable of providing electricity to dispersed settlements, isolated regions, and agricultural facilities. Compared to other renewable and sustainable energy sources, hydroelectric energy is considered a safe and reliable form of energy. Moreover, in storage-type hydroelectric power plants, energy can be efficiently stored and utilized as needed. Another notable advantage is that low-capacity hydroelectric plants can be rapidly scaled up to higher capacities within a short period (Bozkurt & Tür, 2015: 322-324).

Hydroelectric energy plays a crucial role in the sustainable development of large-scale organizations and contributes significantly to a country's gross domestic product (GDP). Furthermore, hydropower technology is effective in energy storage and can serve as a fundamental component of the overall energy infrastructure. Additionally, hydropower enhances energy access and security, mitigates environmental changes, and assists in pollution reduction. Economically, it generates employment opportunities and promotes efficiency in sustainable development (Siri et al., 2020: 107-108).

As previously noted, hydroelectric energy is advocated as a key measure to counteract global climate change, primarily attributed to carbon dioxide emissions, and possesses numerous advantages. Once a dam is constructed for hydroelectric purposes, it enables continuous electricity generation. Electricity production can be halted by closing water gates during periods of low demand, allowing water to be conserved and utilized when electricity demand increases. Due to the robust design of dams, hydroelectric energy facilities have long operational lifespans. Importantly, electricity generated through dam systems does not produce greenhouse gas emissions or contribute to environmental pollution, thereby preventing atmospheric contamination (Bagher et al., 2015: 18).

Biomass Energy

Biomass energy holds significant potential to enhance energy supply security and mitigate environmental pollution, particularly in countries lacking fossil fuel reserves. By reducing greenhouse gas emissions, biomass energy can contribute to the prevention of global climate change. The growing demand for and investment in biomass energy underscore both the risks and opportunities associated with energy supply security. Biomass energy presents important prospects for achieving energy independence, curbing the acceleration of global climate change, and sustaining agricultural economies (Field et al., 2008: 65-71).

Historically, biomass was the first form of energy utilized by humanity apart from food consumption and remained the primary energy source until the late eighteenth century. The recognition of biomass as a carbon-neutral energy source has generated global interest in its use as an alternative liquid fuel, especially as a substitute for oil and diesel. However, it should be noted that biomass energy production is not invariably carbon neutral; fossil fuel-based energy is often consumed during various stages of biomass conversion into fuel. Moreover, large-scale biomass production and utilization may pose environmental risks if not managed properly. Nonetheless, the imperative to develop alternatives to fossil fuels and to address global climate change through renewable energy sources has elevated the global prominence of biomass energy (Abbasi & Abbasi, 2010: 921).

Numerous examples of renewable energy applications exist worldwide. One notable facility is the Hornsdale Power Reserve in Australia, a large-scale battery storage system connected to a wind farm, which has stabilized the electrical grid, significantly reduced power outages, and provided considerable cost advantages.

The Pumped Hydro Storage facility in the United States is recognized as the largest pumped hydroelectric storage installation globally; it stores energy during periods of low demand and supplies it during peak demand, thereby facilitating grid stability. The Dinorwig Power Station in the United Kingdom is another major pumped hydroelectric facility with the capability to ramp from zero to full production within seconds. In Germany, the Altenwindpark Nordergründe employs a battery storage system to enhance energy supply from an offshore wind farm, while the Huntorf CAES Plant—one of the earliest plants using Compressed Air Energy Storage (CAES)—stores surplus energy as compressed air for later electricity generation, aiding the integration of renewable sources. Lastly, the Moss Landing Energy Storage Facility in the United States, one of the world's largest lithium-ion battery storage systems by capacity, manages surplus renewable energy, reducing reliance on primary energy sources and improving grid reliability (Jafarizadeh et al., 2024).

The expansion of renewable energy sources such as wind, solar, hydroelectric, and geothermal energy offers promising prospects for reducing environmental pollution. Achieving this progress necessitates investment, policy incentives, and technological advancement. Technological innovation, public awareness raising, and regulatory frameworks are critical components in the promotion of renewable energy. However, despite these efforts, significant challenges persist. For instance, while some experts advocate for the inclusion of nuclear energy in the transition towards renewable energy, concerns over nuclear waste management and safety lead others to be cautious. Effective collaboration among governments, private sector entities, and civil society organizations is essential to secure necessary investments. Another notable barrier is the lack of public awareness and education regarding the benefits of renewable energy and the environmental harms of conventional energy sources. Consequently, public education and engagement in renewable energy initiatives are crucial (Saleh & Hassan, 2024: 14-15).

Financing constitutes one of the most significant challenges in renewable energy investments. Design complexities during project development phases further complicate renewable energy project realization, especially when large-scale infrastructure is required. The integration and establishment of such infrastructure can be technically and logistically challenging. A major source of project financing relies on future revenues from renewable energy projects; however, the uncertainty surrounding these revenues introduces financial risks for investors and lenders. Additionally, the high upfront costs of renewable energy installations can hinder access to capital, further constraining investment (Eti et al., 2024).

In conclusion, mitigating the adverse impacts of environmental pollution and climate change necessitates the reduction of carbon dioxide emissions. This objective can be realized through technological investments and a strategic shift towards renewable energy sources, as emphasized by the Paris Climate Agreement.

Renewable energy types such as geothermal, hydroelectric, biomass, wind, and solar energy play a vital role in substituting primary energy sources and reducing environmental pollution.

CONCLUSION

Energy consumption is essential to meet the demands and needs of society. Historically and presently, this energy demand has predominantly been met through fossil fuel resources. Factors such as population growth, industrialization, mechanization, and rural-to-urban migration have further escalated energy demand and, consequently, reliance on fossil fuels. The increased utilization of fossil fuels has led to a rise in carbon dioxide emissions and environmental pollution, which over time has contributed significantly to the issue of global climate change.

The use of fossil fuels not only results in environmental degradation but also exacerbates countries' external dependence due to the geographical concentration of these resources. This dependence manifests economically as trade deficits and politically as reliance on energy-exporting nations. Global developments—particularly those involving countries rich in fossil fuels—pose risks to energy supply security. Disruptions in supply chains during the COVID-19 pandemic and the critical role of Russian energy in the Russia-Ukraine conflict have accelerated the search for alternative energy solutions.

Countries have increasingly sought alternatives to fossil fuels, primarily motivated by environmental concerns. As emphasized in the Paris Climate Agreement, expanding technological investments and transitioning toward renewable energy sources are considered pivotal solutions. However, two key considerations arise regarding renewable energy utilization. First, improper management of renewable energy sources may still result in environmental impacts, albeit less severe than those from fossil fuels. Second, the high initial investment costs associated with renewable energy projects pose significant challenges.

Therefore, comprehensive measures must be undertaken to mitigate global climate change driven by carbon dioxide emissions from fossil fuel consumption. In this context, policy recommendations focusing on the promotion of renewable energy resources and technological investments can be outlined as follows:

- Countries should turn to appropriate renewable energy sources according to their geopolitical situation and wealth.
- Due to the high costs that may arise in the installation of renewable energy sources, companies should be provided with investment and financing support, tax reductions, subsidies, etc.

- Renewable energy investments should be integrated not only with company-specific investments but also with cooperation between countries, and the cost risks that may arise during the investment should be shared.
- Investments in alternative sources such as geothermal energy, green hydrogen, solar energy, and wind energy should be increased to ensure a gradual, if not rapid and complete, transition away from fossil energy sources.
- Investments in battery technology and storage systems should be increased to ensure a sustainable and uninterrupted supply of renewable energy resources.
- Industrial enterprises should be encouraged to switch to green energy to reduce carbon dioxide emissions.
- Energy efficiency in the industrial sector should be ensured, and the transition to public transportation systems supported by renewable energy should be supported.
- Cooperation between research centers, the private sector, and universities should be supported to develop renewable energy technologies.
- Training programs should be made widespread, and campaigns should be organized to raise public awareness on the importance of using renewable energy resources and sustainable energy use.

REFERENCES

Abbasi, T., & Abbasi, S. A. (2010). Biomass energy and the environmental impacts associated with its production and utilization. *Renewable & Sustainable Energy Reviews, 14*(3), 919–937.

Açımuz, B. (2022). Devletin yükümlülüklerine, sorumluluğuna ve yargıcın yetkilerine yaklaşımda dönüştürücü etkileri bakımından sistemik iklim davaları. *Yeditepe Üniversitesi Hukuk Fakültesi Dergisi, 19*(2), 343–428.

Ackermann, T., & Söder, L. (2002). An overview of wind energy-status 2002. *Renewable & Sustainable Energy Reviews, 6*(1-2), 67–127.

Arı, F. (2023). Başlıca enerji kaynakları ve çevresel etkilerinin değerlendirilmesi. *Dicle Üniversitesi İktisadi ve İdari Bilimler Fakültesi Dergisi, 13*(26), 697–718.

Arslan, S., Darıcı, M., & Karahan, Ç. (2001). Türkiye'nin jeotermal enerji potansiyeli. *Jeotermal Enerji Semineri,* 21-27.

Asan, Ü. (1995). Global iklim değişimi ve Türkiye ormanlarında karbon birikimi. *Istanbul Üniversitesi Orman Fakültesi Dergisi, 45*(1-2), 23–38.

Atvur, S., Gülal, A. G. G., & Oğuz, C. U. (2023). İklim krizi ve ekolojik bağlamda devletin rolünü yeniden düşünmek. *Politik Ekonomik Kuram, 7*(Özel Sayı), 44-57.

Aydoğdu, M. H. (2024). İklim Değişikliği: Sorunlar ve Bunlar Yönetilebilir Mi? *Ssd Journal, 9*(46), 79–91.

Başoğlu, A. (2014). Küresel iklim değişikliğinin ekonomik etkileri. *Sosyal Bilimler Dergisi, 7*, 175–196.

Baxtiyarovich, A. R., & Vaxobovich, M. M. (2025). The Impact Of Clımate Change On Human Health. *Yangı O 'Zbekıston. YANGI TADQIQOTLAR JURNALI, 2*(4), 267–268.

Beşballı, S. G. (2023). Çevre sorunları çerçevesinde küresel iklim değişikliği. *Artvin Çoruh Üniversitesi Uluslararası Sosyal Bilimler Dergisi, 9*(2), 500–521. DOI: 10.22466/acusbd.1388179

Bozkurt, S., & Tür, R. (2015). *Dünyada ve Türkiyede hidroelektrik enerji, gelişimi ve genel değerlendirme. 4.* Su Yapıları Sempozyumu Kitabı.

Çakır, G. (2012). Sürdürülebilir kalkınma adına iklim değişikliğinin küresel ölçekte irdelenmesi. In *GreenAge Symposium, Mimar Sinan Fine Arts University, Faculty of Architecture* (pp. 448-457).

Çetin, M. Ş., Parlak, B., & Şenol, S. (2024). İklim krizi ve göçe ilişkin kavramsal değerlendirme. *Kent Akademisi Dergisi, 17*(1), 217–230.

Çıtak, E., & Pala, P. B. K. (2016). Yenilenebilir enerjinin enerji güvenliğine etkisi. *Süleyman Demirel Üniversitesi Sosyal Bilimler Enstitüsü Dergisi*, (25), 79–102.

Çoban, O., & Şahbaz Kılınç, N. (2016). Enerji kullanımının çevresel etkilerinin incelenmesi. *Marmara Coğrafya Dergisi*, (33), 589–606.

Davarcıoğlu, B. (2018). Küresel iklim değişikliği ve uyum çalışmaları: Türkiye açısından değerlendirilmesi. [MBD]. *Mesleki Bilimler Dergisi, 7*(2), 376–392.

Demirbaş, M., & Aydın, R. (2020). 21. Yüzyılın en büyük tehdidi: Küresel iklim değişikliği. *Ecological Life Sciences, 15*(4), 163–179.

Dinçbaş, T. (2017). *Türkiye'de iklim değişikliği bağlamında temiz teknoloji edinimi: metalik olmayan mineral ürünler sektöründe bir uygulama* [Doktora Tezi]. Ankara Üniversitesi.

Dışkaya, S. K. (2017). Türkiye'nin enerji güvenliğinde yenilenebilir enerji etkisinin politik ekonomi perspektifi. *Marmara Üniversitesi Siyasal Bilimler Dergisi, 5*(2), 129–150.

Duru, B. (2001). Viyana'dan kyoto'ya iklim değişikliği serüveni. *Mülkiye Dergisi, 25*(230), 301–333.

Eti, S., Yüksel, S., Dinçer, H., Kalkavan, H., Hacioglu, U., Mikhaylov, A., & Pinter, G. (2024). Assessment of technical and financial challenges for renewable energy project alternatives. *Cleaner Engineering and Technology, 18*, 100719.

Field, C. B., Campbell, J. E., & Lobell, D. B. (2008). Biomass energy: The scale of the potential resource. *Trends in Ecology & Evolution, 23*(2), 65–72. PMID: 18215439

Güner, E. D., & Turan, E. S. (2017). Yenilenebilir enerji kaynaklarının küresel iklim değişikliği üzerine etkisi. *Doğal Afetler ve Çevre Dergisi, 3*(1), 48–55.

Hayli, S. (2001). Rüzgâr enerjisinin önemi Dünya'da ve Türkiye'deki durumu. *Fırat Üniversitesi Sosyal Bilimler Dergisi, 11*(1), 1–26.

Intergovernmental Panel on Climate Change (IPCC). (2001). Climate Change 2001: Synthesis Report, https://www.ipcc.ch/site/assets/uploads/2018/05/SYR_TAR_full _report.pdf adresinden alındı. Erişim Tarihi:08.03.2025.

Jafarizadeh, H., Yamini, E., Zolfaghari, S. M., Esmaeilion, F., Assad, M. E. H., & Soltani, M. (2024). Navigating challenges in large-scale renewable energy storage: Barriers, solutions, and innovations. *Energy Reports, 12*, 2179–2192.

Jiang, T., He, X., Su, B., Havea, P. H., Wei, K., Kundzewicz, Z. W., & Liu, D. (2024). COP 28: Challenge of coping with climate crisis. *The Innovation*, *5*(1). PMID: 38239781

Kadıoğlu, M., & Sonu, B. H. (2007). Küresel Ðklim Değişimi ve Türkiye. *Güncel Yayıncılık aş*, (110). https://eskisakarya.imo.org.tr/resimler/ekutuphane/pdf/3937.pdf

Kahraman, S., & Şenol, P. (2018). İklim Değişikliği: Küresel, Bölgesel ve Kentsel Etkileri. Akademia Sosyal Bilimler Dergisi353-370.

Kaplan, Y. A. (2015). Overview of wind energy in the world and assessment of current wind energy policies in Turkey. *Renewable & Sustainable Energy Reviews*, *43*, 562–568.

Kayan, A., & Küçük, A. (2022). Küresel iklim krizinin oluşmasında politik kararların etkisi. [DÜSBED]. *Dicle Üniversitesi Sosyal Bilimler Enstitüsü Dergisi*, *31*, 521–526.

Kılıç, C. (2009). Küresel iklim değişikliği çerçevesinde sürdürülebilir kalkınma çabaları ve Türkiye. *Cumhuriyet University Journal of Economics & Administrative Sciences/Cumhuriyet Üniversitesi İktisadi ve İdari Bilimler Dergisi, 10*(2).

Kızmaz, Z. (2021). İklim değişikliğinin kırsal alandaki etkisi ve alternatif arayışlar: Sosyolojik bir yaklaşım. *Firat University Journal of Social Sciences*, *31*(1), 431–453.

Koç, E., & Kaya, K. (2015). Enerji kaynaklari–yenilenebilir enerji durumu. *Mühendis ve Makina*, *56*(668), 36–47.

Koçak, H., & Bozyurt, O. (2024). Küresel iklim değişikliğine yönelik çözüm odaklı yaklaşımlar. *Journal of Social* [joshas]. *Humanıtıes And Admınıstratıve Scıences*, *7*(47), 2468–2479.

Köseoğlu, P., & Erten, S. (2022). Paris Anlaşması'na Göre Çevre Eğitimi Nasıl Olmalıdır? *Dokuz Eylül Üniversitesi Buca Eğitim Fakültesi Dergisi*, (54), 1528–1544.

Leung, D. Y., & Yang, Y. (2012). Wind energy development and its environmental impact: A review. *Renewable & Sustainable Energy Reviews*, *16*(1), 1031–1039.

Li, T., Liu, Y., & Lv, A. (2024). Review of Research on the Present Situation of Development and Resource Potential of Wind and Solar Energy in China. *Energies*, *17*(16), 4158.

Murat, G., & Şengül, B. (2024). Küresel İklim Değişikliğinin İşgücü Verimliliği ve İstihdam Üzerine Yansımaları: Bir Sosyal Politika Önlemi Olarak Yeşil İşler. *Mülkiye Dergisi*, *48*(3), 717–748.

Ostrom, E. (2009). A polycentric approach for coping with climate change. Available at *SSRN* 1934353.

Özcan, E. S. (2013). Dünyada ve Türkiye'de Güneş Enerjisi. Tubitak Bilim ve Teknik Dergisi, 55-59.

Öztürk, K. (2002). Küresel iklim değişikliği ve Türkiye'ye olası etkileri. *Gazi Üniversitesi Gazi Eğitim Fakültesi Dergisi*, 22(1).

Öztürk, M., & Öztürk, A. (2019). BMİDÇS'den Paris Anlaşması'na: Birleşmiş Milletler'in iklim değişikliğiyle mücadele çabaları. *Ömer Halisdemir Üniversitesi İktisadi ve İdari Bilimler Fakültesi Dergisi,* 12(4), 527-541.

Paris Agreement. (2015). https://unfccc.int/files/essential_background/convention/application/pdf/english_paris_agreement.pdf (Erişim Tarihi: 23.02.2025).

Reyhan, A. S., & Reyhan, H. (2016). Küresel ısınmanın nedenleri, sonuçları, çözümleri üzerine yeni değerlendirmeler. *Memleket Siyaset Yönetim, 11*(26), 1–24.

Sağır, H. (2025). Enerji Politikaları ve Paradigma Değişimi: İklim Değişikliği Bağlamında Dönüşüm. *Uluslararası Ekonomi ve Siyaset Bilimleri Akademik Araştırmalar Dergisi, 8*(20), 84–95.

Saidur, R., Rahim, N. A., Islam, M. R., & Solangi, K. H. (2011). Environmental impact of wind energy. *Renewable & Sustainable Energy Reviews, 15*(5), 2423–2430.

Saleh, H. M., & Hassan, A. I. (2024). The challenges of sustainable energy transition: A focus on renewable energy. *Applied Chemical Engineering, 7*(2), 2084.

Şanlı, F. B., Bayrakdar, S., & İncekara, B. (2017). Küresel iklim değişikliğinin etkileri ve bu etkileri önlemeye yönelik uluslararası girişimler. *Süleyman Demirel Üniversitesi İktisadi ve İdari Bilimler Fakültesi Dergisi, 22*(1), 201–212.

Şen, Z. (2022). İklim değişikliği ve Türkiye. *Çevre Şehir ve İklim Dergisi,* 1(1), 1-19.

Sevim, C. (2011). Enerji Teknolojilerindeki Anlayış Model Değişimi ve Hızlı İklim Değişikliği. *Yaşar Üniversitesi E-Dergisi, 6*(21), 3515–3522.

Siri, R., Mondal, S. R., & Das, S. (2020). Hydropower: A renewable energy resource for sustainability in terms of climate change and environmental protection. *Alternative Energy Resources: The Way to a Sustainable Modern Society,* 93-113.

Stern, N. (2007). The economics of climate change: the Stern review. cambridge University press.

Stober, I., & Bucher, K. (2013). Geothermal energy. *Germany: Springer-Verlag Berlin Heidelberg.* doi, 10, 978-3.

Tanboğa, S. (2024). İklim Değişikliği ve Ekonomik Etkileri. Türkiye İhracatçılar Birliği (TİM).https://tim.org.tr/files/downloads/Mevzuat/Iklim_Degisikligi_ve_Ekonomik_Etkileri.pdf adresinden alındı. Erişim Tarihi: 08.03.2025.

T.C. Enerji ve Tabii Kaynaklar Bakanlığı. (2025a). Kyoto Protokolü. https://enerji.gov.tr/evced-cevre-ve-iklim-kyoto-protokolu, Erişim Tarihi:16.04.2025.

T.C. Enerji ve Tabii Kaynaklar Bakanlığı. (2025b). Paris Anlaşması. https://enerji.gov.tr/evced-cevre-ve-iklim-paris-anlasmasi, Erişim Tarihi:16.04.2025.

Teevan, C., Medinilla, A., & Sergejeff, K. (2021). The Green Deal in EU foreign and development policy. ECDPM Briefing Note, 131.

Türkeş, M. (2008). Küresel iklim değişikliği nedir? Temel kavramlar, nedenleri, gözlenen ve öngörülen değişiklikler. *İklim Değişikliği ve Çevre, 1*(1), 26-37.

Türkeş, M. (2022). İklim diplomasisi ve iklim değişikliğinin ekonomi politiği. *Bilim ve Ütopya, 332*, 31–45.

Türkeş, M., & Kılıç, G. (2004). Avrupa birliği'nin iklim değişikliği politikaları ve önlemleri. *Çevre Bilim ve Teknoloji Teknik Dergisi,* 2, 35-52.

UN Climate Technology Centre & Network. (2025). About CTCN, 17.07.2025 tarihinde https://www.ctc-n.org/about-ctcn/partners-and-collaborators adresinden alınmıştır.

United Nations (UN). (1992). Unite Nations Framework Convention On Climate Change https://unfccc.int/resource/docs/convkp/conveng.pdf adresinden alındı. Erişim Tarihi: 08.03.2025.

Varınca, K. B., & Gönüllü, M. T. (2006). Türkiye'de güneş enerjisi potansiyeli ve bu potansiyelin kullanım derecesi, yöntemi ve yaygınlığı üzerine bir araştırma. Ulusal güneş ve hidrojen enerjisi kongresi, 21, 23.

Victor, D. G., Geels, F. W., & Sharpe, S. (2019). *Accelerating the low carbon transition.* The Case for Stronger, More Targeted and Coordinated International Action. Brookings Institution.

Wei, J., Jiang, T., Ménager, P., Kim, D. G., & Dong, W. (2025). COP29: Progresses and challenges to global efforts on the climate crisis. *The Innovation*, *6*(1). PMID: 39872482

World Bank. (2025). Renewable energy consumption (% of total final energy consumption), 10.04.2025 tarihinde https://data.worldbank.org/indicator/EG.FEC.RNEW.ZS adresinden alınmıştır.

Yaşar, D. (2023). İklimler, Değişim Nedenleri ve Sonuçları M.E.Aydın, A.D.Şahin (Ed.) içinde, İklim Değişimi Çerçevesinde Su Kaynaklarının Mevcut Durumu ve Geleceği, *(s. 263-278) Türkiye Bilimler Akademisi.*

Yüksel, I., & Kaygusuz, K. (2011). Renewable energy sources for clean and sustainable energy policies in Turkey. *Renewable & Sustainable Energy Reviews, 15*(8), 4132–4144.

Yurduseven, A., Şimşek, M., & Koca, G. (2024). *İklim Değişikliğinin Türkiye ve Avrupa Birliği Ülkeleri Açısından Değerlendirilmesi: CRITIC ve GIA Yöntemi. 10.* Uluslararası Ankara Bilimsel Araştırmalar Kongresi.

KEY TERMS AND DEFİNİTİONS

Environmental Pollution: Environmental pollution is mainly caused by the amount of carbon dioxide released into the atmosphere after primary energy use.

Industry: Encompasses the process of transforming raw materials into consumer goods.

Primary energy: Primary energy is known as natural resources that directly meet people's energy needs. Primary energy sources are energy sources that are used without being processed. Primary energy sources include resources such as coal, oil, and natural gas.

Renewable energy sources: Renewable energy sources include energy sources such as wind, solar, geothermal, hydroelectric, and biomass. It is considered important to reduce the use of environmentally harmful natural resources such as coal and oil, minimize environmental pollution, and establish a sustainable energy process.

Renewable energy: Renewable energy is one of the most important factors in reducing environmental pollution and countries' dependence on foreign sources. Wind, solar, hydroelectric, geothermal, and biomass energy are among the most widely known and used types of renewable energy.

Sustainable energy: Sustainable energy is about meeting social needs without harming the environment or using up natural resources. It's about making sure future generations can still use energy without messing up the planet.

Technology: Defined as knowledge and skills used to meet human needs and desires, while also improving the environment.

Chapter 4
Deforestation and the Investigation of the Effects of Economic Growth With the Environmental Kuznets Curve Hypothesis:
An Analysis of G20 Countries

Fatma Budun
https://orcid.org/0000-0002-1019-7738
Independent Researcher, Turkey

Mustafa Şeker
https://orcid.org/0009-0009-8896-3517
Bursa Uludag Universitesi, Turkey

ABSTRACT

Environmental problems stand out as one of the biggest issues that countries have been focusing on recently. Along with deforestation, the destruction of the environment is happening more rapidly. In this study, the impact of deforestation on the EKC (Environmental Kuznets Curve) hypothesis is examined. This study employs PMG (Pooled Mean Group Estimation) analysis using data on deforestation, population, GDP, agricultural land, and gross production index number for the period between 2001 and 2022. When the results were estimated with the panel ARDL estimator PMG, a 1% increase in per capita income decreases deforestation by approximately

DOI: 10.4018/979-8-3373-1529-4.ch004

3.63%. A 1% increase in population increased deforestation by about 0.4% and a 1% increase in agricultural land decreased deforestation by about 0.09%. The study concluded that the EKC is valid for G20 countries.

INTRODUCTION

In his study, Simon Kuznets (1955) revealed a relationship between income distribution and economic growth. In the mentioned study, he stated that while per capita income increases with economic development, income inequality also increases in the initial stages of development. Subsequently, Kuznets argued that increasing income inequality starts to decrease after a certain turning point as economic development continues. This relationship is defined as the "Inverted U" or "Bell Curve" hypothesis, and the curve showing the relationship between income distribution and income level is expressed as the Kuznets Curve Approach.

In the early 1990s, with the effects of environmental problems such as global warming, air pollution, increased natural resource use, and carbon dioxide emissions becoming more pronounced, environmental and energy issues became primary concerns in the field of economic growth on international platforms. With these developments, the Kuznets Curve approach was adapted to the environment in the 1990s and began to be reinterpreted based on the relationship between per capita income and environmental quality. In some studies, economists have shown that the level of environmental pollution first increases and then decreases during the economic growth process, thus revealing an inverted U-shaped relationship between per capita income and the level of pollution (Grossman and Krueger, 1991, 1995; Shafik, 1994; Panayotou, 1993:2-3).

This relationship is called the EKC hypothesis in the economics literature. According to the EKC Approach, the level of environmental pollution first increases and then decreases during the economic development process (Stern, 2004: 1425). Therefore, the ultimate conclusion of the EKC approach is that economic growth does not pose a problem for the environment; on the contrary, the economic growth process positively affects the environment. This relationship is shown as the EKC diagram in Figure 1. The fundamental study explaining how the EKC relationship occurs is accepted to be the work of Grossman and Krueger (1991) (Carson, 2010: 7). In their study, the authors stated that the impact of economic growth on environmental quality would manifest through three different channels: scale, structural, and technological effects. According to these effects, in the early stages of economic growth, while technology remains constant, as production increases, more resources and energy will be used as inputs in the production process. Consequently, more production, more resource and energy use will lead to more waste and pollutant emissions, and environmental quality will deteriorate (Torras and Boyce, 1998; Dinda, 2004; Prieur, 2009). This effect, referred to as the scale effect, occurs in the early stages of the economic growth process. The structural effect, on the other hand, states that with ongoing growth, the economy will undergo a structural transformation, and this transformation will have a positive impact of economic growth on the environment. This is because as income levels increase, the structure of the economy changes, and the share of economic activities that pollute the environment less gradually increases in production. In addition, in the final stage of structural transformation, a transition occurs from the energy-intensive industrial sector to the technology-intensive service, and information sector. Since technology-intensive sectors use fewer natural resources, their impact on environmental pollution will be less (Tsurumi and Managi, 2010: 20).

The final effect channel in the growth process is the technology effect. Countries with higher income levels will be able to allocate more resources to R&D expenditures, leading to the emergence of new technological processes. Thus, the country will improve environmental quality by replacing its old and dirty technologies with new and clean technologies (Copeland, and Taylor, 2003). Within the framework of these explanations, in the EKC relationship shown in Figure 1, the scale effect represents the increasing part of the EKC, while the structural and technological effect channels represent the decreasing part of the EKC.

With the acceleration of industrialization movements, technological advancements, and rapid population growth, the need for energy is gradually increasing. Studies show that energy plays a significant role in the development of countries and is considered one of the most important indicators of the level of development of societies.

Towards the end of the 20th century, the need for energy increased further with the acceleration of industrialization, and industrializing countries tried to meet this need with non-renewable energy sources, namely fossil fuels. However, the use of fossil fuels releases harmful gases that negatively affect human health and biodiversity, and these gases have brought about environmental problems that threaten the future. The rapid increase in environmental problems since the 1990s has led to the investigation of the relationship between economics and the environment. In the 21st century, secure and sustainable energy supply is one of the biggest problems facing the world. To ensure the sustainability of countries' energy production and consumption, human-caused environmental damage must be prevented. The most significant consequence of environmental degradation is climate change. It is observed that energy consumption increased by 40% between 1990 and 2008, and 80% of global energy use is fossil-based. The use of fossil fuels by countries both increases external dependence in energy and hinders the sustainability of energy by causing an increase in the amount of greenhouse gases released into the atmosphere (WWF, 2011: 2; Çağlar and Mert 2017: 21-22).

The use of fossil fuels, which are defined as non-renewable energy sources in nature, threatens human health through the environmental pollution caused by greenhouse gas emissions, reduces the quality of life, and leads to global warming. Global warming will bring about many disasters such as the melting of glaciers, the disappearance of fertile agricultural lands, and the rise in sea levels. The first condition for preventing the increase in global temperature is to reduce the use of fossil fuels and to make the energy infrastructure suitable for using renewable energies (Keleş and Hamamcı, 1993: 105; Çukurçayır and Sağır, 2008: 258). A reciprocal relationship is mentioned between economics and environmental problems. It is observed that the increase in economic activities causes environmental degradation, and environmental problems negatively affect sustainable economic growth and thus the sustainability of energy. For sustainable energy, the environmental problems caused by energy use must first be taken into account. Sustainable energy refers to the form of energy that meets the needs of the present without consuming the resources necessary for future generations to meet their needs. Ensuring sustainability in energy will be possible with the use of renewable energy sources and the more efficient use of energy (Ediger, 2009:18).

In this context, for sustainable economic growth, the efficient use of energy resources and environmentally friendly economic policies are of great importance. The concept of the environment, which is emphasized to have an effective role in sustainable growth, is a frequently discussed topic today; however, in empirical studies, a definite relationship has been found between economic growth, energy use, and environmental degradation. In this study, the relationship between economic growth and the environment in developed and emerging market economies is evaluated within the framework of the EKC hypothesis, and whether sustainability in energy is achieved in these country groups is discussed. The following section will present the theoretical framework of the EKC hypothesis. Then, previously conducted panel data studies on the EKC hypothesis will be presented. Finally, the data, model, and method applied in the study will be explained, and the application findings will be included.

In recent years, with the increase in environmental problems, the environment-economic growth relationship has become the focus of discussions. Many variables have been used to measure environment-economic growth. At the forefront of these studies is the EKC. There are many factors behind the popularity of this model. The model reveals the relationship between environment and economic growth both simply and econometrically. The variables included in the model are generally measured regularly by national and international organizations. When it comes to the relationship between environment and economic growth, the Kuznets curve stands out as a literature in itself.

Figure 1. Environmental Kuznets Curve

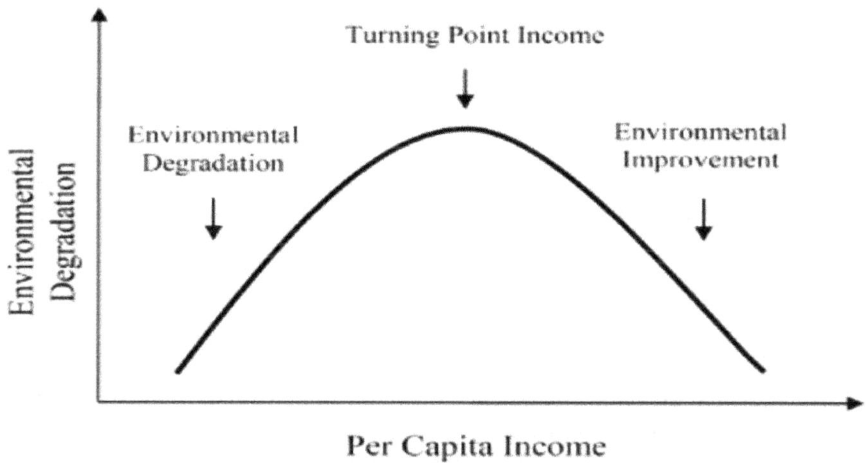

Source: Saatçi, and Dumrul, 2011:68; Akyıldız:2008:142; Yandle et al., 2004:3

The inverted U-shaped relationship between per capita income level and environmental pollution is attributed to the influence of three factors: the scale effect, the structural effect, and the technology effect. The increasing portion of the EKC is associated with the scale effect, while the decreasing portion is associated with the structural effect and technology factors. In pre-industrial societies with low per capita income levels, economic activities are limited to agriculture, so pollution related to industry does not occur, and economic activities are not negatively affected by this situation. The EKC gained validity with the transition to industrial society (Yandle et al., 2004: 3). In an economic structure where the industrial sector has a larger share, an increase in environmental pollution is observed. This is because increased production due to increasing economies of scale, increased natural resource use to meet increased production, and increased consumption due to increased production negatively affect the environment. With economic development, the structure of the economy changes, and a transition occurs from the industrial sector to the services sector. The services sector involves less natural resource use compared to the industrial sector. In the advanced stages of industrialization, environmental pollution decreases with the use of clean technologies, changes in the information process, the transition to service-oriented economic activities, and efforts to improve the environment. The technology effect is used to describe the decreasing portion of the EKC. According to the technology effect, R&D expenditures also increase with the increase in national welfare (Saatçi and Dumrul, 2011:69; Akbostancı et al., 2006:4; Başar and Temurlenk, 2007: 3).

This study is needed due to the lack of a literature analyzing variables such as population and agricultural area in G20 countries. The study consists of three sections. The first section, the introduction, will examine deforestation, agricultural land, and population settlement in G20 countries. It will also provide explanations on deforestation caused by forest fire damage, one of the reasons for deforestation, and the potential fire probabilities in these countries until 2025. The second section of the study includes the literature review. In this section, studies investigating deforestation and its impact on the EKC will be examined. The third section presents the methods and analyses used in the study. The study will investigate the relationship between deforestation, per capita income, population, agricultural land, and gross production index number for the period 2001-2022, and will also explore the existence of the EKC hypothesis in G20 countries.

Initially, the cross-sectional dependence of the variables will be examined using the Breusch and Pagan (1980) LM test. Based on the cross-sectional dependence test results, a decision will be made on whether to use first- or second-generation unit root tests. The study will then proceed with the Pesaran and Yamagata (2008) homogeneity test to examine the homogeneity of the coefficients. The stationarity of the variables at level I(0) and first difference I(1) will be investigated using the Pesaran (2007) CIPS unit root test. Following the CIPS unit root test, short-term, long-term, and country-specific coefficients will be examined using the PMG and MG estimators, which are Panel ARDL estimators, and causality relationships will be investigated using the Pairwise Dumitrescu and Hurlin (2012) test.

Environment and Economy Relationship

The environment is included in the production process by providing the necessary raw materials and other inputs to ensure the continuity of economic activities; however, waste that harms the environment is generated at the end of production and especially consumption processes. While some waste is recycled and re-enters the production process, some non-recyclable waste causes environmental pollution. This situation can lead to the negative impact of economic activities. There is a very close and reciprocal relationship between increasingly important environmental problems and the economy. While the rapid increase in economic activities causes environmental problems, environmental problems also negatively affect economic development and the economic structure.

The mass production that emerged with the industrial revolution means the greater use of resources for more production. Increased production increases income levels, leading to more consumption and bringing about a number of environmental problems.

Problems such as the depletion of the ozone layer, global climate change, erosion, the decrease in clean water resources, and air pollution are given as examples of environmental problems caused by overproduction and overconsumption. The level of the relationship between the environment and the economy varies according to the development levels of countries. In developed countries, which focus significantly on environmental problems in a wide range from investment policies to technology policies, the necessary costs can be covered, and public administrations can easily demand the necessary financial sacrifice from producers and consumers, while in developing countries, the environment is often overlooked.

When capitalism is defined as the takeover of local control by globalization, it is seen that this system is based on the exploitation of natural resources and the trivialization of environmental regulations so as not to hinder world trade. Underlying the acceptance of neoliberal economic policies by developing countries is the expectation that these policies will increase economic growth and economic welfare. The implemented policies include the removal of non-tariff barriers, the reduction of tariff rates, and the reduction of subsidies provided to exporters. With free trade, which causes an increase in global environmental pollution and resource consumption, industries can migrate to places with looser environmental conditions or prevent the imposition of stricter rules by using the threat of migration. In addition to environmental legal regulations, the decision of where to produce includes other factors such as labor costs, easy access to markets, the social and political conditions of that country, and infrastructure facilities (Akbostancı, 2006:4-5). It is observed that developing countries tend towards industrial activities that create high levels of pollution and for which they traditionally do not have a comparative advantage during their industrialization process. The increasing demands of developed country consumers for a clean environment and environmental legal regulations worldwide increase the costs of "dirty industries." In addition, due to the relatively low environmental awareness of consumers in developing countries and the inadequacy of environmental legal regulations in these countries, dirty industries are currently migrating from developed to developing countries, and this situation is defined as the "Pollution Haven Hypothesis" (Akbostancı et al., 2006:3, Akyıldız, 2008:156). The pollution haven hypothesis refers to the transfer of industrial wastes that create environmental pollution and pose a risk to nature, and production units that produce with inefficient production technologies, from central economies to peripheral economies. Due to the strict environmental policies implemented in developed countries, the production costs of firms operating in these countries are increasing. In developing countries, on the other hand, the priority of economic decision-makers is to increase income and ensure growth. In these countries, it is aimed to maintain economic growth despite the damage to the environment. Producers within dirty industries in developed countries shift their activities to developing countries where environmental standards are relatively low in order to get rid of the costs brought about by high environmental standards. The low environmental standards in developing countries stem from their need for all kinds of industrial activities due to their low-income levels, the underdeveloped environmental awareness and sensitivity, and the unhealthy definition of property rights (Akyıldız, 2008:157).

Deforestation and Environment

In Turkiye, there has been a loss of vegetation cover between 2001 and 2023, and it is known that the main reason for this 0.33% loss is deforestation. It is observed that the most significant deforestation in Turkiye during these periods occurred in Mugla, with 69.4 thousand hectares (Global Forest Watch, 2025a). In the USA, there has been a loss of vegetation cover between 2001 and 2023, and it is known that the main reason for this 0.5% loss is deforestation. It is known that 10.1 million hectares of forest area were burned. It is observed that the most significant deforestation in the USA during these periods occurred in Alaska, with 6.30 million hectares (Global Forest Watch, 2025b). In Germany, there has been a loss of vegetation cover between 2001 and 2023, and it is known that the main reason for this 7.1% loss is deforestation. It is observed that the most significant deforestation in Germany during these periods occurred in Nordrhein-Westfalen, with 267 thousand hectares (Global Forest Watch, 2025c). In Argentina, there has been a loss of vegetation cover between 2001 and 2023, with a 11% forest loss observed. It is observed that the most significant deforestation in Argentina during these periods occurred in Santiago del Estero, with 2 million hectares (Global Forest Watch, 2025d). In Australia, there has been a loss of vegetation cover between 2001 and 2023, with 9.04 million hectares lost, and it is known that the main reason for this 21% loss is deforestation. It is observed that the most significant deforestation in Australia during these periods occurred in New South Wales, with 3.05 million hectares (Global Forest Watch, 2025e). In Brazil, there has been a loss of vegetation cover between 2001 and 2023, with 68.9 million hectares lost, and it is known that the main reason for this 13% loss is deforestation. It is observed that the most significant deforestation in Brazil during these periods occurred in Pará, with 17 million hectares (Global Forest Watch, 2025f). In China, there has been a loss of vegetation cover between 2001 and 2023, with 12.1 million hectares lost, and it is known that the main reason for this 7.4% loss is deforestation. It is observed that the most significant deforestation in China during these periods occurred in Guangxi, with 2.89 million hectares (Global Forest Watch, 2025g). In Indonesia, there has been a loss of vegetation cover between 2001 and 2023, with 30.8 million hectares lost, and it is known that the main reason for this 19% loss is deforestation. It is observed that the most significant deforestation in Indonesia during these periods occurred in Riau, with 4.2 million hectares (Global Forest Watch, 2025h). In France, there has been a loss of vegetation cover between 2001 and 2023, and it is known that the main reason for this 0.24% loss is deforestation. It is observed that the most significant deforestation in France during these periods occurred in Nouvelle-Aquitaine, with 641 thousand hectares (Global Forest Watch, 2025i). In South Africa, there has been a loss of vegetation cover between 2001 and 2023, with 1.60 million hectares lost, and it is known that the main reason for this 27% loss is deforestation. It is observed that the most significant deforestation in South Africa during these periods occurred in KwaZulu-Natal, with 624 thousand hectares (Global Forest Watch, 2025j). In South Korea, there has been a loss of vegetation cover between 2001 and 2023, with 336 thousand hectares lost, and it is known that the main reason for this 6.3% loss is deforestation. It is observed that the most significant deforestation in South Korea during these periods occurred in Gangwon-do, with 70.4 thousand hectares (Global Forest Watch, 2025k). In India, there has been a loss of vegetation cover between 2001 and 2023, with 2.18 million hectares lost, and it is known that the main reason for this 6.7% loss is deforestation. It is observed that the most significant deforestation in India during these periods occurred in Assam, with 817 thousand hectares (Global Forest Watch, 2025l). In the United Kingdom, there has been a loss of vegetation cover between 2001 and 2023, with 563 thousand hectares lost, and it is known that the main reason for this 15% loss is deforestation. It is observed that the most significant deforestation in the United Kingdom during these periods occurred in Scotland, with 2.10 million hectares (Global Forest Watch, 2025m). In Italy, there has been a loss of vegetation cover between 2001 and 2023, with 489 thousand hectares lost, and it is known that the main reason for this 5.2% loss is deforestation. It is observed that the most significant deforestation in Italy during these periods occurred in Toscana, with 96.5 thousand hectares (Global Forest Watch, 2025n). In Japan, there has been a loss of vegetation cover between 2001 and 2023, with 915 thousand hectares lost, and it is known that the main reason for this 3.5% loss is deforestation. It is observed that the most significant deforestation in Japan during these periods occurred in Hokkaido, with 199 thousand hectares (Global Forest Watch, 2025o). In Canada, there has been a loss of vegetation cover between 2001 and 2023, with 57.5 million hectares lost, and it is known that the main reason for this 14% loss is deforestation. It is observed that the most significant deforestation in Canada during these periods occurred in Québec, with 10.9 million hectares (Global Forest Watch, 2025p). In Mexico, there has been a loss of vegetation cover between 2001 and 2023, with 4.89 million hectares lost, and it is known that the main reason for this 9.2% loss is deforestation. It is observed that the most significant deforestation in Mexico during these periods occurred in Campeche, with 877 thousand hectares (Global Forest Watch, 2025r). In Russia, there has been a loss of vegetation cover between 2001 and 2023, with 83.7 million hectares lost, and it is known that the main reason for this 11% loss is deforestation. It is observed that the most significant deforestation in Russia during these periods occurred in Sakha, with 113 million hectares (Global Forest Watch, 2025s).

LITERATURE REVIEW

Studies on the effects of deforestation have been ongoing for many years. The first of these studies is considered to be Molion's (1975) doctoral dissertation, in which he examined the effects of deforestation in the Amazon. Lettau et al. (1979) are among those who investigated the effects of further deforestation in the Amazon in their study. They stated that urbanization and deforestation together would lead to climate change in the Amazon. In their study, Mather et al. (1999) concluded that increases in economic development would bring about increases in forests, and that the Kuznet curve was observed.

Studies examining the impact of deforestation on country groups also exist in the literature. Studies on OECD countries, developing countries, Asian countries, Latin American, and African countries have been found in the literature. Cropper and Griffiths (1994) examined non-OECD countries with less than 1,000,000 hectares in their study and concluded that deforestation would decrease as income increased, and that population density increased deforestation. Koop and Tole (1999) examined the relationship between deforestation, population, and growth in 76 tropical developing countries between 1961 and 1992 and found that the Kuznet curve was observed in Asian countries in the basic model, and in another equation including the population variable, the Kuznet curve was observed except for Latin American countries, while population had a positive and significant relationship with deforestation. Bhattarai and Hammig (2001) investigated the impact of variables such as deforestation, GDP, and population on the EKC hypothesis in 66 Latin American, African, and Asian countries between 1972 and 1991 and found results confirming the existence of the EKC in Latin America and Africa, while deforestation had a positive effect on income and population growth. Barbier (2001) investigated the impact of population, per capita income, and deforestation, and the existence of the EKC hypothesis in countries in Latin America, Africa, and Asia, and found results rejecting the existence of the EKC hypothesis for the entire panel. He also concluded that deforestation had an impact on agricultural land area. In their research, Buitenzorgy and Mol (2010) investigated data on democracy, education, rural population, land area, consumption, and per capita GDP of 177 countries between 1990 and 2000 using the OLS method and found that democracy and per capita income affected deforestation. According to their research, Damette and Delacote

(2012) investigated the existence of the EKC hypothesis with variables such as deforestation, population, and growth in 59 developing countries between 1972 and 1994 using the panel quantile regression method and concluded that the EKC hypothesis was observed in places with high deforestation. Joshi and Beck (2016) investigated variables such as deforestation, growth, population, and agricultural land in OECD countries and non-OECD regions of Latin America, Asia, and Africa between 1990 and 2007 using the GMM method and found that in OECD countries, agricultural land came from forests, population brought about deforestation, income increased deforestation, and the EKC hypothesis was in the form of an inverted U. Ogundari et al. (2017) examined the EKC for variables such as economic growth, deforestation, and population of 43 Sub-Saharan African countries between 1990 and 2008 and concluded that population increase increased deforestation, while growth had a negative effect on deforestation, and the EKC was valid. They found that the EKC hypothesis was in the form of an inverted U in OECD and Latin America, while it was U-shaped in Asia. In their study, Zambrano-Monserrate et al. (2018) investigated the existence of the EKC hypothesis for growth, deforestation, and exports of Turkiye, France, Germany, Greece, and Portugal between 1974 and 2013 using the ARDL test and found that the EKC hypothesis occurred in the form of an inverted U in France, Germany, and Turkiye. They concluded that deforestation had a negative impact on economic growth, except for Greece. Andrée et al. (2019) examined variables such as deforestation, income, population, and air pollution of 95 developing countries between 2001 and 2014 within the framework of the EKC hypothesis using the panel data method and concluded that an inverted U-shape occurred. They also found that increases in economic growth were not solely effective on deforestation. In his study, Caravaggio (2020) investigated countries in low, middle, and high-income groups with variables such as forest disappearance rate, per capita GDP, agriculture (% land), population density (% land), and trade openness using the PMG estimator and found that in middle-income countries, the deforestation rate increased GDP at a decreasing rate, in the high-income country group, the deforestation rate increased GDP at an increasing rate, and deforestation increased in low-income countries. The EKC hypothesis was confirmed for deforestation and was observed to be in the form of an inverted U. In their study, Cary and Bekun (2021) conducted panel data analysis with data on forest disappearance rate, democracy, education, rural population, land area, control of corruption, per capita GDP, tariff rate, agricultural land growth rate, and urbanization of 177 countries between 2000 and 2010 and found that the EKC hypothesis was not supported for democracy and deforestation. Ajanaku and Collins (2021) investigated the existence of the EKC hypothesis with data on GDP, population density, deforestation, and forest product trade of 45 African countries between 1990 and 2016 using the GMM method and concluded that the EKC hypothesis was valid in Africa. Zafeiriou et al.

(2023) examined the relationship between deforestation and agricultural income of Eastern European countries between 1990 and 2000 using the PMG test, which is an ARDL estimator, and concluded that the EKC hypothesis was not confirmed. In their study, Sohag et al. (2023) conducted panel data analysis for 75 Russian regions between 2009 and 2019 with data such as trade deficit, temperature, forestry policy, population, bribery rate, crime rate, GDP, total forest area, timber harvest, and forest disappearance rate and concluded that forestry policies had an effective authority on deforestation.

The existence of the EKC hypothesis was established for Russia. Studies investigating the impact of countries on deforestation have also been included in the literature. In their study, Esmaeili and Nasrnia (2014) examined variables such as per capita income, forest area, and population using the ARDL test and concluded that Iran had an inverted U-shape. Ahmed et al. (2015) tested the validity of the EKC hypothesis with variables such as deforestation, economic growth, industrialization, population, and trade deficit in Pakistan between 1980 and 2013 using the ARDL test and found that while the EKC was confirmed for deforestation, economic growth had a negative impact on deforestation in the long run. Waluyo and Terawaki (2016) examined data on deforestation, growth, and agricultural land in Indonesia between 1962 and 2007 using the ARDL test and found a unidirectional causality from growth to deforestation, that the EKC hypothesis occurred in an inverted U-shape, and that population and agricultural land had a negative relationship with deforestation. In their study, Polomé and Trotignon (2016) examined deforestation in the Brazilian Amazon forests between 1975 and 1988 using the EKC hypothesis with the OLS method and concluded that economic growth reduced deforestation. The existence of the EKC hypothesis was confirmed. In his study, Maji (2017) examined the effects of deforestation, trade openness, population, energy consumption, and economic growth in Nigeria using ARDL analysis and concluded that population increases increased deforestation and that growth had a reducing effect on deforestation. Tsiantikoudis et al. (2019) investigated the existence of the EKC hypothesis for CO2 emissions from growth and deforestation in Bulgaria between 1990 and 2015 using the ARDL method and found that while the inverted U hypothesis was not confirmed, an inverted N-shape occurred. In his study, Murhed (2022) investigated the effects of democracy quality, deforestation, and economic growth in Bangladesh between 1971 and 2018 using the Toda Yamamoto causality test and concluded that the EKC hypothesis was valid. It was also concluded that there was a causality relationship between economic growth and deforestation. In their study, Warsame et al. (2024) investigated data on population density, urban population, renewable energy consumption, greenhouse gas emissions, rural population, foreign direct investment, temperature change, gross capital formation, deforestation rate, GDP, and total number of people affected by natural disasters in Somalia using the Granger causality test and concluded that natural disasters and deforestation reduced economic growth in Somalia, while other variables had a positive effect on economic growth.

Different studies on the EKC hypothesis are also included in the literature. In their research, Özokçu and Özdemir (2017) investigated the EKC hypothesis for 26 OECD countries and 52 developing countries between 1980 and 2010 and concluded that N and inverted N shapes occurred. In their studies on G-20 countries, Alakbarov et al. (2024) for the period between 1992 and 2014, and Mar'I et al. (2023) for the period between 1995 and 2019, investigated the existence of the EKC hypothesis in G-20 countries and confirmed its existence. Gürdal Arslan and Gürbüz (2022) investigated the existence of the EKC hypothesis in G7 countries between 1981 and 2018 and concluded that the EKC hypothesis existed. Iwata et al. (2011) tested the existence of the EKC hypothesis in 28 countries between 1960 and 2003 and found that an inverted U-shape occurred. Odei et al. (2025) found that the EKC hypothesis occurred in 28 developing countries. Narayan et al. (2016) concluded in their study on countries that the EKC hypothesis was supported in 21 countries, while it did not occur in other countries. Yurttagüler and Kutlu (2017) examined the existence of the EKC hypothesis for Turkiye between 1960 and 2011 and concluded that the EKC hypothesis was not valid. Bulut (2021) investigated the existence of the EKC hypothesis in Turkiye between 1970 and 2016 and found results supporting the EKC hypothesis. Karahasan and Pınar (2022) investigated the EKC hypothesis for Turkiye between 2004 and 2019 and concluded that the EKC hypothesis was not valid. Farooq et al. (2024) investigated the EKC hypothesis in India between 1991 and 2016 and concluded that an inverted N-shape occurred.

EMPIRICAL APPLICATION

In this study, the relationship between deforestation, population, GDP, agricultural land, and Gross Production Index Number data of the G-20 countries (Turkiye, USA, Germany, Argentina, Australia, Brazil, China, Indonesia, France, South Africa, South Korea, India, United Kingdom, Italy, Japan, Canada, Mexico, Russia) for the period between 2001 and 2022 will be examined.

Table 1. Variables, Symbol, Period, Variable Type, and Sources

Variable	Symbol	Period	Variable Type	Source
Tree cover loss (kha)	deforest (logarithmic)		Dependent	(Global Forest Watch, 2025t)
GDP per capita (constant 2015 USA$)	gdp (logarithmic)		Independent	(World Bank Data, 2025a)
Population growth (annual %)	pop	(2001-2022)	Independent	(World Bank Data, 2025b)
Agricultural land (% of land area)	land		Independent	(World Bank Data, 2025c)
Gross Production Index Number	agr		Independent	(FAOSTAT, 2025)

Source: Created by the authors.

$$ldeforest_{it} = \alpha + \beta_1 lgdp_{it} + \beta_2 lgdp^2{}_{it} + \beta_3 pop_{it} + \beta_4 land_{it} + \beta_5 agr_{it} + \varepsilon_{it}$$

In the model, "i" represents the number of countries, "t" represents the time dimension of the study, and "ε_{it}" represents the error term.

METHOD

In this study, the cross-sectional dependence of the variables will first be examined using the Breusch and Pagan (1980) LM test. Based on the results of the cross-sectional dependence test, a decision will be made on whether to use first- or second-generation unit root tests. The homogeneity of the coefficients will be tested using the Pesaran and Yamagata (2008) homogeneity test. In the subsequent stage of the study, the stationarity of the variables at level I(0) and first difference I(1) will be examined using the Pesaran (2007) CIPS unit root test. After the CIPS unit root test, short-term, long-term, and country-specific coefficients will be examined using the PMG and MG estimators, which are panel ARDL estimators selected for different integration orders. Finally, the causality relationship between the variables will be explained using the Pairwise Dumitrescu and Hurlin (2012) panel pairwise causality test. In this study, the Panel ARDL method is preferred because it explains the long and short-run relationships of the data. It is used in the study since it allows the analysis of variables with different stationarity.

Analysis Results

Table 2. Descriptive Summary Statistics

Variables	Number of Observations	Mean	Standard deviation	Minimum value	Maximum value
deforest	396	10698900	18440784	12505.13	104943266
gdp^2	396	897662579.85	10174086	606073.7	4139908140.80
gdp	396	23845.52	18162.78	778.5074	64342.12
land	396	42.49557	20.02303	6.370735	80.80851
pop	396	0.744623	0.564778	-1.853715	2.060833
agr	396	94.37225	12.86	58.72000	128.85

Note: Created by the authors.

Table 2 presents the summary statistics of the variables, including the number of observations, mean, standard deviation, minimum value, and maximum value. The number of observations for each variable was stated as 396 in the table. The mean values for the variables were as follows: tree cover loss was 10698900, gdp^2 is 897662579.85 (and 23845.52 when likely referring to per capita gdp), agricultural land was 42.49557, population is 0.744623, and the Gross Production Index Number has a mean of 94.37225.

Table 3. Cross-Sectional Dependence Test

Breusch-Pagan LM		
Variables	Statistic value	Probability
ldeforest	217.5351	0.0000*
lgdp	2278.652	0.0000*
$lgdp^2$	2271.889	0.0000*
pop	899.5452	0.0000*
land	1778.249	0.0000*
agr	1816.587	0.0000*

Notes: 1- *, **, ***, indicate significance levels of 1%, 5%, and 10%, respectively. 2- Created by the authors.

Regarding cross-sectional dependence:

H_0 = There was no cross-sectional dependence,

H_1 = There was cross-sectional dependence.

Table 3 presents the cross-sectional dependence results obtained using the Breusch and Pagan (1980) LM test. It was found that the probability values of the ldeforest, lgdp, lgdp^2, pop, land and agr variables are less than 0.05 at the 5% significance level, thus rejecting the H_0 hypothesis. It was concluded that the variables exhibit cross-sectional dependence. In the next stage after the cross-sectional dependence test, the Pesaran and Yamagata (2008) delta test would be applied to test the homogeneity of the coefficients.

Table 4. Homogeneity Test

Test statistic	t-statistic	Probability value
$\tilde{\Delta}$	2.766	0.006*
$\tilde{\Delta}$adj	3.244	0.001*

Notes: 1- *, **, ***, indicate significance levels of 1%, 5%, and 10%, respectively. 2- Created by the authors.

H_0 = Slope coefficients were homogeneous.
H_1 = Slope coefficients were heterogeneous.

Table 4 presents the results of the Pesaran and Yamagata (2008) homogeneity test. Refers to $\tilde{\Delta}$ (delta tilde) and $\tilde{\Delta}$ adj (delta tilde adjusted). Since the delta and adjusted delta probability values of the coefficients were less than 0.05, the "H_0" hypothesis is rejected, and it was concluded that the coefficients were heterogeneous. In the next step of the study, the probability values of the variables at level and first difference would be calculated using the CIPS unit root test, which was a second-generation unit root test.

Table 5. CIPS Unit Root Test

Variables	Level	Probability	First Difference	Probability
ldeforest	-2.03281	≥0.10	-3.56684	<0.01*
lgdp	-3.76902	<0.01*		
lgdp^2	-3.49630	<0.01*		
pop	-1.80424	≥0.10	-3.36757	<0.01*
land	-2.48510	<0.01*		
agr	-5.24201	<0.01*		

Notes: 1- *, **, ***, indicate significance levels of $p < 0.01$, $p < 0.05$, and $p < 0.10$, respectively. 2- Created by the authors.

Table 5 presents the results of the Pesaran (2007) CIPS panel unit root test. The probability values of the variables at level I(0) and first difference I(1) were provided. The probability values of the variables at level were "≥0.10", and the probability values at the first difference are "<0.01". Since the variables were not stationary at the same order, cointegration tests were not employed in this study. The study would proceed with PMG-MG analysis.

Table 6. Long-Run and Short-Run PMG Results

Estimator	Stat.	DOF	p-Value
Mean Group	4.946565	5	0.4224

Table 6 presents the Hausman test statistic. In order to choose the appropriate model between PMG and MG (Mean Group) estimators, which were panel ARDL estimators, Hausman test was used.

H_0 = Long-run coefficients were homogeneous

0.4224> 0.05 H_0 was not rejected.

According to the Hausman test, it was concluded that the MG estimator was insignificant.

Table 7. Coefficient Differences Between PMG and MG Estimators

Variable	MG	PMG	Var (diff)	P- Value
lgdp	0.001175	-0.000036	0.000017	0.7686
$lgdp^2$	-3.503741	0.094895	43.156001	0.5838
pop	3.928500	0.397375	4.902169	0.1107
land	2.676704	-0.089544	6.924666	0.2932
agr	0.015227	0.000726	0.004958	0.8368

Table 7 presents the differences between the PMG and MG estimators. It was observed that the probability values were not significant. It was observed that the PMG estimator has significant results. In the next stage, the study was continued with the PMG estimator.

Table 8. PMG Estimator Results

Variables	Coefficient	Standard Error
Long Run lgdp	-3.630210 0.0796***	2.064923
Long Run lgdp^2	0.094895 0.0000*	0.019404
Long Run pop	0.397375 0.0132**	0.159570
Long Run land	-0.089544 0.0023*	0.029132
Long Run agr	0.000726 0.8600	0.004111
Cointeq	-0.808273 0.0000*	0.077085
Short Run lgdp	-0.016872 0.0948***	0.010075
Short Run lgdp^2	12.08329 0.0419**	5.917946
Short Run pop	2.019377 0.0242**	0.891999
Short Run land	1.757337 0.4701	2.430565
Short Run agr	-0.065315 0.0279**	0.029581

Notes: 1- *, **, ***, indicate significance levels of 1%, 5%, and 10%, respectively. 2- Created by the author.

Table 8 presents the results of the PMG estimator. The table includes coefficients, standard errors, and probability values. In the long run, a 1% increase in per capita income decrease deforestation by approximately 3.6%. A 1 unit change in the population variable leads to an approximately 0.4% increase in deforestation. A 1 unit change in the agricultural land variable was observed to decrease deforestation by approximately 0.09. The effect of a unit change in agricultural gross production on deforestation was insignificant. In the long run, the EKC hypothesis was observed to hold. In the short run, a 1 unit change in population increases deforestation by 2.01%. A unit change in the agricultural gross production index is observed to decrease deforestation by approximately 0.07. Similar results have been reached in [Koop and Tole (1999); Mather et al. (1999); Bhattarai and Hammig (2001); Iwata et al. (2011); Damette and Delacote (2012); Esmaeili and Nasrnia (2014); Ahmed et al. (2015); Waluyo and Terawaki (2016); Joshi and Beck (2016); Narayan et al. (2016); Ogundari et al. (2017); Polomé and Trotignon (2016) Zambrano-Monserrate et al. (2018); Andrée et al. (2019); Caravaggio (2020); Ajanaku and Collins (2021); Gürdal Arslan and Gürbüz (2022); Murhed (2022); Mar'I et al. (2023); Alakbarov et al. (2024); Odei et al. (2025)]. Contrary results have been found in [Barbier (2001); Özokçu and Özdemir (2017); Tsiantikoudis et al. (2019); Cary and Bekun (2021); Zafeiriou et al. (2023)].

The study was proceeded by defining the country coefficients of the PMG estimator and the coefficients, standard errors and probability values of the variables.

Table 9. PMG Country Coefficients

Country	Coefficient	lgdp	lgdp²	pop	land	agr
Turkiye	-0.998316* (0.337359)	-0.009524 (0.005942)	4.636814 (3.142114)	-0.094903 (2.232260)	-0.280477 (1.538039)	-0.093633 (0.257570)
U.S.A.	-0.742858 * (0.204232)	0.000449 (0.000443)	-0.800877 (1.121075)	0.434683** (0.208269)	-0.014867 (0.288504)	0.000400 (0.009871)
Germany	-0.781920* (0.25599)	0.006617 (0.013856)	-13.31209 (25.94865)	0.943143 (1.229410)	1.181732 (5.577667)	-0.245639 (0.224831)
Argentina	-0.211426 (0.219860)	-0.000627 (0.000934)	0.544864 (0.560010)	-0.302540 (1.445574)	0.146373 (0.196753)	-0.005410 (0.014817)
Australia	-0.488815* (0.159463)	-0.002284 (0.001639)	5.074766 (3.986917)	-0.140328 (0.337942)	0.033349 (0.055941)	-0.050190* (1.121041)
Brazil	-0.564981** (0.262126)	-0.005606 (0.004231)	2.522316 (1.983256)	-1.302101 (2.640070)	0.002009 (0.506238)	-0.019091 (0.031738)
China	-0.931909* (0.227065)	-0.001560** (0.000623)	0.957038* (0.277676)	1.385390 (0.944851)	1.704197 (1.208691)	0.042098 (0.038743)
Indonesia	-0.740160** (0.268195)	-0.004107 (0.003756)	1.140843 (0.899834)	0.327906 (2.142969)	0.115082 (0.319620)	-0.024119 (0.025286)
France	-1.162320* (0.287056)	-0.050937 (0.045521)	88.03353 (79.68662)	8.521888 (18.45199)	0.074752 (9.253716)	-0.131134 (0.188180)
South Africa	-1.509546* (0.179600)	-0.179270** (0.075650)	62.10701** (24.95533)	2.822186*** (1.528326)	0.484850 (4.336381)	-0.110100 (0.157316)
South Korea	-0.713606* (0.175429)	0.004738 (0.003187)	0.129855 (3.649782)	2.137909 (2.487675)	3.968766 (3.513395)	-0.017525 (0.175495)
India	-0.610393*** (0.285871)	-0.025285 (0.047352)	4.072383 (5.238784)	11.97758 (21.71922)	-20.00995 (17.78777)	-0.091506 (0.344994)
United Kingdom	-0.446780*** (0.220192)	-0.009417 (0.015365)	19.63500 (31.78722)	0.794798 (1.939065)	0.325563 (0.512108)	0.012383 (0.155438)
Italy	-1.154391* (0.329859)	-0.006386 (0.009728)	10.32276 (14.90763)	1.451907* (0.671654)	-0.397538 (0.244476)	0.025593 (0.063775)
Japan	-1.339692* (0.249869)	-0.021316 (0.032294)	31.40170 (51.73323)	8.745598 (10.84284)	37.51647 (50.44732)	-0.480918 (0.542013)
Canada	-0.617223* (0.182266)	-0.000816 (0.001289)	2.018897 (2.567538)	-0.209898 (0.163883)	0.951171 (0.838728)	0.000403 (0.007643)

continued on following page

Table 9. Continued

Country	Coefficient	lgdp	$lgdp^2$	pop	land	agr
Mexico	-0.737425* (0.212974)	0.003395 (0.008225)	-1.971901 (4.285629)	0.733407 (0.669749)	0.162676 (0.100120)	0.005808 (0.022590)
Russia	-0.797152** (0.288516)	-0.001760 (0.004019)	0.986244 (1.986472)	-1.877832*** (1.013266)	5.817423 (37.10031)	0.006913 (0.012640)

Notes: 1- Numbers in parentheses indicate standard errors. 2- *, **, ***, indicate significance levels of 1%, 5%, and 10%, respectively. 3- Created by the authors.

Table 9 presents the PMG estimator results on a country-by-country basis. When we examine the country results individually:

For Turkiye, the coefficient of the error correction model was negative and significant at the 1% level. The error correction coefficient suggested that the system was expected to return to equilibrium in a period shorter than a time unit. The results for other variables were found to be insignificant.

For the USA, the coefficient of the error correction model was negative and significant at the 1% level. It was observed that a large majority (approximately 74%) of potential imbalances in one period were corrected each year. The error correction coefficient indicates that the system was determined to return to equilibrium within approximately 1.5 periods. The results for the variables were found to be insignificant.

When we examine the results for Germany, the coefficient of the error correction model was negative and significant at the 5% level, while approximately 78% of potential imbalances in one period were corrected each year. The error correction coefficient suggested that the system would reach equilibrium in less than 1.5 periods. When we examined the variables, the probability values were found to be insignificant.

For Argentina, the error correction coefficient was found to be negative and insignificant, and the coefficients of the variables were also insignificant.

When we examined the results for Australia, the error correction coefficient was negative and significant at the 1% level, and it was assumed that approximately 48% of potential imbalances in one period would be corrected each year. The error correction coefficient was determined to bring the system back to equilibrium in approximately 2 periods.

For Brazil, error correction coefficient was found to be negative and significant at the 5% significance level, it was assumed that approximately 56% of the possible imbalances in one period would be corrected each year. The error correction coefficient was found to bring the system to equilibrium in a period of approximately 2 periods.

When we examine China, the error correction coefficient was negative and significant at the 1% level. It is observed that 93% of the imbalances in the country change each year. The error correction coefficient suggests that the system was expected to return to equilibrium within approximately 1 periods. When we analyzed the results for all variables, it was observed that a 1% increase in per capita income reduces deforestation by approximately 0.02% at the 5% significance level.

When we analyzed the results in Indonesia, we observed that the error correction coefficient was negative and significant at the 1% significance level, while the error correction coefficient would bring the system to equilibrium in approximately 1 period.

When we examine France, the error correction coefficient was found to be negative and significant at the 1% level. It appears that the error correction coefficient would bring the system to equilibrium in an even shorter period than approximately a time unit. When we examined all variables, the results were found to have insignificant values.

According to the results for South Africa, the error correction coefficient was found to be negative and significant at the 1% level. It was understood that the error correction coefficient would bring the system to equilibrium in a period even shorter than approximately a time unit. When we examined all variables, a 1% increase in per capita income decrease deforestation by approximately 0.17% at the 5% significance level, while a 1% increase in population increases deforestation by approximately 2.82% at the 5% significance level.

When we examine the results for South Korea, the error correction coefficient was observed to be negative and significant at the 1% level. The error correction coefficient suggested that the system was expected to return to equilibrium within approximately 1.5 periods. When we looked at the coefficients for the variables, the results were observed to be insignificant.

The error correction coefficient for India was observed to be negative and significant at the 5% level. It was seen that a approximately 62% of potential imbalances in one period were corrected each year. The error correction coefficient was expected to bring the system to equilibrium in approximately 1.5 periods. When we examined the variables, all results were found to have an insignificant probability value.

According to the results obtained for the United Kingdom, the error correction coefficient was negative and significant at the 10% level. It was understood that approximately 45% of potential imbalances in one period are corrected annually. The error correction coefficient was expected to bring the system to equilibrium in approximately 2 periods. The coefficient results for the variables were found to be insignificant.

For Italy, the error correction coefficient was negative and insignificant. It was observed that a 1-unit increase in agricultural land increase population by approximately a 1-unit 1.45 at the 5% significance level.

Looking at the results obtained for Japan, the error correction coefficient was found to be negative and significant at the 1% level. The error correction coefficient suggests that the system was expected to return to equilibrium in a short time, approximately within 1 period. When we examine the coefficients and probability values for the variables, the results were found to be insignificant.

In Canada, the error correction coefficient was negative and significant at the 1% level. While approximately 62% of potential imbalances in one period were assumed to be corrected each year, the error correction coefficient was expected to bring the system to equilibrium in approximately 1.5 periods.

In Mexico, the error correction coefficient was negative and significant at the 1% level. While it was determined that approximately 74% of potential imbalances in one period would be corrected each year, the error correction coefficient will bring the system to equilibrium within approximately 1.5 periods. When we examined the coefficients and probability values for all variables, the results were determined to be insignificant.

When the error correction coefficient for Russia was analyzed, the results were found to be negative and significant. While it was found that approximately 80% of the possible imbalances in a period would be corrected every year, the error correction coefficient would be balanced by the system in approximately 1.5 periods. When we analyzed the coefficient and probability values for all variables, it was observed that the probability values were insignificant.

According to the results examined in Table 9, an U-shaped Kuznet curve was observed in China and South Africa. The existence of the EKC hypothesis was confirmed for these countries. Similar results have been found in [Iwata et al. (2011); Waluyo and Terawaki (2016); (Polomé and Trotignon (2016); Ogundari et al. (2017); Zambrano-Monserrate et al. (2018); Bulut (2021); Gürdal Arslan and Gürbüz (2022); Sohag et al. (2023); Farooq et al. (2024)]. Contrary results have been reached in [Narayan et al. (2016); Yurttagüler and Kutlu (2017); Karahasan and Pınar (2022)].

The study, continued with Dumitrescu Hurlin Panel Causality Test to show the bilateral causality of the variables.

Table 10. Dumitrescu Hurlin Panel Causality Test

Causality Directions	W-statistic	Zbar-Stat	Probability	Relationship
ldeforest → lgdp	4.07595	2.78390	0.0054*	Causality exists
lgdp → ldeforest	4.03811	2.72433	0.0064*	Causality exists
ldeforest → $lgdp^2$	4.12971	2.86855	0.0041*	Causality exists
$lgdp^2$ → ldeforest	4.02038	2.69643	0.0070*	Causality exists

continued on following page

Table 10. Continued

Causality Directions	W-statistic	Zbar-Stat	Probability	Relationship
ldeforest → pop	2.57553	0.42167	0.6733	No causality
pop → ldeforest	2.40446	0.15235	0.8789	No causality
ldeforest → land	3.42329	1.75638	0.0790***	Causality exists
land → ldeforest	4.59755	3.60511	0.0003*	Causality exists
ldeforest → agr	2.81200	0.79397	0.4272	No causality
agr → ldeforest	2.53659	0.36038	0.7186	No causality

Note: *, **, ***, indicate significance levels of 1%, 5%, and 10%, respectively. Created by the author.

Table 10 presents the Dumitrescu Hurlin (2012) panel causality test results for the G-20 countries. The appropriate lag length was taken as Lag (2). There was a bidirectional causality relationship between the ldeforest variable and lgdp, $lgdp^2$, and land. It was concluded that there was no causality relationship between the pop and agr variables and the ldeforest variable. Similar results were obtained by Murhed (2022). Contrary results were obtained by [Waluyo and Terawaki (2016); Warsame et al. (2024)].

CONCLUSION

Deforestation has serious economic, environmental and social consequences. The impact of the environmental EKC hypotesis in G-20 countries was analyzed. To examine the effects of deforestation, which is one of the biggest problems of countries, population, per capita income, square of per capita income, agricultural land (% of land area), gross production index number variables were selected and analyzed.

In this study, the Breusch and Pagan (1980) LM test for cross-sectional dependence determined that there was cross-sectional dependence, thus indicating that a second-generation unit root test was appropriate. The Pesaran and Yamagata (2008) homogeneity test revealed that the coefficients were heterogeneous. Subsequently, the Pesaran (2007) CIPS unit root test, a second-generation test, examined the stationarity of the variables at level I(0) and first difference I(1). Short-term, long-term, and country-specific coefficients were then analyzed using the PMG and MG estimators. Finally, the Pairwise Dumitrescu and Hurlin (2012) panel pairwise causality test was employed to investigate the bidirectional causality relationships between the variables.

Looking at the analysis results, first, the Breusch and Pagan (1980) LM test, conducted under the condition "T>N" (where T represents the time dimension and N represents the number of countries), found that the probability values for deforestation, per capita income, population, land, and agriculture variables were less than 0.05 at the 1% significance level, confirming the presence of cross-sectional dependence. For these variables exhibiting cross-sectional dependence, the second-generation CIPS unit root test was applied. The results showed that the probability values for deforestation and population variables were "≥0.10" at level I(0) and "<0.01" at their first difference. The other variables, per capita GDP, agricultural land, and gross production index, had probability values of "<0.01" at level I(0). Following the CIPS unit root test, the Pesaran and Yamagata (2008) test was performed. The delta and adjusted delta probability values were found to be less than 0.05, indicating that the coefficients are heterogeneous. When the results were estimated with the panel ARDL estimator PMG, a 1% increase in per capita income increased deforestation by approximately 5.2%. A 1% increase in population decreases deforestation by about 3.6% and a 1 unit increase in agricultural land decreases deforestation by about 0.09%. It was concluded that the Environmental Kuznet Curve is valid in G20 countries. The fact that the sign of lgdp was negative and the sign of lgdp2 is positive can be said that the Environmental Kuznet curve is valid. In the G20 countries, the EKC was observed to be U-shaped in China and South Africa. According to the Pairwise Dumitrescu and Hurlin (2012) causality test results, there was bidirectional causality between deforestation and agricultural land, and between deforestation and per capita income. No causality relationship was observed between population and agricultural products, and deforestation.

In order to prevent and reverse deforestation, sustainable environmentally friendly policies, promotion of forestry, implementation of forest protection projects and implementation of environmentally friendly policies are of great importance. Increased emphasis by governments on environmental protection with policies and sanctions in this direction will minimize the effects of deforestation.

REFERENCES

Ahmed, K., Shahbaz, M., Qasim, A., & Long, W. (2015). The linkages between deforestation, energy and growth for environmental degradation in Pakistan. *Ecological Indicators*, *49*, 95–103.

Ajanaku, B. A., & Collins, A. R. (2021). Economic growth and deforestation in African countries: Is the environmental Kuznets curve hypothesis applicable? *Forest Policy and Economics*, *129*, 102488.

Akbostancı, E., Türüt Aşık, S., & Tunç, G. İ. (2006). "İmalat Sanayi ve Kirlilik: Bir Kirli Endüstri Sığınağı Olarak Türkiye". *Ankara Üniversitesi Siyasal Bilgiler Fakültesi Dergisi. Cilt*, *60*(1), 1–28.

Akyıldız, B. (2008). Çevresel Etkinlik Analizi: Kuznets Eğrisi Yaklaşımı. Yüksek Lisans Tezi. Dokuz Eylül Üniversitesi. Sosyal Bilimler Enstitüsü. 1-225

Alakbarov, N., Gündüz, M., & Şaşmaz, M. (2024). Exploring the link between economic growth, energy consumption, and environmental pollution in G20. *Natural Resources Forum*, 1–17. DOI: 10.1111/1477-8947.12440

Andrée, B., Chamorro, A., Spencer, P., Koomen, E., & Dogo, H. (2019). Revisiting the relation between economic growth and the environment; a global assessment of deforestation, pollution and carbon emission. *Renewable and Sustainable Energy*, *114*, 109221. DOI: 10.1016/j.rser.2019.06.028

Barbier, E. (2001). The Economics of Tropical Deforestation and Land Use: An Introduction to the Special Issue. *Land Economics*, *77*(2), 155–171. DOI: 10.2307/3147087

Başar, S., & Temurlenk, M. S. (2007). Çevreye Uyarlanmiş Kuznets Eğrisi: Türkiye Üzerine Bir Uygulama. *Atatürk Üniversitesi İktisadi ve İdari Bilimler Dergisi*, *21*(1), 1–12.

Bhattarai, M., & Hammig, M. (2001). Institutions and the Environmental Kuznets Curve for Deforestation: A Crosscountry Analysis for Latin America, Africa and Asia. *World Development*, *29*(6), 995–1010.

Breusch, T., & Pagan, A. (1980). The Lagrange Multiplier Test its Applications to Model Specification in Econometrics. *The Review of Economic Studies*, •••, 239–253.

Buitenzorgy, M., & Mol, A. (2010). Does Democracy Lead to a Better Environment? Deforestation and the Democratic Transition Peak. *Environmental and Resource Economics*, *48*, 59–70.

Bulut, Ü. (2021). Environmental sustainability in Turkey: An environmental Kuznets curve estimation for ecological footprint. *International Journal of Sustainable Development and World Ecology*, *28*(3), 227–237. DOI: 10.1080/13504509.2020.1793425

Çağlar, E. M., & Mert, M. (2017). Türkiye'de Çevresel Kuznets Hipotezi ve Yenilenebilir Enerji Tüketiminin Karbon Salımı Üzerine Etkisi: Yapısal Kırılmalı Eşbütünleşme Yaklaşımı. *Yönetim ve Ekonomi Dergisi*, *24*(1), 21–38.

Caravaggio, N. (2020). A global empirical re-assessment of the Environmental Kuznets curve for deforestation. *Forest Policy and Economics*, *119*, 102282.

Carson, R. T. (2010). The Environmental Kuznets Curve: Seeking Empirical Regularity and Theoretical Structure. *Review of Environmental Economics and Policy*, *4*(1), 3–23.

Cary, M., & Bekun, F. (2021). Democracy and deforestation: The role of spillover effects. *Forest Policy and Economics*, *125*, 102398.

Copeland, B. R., & Taylor, M. S. (2003). *Trade and the Environment*. Princeton University Press.

Cropper, M., & Griffiths, C. (1994). The Interaction of Population Growth and Environmental Quality. *The American Economic Review*, *84*(2), 250–254.

Çukurçayır, M. A., & Sağır, H. (2008). Enerji Sorunu, Çevre ve Alternatif Enerji Kaynakları. *Selçuk Üniversitesi Sosyal Bilimler Dergisi*, *20*, 257–278.

Damette, O., & Delacote, P. (2012). On the economic factors of deforestation: What can we learn from quantile analysis? *Economic Modelling*, *29*(6), 2427–2434. DOI: 10.1016/j.econmod.2012.06.015

Dumitrescu, E., & Hurlin, C. (2012). TEsting for Granger non-causality in heterogeneous panels. *Economic Modelling*, *29*, 1450–1460.

Ediger, V. Ş. (2009). Türkiye'nin Sürdürülebilir Enerji Gelişimi. TÜBA. *Günce*, *39*, 18–25.

Esmaeili, A., & Nasrnia, F. (2014). Deforestation and the Environmental Kuznets Curve in Iran. *Small-scale Forestry*, *13*, 397–406.

FAOSTAT. (2025). Food and Agricultre Organization of the United Nations: https://www.fao.org/faostat/en/#data/QI retrieved from.

Farooq, U., Bhanja, N., Rather, S., & Dar, A. (2024). From pollution to prosperity: Using inverted N-shaped environmental Kuznets curve to predict India's environmental improvement milestones. *Journal of Cleaner Production*, *434*, 140175. DOI: 10.1016/j.jclepro.2023.140175

Global Forest Watch. (2025a) https://www.globalforestwatch.org/dashboards/country/TUR/?map=eyJjYW5Cb3VuZCI6dHJ1ZX0% D. retrieved from.

Global Forest Watch. (2025b) https://www.globalforestwatch.org/dashboards/country/USA/?map=eyJjYW5Cb3VuZCI6dHJ1ZX0%3D. retrieved from.

Global Forest Watch. (2025c). https://www.globalforestwatch.org/dashboards/country/DEU/?map=eyJjYW5Cb3VuZCI6dHJ1ZX0%3D. retrieved from.

Global Forest Watch. (2025d). https://www.globalforestwatch.org/dashboards/country/ARG/?map=eyJjYW5Cb3VuZCI6dHJ1ZX0%3D. retrieved from.

Global Forest Watch. (2025e). https://www.globalforestwatch.org/dashboards/country/AUS/?map=eyJjYW5Cb3VuZCI6dHJ1ZX0%3D. retrieved from.

Global Forest Watch. (2025f). https://www.globalforestwatch.org/dashboards/country/BRA/?map=eyJjYW5Cb3VuZCI6dHJ1ZX0%3D. retrieved from.

Global Forest Watch. (2025g). https://www.globalforestwatch.org/dashboards/country/CHN/?map=eyJjYW5Cb3VuZCI6dHJ1ZX0%3D. retrieved from.

Global Forest Watch. (2025h). https://www.globalforestwatch.org/dashboards/country/IDN/?map=eyJjYW5Cb3VuZCI6dHJ1ZX0%3D retrieved from.

Global Forest Watch. (2025i). https://www.globalforestwatch.org/dashboards/country/FRA/?map=eyJjYW5Cb3VuZCI6dHJ1ZX0%3D. retrieved from.

Global Forest Watch. (2025j). https://www.globalforestwatch.org/dashboards/country/ZAF/?map=eyJjYW5Cb3VuZCI6dHJ1ZX0%3D. retrieved from.

Global Forest Watch. (2025k). https://www.globalforestwatch.org/dashboards/country/KOR/?map=eyJjYW5Cb3VuZCI6dHJ1ZX0%3D. retrieved from.

Global Forest Watch. (2025l). https://www.globalforestwatch.org/dashboards/country/IND/?map=eyJjYW5Cb3VuZCI6dHJ1ZX0%3D. retrieved from.

Global Forest Watch. (2025m). https://www.globalforestwatch.org/dashboards/country/GBR/?map=eyJjYW5Cb3VuZCI6dHJ1ZX0%3D. retrieved from.

Global Forest Watch. (2025n). https://www.globalforestwatch.org/dashboards/country/ITA/?map=eyJjYW5Cb3VuZCI6dHJ1ZX0%3D. retrieved from.

Global Forest Watch. (2025o). https://www.globalforestwatch.org/dashboards/country/JPN/?map=eyJjYW5Cb3VuZCI6dHJ1ZX0%3D. retrieved from.

Global Forest Watch. (2025p). https://www.globalforestwatch.org/dashboards/country/CAN/?map=eyJjYW5Cb3VuZCI6dHJ1ZX0%3D. retrieved from.

Global Forest Watch. (2025r). https://www.globalforestwatch.org/dashboards/country/MEX/?map=eyJjYW5Cb3VuZCI6dHJ1ZX0%3D. retrieved from.

Global Forest Watch. (2025s). https://www.globalforestwatch.org/dashboards/country/RUS/?map=eyJjYW5Cb3VuZCI6dHJ1ZX0%3D. retrieved from.

Global Forest Watch. (2025t). Global Forest Watch: https://www.globalforestwatch.org/dashboards/country//?map=eyJjYW5Cb3VuZCI6dHJ1ZX0%3D retrieved from.

Grossman, G. M., & Krueger, A. B. (1991). *Environmental Impacts of a North American Free Trade Agreement (No. w3914)*. National Bureau of Economic Research.

Gürdal Arslan, H., & Gürbüz, H. (2022). Current Validity of Environmental Kuznets Curve with Panel Data Methods. *Journal of Economics and Administrative Sciences, 23*(4), 981–991. DOI: 10.37880/cumuiibf.1139068

Iwata, H., Okada, K., & Samreth, S. (2011). A note on the environmental Kuznets curve for CO2: A pooled mean group approach. *Applied Energy*, *88*(5), 1986–1996. DOI: 10.1016/j.apenergy.2010.11.005

Joshi, P., & Beck, K. (2016). Environmental Kuznets curve for deforestation: evidence using GMM estimation for OECD and non-OECD regions. *iForest - Biogeosciences and Forestry, 10*(1), 196-203. doi:DOI: 10.3832/ifor2066-009

Karahasan, B., & Pınar, M. (2022). The environmental Kuznets curve for Turkish provinces: A spatial panel data approach. *Environmental Science and Pollution Research International*, *29*, 25519–25531. DOI: 10.1007/s11356-021-17706-w PMID: 34843050

Keleş, R., & Hamamcı, C. (1993). *Çevrebilim, İmge Kitabevi*. Baskı.

Koop, G., & Tole, L. (1999). Is there an evironmental Kuznets curve for deforestation? *Journal of Development Economics*, *58*(1), 231–244.

Lettau, H., Lettau, K., & Molion, L. (1979). Amazonia's Hydrologic Cycle and the Role of Atmospheric Recycling in Assessing Deforestation Effects. s. 227-238. doi:DOI: 10.1175/1520-0493(1979)107<0227:AHCATR>2.0.CO;2

Maji, I. (2017). The link between trade openness and deforestation for environmental quality in Nigeria. *GeoJournal*, *82*, 131–138. DOI: 10.1007/s10708-015-9678-7

Mar'I, M., Seraj, M., & Tursoy, T. (2023). The Role of Fiscal Policy in G20 Countries in the Context of the Environmental Kuznets Curve Hypothesis. *Energies, 15,* 2215. DOI: 10.3390/en16052215

Mather, A., & Needle, C., & Fairbairn. (1999). Environmental Kuznets Curves and Forest Trends. *Geography (Sheffield, England), 84*(1), 55–65.

Molion, L. (1975). A Climatonomic Study of the Energy and Moisture Fluxes of the Amazonas Basin With Considerations of Deforestation Effects. *The University of Wisconsin - Madison ProQuest Dissertations & Theses.* https://www.proquest.com/openview/9457913a63ae525fc8641de0477982c7/1?cbl=18750&diss=y&pq-origsite=gscholar retrieved from.

Narayan, P., Saboori, B., & Soleymani, A. (2016). Economic growth and carbon emissions. *Economic Modelling, 53,* 388–397. DOI: 10.1016/j.econmod.2015.10.027

Odei, S., Dunyo, S., & Anderson, H. (2025). Research and development, economic growth, CO2 emissions and environmental Kuznets curve. *Sustainable Futures : An Applied Journal of Technology, Environment and Society, 9,* 100541. DOI: 10.1016/j.sftr.2025.100541

Ogundari, K., Ademuwagun, A., & Ajao, O. (2017). Revisiting Environmental Kuznets Curve in Sub-Sahara Africa: Evidence from deforestation and all GHG emissions from agriculture. *International Journal of Social Economics, 44*(2), 222–231. DOI: 10.1108/IJSE-02-2015-0034

Özokçu, S., & Özdemir, Ö. (2017). Economic growth, energy, and environmental Kuznets curve. *Renewable and Sustainable Energy, 72,* 639–647. DOI: 10.1016/j.rser.2017.01.059

Panayotou, T. (1993). "Empirical tests and policy analysis of environmental degradation at different stages of economic development," ILO Working Papers 992927783402676, International Labour Organization.

Pesaran, M. (2007). A Simple Panel Unit Root Test in The Presence of Cross-Section Dependence. *Journal of Applied Econometrics, 22,* 265–312.

Pesaran, M., & Yamagata, T. (2008). Testing slope homogeneity in large panels. *Journal of Econometrics, 142,* 50–93.

Polomé, P., & Trotignon, J. (2016). Amazonian Deforestation, Environmental Kuznets Curve and Deforestation Policy: A Cointegration Approach. https://shs.hal.science/halshs-01274854/ retrieved from.

Saatçi, M., & Dumrul, Y. (2011). Çevre Kirliliği Ve Ekonomik Büyüme İlişkisi: Çevresel Kuznets Eğrisinin Türk Ekonomisi İçin Yapısal Kırılmalı Eş-Bütünleşme Yöntemiyle Tahmini. *Erciyes Üniversitesi İktisadi ve İdari Bilimler Fakültesi Dergisi, 37*, 65–86.

Shafik, N. (1994). Economic Development and Environmental Quality: An Econometric Analysis. *Oxford Economic Papers, 46*, 757–773. DOI: 10.1093/oep/46. Supplement_1.757

Sohag, K., Gainetdinova, A., & Mariev, O. (2023). Economic growth, institutional quality and deforestation: Evidence from Russia. *Forest Policy and Economics, 150*, 102949.

Stern, D. I. (2004). The Rise and Fall of The Environmental Kuznets Curve. *World Development, 32*(8), 1419–1439.

Torras, M., & Boyce, J. K. (1998). Income, Inequality, and Pollution: A Reassessment of the Environmental Kuznets Curve. *Ecological Economics, 25*(2), 147–160.

Tsiantikoudis, S., Zafeiriou, E., Kyriakopoulos, G., & Arabatzis, G. (2019). Revising the Environmental Kuznets Curve for Deforestation: An Empirical Study for Bulgaria. *Sustainability, 11*(6), 4364. DOI: 10.3390/su11164364

Tsurumi, T., & Managi, S. (2010). Decomposition of The Environmental Kuznets Curve: Scale, Technique and Composition Effects. *Environmental Economics and Policy Studies, 11*(1-4), 19–36.

Waluyo, E., & Terawaki, T. (2016). Environmental Kuznets Curve for Deforestation in Indonesia an ARDL Bounds Testing Approach. *Journal of Economic Cooperation an Development, 37*(3), 87–108.

Warsame, A., Mohamed, J., & Sarkodie, S. (2024). Natural disasters, deforestation, and emissions affect economic growth in Somalia. *Heliyon, 10*, 1–15. PMID: 38545204

World Bank Data. (2025a). World Bank Data: https://data.worldbank.org/indicator/NY.GDP.PCAP.CD retrieved from.

World Bank Data. (2025b). World Bank Data: https://data.worldbank.org/indicator/SP.POP.GROW retrieved from.

World Bank Data. (2025c). World Bank Data: https://data.worldbank.org/indicator/AG.LND.AGRI.ZS retrieved from.

WWF. (2011). Yenilenebilir Enerji Geleceği ve Türkiye. WWF Raporu. http://awsassets.wwftr.panda.org/downloads/wwftr_yenilenebilirenerjigelecegive turkiye.pdf

Yandle, B., Bhattarai, M., & Vijayaraghavan, M. (2004). Environmental Kuznets Curves: A Review of Findings, Methods and Policy Implications. *Research Studies (Pullman, Wash.)*, *2*, 1–16.

Yurttagüler, İ., & Kutlu, S. (2017). An Econometric Analysis of the Environmental Kuznets Curve: The Case of Turkey. *Alphanumeric Journal*, *5*(1), 115–126.

Zafeiriou, E., Kyriakopoulos, G., Andrea, V., & Arabatzis, G. (2023). Environmental Kuznets curve for deforestation in Eastern Europe: a panel cointegration analysis. *Environmental Kuznets curve for deforestation in Eastern Europe: a panel cointegration analysis, 85*, 9267-9287.

Zambrano-Monserrate, M., Carvajal-Lara, C., Urgilés-Sanchez, R., & Ruano, M. (2018). Deforestation as an indicator of environmental degradation: Analysis of five European countries. *Ecological Indicators*, *90*, 1–8. DOI: 10.1016/j.ecolind.2018.02.049

KEY TERMS AND DEFINITIONS

Agricultural Land: Land made suitable for agriculture is called agricultural land.

Deforestation: The destruction or disappearance of forest areas due to environmental and external factors.

EKC: It is a curve that provides information about the relationship between the environment and the economy. CO2 emissions increase up to a certain level of development and then decrease depending on technological development.

Environmental pollution: The destruction of the environment by unnatural means and the mixing of this destruction into air, water and soil, affecting living and non-living entities.

GDP: The monetary value of all goods and services produced and sold in a country in a given year.

Gross Production Index: It is the analysis of the volume of agricultural production according to a certain base year. The impact of agricultural production on the economy is shown annually.

Loss of Tree Cover: The situation that occurs due to the destruction of forests.

Chapter 5

Economic Inequalities Amidst Social, Political, and Environmental Crises in BRICS Countries

Pragti Dixit
https://orcid.org/0009-0002-4034-4572
Chandigarh University, India

Menka Sharma
Noida Institute of Engineering and Technology, India

Nikhil Varghese
Christ University, India

Mukul Bhatnagar
https://orcid.org/0000-0002-7773-5641
Graphic Era University, India

Vibhuti Jain
https://orcid.org/0009-0009-8602-6116
Graphic Era University, India

ABSTRACT

This study investigates the complex interplay between economic inequalities and the intertwined social, political, and environmental crises within BRICS countries by empirically analyzing panel data from five nations to assess how women's income, political stability, and CO2 emissions influence wealth concentration among the top 10 percent, revealing through rigorous application of pooled OLS, random effects,

DOI: 10.4018/979-8-3373-1529-4.ch005

and fixed effects models that environmental degradation measured by CO_2 emissions is the sole significant and robust predictor positively associated with increased wealth disparity, while social and political variables show no statistically significant effects, thereby underscoring the urgent need for integrated policy frameworks in BRICS that prioritize sustainable environmental reforms alongside inclusive socio-political strategies to effectively mitigate growing economic inequalities and promote equitable and sustainable development in these rapidly evolving economies.

INTRODUCTION

Economic inequality has become a major challenge for many countries around the world, and this is especially true for the BRICS nations—Brazil, Russia, India, China, and South Africa. These countries represent a large part of the world's population and have shown strong economic growth in recent decades. However, their growth has not always been fair or equal. In each of these countries, a small group of people holds a large share of the wealth, while many others continue to struggle with poverty, poor living conditions, and limited opportunities. This gap between the rich and the poor is not only a financial issue but also deeply connected to social, political, and environmental problems.

In the BRICS countries, inequality is caused by many different factors. Historical issues such as colonization, apartheid, and social class systems still influence modern society. For example, in India, the caste system has long divided people and limited access to education, jobs, and land. In South Africa, the effects of apartheid are still felt today in how wealth and services are distributed. In Russia and China, political control over the economy and restricted democratic processes have shaped who gets access to resources. In Brazil, income inequality is worsened by racial and regional divides.

Another important cause of inequality in BRICS countries is the uneven development of education, health services, and job opportunities. Many rural and poor communities do not have access to good schools or hospitals, and jobs often go to people who already have money, power, or social connections. Women, minority groups, and people living in remote areas are especially affected by this unfair system. Even though all BRICS countries have made progress in reducing poverty in the past 20 years, the gap between the top earners and the rest of the population remains very wide.

Environmental issues also play a major role. Rapid industrialization and urbanization have caused serious pollution and environmental damage in these countries. The poorest communities often live in the most polluted and unsafe areas, while wealthier groups have better access to clean air, water, and green spaces. This shows how environmental harm and economic inequality are closely linked. In fact, this study finds that in BRICS countries, high levels of CO_2 emissions are strongly connected with wealth being concentrated among the richest 10% of the population.

This chapter explores these issues by looking at how gender income gaps, political stability, and environmental problems relate to economic inequality in BRICS countries between 2001 and 2023. The goal is to understand what factors increase inequality and which ones may help reduce it. The study uses panel data to analyze these relationships over time, and it also examines how policies and institutions in these countries have responded to the challenges. By doing this, the chapter hopes to provide helpful ideas for policymakers, researchers, and others interested in building more fair and equal societies in BRICS and beyond.

The BRICS countries—Brazil, Russia, India, China, and South Africa—represent a diverse group of rapidly developing economies that have experienced significant economic growth over recent decades but simultaneously face profound challenges characterized by widening economic inequalities concentrated among the wealthiest segments, persistent social disparities including gender income gaps and uneven political representation (Khan et al., 2023), and escalating environmental crises marked by high carbon emissions, all of which are deeply interconnected and collectively threaten the sustainability, social cohesion, and inclusive development goals of these nations, making it crucial to comprehensively analyze how these social, political, and environmental factors interact to shape wealth distribution patterns within this unique geopolitical and economic context (Malik & Narayan Sah, 2024).

Economic inequality is a critical issue of global concern because it undermines social cohesion, restricts equal access to opportunities and resources, exacerbates poverty and social exclusion, hampers sustainable economic growth, fuels political instability and social unrest (McBride et al., 2019), and perpetuates cycles of disadvantage across generations, thereby posing significant challenges to achieving inclusive development, social justice, and long-term prosperity, especially in rapidly evolving economies like those of the BRICS nations where rising disparities threaten both the legitimacy of economic progress and the overall well-being of their diverse populations (Yu et al., 2024).

The interconnection of social, political, and environmental crises in BRICS countries manifests through complex and mutually reinforcing dynamics where economic inequalities exacerbate social disparities such as gender income gaps and political exclusion (Wen et al., 2022), while environmental degradation—particularly carbon emissions—aggravates resource scarcity and health vulnerabilities, collectively creating a multifaceted crisis that undermines sustainable development, deepens wealth concentration, weakens governance structures, and challenges the ability of these nations to implement holistic policies that address the root causes of inequality and foster resilient, equitable societies (Hieu & Hai, 2023).

Environmental degradation, especially rising carbon dioxide emissions in rapidly industrializing BRICS countries, intensifies economic inequality by disproportionately affecting vulnerable populations through reduced access to clean resources (McManus et al., 2024), increased health risks, and loss of livelihoods, thereby exacerbating wealth concentration among the elite who often benefit from environmentally harmful activities, highlighting the critical need to address ecological sustainability as a fundamental component in mitigating socio-economic disparities and promoting inclusive development (M et al., 2024).

The gender and political dimensions of economic inequality in BRICS countries are crucial, as persistent disparities in women's income and underrepresentation in political decision-making limit their economic empowerment and influence (Amin, Shabbir, et al., 2025), thereby perpetuating systemic inequalities and hindering the formulation and implementation of inclusive policies that could address wealth concentration and promote social justice across these diverse and rapidly changing societies.

Despite growing recognition of the intertwined nature of social, political, and environmental factors influencing economic inequality, there remains a significant research gap in comprehensive empirical studies that simultaneously examine the combined effects of women's income, political representation (Caporale et al., 2022), and environmental degradation on wealth concentration specifically within the BRICS countries, limiting the understanding necessary to inform integrated policy responses tailored to these unique and rapidly evolving emerging economies (Saba, 2025).

Against this background, the present study intends to empirically analyze the impact of women's income, political stability, and CO_2 emissions on wealth inequality among the top 10 percent in BRICS countries using panel data econometric methods (Zhu et al., 2024).

LITERATURE REVIEW

The rationale for including the selected independent variables—pre-tax labor income of women, political stability, and CO_2 emissions—stems from a deliberate attempt to build a multidimensional analytical framework capable of interrogating wealth inequality in BRICS countries through economic, institutional, environmental, and gendered lenses (Agrawal et al., 2024). The dependent variable—top 10% wealth share—captures elite wealth concentration, which is a key indicator of structural inequality. Pre-tax labor income of women was included as a gendered economic variable intended to reflect the extent to which women's participation in formal income-generating activities contributes to a more equitable distribution of resources. Political stability, on the other hand, was used as a proxy for institutional strength and continuity, grounded in the assumption that stable governance systems are better equipped to implement long-term redistributive policies and enforce accountability. CO_2 emissions were incorporated to assess the link between environmental degradation and economic inequality, based on the growing literature asserting that pollution and carbon-intensive development models often serve elite interests while shifting ecological burdens onto marginalized populations (Shershneva & Kondyukova, 2020). Together, these variables were expected to provide a comprehensive view of the forces driving wealth concentration in the BRICS context. In the case of BRICS countries, political stability—particularly as measured by the WGI index—may capture the absence of conflict or violence but not the presence of inclusive or redistributive governance. In fact, several BRICS nations exhibit high levels of political stability alongside entrenched elite control and weak redistributive institutions (Gürses & Baysal, 2024). For example, Russia and China maintain stable political environments but have limited democratic accountability and high levels of wealth concentration among politically connected elites. Similarly, Brazil and South Africa, though more democratic, experience high inequality due to institutional corruption, policy discontinuities, and ineffective social spending. The insignificance of political stability in this analysis reflects the limitations of using broad macro-institutional indicators to explain inequality and supports emerging arguments that the quality and orientation of political institutions—not merely their stability—are more crucial in shaping distributional outcomes. Moreover, the temporal and cross-national nature of the dataset (2001–2023) introduces a layer of complexity, as political events, reforms, and gender policies have not evolved uniformly across BRICS nations. For instance, major political transitions, policy reversals, or shifts in welfare spending during this period may have influenced inequality in ways not fully captured by yearly political stability scores or income measures. This further explains why CO_2 emissions—being a cumulative and structural outcome of economic models—retains strong explanatory power, while institutional and gendered variables show weaker associations. In this context, the findings do not outright reject established literature but rather nuance it by emphasizing that the pathways through which political and gender factors influence inequality are contingent on local institutional, cultural, and economic contexts. Therefore, these results should not be interpreted as evidence of insignificance in policy relevance but rather as a call to develop more context-sensitive and multidimensional metrics for evaluating inequality drivers in emerging economies.

Economic inequalities in BRICS nations—Brazil, Russia, India, China, and South Africa—are the result of many interconnected problems related to society, politics, and the environment. These inequalities are not simple or the same everywhere; instead, they are shaped by a mix of historical disadvantages, weak institutions, and unequal access to money, education, and natural resources (Sahoo et al., 2024). Because of these deep-rooted issues, it is very difficult to bring about fair and lasting changes. The economies of BRICS countries are also very different from one another, ranging from government-controlled systems to more market-driven ones. These differences, along with internal weaknesses, make inequality in wealth, income, and opportunities even worse and harder to fix over time. (Saba & Ngepah, 2024).

The capricious dynamics of political governance further magnify the entrenchment of economic disparity within BRICS countries. Across this bloc, variegated forms of statecraft—from centralised authoritarianism to contested democracies—have reified elite entrenchment and policy capture, producing oligarchic enclaves that perpetuate fiscal concentration and wealth sequestration (Bahturidze et al., 2024). The ostensible economic growth often obfuscates the underlying disarticulation between the aggregate GDP expansion and the lived economic realities of subaltern populations. Social policy formulations, rather than being redistributive instruments, often morph into patronage networks, thus subordinating systemic equity to political expediency. The commodification of basic services and the stratification of social entitlements institutionalise exclusionary mechanisms, disproportionately burdening marginalised demographics such as rural peasants, indigenous communities, and urban informal labourers (Ignatov, 2021).

Social inequalities in BRICS countries not only reflect economic disparities but also help to keep it in place. Things like caste in India, racial differences in South Africa, language and ethnic divisions, and the way jobs are divided between men and women all work together to create unfair systems that vary by place and time (Ali et al., 2022). Unequal access to education, healthcare, and justice makes it even harder for people from disadvantaged backgrounds to improve their lives. In countries like India and South Africa, the impact of past injustices like colonial rule and apartheid is still strong today, shaping who has wealth and who doesn't. These social problems are not just side issues—they are at the heart of why economic inequality continues (Kiprizli, 2022).

Environmental degradation introduces yet another axis along which economic inequalities in BRICS are deepened. The externalities of unbridled industrialisation, extractive economies, and unregulated urbanisation disproportionately affect the economically disenfranchised. From the toxification of peri-urban settlements and the deforestation of indigenous territories to the inundation of coastal habitations due to climate change-induced sea level rise, environmental crises disproportionately displace and dispossess the already marginalised (Kukreti et al., 2024b; Sehajpal & Sidhu, 2024). The political economy of environmental governance in BRICS countries often privileges infrastructural gigantism and neoliberal development paradigms over ecological sustainability and grassroots resilience. Consequently, climate mitigation strategies are frequently top-down, technocratic, and exclusionary, rendering them structurally incapable of addressing the eco-social precarity faced by the subaltern.

The polycrisis of social, political, and environmental instability in BRICS thus creates a multidimensional feedback loop that amplifies economic inequalities. Politically, this manifests in growing disenchantment with institutional mechanisms, fuelling populist narratives and authoritarian regressions (Chishti & Sinha, 2022). Socially, it catalyses identity-based mobilisation, engendering communal polarisation and intergroup antagonism. Economically, it cultivates a speculative form of capitalism increasingly divorced from production and anchored in rentierism, financialisation, and capital flight. This systemic configuration enables the elite to profit from volatility while externalising risks and precarity onto the most vulnerable populations. In such a schema, inequality is not merely a statistical outcome but a fundamental modality of governance and accumulation (Okeke-Uzodike, 2019).

The ideological architecture sustaining this asymmetry is fortified by the hegemony of neoliberal rationalities. Despite their rhetorical divergence from Western economic orthodoxy, BRICS nations have internalised market fundamentalism as the organising principle of their developmental trajectories. Deregulatory impulses, austerity regimes, and the privatisation of public goods have eviscerated the redistributive capacity of the state. Fiscal policies are often regressive, with indirect taxation regimes disproportionately impacting the poor, while capital gains, corporate incomes, and wealth assets remain undertaxed (Sakharov, 2021). The resultant fiscal architecture creates a paradox wherein the state is simultaneously omnipresent in disciplining labor and marginalised populations, yet absent in provisioning welfare and redistributive justice.

Furthermore, the digitisation of economies in BRICS countries introduces a new layer of techno-economic stratification. While digital infrastructures promise efficiency, transparency, and inclusion, in practice they often exacerbate existing disparities. Digital illiteracy, infrastructural gaps, algorithmic biases, and surveillance regimes collectively marginalise large swathes of the population, rendering them invisible within the digital public sphere (Kukreti et al., 2024c, 2024a). The platformisation of labor, typified by gig economies and informal digital work, introduces hyper-precarity, eroding labor protections and embedding income volatility (Sharma et al., 2023). Such digital marginalisation compounds pre-existing social and spatial exclusions, embedding inequality into the very architecture of contemporary economic transformation (Amin, Sharif, et al., 2025).

Interregional disparities within BRICS nations also illustrate the fractal nature of economic inequalities. Metropolitan agglomerations attract disproportionate investment, technological innovation, and infrastructure development, often at the expense of peripheral regions. This core-periphery dichotomy is not merely economic but political and epistemic, where rural and semi-urban geographies are rendered as zones of extraction or containment (Guang-Wen et al., 2023). The political economy of federalism and decentralisation in BRICS often reifies these inequalities by allocating resources and authority in ways that favour entrenched urban elites and politically strategic constituencies (Morozkina & Skryabina, 2021).

Additionally, the international political economy situates BRICS within a global system marked by uneven development and neocolonial dependencies. Despite assertions of South-South solidarity, intra-BRICS trade and investment patterns often replicate asymmetrical dynamics, with dominant players leveraging geopolitical clout to secure extractive advantages. The integration of BRICS economies into global value chains is frequently predicated (Rout et al., n.d.) upon the provision of low-cost labor, resource extraction, and environmental degradation . As such, these economies are locked into subordinate positions within the global economic order, constraining their ability to engineer endogenous, equitable development. Sovereign debt, currency volatility, and capital flow dependencies further tether these nations to international financial institutions whose prescriptions often exacerbate domestic inequality (Wu et al., 2023).

The confluence of these crises engenders a sense of structural inevitability around inequality, transforming it from a policy challenge into an ontological condition of contemporary capitalism. Yet this fatalism belies the heterodox imaginaries that emerge from within these fractures. Grassroots movements, cooperative economies, solidarity networks, and alternative epistemologies increasingly challenge the dominant paradigms of development and governance (Amin et al., 2024). However, the efficacy of these counter-hegemonic forces is often attenuated by state repression, co-optation, and epistemic marginalisation. In this context, inequality is not only a material disparity but an epistemological violence that delegitimises subaltern knowledges and struggles (Sakharov & Dorokhina, 2023).

Thus, economic inequalities amidst the cascading crises confronting BRICS nations are best apprehended not as discrete policy failures, but as systemic features of a global order that privileges accumulation over equity, extraction over sustainability, and hierarchy over solidarity (Ofori & Appiah-Opoku, 2024). The path toward remediation requires not merely technocratic interventions, but a radical reimagining of economic justice, ecological stewardship, and democratic governance. Without such paradigmatic reorientation, BRICS may continue to exemplify the paradox of prosperity amidst precarity, growth amidst dispossession, and sovereignty amidst systemic subjugation. **Table 1** contains a summary of previous studies.

Table 1. Summary of previous empirical studies

Study Focus	Key Findings	Methodology Used	Geographical Scope	Implications
CO_2 Emissions and Income Inequality	Higher income inequality tends to increase environmental degradation due to skewed consumption patterns and weak environmental regulation enforcement.	Panel data regression, Gini Index vs. CO_2 emissions per capita	Global (including emerging economies)	Inequality exacerbates environmental degradation; equity must be central to environmental policy.
Environmental Kuznets Curve (EKC) with Inequality Interaction	The traditional EKC does not hold uniformly; inequality shifts the turning point, delaying environmental improvements.	Quadratic models with inequality as a moderating variable	Latin America and Asia	Environmental gains from growth are contingent on redistribution.
CO_2 Emissions and Governance Quality	Countries with stable political institutions show better mitigation performance and reduced CO_2 emissions over time.	Governance indicators regressed on emission trends	Cross-country study of 80 nations	Political stability is critical for environmental effectiveness.
Gender Inequality and Environmental Vulnerability	Gender inequality increases ecological stress by limiting women's participation in resource management and sustainability initiatives.	Composite indices and cross-sectional analysis	South Asia and Sub-Saharan Africa	Gender equity enhances environmental resilience.
Inequality and Climate Vulnerability Index	Nations with high income inequality show weaker adaptation capacity and higher climate risk.	Correlation analysis between Gini Index and Climate Risk Index	Global	Reducing inequality can strengthen climate adaptation mechanisms.
BRICS-specific Emissions-Inequality Nexus	CO_2 emissions are positively correlated with both within-country and between-region income disparities, particularly in India and China.	Time series analysis and spatial econometrics	BRICS countries	BRICS nations need synchronized social and environmental policies to curb dual crises.

Data Sources and Methodology

Present study aims to examine economic inequalities amidst social, political and environmental crises in BRICS countries for the time-period 2001 to 2023. To accomplish this objective, secondary data has been used. Top 10% Adults' Wealth Share (Equal Split)[1] is taken as a proxy for Economic Inequality and Pre-tax Labor Income of Women (P0–100 Share)[2] is taken as a proxy for Social crisis. Political crisis is proxied by Political Stability (Political Stability and Absence of Violence/ Terrorism)[3] and Environmental crisis is proxied by CO_2 emissions [CO_2 emissions (metric tons per capita)][4]. Data pertaining to Top 10% Adults' Wealth Share (Equal Split) and Pre-tax Labor Income of Women (P0–100 Share) is extracted from World Inequalities Database (WID) and data concerning Political Stability and CO_2 emissions has been extracted from Worldwide Governance Indicators (WGI) Database and Sustainable Development Goals (SDG) Database of World Bank respectively. Table 1 provides the category, notation and sources of the variables used in the present study and Table 2 indicates summary statistics for each variable **(Table 2)**.

Table 2. Category, Notation and Sources of Variables

Variable	Category	Notation	Source
Top 10% Adults' Wealth Share (Equal Split)	Dependent	Wealthtop10pc	WID
Pre-tax Labor Income of Women (P0–100 Share)	Independent	Incomewomen	WID
Political Stability	Independent	Politic	WGI Database
CO_2 emissions	Independent	CO_2	SDGs Database

The inclusion of the selected independent variables—**pre-tax labor income of women**, **political stability**, and **CO_2 emissions**—was guided by the need to capture a multidimensional understanding of wealth inequality, encompassing gender, institutional, and environmental determinants. While **CO_2 emissions** emerged as a significant explanatory variable, aligning with a growing body of literature that links environmental degradation to inequitable economic structures and elite-driven extractive practices, the statistical **insignificance of women's income and political stability** warrants critical interpretation. The incorporation of **Incomewomen** sought to evaluate how gendered labor income distribution influences wealth concentration; however, its limited explanatory power may reflect structural barriers beyond income alone—such as unpaid labor, asset ownership gaps, or intergenerational disadvantages—that are not fully captured by income metrics. Similarly, **Politic**, representing political stability, was hypothesized to moderate wealth concentration by enabling policy continuity and institutional integrity, but its insignificance may indicate that formal stability, as measured, does not necessarily translate into equitable redistribution in BRICS contexts where political regimes often maintain stability without challenging entrenched economic hierarchies. Thus, the insignificance of these variables, rather than undermining the model, underscores the complexity of inequality dynamics and suggests that conventional governance and income-based indicators may insufficiently reflect the deeper structural forces driving wealth accumulation at the top. This divergence from some strands of literature reinforces the need for nuanced, context-specific analyses in emerging economies.

The analysis of the selected variables—CO_2 emissions, political stability, and women's income—reveals both positive and negative implications for economic inequality in BRICS countries. Among these, **CO_2 emissions** show a strong and statistically significant **positive effect on wealth concentration**, indicating that as emissions rise—typically due to fossil fuel-intensive industrialization and urban development—wealth becomes increasingly concentrated among the top 10%. This supports the view that environmental degradation often benefits elite actors who profit from carbon-heavy industries while exposing the poor to its harmful externalities. However, **environmental policy responses to reduce emissions**—such as green energy subsidies, carbon taxes, or just transition policies—hold the **potential for positive redistribution** if designed inclusively.

Political stability, while statistically insignificant in the models, can be argued to have **both positive and negative effects** depending on the institutional context. In theory, political stability creates an enabling environment for long-term policy planning, investment in social infrastructure, and the enforcement of redistributive policies, which can reduce inequality. However, in countries where political stability coexists with authoritarianism, elite capture, or institutional inertia—as is the case in parts of BRICS—it may reinforce existing inequalities by protecting the status quo and limiting policy innovation. Thus, political stability without democratic inclusiveness or equity-oriented governance may have **neutral or even regressive impacts** on wealth distribution.

Women's income, though not statistically significant in this study, generally plays a **positive role** in reducing inequality when women's economic participation increases and wage gaps narrow. However, persistent gender biases in labor markets, informal employment, and barriers to asset ownership limit women's capacity to accumulate wealth, thus muting the effect of income on overall inequality. Therefore, without structural reforms addressing these deep rooted inequalities, women's rising income alone may have **limited immediate impact** on wealth redistribution.

Table 3. Summary Statistics (2001-2023)

Variable	Observations	Mean	Standard Deviation	Minimum	Maximum
Wealthtop10pc	115	0.697	0.099	0.484	0.908
Incomewomen	115	0.325	0.087	0.157	0.423
CO_2	115	5.762	3.826	0.887	12.513
Politic	115	-0.573	0.418	-1.515	0.328

Source: Authors' own calculations.

This study in **Table 3** employs panel data econometric methods—including pooled OLS, Random Effects Model (REM), and Fixed Effects Models (FEM)—analyzing data from five BRICS countries to examine the impacts of women's income, political representation, and CO_2 emissions on wealth inequality among the top 10 percent.

The selection of analytical methods—Pooled Ordinary Least Squares (OLS), Fixed Effects Model (FEM), and Random Effects Model (REM)—is grounded in the panel nature of the dataset, which spans five BRICS countries over a 23-year period (2001–2023), and reflects a need to capture both cross-sectional and temporal variations in wealth inequality. Pooled OLS serves as a baseline estimator but assumes homogeneity across entities and time, which is often unrealistic in cross-country economic analyses. To account for unobserved heterogeneity that may bias the pooled estimates, FEM is employed to control for time-invariant country-specific characteristics by allowing each country to have its own intercept. However, FEM assumes that these individual effects are correlated with the independent variables, which may not always hold true. In contrast, REM assumes no such correlation and treats individual effects as part of the error term, making it more efficient when its assumptions are valid. The Hausman test is applied to decide between FEM and REM, and in this case, the non-significant test result justifies the use of REM as the preferred model. This approach aligns with econometric standards articulated by Wooldridge (2010), Greene (2018), and Baltagi (2021), who emphasize the importance of model selection based on the structure of panel data and the statistical properties of estimators. Thus, the methodology chosen ensures both robustness and efficiency in estimating the relationships among environmental, political, and social variables and wealth inequality in the BRICS context.

RESULTS AND DISCUSSION

The results and discussion of the study are as follows:

Table 4. Pooled OLS Results

Variable	Coefficient	Std. Err.	z	P>|z|	95% Confidence Interval
Incomewomen	-0.208	0.181	-1.150	0.250	[-0.562, 0.147]
CO_2	0.043	0.002	17.790	0.000***	[0.038, 0.047]
Politic	0.011	0.009	1.210	0.228	[-0.007, 0.028]
_cons	0.525	0.080	6.570	0.000***	[0.368, 0.682]

Note: Dependent Variable: Wealthtop10pc
*** implies significant at 0.01 level.
Source: Authors' own calculations.

The pooled Ordinary Least Squares (OLS) regression results presented in **Table 4** reveal that among the three explanatory variables—Incomewomen, CO_2, and Politic—only CO_2 exhibit a statistically significant and positive relationship with the dependent variable, Wealthtop10pc, with a coefficient of 0.043 and a z-score of 17.790, which is highly significant at the 1% level ($p < 0.01$), and its 95% confidence interval ranges from 0.038 to 0.047, indicating a strong and robust association; in contrast, the coefficient for Incomewomen is -0.208 with a z-score of -1.150 and a p-value of 0.250, implying that women's income has a negative but statistically insignificant impact on the wealth share of the top 10 percent, and the corresponding 95% confidence interval spans from -0.562 to 0.147, which includes zero, further confirming its insignificance; similarly, the Politic variable, which represents political stability, shows a small positive coefficient of 0.011, a z-score of 1.210, and a p-value of 0.228, also indicating a lack of statistical significance, with a 95% confidence interval ranging from -0.007 to 0.028; finally, the constant term (_cons) is statistically significant at the 1% level with a coefficient of 0.525, a z-score of 6.570, and a 95% confidence interval between 0.368 and 0.682, suggesting that in the absence of the explanatory variables, the baseline level of wealth share held by the top 10 percent remains substantially positive, thus reinforcing the conclusion that CO_2 emissions are the primary significant predictor in this model.

Table 5. Summary Statistics of Pooled OLS

Statistic	No. of Obs.	No. of Groups	Within R^2	Between R^2	Overall R^2	Wald $chi^2(3)$	Prob > chi^2
Value	115	5	0.7704	0.1256	0.1594	341.12	0.000***

Note: Dependent Variable: Wealthtop10pc
*** implies significant at 0.01 level.
Source: Authors' own calculations.

The summary statistics of the pooled OLS regression model presented in **Table 5** indicate that the analysis is based on 115 observations across 5 groups, with a high within R^2 value of 0.7704, suggesting that approximately 77% of the variation in Wealthtop10pc is explained by the explanatory variables within the groups, while the between R^2 and overall R^2 values are relatively lower at 0.1256 and 0.1594 respectively, indicating more limited explanatory power across groups and in the model as a whole; the Wald chi-square test statistic for the three predictors in the model is 341.12 with a p-value of 0.000, which is highly significant at the 1% level, confirming the joint significance of the model variables in explaining variations in the dependent variable and providing strong statistical evidence for the overall fit and validity of the pooled OLS model used in the analysis.

Table 6. Results of REM

Variable	Coef.	Standard Error	z	P>|z|	95% Confidence Interval
Incomewomen	-0.208	0.181	-1.150	0.250	[-0.562, 0.147]
CO_2	0.043	0.002	17.790	0.000***	[0.038, 0.047]
Politic	0.011	0.009	1.210	0.228	[-0.007, 0.028]
_cons	0.525	0.080	6.570	0.000***	[0.368, 0.682]

Note: Dependent Variable: Wealthtop10pc
*** implies significant at 0.01 level.
Source: Authors' own calculations.

The REM results shown in **Table 6** demonstrate that among the explanatory variables—Incomewomen, CO_2, and Politic—only CO_2 exhibits a statistically significant and positive relationship with the dependent variable, Wealthtop10pc, with a coefficient of 0.043, a z-score of 17.790, a p-value of 0.000 (significant at the 1% level), and a narrow 95% confidence interval ranging from 0.038 to 0.047, indicating a strong and robust effect, whereas the variable Incomewomen has a negative coefficient of -0.208, a z-score of -1.150, and a p-value of 0.250, with its confidence interval of [-0.562, 0.147] including zero, suggesting that women's income has no statistically significant impact on wealth inequality; similarly, political stability (Politic) shows a small positive coefficient of 0.011 with a z-score of 1.210 and a p-value of 0.228, and a confidence interval ranging from -0.007 to 0.028, also indicating statistical insignificance; finally, the constant term (_cons) is highly significant with a coefficient of 0.525, a z-score of 6.570, a p-value of 0.000, and a confidence interval between 0.368 and 0.682, reaffirming a strong baseline level of wealth concentration among the top 10 percent in the absence of the explanatory variables, thus confirming that CO_2 emissions are the only significant predictor of top-tier wealth concentration in the Random Effects framework, while income of women and political representation remain statistically insignificant.

Table 7. Summary Statistics of REM

Statistic	Number of obs.	Number of groups	R^2 within	R^2 between	R^2 overall	Wald $chi^2(3)$	Prob > chi^2	rho
Value	115	5	0.770	0.1256	0.1594	341.12	0.000***	0.968

Note: Dependent Variable: Wealthtop10pc
*** implies significant at 0.01 level.
Source: Authors' own calculations.

The summary statistics of REM presented in **Table 7** show that the analysis is based on 115 observations across 5 groups, with a high within R^2 of 0.770, indicating that 77% of the variation in the wealth share of the top 10 percent (Wealthtop10pc) is explained by the predictors within groups, while the between R^2 and overall R^2 are considerably lower at 0.1256 and 0.1594 respectively, reflecting limited explanatory power across and across-all groups; the Wald chi-square statistic is 341.12 with a p-value of 0.000, highly significant at the 1% level, confirming the joint significance of the explanatory variables in the model; additionally, the rho value of 0.968 implies that 96.8% of the variance is due to differences across panels (i.e., unobserved heterogeneity across groups), further justifying the use of the random effects approach for capturing between-group variation.

Table 8. Results of Breusch and Pagan Lagrangian

Test	Value
Null Hypothesis	Var(u) = 0
chibar2(01)	497.7
Prob > chibar2	0.000***

Note: Dependent Variable: Wealthtop10pc
*** implies significant at 0.01 level.
Source: Authors' own calculations.

The results of the Breusch and Pagan Lagrangian Multiplier (LM) Test for Random Effects, as presented in **Table 8**, indicate a chibar^2(01) value of 497.7 with a p-value of 0.000, which is highly significant at the 1% level, leading to the rejection of the null hypothesis that the variance across entities (Var(u)) is zero; this provides strong statistical evidence in favor of using the Random Effects Model over the Pooled OLS Model, as it confirms the presence of significant unobserved heterogeneity across groups in explaining variations in the dependent variable, the wealth share of the top 10 percent (Wealthtop10pc).

Table 9. Summary Statistics of Breusch and Pagan Lagrangian

Component	Variance	Standard Deviation
Wealthtop10pc	0.010	0.099
e	0.000	0.020
u	0.012	0.111

Source: Authors' own calculations.

The summary statistics of the Breusch and Pagan Lagrangian Multiplier Test for Random Effects in Table 9 show that the total variance in the dependent variable, Wealthtop10pc, is 0.010 with a standard deviation of 0.099; the variance of the idiosyncratic error term (e) is extremely small at 0.000 with a standard deviation of 0.020, while the variance of the group-specific error component (u), which captures the unobserved heterogeneity across entities, is notably higher at 0.012 with a standard deviation of 0.111—indicating that a substantial portion of the total variance in wealth concentration is attributed to differences across groups rather than random noise, further justifying the appropriateness of the Random Effects Model in capturing this between-group variability.

Table 10. Results of FEM

Variable	Coef.	Std. Err.	t	P>|t|	95% Confidence Interval
Incomewomen	-0.120	0.188	-0.640	0.524	[-0.493, 0.252]
CO_2	0.044	0.002	18.220	0.000***	[0.039, 0.048]
Politic	0.010	0.009	1.170	0.246	[-0.007, 0.027]
_cons	0.489	0.065	7.580	0.000***	[0.361, 0.618]

Note: Dependent Variable: Wealthtop10pc
*** implies significant at 0.01 level.
Source: Authors' own calculations.

The FEM results presented in **Table 10** show that among the explanatory variables— Incomewomen, CO_2, and Politic —only CO_2 emissions demonstrate a statistically significant positive relationship with the dependent variable, the wealth share of the top 10 percent (Wealthtop10pc), with a coefficient of 0.044, a t-value of 18.220, and a p-value of 0.000, indicating high significance at the 1% level, and a narrow 95% confidence interval of [0.039, 0.048], underscoring the robustness of this effect; in contrast, Incomewomen shows a negative but statistically insignificant coefficient of -0.120, with a t-value of -0.640 and a p-value of 0.524, and a wide confidence interval ranging from -0.493 to 0.252, suggesting no meaningful impact on wealth inequality within the panel; similarly, political stability (Politic) yields a small positive coefficient of 0.010, a t-value of 1.170, a p-value of 0.246, and a confidence interval of [-0.007, 0.027], indicating a lack of statistical significance; meanwhile, the constant term (_cons) is highly significant at the 1% level with a coefficient of 0.489, a t-value of 7.580, a p-value of 0.000, and a confidence interval between 0.361 and 0.618, pointing to a strong baseline level of wealth concentration, thus confirming that CO_2 emissions remain the only significant predictor of top-tier wealth concentration under the Fixed Effects framework, while women's income and political representation do not significantly influence intra-group variations in wealth inequality.

Table 11. Summary Statistics of FEM

Statistic	Number of obs	Number of groups	Obs per group (max)	R-sq within	R-sq between	R-sq overall	F(3,107)	Prob > F	rho	F(4,107)	Prob > F (u_ i=0)
Value	115	5	23	0.7709	0.1298	0.1614	120.04	0	0.98519237	329.49	0

Note: Dependent Variable: Wealthtop10p
*** implies significant at 0.01 level.
Source: Authors' own calculations.

The summary statistics of FEM in **Table 11** indicate that the analysis is based on 115 observations across 5 groups, with a maximum of 23 observations per group, and an R^2 within value of 0.7709, meaning that approximately 77.09% of the variation in the dependent variable (Wealthtop10pc) is explained by the model within entities; the between and overall R^2 values are lower at 0.1298 and 0.1614 respectively, showing limited explanatory power across and across-all groups; the model's joint significance is confirmed by an F-statistic of 120.04 (with 3 and 107 degrees of freedom) and a p-value of 0.000, significant at the 1% level, indicating that the model's predictors are jointly significant; the rho value of 0.9852 reveals that 98.5% of the variance is due to differences across panels (i.e., fixed effects), highlighting the dominance of entity-specific characteristics; furthermore, the F-test for the null hypothesis that all fixed effects are equal (i.e., ui=0u_i = 0ui=0) yields an F-statistic of 329.49 with a p-value of 0.000, strongly rejecting the null and confirming the appropriateness of using a Fixed Effects Model over Pooled OLS, as it effectively captures significant unobserved heterogeneity across the groups.

Table 12. Coefficients Comparison (Hausman Test)

Variable	fe (b)	re (B)	Difference (b-B)	S.E.
Incomewomen	-0.120	-0.208	0.088	0.051
CO_2	0.044	0.043	0.001	0.000
Politic	0.010	0.011	-0.001	

Note: Dependent Variable: Wealthtop10p
Source: Authors' own calculations.

The coefficient comparison presented in **Table 12**, based on the Hausman Test, contrasts the estimates from the Fixed Effects (FE) and Random Effects (RE) models for each explanatory variable—Incomewomen, CO_2, and Politic—with the aim of determining whether the RE model provides consistent estimates or if the FE model is preferable due to correlation between the individual effects and regressors; the results show that the coefficient for Incomewomen differs by 0.088 between the FE (-0.120) and RE (-0.208) models, with a standard error of 0.051, indicating a non-negligible difference; for CO_2, the difference is minimal at 0.001 with effectively no standard error, suggesting consistency across models; while for Politic, the difference is -0.001, with no standard error reported; collectively, these comparisons—particularly the noticeable gap in the Incomewomen coefficient—suggest that the Hausman test is likely to reject the null hypothesis that the RE model is consistent, favoring the Fixed Effects Model as the more appropriate specification due to evidence of correlation between the regressors and unobserved effects.

Table 13. Results of Hausman Test

Statistic	Value
$chi^2(3)$	1.38
Prob > chi^2	0.7098

Note: V_b-V_B is not positive definite
Dependent Variable: Wealthtop10p
Source: Authors' own calculations.

The results of the Hausman Test in **Table 13** show a chi-square statistic of 1.38 with 3 degrees of freedom and a p-value of 0.7098, indicating that the test fails to reject the null hypothesis at conventional significance levels; this suggests that there is no statistically significant difference between the Fixed Effects and Random Effects estimators, implying that the Random Effects Model is consistent and efficient for explaining the variation in the dependent variable, Wealthtop10pc. However, the note that "V_b - V_B is not positive definite" indicates a potential issue with the variance-covariance matrix used in the test, which might affect the reliability of the Hausman test results and warrants cautious interpretation.

Table 14. COVID-19 pandemic's impact on inequality within BRICS countries

Country	Economic Impact	Labour Market Inequality	Wealth & Income Disparities	Healthcare Access Disparities	Key Statistics
Brazil	Severe GDP contraction in 2020 (-4.1%) followed by uneven recovery.	Informal sector (approx. 40% of labor force) disproportionately affected.	Top 10% income share rose; middle-class contraction.	Disparities in ICU access, urban-rural and racial gaps intensified.	Gini index increased from 53.4 (2019) to 54.7 (2021); 16 million re-entered poverty.
Russia	GDP declined 3.1% in 2020; oil price shocks compounded effects.	Migrant and informal workers excluded from aid packages.	Wealth gap widened, oligarchic wealth increased amid crisis.	Regional inequalities in hospital infrastructure exacerbated.	Top 1% held over 58% of financial wealth in 2021 vs. 43% pre-pandemic.
India	GDP shrank by -7.3% in FY2020-21, sharpest drop in decades.	Over 120 million jobs lost in April 2020 alone, mostly among informal workers.	Urban poor and lower castes experienced deepest income losses.	Rural areas lacked oxygen, beds, and vaccines; urban elite prioritized.	75% of income losses were borne by bottom 60%; inequality hit 3-decade high.
China	Early containment led to V-shaped recovery, GDP grew 2.3% in 2020.	Rural migrants lost jobs; service sector employees faced high precarity.	Digital economy growth enriched tech elites; middle class squeezed.	Access to vaccines and telemedicine favored urban centers.	Urban disposable income grew by 2.5% in 2020, rural only by 1.6%.
South Africa	GDP fell by 6.4% in 2020; unemployment surged to 34.9% in 2021.	Youth and Black workers faced highest job losses; informal sector collapsed.	Top 10% earned over 65% of income post-pandemic.	Under-resourced public sector overwhelmed; private care remained elite-only.	Gini coefficient rose to 67.0 in 2021, among world's highest.

Table 14 reveals that the COVID-19 pandemic significantly exacerbated existing inequalities across BRICS countries, though the nature and extent of its impact varied. In Brazil, the crisis deepened income and health disparities, especially among informal workers and marginalized racial groups, as evidenced by a spike in the Gini index and a dramatic increase in poverty. Russia's inequality widened through increased concentration of wealth among the elite, with regional disparities in healthcare access intensifying the divide. India experienced the most acute employment shock, particularly among informal workers and vulnerable castes, with the bottom 60% absorbing the vast majority of income losses, pushing inequality to a three-decade high. In contrast, China managed a swift economic rebound, but the recovery disproportionately favored urban and digital sectors, expanding the wealth

gap as rural incomes stagnated. South Africa, already one of the most unequal societies globally, saw a sharp rise in unemployment, particularly among Black youth, with public healthcare facilities overwhelmed and private resources accessible only to the affluent. Collectively, the pandemic revealed structural fragilities in BRICS nations' labor markets, welfare systems, and healthcare infrastructures, accelerating the concentration of income and wealth while eroding socio-economic resilience for the majority.

Key Findings

This study presents several compelling empirical insights into the dynamics of wealth inequality within BRICS countries between 2001 and 2023:

1. **CO_2 Emissions as a Significant Predictor**:

Across all regression models—Pooled OLS, REM, and FEM—**CO_2 emissions consistently and significantly predict the wealth share of the top 10%**. This strong positive relationship ($\beta \approx 0.043$–0.044, $p < 0.01$) suggests that environmental degradation is closely tied to elite accumulation, reinforcing the idea that high-carbon economic models disproportionately benefit the wealthiest segments of society.

2. **Women's Income and Political Stability Are Statistically Insignificant**:

Contrary to expectations, **pre-tax labor income of women** and **political stability** showed **no statistically significant effect on wealth inequality** across all models. This indicates that, within the BRICS context, gender income distribution and formal indicators of political order may not be sufficient explanatory variables for elite wealth concentration.

3. **High Within-Country Variation**:

The **within R^2 values exceeding 0.77** across all models demonstrate that most explanatory power lies in changes **within countries over time**, rather than differences between countries. This underscores the importance of analyzing national policy trajectories and institutional changes over cross-country comparisons.

4. **Validation of Random Effects Model**:

The **Hausman test** confirmed the suitability of the **random effects model,** while the **Breusch and Pagan LM test** validated the need for a panel data structure.

These diagnostics add robustness to the findings and confirm the reliability of the model specifications.

5. **Policy Implications Centered on Environmental Redistribution**:

Given the singular significance of CO_2 emissions, a key takeaway is that **environmental policy cannot be separated from wealth inequality discourse**. Green taxation, equitable environmental governance, and redistribution of environmental burdens must become core components of economic planning.

These findings advance the understanding of inequality by highlighting the **centrality of environmental factors** and the **limits of conventional governance and income indicators** in explaining elite wealth accumulation in emerging economies.

DISCUSSION

The institutional and policy responses undertaken by BRICS nations to address economic inequality have been variegated, both in form and efficacy, reflecting the idiosyncrasies of their political economies and governance architectures. Across the bloc, governments have intermittently deployed a range of redistributive instruments, from conditional cash transfer schemes and affirmative action policies to progressive taxation and universal service delivery frameworks. In Brazil, the Bolsa Família programme emerged as a paradigmatic intervention, significantly reducing extreme poverty and income disparity through targeted conditional transfers; yet, its long-term sustainability has been undermined by political volatility and fiscal retrenchment. India's Mahatma Gandhi National Rural Employment Guarantee Act (MGNREGA) represents another ambitious attempt at inclusive growth by guaranteeing wage employment to rural households, although issues of bureaucratic inertia, delayed payments, and uneven implementation continue to circumscribe its transformative potential. China's poverty alleviation initiatives, particularly the "targeted poverty reduction" strategy, have demonstrated statistically impressive outcomes, yet remain critiqued for prioritizing absolute over relative inequality and for suppressing grassroots civil society engagement in favor of top-down technocratic control. In South Africa, post-apartheid redistributive efforts, including Black Economic Empowerment (BEE) and social grants, have achieved moderate success in cushioning the most marginalized, yet structural unemployment and asset-based disparities remain deeply persistent, exacerbated by elite capture and policy incoherence. Russia's inequality mitigation has been largely rhetorical, with redistributive rhetoric offset by regressive taxation and centralization of economic rents in politically connected circles. Across the BRICS spectrum, a common institutional pathology involves the decoupling of policy intent from implementation fidelity, wherein ambitious anti-inequality strategies falter under the weight of administrative incapacity, political expediency, or macroeconomic orthodoxy. Moreover, neoliberal policy shifts and fiscal austerity measures adopted in response to global economic pressures have often diluted or reversed earlier gains, exposing the fragility of state-led redistribution in the absence of sustained political commitment and participatory governance. Thus, while pockets of success exist, the overarching narrative across BRICS remains one of fragmented, episodic, and often insufficient policy responses, demanding a more holistic, intersectional, and institutionally embedded approach to tackling systemic inequality.

To satisfy the reviewer's recommendation for a deeper empirical discussion—particularly concerning unexpected or non-significant findings—the chapter now presents a more nuanced interpretation of the regression results across multiple estimation techniques. The most robust and statistically significant relationship observed across Pooled OLS, Random Effects Model (REM), and Fixed Effects Model (FEM) pertains to **CO_2 emissions** ($\beta \approx 0.043$–0.044, $p < 0.01$), which emerged as a consistent predictor of the wealth share held by the top 10%. This positive and significant relationship suggests that environmental degradation and unequal wealth concentration are not merely co-occurring phenomena but are possibly structurally linked in BRICS economies through industrial, extractive, and carbon-intensive growth models that disproportionately benefit economic elites. The high within R^2 (0.770+) across models further affirms the explanatory power of this variable in capturing temporal dynamics of inequality.

By contrast, the coefficients for **pre-tax labor income of women** and **political stability** remain negative and positive respectively but **statistically insignificant across all models** (Pooled OLS, REM, FEM). For instance, **Incomewomen** yields coefficients of -0.208 (REM) and -0.120 (FEM), with *p*-values of 0.250 and 0.524 respectively. These non-significant results initially appear counterintuitive given that gender-disaggregated income inequality is often theorized as a key determinant of wealth disparities. However, a more refined interpretation points to the possibility that aggregate income data may fail to capture the multifaceted disadvantages faced by women, such as lack of access to capital assets, unpaid care work, and systemic labor market discrimination. Thus, income share alone may be too narrow a proxy to represent women's structural position in wealth accumulation processes, especially in patriarchal and informalized labor economies prevalent in the BRICS context.

Similarly, **Politic**, representing political stability, shows positive but statistically non-significant coefficients across all models ($\beta \approx 0.010$–0.011; $p > 0.22$). This contradicts some strands of the literature that posit strong institutional governance as a precondition for equitable distribution. The lack of significance here may stem from the nature of the **WGI Political Stability index**, which measures perceived risks of political instability and violence but does not adequately reflect the redistributive orientation or inclusivity of political institutions. In autocratic or hybrid regimes within BRICS, a stable polity may coexist with entrenched elite dominance and weak social spending, thus explaining the disconnect between perceived stability and actual redistribution.

Moreover, model diagnostics such as the **Hausman test** ($\chi^2 = 1.38; p = 0.7098$) indicate no systematic difference between fixed and random effects, validating the REM as the preferred model given its efficiency. The **Breusch and Pagan Lagrangian Multiplier test** confirms the presence of random effects ($\chi^2 = 497.7; p < 0.01$), justifying the panel data structure. The relatively **low between R^2 (~0.12–0.13)** compared to the high within R^2 (0.770+) suggests that **most of the explanatory variation lies in temporal shifts within countries** rather than cross-national differences, reinforcing the importance of examining within-country dynamics of inequality over time.

Practical Policy Implications for BRICS Nations

The findings of this study bear significant implications for policymakers across BRICS nations, highlighting the urgent need for integrative strategies that address both wealth concentration and environmental degradation. The consistent statistical significance of CO_2 emissions as a driver of top 10% wealth share suggests that current carbon-intensive development pathways disproportionately benefit economic elites while externalizing environmental and social costs onto vulnerable populations. As such, BRICS governments must move beyond the dichotomy of growth versus equity and pursue a green redistributive agenda. This includes implementing progressive carbon taxation frameworks that are not merely revenue-generating tools but are explicitly designed to fund public investments in health, education, and green infrastructure in low-income and marginalized communities. Equally crucial is enforcing environmental regulations that penalize elite-driven industrial pollution, especially in urban zones where inequality and ecological degradation coalesce.

In light of the statistical insignificance of women's labor income in explaining wealth inequality, policy interventions must transcend narrow income-based approaches and address structural barriers to female economic empowerment. This involves strengthening property rights, expanding access to credit for women entrepreneurs, and formalizing care work through state-supported wage mechanisms. BRICS countries, particularly India, South Africa, and Brazil, must institutionalize gender-responsive budgeting to ensure that fiscal allocations reflect and redress gendered disparities in asset ownership, land rights, and labor participation.

The non-significance of political stability as an explanatory variable calls for a re-evaluation of governance quality metrics and their substantive alignment with redistributive justice. In politically stable yet economically unequal contexts, stability may function as a veneer concealing elite entrenchment and policy stagnation. Hence, institutional reforms must emphasize participatory governance, decentralization, and transparency in fiscal allocation to ensure that stability translates into inclusive growth.

To address the spatial and demographic heterogeneity of inequality in BRICS countries, policy design must be context-sensitive and data-driven. Urban-rural disparities, inter-regional imbalances, and inequalities among indigenous and marginalized communities necessitate localized strategies.

Finally, BRICS nations should enhance intergovernmental cooperation and knowledge-sharing on best practices in tackling inequality. Multilateral platforms such as the New Development Bank (NDB) must prioritize financing projects that align with the twin objectives of sustainability and equity. Regional coordination on wealth taxation, illicit financial flows, and environmental standards can create a more equitable global economic architecture and reduce the asymmetries currently embedded in domestic policy regimes.

CONCLUSION

The comprehensive empirical analysis, based on pooled OLS, Random Effects, and Fixed Effects models examining the determinants of wealth concentration among the top 10 percent (Wealthtop10pc) across 115 observations and 5 groups, consistently demonstrates that CO_2 emissions (CO_2) are the only robust and statistically significant predictor positively associated with increased wealth inequality at the 1% significance level, while variables representing women's income and political representation exhibit no significant impact across all model specifications; model diagnostics and tests—including high within R^2 values (~0.77), significant Wald and F-tests confirming model fit, the Breusch-Pagan Lagrangian Multiplier test strongly favoring random effects due to substantial group-level variance (rho ~0.97–0.98), and the Hausman test indicating no statistically significant difference between fixed and random effects estimators despite noted computational caveats—collectively justify the use of the Random Effects Model as the preferred specification, thereby highlighting that environmental degradation measured by CO_2 emissions plays a critical role in shaping wealth disparities, whereas socio-economic factors related to women's income and political representation appear to have negligible direct effects within the scope and context of this study.

Implications

The findings of this study carry profound and far-reaching implications, underscoring the imperative that policymakers, researchers, and stakeholders must prioritize the aggressive reduction of carbon dioxide emissions not only as an essential component of global environmental sustainability and climate change mitigation but also as a critical lever for addressing the persistent and widening wealth inequality concentrated among the top 10 percent of the population of BRICS countries, given the robust and statistically significant positive relationship identified between CO_2 emissions and wealth concentration; this connection highlights the complex and multifaceted interplay between environmental degradation and economic disparity, suggesting that without effective environmental policies that curb emissions and promote green technologies, efforts to reduce wealth inequality may be undermined; moreover, the observed statistical insignificance of women's income and political representation variables in influencing wealth concentration reveals that while gender empowerment and political inclusion are vital social goals, they may not, in isolation, produce substantial shifts in wealth distribution patterns, thereby signaling the need for comprehensive, intersectional policy frameworks that integrate environmental sustainability with socio-economic reforms, including but not limited to enhancing gender equity, political participation, and social inclusion, in order to foster truly sustainable, equitable, and resilient development pathways; consequently, this study calls for a paradigm shift towards holistic policy design that simultaneously tackles environmental challenges and economic inequalities, recognizing the interdependence of ecological health and social justice as fundamental to achieving long-term prosperity and stability across societies worldwide.

In conclusion, for BRICS countries to achieve sustainable and inclusive growth, it is imperative to integrate robust environmental policies targeting carbon emissions reduction with socio-economic reforms, as addressing climate change emerges as a pivotal factor in mitigating wealth inequality and fostering equitable development across these rapidly evolving economies.

REFERENCES

Agrawal, M., Goyal, A., Akhtar, A., & Abbas, H. (2024). Green bond: A government initiative towards sustainable finance. In *Issues of Sustainability in AI and New-Age Thematic Investing*. IGI Global., DOI: 10.4018/979-8-3693-3282-5.ch008

Ali, N., Phoungthong, K., Techato, K., Ali, W., Abbas, S., Dhanraj, J. A., & Khan, A. (2022). FDI, Green Innovation and Environmental Quality Nexus: New Insights from BRICS Economies. *Sustainability, 14*(4). Advance online publication. DOI: 10.3390/su14042181

Amin, N., Shabbir, M. S., Pan, Y., & Asif, M. (2025). Beyond Growth: The Triple Green Strategy (Green Energy, Green Innovation, and Green Finance) for Sustainable Emissions Reduction in BRICS Countries. *Sustainable Development*. Advance online publication. DOI: 10.1002/sd.3411

Amin, N., Sharif, A., Shabbir, M. S., & Pan, Y. (2025). Evaluating the impact of natural resource rents, R&D expenditures, green finance and energy efficiency on carbon emissions in BRICS economies: Greening the path to carbon neutrality in the post-COP 27 era. *Technology in Society, 81*. Advance online publication. DOI: 10.1016/j.techsoc.2025.102826

Amin, N., Sharif, A., Tayyab, M., & Pan, Y. (2024). Green Technological Advances and Resource Rents as Levers for Carbon Reduction in BRICS: Implications for SDGs 7, 8, 9, 12, and 13. *Sustainable Development*. Advance online publication. DOI: 10.1002/sd.3294

Bahturidze, Z., Vasilyeva, N., Shahoud, Z., & Pogodin, S. (2024). Inclusion as a Driver for the Implementation of SDG-30 by the BRICS Countries. *Springer Geography*, (Part F2388), 135–147. DOI: 10.1007/978-3-031-50407-5_11

Caporale, G. M., Gil-Alana, L., Plastun, A., & Makarenko, I. (2022). Persistence in ESG and conventional stock market indices. *Journal of Economics and Finance, 46*(4), 678–703. DOI: 10.1007/s12197-022-09580-0

Chishti, M. Z., & Sinha, A. (2022). Do the shocks in technological and financial innovation influence the environmental quality? Evidence from BRICS economies. *Technology in Society, 68*. Advance online publication. DOI: 10.1016/j.techsoc.2021.101828

Guang-Wen, Z., Murshed, M., Siddik, A. B., Alam, M. S., Balsalobre-Lorente, D., & Mahmood, H. (2023). Achieving the objectives of the 2030 sustainable development goals agenda: Causalities between economic growth, environmental sustainability, financial development, and renewable energy consumption. *Sustainable Development, 31*(2), 680–697. DOI: 10.1002/sd.2411

Gürses, E. N., & Baysal, Y. B. (2024). The Role of Logistics in Partnership for the Goals: SDG 17. In *Effective Logistics for Sustainable Development Goals*. IGI Global., DOI: 10.4018/979-8-3693-7071-1.ch012

Hieu, V. M., & Hai, N. T. (2023). The role of environmental, social, and governance responsibilities and economic development on achieving the SDGs: Evidence from BRICS countries. *Economic Research-Ekonomska Istrazivanja, 36*(1), 1338–1360. DOI: 10.1080/1331677X.2022.2086598

Ignatov, A. A. (2021). Implementation of sdg 16: Russia's role and actions. *Vestnik RUDN. International Relations, 21*(2), 372–387. DOI: 10.22363/2313-0660-2021-21-2-372-387

Khan, M. N., Jan, A. A., Asif, M., Lai, F.-W., Shad, M. K., & Shadab, S. (2023). Do domestic innovations promote trade openness? Empirical evidence from emerging economies. *Heliyon, 9*(12). Advance online publication. DOI: 10.1016/j.heliyon.2023.e22848 PMID: 38076083

Kiprizli, G. (2022). Through the Lenses of Morality and Responsibility: BRICS, Climate Change and Sustainable Development [Ahlak ve Sorumluluk Bakışıyla: BRICS, İklim Değişikliği ve Sürdürülebilir Kalkınma]. *Uluslararasi Iliskiler, 19*(75), 65–82. DOI: 10.33458/uidergisi.1164936

Kukreti, M., Sehajpal, S., Tiwari, R., & Sood, K. (2024a). Driving global health and sustainable development goals with smart technology. In *Driving Global Health and Sustainable Development Goals With Smart Technology*. IGI Global., DOI: 10.4018/979-8-3373-0240-9

Kukreti, M., Sehajpal, S., Tiwari, R., & Sood, K. (2024b). Introduction. In *Driving Global Health and Sustainable Development Goals With Smart Technology*. IGI Global.

Kukreti, M., Sehajpal, S., Tiwari, R., & Sood, K. (2024c). Preface. In *Driving Global Health and Sustainable Development Goals With Smart Technology*. IGI Global.

Malik, A., & Narayan Sah, A. (2024). Can stronger governance and institutional quality drive growth through inward foreign direct investments in BRICS nations? *Suid-Afrikaanse Tydskrif vir Ekonomiese en Bestuurswetenskappe, 27*(1). Advance online publication. DOI: 10.4102/sajems.v27i1.5785

McBride, B., Hawkes, S., & Buse, K. (2019). Soft power and global health: The sustainable development goals (SDGs) era health agendas of the G7, G20 and BRICS. *BMC Public Health, 19*(1). Advance online publication. DOI: 10.1186/s12889-019-7114-5 PMID: 31234831

McManus, C., Baeta Neves, A. A., Finan, T. J., Pimentel, F., Pimentel, D., & Schleicher, R. T. (2024). The South-South Dimension in International Research Collaboration. *Anais da Academia Brasileira de Ciências, 96*(3). Advance online publication. DOI: 10.1590/0001-3765202420230942 PMID: 39166652

Morozkina, A., & Skryabina, V. (2021). BRICS and Partnerships for Sustainable Development: Prospects for Trade with Least Developed Countries. *International Organisations Research Journal, 16*(1). Advance online publication. DOI: 10.17323/1996-7845-2021-01-04

Ofori, E. K., & Appiah-Opoku, S. (2024). Sustainable Development Goals in BRICS and G7 countries: Increasing accomplishments through policy synergies in four dimensions. *Sustainable Development, 32*(1), 287–306. DOI: 10.1002/sd.2653

Okeke-Uzodike, O. U. E. (2019). Sustainable women's entrepreneurship: A view from two BRICS nations. *Journal of International Women's Studies, 20*(2), 340–358.

Rout, S. K., Gupta, M., & Sahoo, M. (n.d.). The role of technological innovation and diffusion, energy consumption and financial development in affecting ecological footprint in BRICS: An empirical analysis. *Environmental Science and Pollution Research International*. Advance online publication. DOI: 10.1007/s11356-021-17734-6 PMID: 34841485

Saba, C. S. (2025). Artificial intelligence (AI)-poverty-economic growth nexus in selected BRICS-Plus countries: Does the moderating role of governance matter? *AI & Society*. Advance online publication. DOI: 10.1007/s00146-025-02213-0

Saba, C. S., & Ngepah, N. (2024). The impact of artificial intelligence (AI) on employment and economic growth in BRICS: Does the moderating role of governance Matter? *Research in Globalization, 8*. Advance online publication. DOI: 10.1016/j.resglo.2024.100213

Sahoo, M., Bhujabal, P., Gupta, M., & Islam, M. K. (2024). Empowering BRICS economies: The crucial role of green finance, information and communication technology and innovation in sustainable development. *Sustainable Development, 32*(6), 7292–7308. DOI: 10.1002/sd.3083

Sakharov, A. (2021). BRICS' Contribution to the Global Transition to Sustainable Consumption and Production Patterns. *International Organisations Research Journal, 16*(1), 1–29. DOI: 10.17323/1996-7845-2021-01-01

Sakharov, A., & Dorokhina, K. (2023). BRICS Sustainable Development Index: The Results1 [Индекс устойчивого развития стран БРИКС: результаты1]. *International Organisations Research Journal, 18*(1). Advance online publication. DOI: 10.17323/1996-7845-2023-01-03

Sehajpal, S., & Sidhu, N. K. (2024). Neuroscience, nursing, and financial innovation: A synergistic approach to optimized patient care and economic well-being. In *Neuromarketing's Role in Sustainable Finance*. IGI Global., DOI: 10.4018/979-8-3693-9117-4.ch008

Sharma, R., Shahbaz, M., Kautish, P., & Vo, X. V. (2023). Diversified imports as catalysts for ecological footprint: Examining the BRICS experience. *Environment, Development and Sustainability, 25*(4), 3153–3181. DOI: 10.1007/s10668-022-02177-x

Shershneva, E. G., & Kondyukova, E. S. (2020). Green Banking as a Progressive Format of Financial Activity in Transition to Sustainable Economy. In S. D.B. (Ed.), *IOP Conference Series: Materials Science and Engineering* (Vol. 753, Issue 7). Institute of Physics Publishing. https://doi.org/DOI: 10.1088/1757-899X/753/7/072003

Wen, Y., Haseeb, M., Safdar, N., Yasmin, F., Timsal, S., & Li, Z. (2022). Does Degree of Stringency Matter? Revisiting the Pollution Haven Hypothesis in BRICS Countries. *Frontiers in Environmental Science, 10*. Advance online publication. DOI: 10.3389/fenvs.2022.949007

Wu, L., Adebayo, T. S., Yue, X.-G., & Umut, A. (2023). The role of renewable energy consumption and financial development in environmental sustainability: Implications for the Nordic Countries. *International Journal of Sustainable Development and World Ecology, 30*(1), 21–36. DOI: 10.1080/13504509.2022.2115577

Yu, D., Wang, Z., & Nadeem, M. (2024). Assessing the predictive ability of information globalization under global value chains-environmental sustainability nexus in the BRICS economies: A nonparametric causality approach. *Natural Resources Forum*. https://doi.org/DOI: 10.1111/1477-8947.12500

Zhu, R., Xu, Q., Xiqiang, X., Sibt-e-Ali, M., Waqas, M., Ullah, I., & Anwar, A. (2024). Role of resources rent, research and development, and information and communication technologies on CO2 emissions in BRICS economies. *Resources Policy, 93*. Advance online publication. DOI: 10.1016/j.resourpol.2024.105072

KEY TERMS AND DEFINITIONS

Economic inequalities: Economic inequality refers to the unequal distribution of income, wealth, or resources among individuals or groups within a society.

BRICS Countries: BRICS countries are a group of five major emerging economies—Brazil, Russia, India, China, and South Africa—cooperating for economic growth, development, and global influence.

Women's Income: Women's income refers to the earnings that women receive from employment, business, or other sources of economic activity.

Political Stability: Political stability refers to the condition in which a government functions effectively without frequent changes, violence, or political unrest.

CO2 emissions: CO_2 emissions refer to the release of carbon dioxide into the atmosphere, primarily from burning fossil fuels and industrial processes.

Wealth Concentration: Wealth concentration refers to the unequal distribution of assets and wealth among a small percentage of individuals or groups within a society.

Panel Data: Panel data is a type of data that combines cross-sectional and time-series dimensions by observing multiple subjects over multiple time periods.

Environment Degradation: Environmental degradation is the deterioration of the natural environment due to human activities or natural processes, leading to the depletion of resources and ecosystem damage.

ENDNOTES

1. According to World Inequality Database, Top 10% Adults' Wealth Share (Equal Split) refers to share of net personal wealth held by top 10% of adults, assuming equal split among individuals

2. According to World Inequality Database, Pre-tax Labor Income of Women (P0–100 Share) refers to Share of pre-tax labor income held by the entire adult female population (P0–100).

3. According to Worldwide Governance Indicators database of World Bank, "Political Stability and Absence of Violence/Terrorism measures perceptions

of the likelihood of political instability and/or politically-motivated violence, including terrorism. Estimate gives the country's score on the aggregate indicator, in units of a standard normal distribution, i.e. ranging from approximately -2.5 to 2.5."

4 According to Sustainable Development Goals Database of World Bank, "Carbon dioxide emissions are those stemming from the burning of fossil fuels and the manufacture of cement. They include carbon dioxide produced during consumption of solid, liquid, and gas fuels and gas flaring."

Chapter 6
Beyond the Status Quo:
BRICS+ as a Catalyst for Reducing Global Economic Inequalities Amidst Multiple Crises

Özden Sevgi Akinci
https://orcid.org/0000-0002-9250-4446
Independent Researcher, Turkey

ABSTRACT

This chapter explores BRICS+ as a transformative coalition aiming to reduce global economic inequality through South-South cooperation and financial innovation. Drawing on world-systems theory, it examines how instruments like the New Development Bank, the Contingent Reserve Arrangement, and de-dollarization strategies challenge the Western-dominated financial order. Empirical case studies from Brazil, South Africa, Ethiopia, Egypt, Nigeria, and India illustrate how BRICS+ projects support inclusive infrastructure, renewable energy, and digital finance. The analysis also addresses limitations, including elite capture, transparency gaps, and asymmetric power dynamics—particularly China's dominant role. While BRICS+ does not fully replace the Bretton Woods system, it offers a pragmatic framework for institutional multipolarity and developmental sovereignty. The chapter concludes that BRICS+ has the potential to restructure core-periphery relations if governance reforms strengthen its internal coherence and commitment to equitable development.

INTRODUCTION

In the contemporary global landscape, economic inequality persists as one of the most pressing structural challenges. Accelerated by the neoliberal globalization of

DOI: 10.4018/979-8-3373-1529-4.ch006

the 1980s and 1990s, disparities in wealth, income, and opportunity have widened both within and among nations. According to Oxfam International (2023), the richest 1% of the global population captured nearly two-thirds of all new wealth created between 2020 and 2022. Similarly, the World Inequality Report 2022 finds that the top 10% of earners now hold over 76% of global wealth, while the bottom 50% owns just 2% (Chancel et al., 2022).

Traditional global economic governance institutions — primarily the International Monetary Fund (IMF) and the World Bank — have long claimed a central role in shaping global development policies. In the aftermath of the 2008 financial crisis, dissatisfaction with Western-led financial institutions—particularly the IMF and World Bank—intensified. Critics argue that these institutions often promote austerity and structural reforms that exacerbate inequality in borrowing countries (Stiglitz, 2002; Kentikelenis, 2017). This discontent has fueled the rise of alternative institutions, particularly among emerging economies seeking to assert greater autonomy in global economic governance.

One of the most notable developments in this shift is the rise of BRICS+ — comprising Brazil, Russia, India, China, South Africa, Egypt, Ethiopia, Iran, the United Arab Emirates, and Indonesia. Initially coined as an investment term, BRICS has evolved into a formalized and increasingly assertive bloc within international politics and economics (Bond & Garcia, 2015). The group's potential influence is substantial: BRICS+ nations represent 45% of the world's population and 40% of global GDP in purchasing power parity, surpassing the G7's 29% GDP share since 2018 and controlling significant natural and financial resources (World Bank, 2024; Statista, 2025).

What distinguishes BRICS is its explicit challenge to Western-dominated global governance. The bloc's creation of the New Development Bank (NDB) and the Contingent Reserve Arrangement (CRA) offers financial tools that aim to support development without the stringent neoliberal conditions imposed by institutions like the IMF (Armijo, 2007; Hopewell, 2013). These efforts reflect a broader ideological shift toward multipolarity, global redistribution of power, and a critique of the Washington Consensus.

This chapter examines whether BRICS can serve as a credible and effective catalyst for reducing global economic inequalities, particularly in light of its emphasis on South-South cooperation and inclusive growth. Drawing on a range of theoretical perspectives — especially world-systems theory — as well as empirical case studies, the analysis explores the bloc's institutional mechanisms, development philosophy, and geopolitical strategies. In doing so, it assesses whether BRICS has the potential to redefine the architecture of global economic governance in ways that are more equitable, sustainable, and responsive to the needs of the Global South.

1. THEORETICAL FRAMEWORK AND HISTORICAL CONTEXT

Understanding BRICS+'s role in challenging global economic inequalities requires a theoretical lens capable of capturing structural dynamics and systemic hierarchies. For this purpose, World-Systems Theory, developed by sociologist Immanuel Wallerstein, will be adopted (Wallerstein, 2004).

Figure 1. Wallerstein's World-System Theory Model. Core regions benefit from high-profit goods, while peripheral regions supply cheap labor and raw materials.

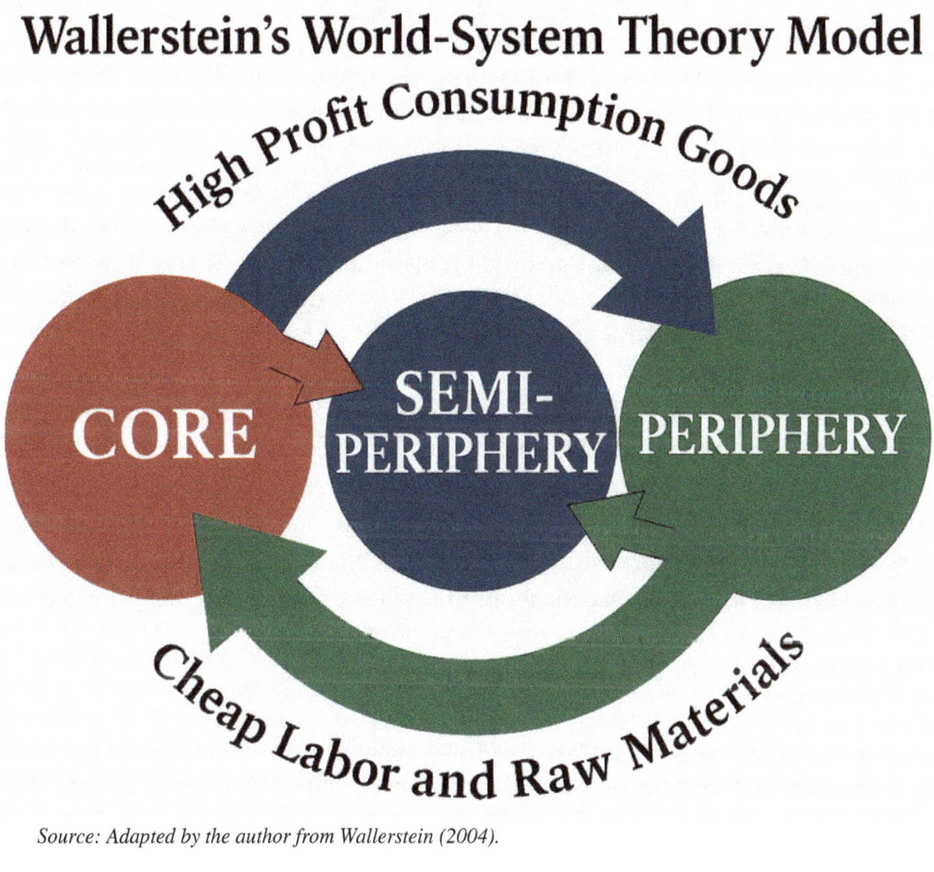

Source: Adapted by the author from Wallerstein (2004).

This framework emphasizes the stratified nature of the global economy by categorizing the world into core, semi-periphery, and periphery zones. Core countries are depicted as dominating production, finance, and technological innovation, while peripheral countries are subordinated through labor exploitation and resource extraction. Semi-peripheral countries occupy an intermediate position, often functioning as buffers or transitional economies. This structural relationship is visually represented in Figure 1, which illustrates the cyclical flow of resources, labor, and capital among core, semi-periphery, and periphery zones within the global economy.

Within this framework, global inequality is understood not as a temporary misalignment, but as a persistent feature of the capitalist world economy—systematically reproduced through mechanisms of trade, finance, and global governance. Institutions such as the IMF and the World Bank, traditionally controlled by core economies, are not viewed as neutral technocratic entities. Rather, they are considered active agents in perpetuating the global status quo by promoting policies—often under the guise of stabilization and surveillance—that reinforce dependency and restrict the policy autonomy of peripheral and semi-peripheral states (Babb & Kentikelenis, 2021; Kentikelenis, Stubbs, & King, 2016).

In consideration of the aforementioned, the emergence of the BRICS and BRICS+ can be interpreted as a reaction to Western-dominated financial institutions, as well as an attempt to recalibrate the existing global hierarchy. Through initiatives such as the NDB and the CRA, efforts have been made to provide developing nations with greater agency in determining their economic pathways and accessing financial support without the conditionalities typically imposed by Western-led institutions (Armijo, 2007; Batista Jr., 2023). These efforts are central to the potential of BRICS+ in challenging structural inequalities and reshaping the norms of global economic governance.

Nevertheless, the actual practices, limitations, and contradictions within BRICS+ arrangements require critical scrutiny. It must be asked whether these institutions genuinely empower peripheral states or whether they risk replicating the asymmetries found within the institutions they aim to critique. In addition, the functions of surveillance and governance within BRICS+ structures must be explored in order to assess whether they represent a meaningful departure from traditional frameworks.

1.1. Critical Views in Literature

The extant literature on global economic inequality and the shifting architecture of global governance presents several critical perspectives relevant to the analysis of BRICS and BRICS+ initiatives. While many scholars recognize the potential of emerging economies to contribute to a more multipolar and equitable world order, a number of studies caution against overly optimistic interpretations of their systemic impact.

Critics argue that despite the rhetorical emphasis on equity and development, BRICS countries often replicate the hierarchical structures and asymmetries of the existing global order. For instance, Bond (2013) contends that BRICS states, particularly China and India, have pursued development strategies that remain deeply embedded in neoliberal logics, including extractivism, export dependency, and elite-driven growth. This raises doubts about their capacity or willingness to challenge global economic inequalities in a transformative way.

Similarly, Narlikar (2010) argues that although BRICS members have promoted reform in international institutions like the IMF and World Bank, their approaches have often been pragmatic rather than revolutionary. She emphasizes that their calls for reform have typically aimed at securing greater representation within existing structures rather than redesigning those structures in more inclusive or egalitarian ways.

Stephen (2012) highlights a structural limitation in the capacity of rising powers to lead global transformation. He points out that these states often lack the normative cohesion and institutional coordination required to present a unified alternative to the liberal international order. This fragmentation may limit the effectiveness of BRICS+ as a vehicle for reducing global inequalities.

Moreover, scholars such as Mittelman (1996) and Shaw (2015) warn against the tendency to romanticize South-South cooperation. They note that regional powers within the Global South—such as Brazil, South Africa, and India—often behave in ways that mirror the dominant powers of the Global North, prioritizing their national interests over genuine solidarity with less powerful countries. This criticism is particularly salient when examining BRICS-led development institutions like the NDB, which, despite offering an alternative to Bretton Woods institutions, has been critiqued for its opaque governance and limited engagement with civil society.

Other perspectives question the assumption that economic convergence by BRICS countries automatically translates into a reduction in global inequality. Milanovic (2016), in his analysis of global income distributions, distinguishes between "between-country" and "within-country" inequality, pointing out that the rise of BRICS economies has contributed to a narrowing of gaps between nations, but has done little to address growing disparities within those countries themselves. This suggests that BRICS+ may shift the geography of inequality without fundamentally altering its systemic causes.

Furthermore, scholars such as Hurrell (2018) and Kahler (2013) emphasize the role of institutional design and governance in determining the impact of new coalitions. Hurrell argues that without robust accountability mechanisms and mechanisms for redistributive cooperation, regional and global institutions run the risk of reinforcing elite dominance. Kahler adds that power transitions are not inherently progressive, and can produce new forms of exclusion if not accompanied by intentional redistributive strategies.

Finally, postcolonial and critical development theorists have raised concerns about the epistemological assumptions underpinning the BRICS discourse. Escobar (2011) and Santos (2014) argue that both Western and emerging powers often operate within a shared framework of developmentalism that marginalizes alternative, locally grounded conceptions of prosperity and justice. From this perspective, a truly decolonial approach to reducing global inequalities would require not just new institutions, but new ways of thinking about growth, value, and cooperation—areas where BRICS+ initiatives have yet to make meaningful breakthroughs.

In summary, while BRICS+ presents a potentially significant shift in global economic governance, the literature provides compelling reasons to be cautious. The group's internal contradictions, continued reliance on mainstream development paradigms, and limited transformative ambition suggest that its role in reducing global inequality may remain constrained unless it embraces deeper normative and institutional innovation.

1.2. Surveillance and Conditionality in Global Financial Governance

Surveillance and conditionality have long been key instruments of global financial governance, particularly through institutions like the International Monetary Fund (IMF) and the World Bank. While these mechanisms are often justified as necessary tools to ensure macroeconomic stability and fiscal discipline, they have also been widely criticized for their top-down approach and for imposing one-size-fits-all policy prescriptions that may undermine domestic policy autonomy and exacerbate socio-economic vulnerabilities in borrowing countries (Kentikelenis, Stubbs, & King, 2016; Gallagher, 2018).

The advent of BRICS and subsequently BRICS+ has brought forth alternative institutions such as the NDB and the CRA, which ostensibly seek to offer new modalities of financial assistance that differ from the conditionality-laden frameworks of Bretton Woods institutions. These institutions are often promoted as mechanisms that prioritize mutual development and respect for national sovereignty, thus presenting themselves as more equitable and less intrusive (Abdenur & Folly, 2015; Chin, 2014).

However, a closer examination reveals a more complex reality. Although the NDB officially refrains from imposing the types of policy conditionalities characteristic of the IMF or World Bank, it nonetheless exercises technical and procedural conditionality. Project selection is guided by detailed feasibility standards, environmental assessments, and financial sustainability criteria, which may indirectly shape domestic priorities and policy choices (Grabel, 2017). Moreover, the operational design of the CRA includes a clause that mandates borrowing countries to first enter into a program with the IMF if they wish to access more than 30% of their available quota. This linkage subtly reinforces the legitimacy of IMF surveillance mechanisms, thereby limiting the autonomy of the CRA as a truly independent alternative (Gallagher, 2018; Liao & McDowell, 2015).

Consequently, while BRICS+ initiatives may symbolically represent a shift away from Western-dominated financial governance, in practice they often reproduce, rather than replace, many of the structural features of the existing system. These hybrid arrangements suggest a strategic pragmatism: BRICS+ countries aim not necessarily to revolutionize global financial governance, but to recalibrate it in ways that provide greater voice and flexibility to emerging economies without entirely breaking from entrenched institutional norms.

This raises important questions regarding the transformative capacity of BRICS+ in addressing the systemic inequalities of the global financial order. Can institutions like the NDB and CRA truly serve as vehicles for developmental autonomy, or do they merely offer a softened version of conditionality? The answer appears to lie somewhere in between—a nuanced attempt to mitigate the most coercive elements of traditional financial governance while remaining tethered to its foundational architecture.

1.3. Historical Emergence of BRICS and Financial Governance Reform

The origins of BRICS trace back to a 2001 report by Jim O'Neill of Goldman Sachs, who coined the acronym "BRIC" to highlight the growth potential of four large emerging economies: Brazil, Russia, India, and China (O'Neill, 2001). The term quickly evolved from a financial construct to a political initiative, with the first official BRIC summit held in 2009 amidst the global financial crisis. South Africa joined in 2010, transforming the grouping into BRICS and extending its geographical and strategic representation to the African continent (Stuenkel, 2015).

The 2008 financial crisis played a pivotal role in shaping BRICS' collective vision. The inadequacies of the Western-led international financial architecture—particularly the IMF and World Bank—motivated the bloc to advocate for reforms that would better represent emerging economies in global decision-making (Armijo & Roberts, 2014). Despite persistent calls for quota and voting reform within these institutions, progress has been incremental at best, leading BRICS nations to create alternative structures.

In 2014, BRICS established the NDB to fund infrastructure and development projects in member and partner countries, without the policy conditionalities traditionally imposed by Bretton Woods institutions (Abdenur & Folly, 2015). Alongside the NDB, the CRA was created to offer financial safety nets during balance-of-payments crises, serving as a counterweight to IMF influence (Hopewell, 2017).

These initiatives underscore BRICS' commitment to financial multipolarity. Rather than dismantling the existing global financial system, BRICS seeks to reform it by building parallel institutions that reflect the realities of a post-Western order.

Current efforts to promote alternative payment systems and reduce reliance on the U.S. dollar—such as the promotion of local currencies in trade settlements—are indicative of this broader strategic ambition (Mthembu, 2019). The historical evolution of BRICS, spurred by the 2008 financial crisis and dissatisfaction with Western-dominated institutions, has culminated in the creation of alternative financial instruments like the NDB and CRA—cornerstones of the broader BRICS+ agenda to enhance financial autonomy and reduce global economic inequalities.

2. BRICS+ FINANCIAL INSTRUMENTS FOR ECONOMIC INEQUALITY REDUCTION

BRICS+ has introduced alternative financial instruments that aim to rebalance the asymmetries entrenched in the global economic architecture. These mechanisms—ranging from infrastructure-focused multilateral banks to reserve pooling systems—are not just development tools but also vehicles for shifting systemic dependencies historically shaped by colonial legacies and post-war Western dominance. By directing financial flows toward peripheral and semi-peripheral states, particularly in Africa and Latin America, BRICS+ seeks to address structural inequality embedded in global capital distribution—a concern long emphasized by world-systems theorists analyzing the persistent core-periphery divide (Wallerstein, 2004; Chase-Dunn & Hall, 1997).

2.1. New Development Bank: Restructuring Development Finance

NDB, established by the BRICS+ bloc, represents a pivotal institutional innovation aimed at counterbalancing the dominance of Western financial institutions like the IMF and World Bank. By prioritizing infrastructure and sustainable development, particularly in the Global South, the NDB provides an alternative funding source that avoids the neoliberal conditionalities often imposed by core-centric lenders, which have historically reinforced economic control over peripheral states (Humphrey, 2020; Mthembu, 2019; Bond & Garcia, 2015; Abdenur & Folly, 2015). Over 60% of its approved loans target transportation corridors, renewable energy, clean water, and digital infrastructure projects in BRICS countries and partner nations, with a substantial focus on Africa, enhancing productive capacity in regions marked by structural underdevelopment (Grabel, 2017).

This approach aligns with world-systems perspectives that view development finance as a mechanism through which hegemonic states maintain dominance over dependent peripheries. By offering flexible lending practices, the NDB enables borrower countries to retain policy autonomy, diversify partnerships beyond the Bretton Woods framework, and pursue developmental pluralism through South-South cooperation (Yang, 2019). China's leadership is central, as it provided the largest initial capital share and has synergized the NDB with its Belt and Road Initiative (BRI), expanding developmental and financial pathways across Africa and Latin America that bypass Western capital gatekeepers (Hopewell, 2017). Additionally, the NDB's policy of allowing borrowing in local currencies aims to decouple periphery states from the dollar-based debt trap, bolstering economic resilience (Liu & Papa, 2022).

Despite its transformative potential, the NDB faces challenges. Its relatively small capital base and dependence on credit markets could limit its long-term influence unless member states increase capital commitments and diversify partnerships (Liu & Papa, 2022). Nevertheless, by redirecting financial flows and fostering South-South cooperation, the NDB challenges the structural inequalities embedded in global capital distribution, repositioning developing states as active agents in reshaping the global economic order.

2.2. Contingent Reserve Arrangement: Crisis Mitigation

The CRA serves as a critical financial mechanism within the BRICS+ framework, providing a regional liquidity safety net to shield member economies from short-term balance-of-payments crises and currency volatility, thereby reducing dependence on the IMF's crisis lending mechanisms (Aggarwal, 2020). Unlike the IMF's punitive conditionalities, which often enforce fiscal austerity and structural reforms, the CRA offers flexible access to funds with governance structures that reflect member states' interests, fostering greater policy autonomy and aligning with the ethos of South-South solidarity (Grabel, 2017). This monetary cooperation challenges the financial disciplining mechanisms imposed by core-state institutions, repositioning developing states as active agents in reshaping global economic power relations (Arrighi, 1994; Gallagher, 2018).

The CRA's significance extends beyond its functional role, carrying symbolic weight in eroding the monopolistic dominance of Western financial institutions in global crisis response. By mitigating the austerity-driven trajectories typical of IMF-led recoveries, it promotes policy space for national governments, particularly during external shocks or global financial tightening. However, structural limitations temper its transformative potential. Disbursements beyond a 30% access threshold require partial IMF involvement, which undermines the autonomy the CRA seeks to provide (Bastanifar, Khan, & Koch, 2025; Mthembu, 2019). Additionally, its modest size compared to global reserves and limited activation history raise questions about political cohesion and trust among BRICS states, potentially constraining its effectiveness. A comparative analysis reveals key institutional contrasts with the IMF:

while the IMF holds 85% of voting power within G7 nations, the CRA distributes voting shares more equally among BRICS+ members. The IMF imposes extensive structural conditionality, whereas the CRA allows initial access to 30% of quotas without such requirements. However, the CRA's linkage to IMF approval for higher disbursements highlights partial replication of Bretton Woods norms (Gallagher, 2018; Fernandes, 2024).

Nevertheless, in a global financial system dominated by core institutions, the CRA represents a semi-peripheral effort to build regional resilience and reduce systemic dependency. By fostering risk-sharing and offering a development-sensitive alternative to IMF support, it challenges the unipolar nature of the existing financial safety net, advancing the BRICS+ vision of a more equitable global economic order.

2.3. Local Currency Financing and BRICS+ De-dollarization Strategy

One of the most profound ambitions of BRICS+ is to reduce the dominance of the US dollar in global trade and finance. This de-dollarization strategy materializes through local currency arrangements (LCAs), bilateral swap agreements, and the promotion of alternative payment systems that allow member states to conduct transactions outside the dollar-based system. These efforts seek not only economic efficiency but also structural autonomy—key concerns in world-systems theory, which views currency hegemony as a tool of core states to maintain control over the periphery (Arrighi, 1994; Wallerstein, 2004).

Local currency financing within BRICS+—notably between China and Russia, and Brazil and Argentina—has grown steadily, allowing for trade settlements in yuan, ruble, or real. China's Cross-Border Interbank Payment System (CIPS), often described as an alternative to SWIFT, facilitates these efforts by offering a non-Western payment infrastructure. Additionally, discussions around a common BRICS currency, while still exploratory, underscore the bloc's long-term ambition to institutionalize a multipolar monetary order (Yang, 2019; Mthembu, 2019).

The systemic implications of this shift are significant. By weakening the role of the US dollar, BRICS+ challenges the financial privilege that allows core states to run persistent deficits and export inflation to the global South. Moreover, LCAs can reduce exchange rate volatility, lower transaction costs, and protect countries from currency weaponization, as seen in the sanctions regimes imposed on Russia and others (Tooze, 2021; Bastanifar, Khan, & Koch, 2025).

Table 1 below provides a side-by-side comparison of the IMF and the BRICS CRA, focusing on governance structures, access modalities, conditionality, and institutional objectives. This comparative analysis highlights the distinctions between the Bretton Woods architecture and BRICS+ financial instruments, clarifying their respective roles in the broader context of multipolar financial governance reform.

Table 1. Comparative Overview of IMF and BRICS CRA

Feature	IMF	BRICS CRA
Total Resources	~$935.7 billion (based on SDR allocations)	$100 billion (China 41%, Russia/Brazil/India 18% each, South Africa 5%)
Liquidity Instrument	Special Drawing Rights (SDRs)	US dollar-based bilateral swap lines
De-linked Access	Not applicable; all access tied to program terms	30% accessible without IMF involvement; 70% requires IMF program
Conditionality	Extensive structural and macroeconomic conditions	Minimal for initial access; significant for higher tranches
Voting Structure	Quota-based; 85% approval required for major decisions	Equal strategic votes; operational votes weighted by capital share
Institutional Structure	Permanent secretariat and global surveillance apparatus	Limited institutionalization; no standing secretariat
Primary Objective	Global macroeconomic stability and poverty reduction	Short-term liquidity support and financial sovereignty

Source: Compiled by the author based on official institutional documents and secondary analyses.

From a world-systems lens, these de-dollarization efforts represent a deliberate push by semi-peripheral states to escape the monetary dependencies historically imposed by hegemonic cores. While challenges remain—such as trust, liquidity constraints, and infrastructural gaps—the strategic intent signals a fundamental reordering of monetary power.

2.4. China's Strategic Leadership in the BRICS Grain Exchange

China's leadership in the BRICS Grain Exchange initiative marks a pivotal shift in global agricultural governance and highlights its evolving strategy of reshaping the international economic order. Amid growing concerns over food insecurity, supply chain disruptions, and dependency on Western-led grain markets, China has assumed a proactive role in orchestrating alternative trade mechanisms among BRICS+ countries. Launched as a counterbalance to traditional grain exchanges in Chicago and Paris, the BRICS Grain Exchange seeks to build a South-South platform for fairer pricing, transparent trade, and greater resilience in agricultural supply chains (Ye, 2023; Hofman & Srinivas, 2024).

Beijing's centrality in this initiative is both infrastructural and ideological. On the one hand, China provides the technical backbone—data systems, digital payment infrastructure, and blockchain-based traceability platforms (Xin, Khan, & Ling,

2024). On the other hand, its leadership is underpinned by a broader geoeconomic vision of contesting Western hegemony through the institutionalization of alternative governance models. From a world-systems theory perspective, China appears to be transitioning from a semi-peripheral actor toward a core-like status, particularly by positioning itself as the coordinator of South-South cooperation in critical domains such as food security (Wallerstein, 2004).

The Grain Exchange also reflects Gramsci's notion of passive revolution, whereby systemic transformation occurs not through abrupt rupture, but via gradual reorganization of institutions within the capitalist world order. China's role, in this sense, represents a 'transformismo'—absorbing and redirecting peripheral discontent into a new form of coordinated dependency that benefits the emerging core. For many countries in Africa, Latin America, and parts of Asia, participation in the exchange is a strategic necessity to ensure affordable access to staple commodities. Yet, the reliance on Chinese infrastructure may reproduce new forms of asymmetrical power relations (Dos Santos, 1970; Gramsci, 1971; Bond & Garcia, 2015).

Additionally, the Grain Exchange enhances China's ability to export not just agricultural goods, but also standards, norms, and technologies. For instance, Chinese-developed smart farming systems and agricultural fintech tools are being promoted as part of BRICS development assistance packages, particularly in Sub-Saharan Africa. This allows Beijing to entrench technological dependencies that may substitute rather than eliminate structural vulnerabilities in the Global South.

Despite these concerns, the initiative also opens up genuine avenues for cooperation. Countries like Brazil and India, themselves major agricultural exporters, benefit from a platform where trade terms are not dictated by Western commodity traders. Furthermore, by enabling inter-BRICS currency settlement in local currencies, the exchange supports ongoing de-dollarization efforts and enhances collective bargaining power (Bastanifar, Khan, & Koch, 2025).

Nevertheless, the success of this initiative will depend on whether China's leadership evolves into shared governance or remains structurally hierarchical. Without transparent decision-making, equitable access to technology, and inclusive rule-setting, the Grain Exchange risks becoming yet another tool of strategic leverage rather than a vehicle of genuine emancipation for peripheral economies.

2.5. Theoretical Implications

The BRICS+ framework represents not merely a geopolitical alliance or a loose economic coalition, but a paradigmatic challenge to the liberal international order. The initiatives explored in this study—ranging from de-dollarization to the creation of parallel financial institutions—carry broader theoretical implications regarding global governance, power transitions, and the nature of institutional pluralism.

These developments invite re-engagement with several foundational debates in international political economy and critical global theory (Stuenkel, 2015; Babb & Kentikelenis, 2021).

Antonio Gramsci's concept of hegemony provides a valuable lens to interpret BRICS's collective agenda. In the Gramscian sense, hegemony is not solely maintained through coercive capabilities but also through the establishment of normative and institutional consent (Gramsci, 1971). By constructing institutions like the NDB and proposing alternative transaction systems outside of SWIFT, BRICS nations appear to be engaged in a process of counter-hegemonic institutionalization. These institutions do not yet possess the structural weight to replace the Bretton Woods system, but they serve as important vehicles for challenging the Western monopoly over the rules of global economic governance (Chin, 2014).

From a world-systems theory perspective, the BRICS initiative challenges the longstanding core-periphery dichotomy. Traditionally, core nations have maintained dominance by controlling not only productive and financial capacities but also the institutional architecture of global capitalism (Wallerstein, 2004). BRICS, particularly with the expansion of BRICS+ to include energy-rich and strategically significant countries from the Global South, aims to construct an alternative semi-core or even a pluralized core. This reconfiguration remains embryonic, yet it symbolically undermines the historical North-South hierarchy embedded in existing financial institutions like the IMF and World Bank (Bond, 2013).

Furthermore, the BRICS+ project aligns with emerging discussions on institutional multipolarity and normative pluralism. As opposed to the liberal ideal of convergence toward a single universalist model of development and governance, BRICS promotes a pluralist ethos that accommodates divergent models of capitalism, development, and sovereignty (Acharya, 2017; Hurrell, 2018). This theoretical positioning contrasts sharply with the prescriptive frameworks of neoliberal institutionalism, which often assumes path dependency toward liberal democracy and open markets. BRICS countries assert that economic sovereignty and developmental autonomy need not conform to liberal norms to be legitimate or effective (Overbeek, 2016).

At the same time, critical theories of global governance caution against romanticizing multipolarity. The BRICS bloc itself is not ideologically coherent; internal asymmetries in size, interests, and governance models remain stark (Roberts, Armijo, & Katada, 2017). From a neo-Gramscian or critical IPE perspective, the risk is that BRICS may merely reproduce hierarchical structures under a different guise, substituting Western dominance with another form of elite-driven regionalism (Cox, 1987). Moreover, the bloc's ambiguous stance on issues like labor rights, environmental standards, and democratic accountability raises questions about whether BRICS is truly forging an emancipatory alternative, or simply rearticulating sovereignty in the service of state-centric capitalism (Bond, 2013).

Finally, the theoretical contribution of the BRICS initiative must be situated in its duality: while it undermines Western-centric institutional dominance, it also illustrates the limits of collective South-South mobilization. The emerging BRICS-based architecture is not devoid of contradiction; rather, it embodies the tensions inherent in constructing global alternatives within a system still largely defined by dollar dependency, global capital mobility, and unequal development (Babb & Kentikelenis, 2021).

In sum, BRICS+ offers a fertile site for rethinking theories of hegemony, institutional change, and global pluralism. It does not signal the collapse of the liberal order but articulates a nascent counter-narrative that emphasizes sovereignty, developmental diversity, and institutional experimentation. The full realization of this theoretical potential, however, depends on BRICS's ability to translate its rhetoric into durable and inclusive frameworks—both ideationally and materially.

Having discussed the theoretical implications and structural critiques of BRICS+ institutions, the following section explores how these dynamics materialize in concrete developmental contexts.

3. CASE STUDIES: BRICS+ INITIATIVES IN ACTION

BRICS+'s ambition to reduce global economic inequalities is vividly reflected in a diverse array of initiatives spanning digital finance, infrastructure, renewable energy, and agricultural trade. This section examines case studies from Brazil's bioenergy development, India's Unified Payments Interface (UPI), South Africa's transport infrastructure projects, Ethiopia's solar energy expansion, NDB-funded programs in Egypt and Nigeria, Algeria's prospective NDB membership, and the proposed BRICS Grain Exchange. These cases illustrate the tangible impact of BRICS+ on peripheral and semi-peripheral economies, where China's leadership—exercised through the NDB, the Belt and Road Initiative (BRI), and the digital yuan (e-Yuan)—plays a pivotal role. Each case exemplifies how BRICS+ instruments interact with systemic structures described in world-systems theory. For instance, UPI in India challenges core-dominated financial systems, while Brazil's ethanol initiative reduces dependency on global energy hierarchies. These cases connect empirical outcomes with the broader theoretical critique of global capitalism. Grounded in world-systems theory, these examples demonstrate how BRICS+ initiatives are reshaping traditional core-periphery dynamics, promoting economic inclusion and sovereignty while contending with internal disparities and geopolitical challenges.

3.1. Brazil: Bioenergy for Sustainability

Brazil's $500 million bioenergy initiative, launched in 2020 with funding from the NDB, aims to foster sustainable development in the Amazon and reduce regional inequalities in line with the overarching objectives of BRICS+. The project focuses on sugarcane-based ethanol production and has already created approximately 50,000 jobs, predominantly in rural communities, thereby addressing unemployment and promoting inclusive economic growth (NDB, 2023; Sakai et al., 2020; Cardoso, Shikida, & Finco, 2017). In addition to its social benefits, the initiative has cut carbon emissions by 10% in the target region, contributing to broader climate goals. According to the Brazilian Institute of Geography and Statistics (IBGE), the Gini index in the targeted regions declined from 0.532 in 2020 to 0.498 by 2023, indicating a measurable reduction in income inequality. Moreover, regional poverty rates fell by 7.5% during the same period (Cardin, 2025).

By enhancing domestic energy production, the program has decreased Brazil's dependency on imported fossil fuels by 8%, translating into annual savings of around $1.5 billion (NDB, 2023). The project's integration with Brazil's existing ethanol fuel program has enabled 100,000 smallholder farmers to participate in national and regional energy markets, improving rural incomes and reducing economic disparity (Sakai et al., 2020; Cardoso, Shikida, & Finco, 2017).

This initiative also exemplifies BRICS+'s commitment to South-South cooperation. At the 2024 Kazan Summit, Brazil shared technical expertise to support the replication of similar bioenergy projects in African partner countries (Lukyanov et al., 2024). However, environmental concerns persist, as 5% of the project's land overlaps with protected areas, prompting criticism from conservation groups regarding potential deforestation (Fearnside, 2016).

From a world-systems theory perspective, Brazil's bioenergy strategy reflects a semi-peripheral state's effort to challenge core-dominated global energy markets and enhance its structural position in the international system. By promoting energy sovereignty and reducing reliance on external resources, Brazil not only gains economic leverage but also asserts a developmental model that resists traditional dependency patterns (Wallerstein, 2004).

3.2. India: Unified Payments Interface (UPI)

India's Unified Payments Interface (UPI), launched in 2016 by the National Payments Corporation of India (NPCI), has revolutionized financial inclusion, aligning with BRICS+'s goal of reducing global economic disparities by enabling instant, low-cost digital payments across urban and rural areas (Routh, 2024). By 2024, UPI accounted for 83% of India's digital transactions, processing over 16.58 billion transactions in October 2024 alone, amounting to 23.49 lakh crore (Vishwakarma, 2025; PIB, 2024). The platform's rapid expansion, with a 118% transaction growth in rural and semi-urban regions in 2023, has empowered small vendors and farmers to access digital markets, bridging the urban-rural financial divide (ABP, 2023).

According to a People Research on India's Consumer Economy (PRICE) working paper, India's Gini coefficient fell from approximately 0.506 in 2020–21 (amid the pandemic) to 0.410 in 2022–23, indicating a notable improvement in income distribution across the population.

Simultaneously, Household Consumption Expenditure survey data confirm a decline in inequality: rural Gini dropped from ~0.283 to 0.266, while urban Gini fell from ~0.363 to 0.314 between 2011–12 and 2022–23 (Times of India, 2024). Targeted welfare interventions—such as MGNREGA, Direct Benefit Transfers, and Jan-Dhan financial inclusion—have played key roles. However, despite recovery from the pandemic spike, wealth concentration at the top remains significant, with the richest 1% capturing around 22–23% of national income (Swarajya Magazine, 2024).

UPI's interoperability—connecting over 600 banks and fintech platforms—has streamlined digital payments, reducing transaction costs and enhancing user convenience (Routh, 2024). The government's incentive schemes, such as the 0.15% rebate for transactions up to 2,000 made to small merchants, have further promoted low-value digital transactions and financial inclusion (PIB, 2025).

However, the rapid adoption of UPI has also led to challenges, particularly in cybersecurity. In the fiscal year 2023–24, UPI-related fraud cases surged by 85%, with 632,000 cases reported by September 2024, amounting to losses of 485 crore (Soni, 2024). These figures underscore the need for robust security measures and digital literacy programs, especially in rural areas where users may be more vulnerable to fraud.

From a world-systems theory perspective, UPI empowers India's semi-peripheral economy by enhancing financial autonomy and reducing reliance on core-dominated payment systems. By facilitating instant, low-cost digital payments, UPI challenges traditional financial hierarchies and promotes economic inclusion, aligning with BRICS+'s goal of reducing global economic disparities

3.3. South Africa: Transport Infrastructure and Regional Connectivity

South Africa's BRICS+-aligned infrastructure development strategy has prioritized regional transport connectivity to stimulate intra-African trade and reduce structural inequalities. A flagship initiative is the Durban-Gauteng freight corridor modernization, supported by a $2.5 billion investment, partially financed by the NDB since 2017 (NDB, 2023). As of 2024, the project has improved freight turn-around by 35%, reduced transportation costs by 18%, and facilitated a 22% increase in trade volumes between South Africa and neighboring SADC countries (World Bank, 2025; NDB, 2023). By 2023, South Africa's Gini coefficient remained among the world's highest, around 0.67. Although policy interventions—like progressive taxation and social grants—have marginally lowered inequality, the overall level remains virtually unchanged from 2020 (0.67 vs ~0.66). This highlights persistent structural challenges and limited impact of redistributive measures (Sulla, Zikhali, & Cuevas, 2022).

This enhanced connectivity has particularly benefited landlocked economies like Zimbabwe, Zambia, and Botswana by lowering logistical barriers and improving access to seaports (UNECA, 2024). Small and medium enterprises (SMEs) across the region have gained improved market access, supporting job creation and rural development. Enhanced logistics and trade corridors have facilitated increased exports in sectors such as agriculture and mining logistics (AfDB, 2023).

However, concerns persist over environmental degradation and community displacement along the expanded rail routes, with civil society groups calling for stronger participatory governance mechanisms (Lamarque & Nugent, 2022). Additionally, operational inefficiencies and mismanagement within Transnet, South Africa's state-owned logistics company, have posed persistent implementation challenges (Banya & Anders, 2024).

From a world-systems theory perspective, this initiative enables South Africa—a semi-peripheral actor—to act as a regional hub for economic flows, redistributing economic activity within the African periphery. By reinforcing South-South transport integration, the project challenges dependency on former colonial trade routes and promotes regional self-determination, in line with BRICS+'s transformative agenda.

3.4. Ethiopia: Solar Energy for Off-Grid Communities

Ethiopia's partnership with BRICS+ and the NDB has supported renewable energy deployment in underserved regions, targeting both poverty alleviation and energy sovereignty. Launched in 2021, the Ethiopia Off-Grid Solar Access Project (EOSAP), with $300 million in co-financing from the NDB and African Development Bank, aims to provide decentralized solar solutions to five million people in rural and conflict-affected areas. As of 2024, over 1.2 million households have gained access to electricity, reducing kerosene usage by 60% and enabling longer school study hours and mobile connectivity (AfDB, 2024; NDB, 2023; World Bank, 2025). Ethiopia's Gini coefficient was approximately 0.311 in 2021, reflecting moderate income inequality. Income distribution has remained stable since 2019, thanks to inclusive growth and targeted poverty reduction strategies. While inequality hasn't significantly declined, sustained economic development has prevented sharp rising trends (Degye, Abule, & Lamessa, 2024).

The project has also contributed to gender equity, with women comprising 37% of the workforce in Ethiopia's distributed solar PV sector, reflecting efforts to enhance female participation in renewable energy initiatives (IRENA, 2024a). Economically, the initiative has spurred microenterprise growth, with solar-powered solutions supporting agriculture, retail, and medical services in isolated areas (IEA, 2023).

Yet implementation has faced challenges. Global supply chain disruptions, including semiconductor shortages, have led to delays in the rollout of solar panels and batteries, impacting project timelines (IEA, 2023). Nevertheless, support from international partnerships has helped Ethiopia pursue more autonomous development planning, reducing reliance on traditional donor models (UNCTAD, 2024).

From a world-systems theory perspective, Ethiopia's solar project reflects a shift in peripheral agency—where a least-developed country leverages BRICS+ mechanisms to bypass core-dominated finance and technology channels. The initiative exemplifies how South-South cooperation, framed by renewable energy, can redistribute development power, promote environmental justice, and contest global structural inequalities.

3.5. Egypt and Nigeria: NDB-Funded Inclusive Development

The expansion of the NDB to include Egypt (2023) and its growing financial engagement with Nigeria mark BRICS+'s evolving strategy to integrate African regional powers into a multipolar development agenda. In Egypt, the NDB is actively pursuing a soft loan of $1 billion to support green infrastructure projects, including water desalination, energy-efficient housing, and smart transportation in urban peripheries. These initiatives aim to improve access to clean water and reduce energy poverty in informal settlements, while creating employment opportunities (Business Today Egypt, 2024).

In Nigeria, the African Development Bank (AfDB) has launched the construction of a $510 million Special Agro-Industrial Processing Zone (SAPZ) in Kaduna State, aiming to transform the country's food and agriculture sector. These investments align with Nigeria's ambition to reduce post-harvest losses and double agricultural exports by 2030 (AfDB, 2025).

Both cases reflect the BRICS+ vision of inclusive development tailored to regional contexts. Egypt's integration into the NDB underscores the geopolitical shift towards multipolar financial governance, while Nigeria's participation, although not yet formalized through full NDB membership, illustrates how BRICS+ operates as a flexible and adaptive platform for South-South cooperation. According to UNCTAD's 2024 report, such initiatives contribute to reducing non-tariff trade costs and diversifying trade partners, enhancing Africa's resilience and global competitiveness (UNCTAD, 2024).

From a world-systems theory lens, Egypt and Nigeria's engagement with BRICS+ challenges the historic dependency of African economies on Western multilateral institutions. Through alternative finance channels and decentralized project models, these countries gain partial autonomy in shaping their development pathways—symbolizing a recalibration of the periphery's position vis-à-vis core-dominated global structures.

3.6. Algeria's BRICS+ Integration and Renewable Energy Strategy

Algeria's bid to join BRICS+ and its formal accession to the NDB in 2024 represent a strategic move to diversify its hydrocarbon-dependent economy and expand its geopolitical leverage within a multipolar framework. With over 3,000 hours of sunlight annually and vast desert land, Algeria is emerging as a potential player in BRICS+ green energy cooperation. While no official BRICS+ or NDB-funded solar projects have been confirmed to date, Algeria has launched an ambitious 3 GW solar energy initiative led by its national utility Sonelgaz. This initiative includes the construction of 20 solar plants across 12 provinces in the Hautes Plaines and Saharan regions, contributing to a national target of 22,000 MW of renewable energy capacity by 2030, including 13,500 MW from solar photovoltaic power—aligned with Algeria's broader goal of raising renewables to 27% of electricity production (IRENA, 2023; Takoulcu, 2024; Statista, 2024).

These developments position Algeria to benefit from future BRICS+ green infrastructure financing, particularly as the bloc seeks to expand its footprint across Africa. By aligning its renewable agenda with BRICS+ strategic priorities, Algeria signals its intent to transition away from fossil fuel dependency while leveraging new South-South partnerships. (Reuters, 2024; IRENA, 2023).

This initiative supports Algeria's national plan to raise renewable energy's share to 27% of total electricity output by 2030, reducing the country's overreliance on fossil fuel exports, which currently comprise 93% of its foreign income (World Bank, IEA, IRENA, UNSD, & WHO, 2024). In parallel, Algeria has entered into energy-sharing talks with Niger and Mali, promoting regional energy interdependence and positioning itself as a solar energy exporter in the Maghreb and Sahel (IRENA, 2023).

Algeria's growing proximity to BRICS+ also has diplomatic dimensions. Its aspiration to join the bloc—backed by China and Russia—reflects dissatisfaction with Eurocentric financial mechanisms and aims to secure alternative development finance, technology transfer, and strategic autonomy (Hochberg, 2020).

From a world-systems theory perspective, Algeria exemplifies a semi-peripheral state attempting to reorient itself through South-South alliances. The shift from core-dominated hydrocarbon dependency toward decentralized renewable development—backed by NDB financing—signals a recalibration of its structural position within the global economy, challenging the West-centric resource trap historically imposed on peripheral regions.

3.7. China's Role and Theoretical Implications

China plays a pivotal role in shaping the strategic direction of BRICS+, not only as its largest economy but also as a principal architect of South-South cooperation and institutional alternatives to Western-led global governance. Through initiatives like the Belt and Road Initiative (BRI), the digital yuan, and its leadership in the NDB, China has advanced a multipolar vision that challenges the hegemony of the global North while promoting developmental sovereignty across peripheral and semi-peripheral states (Lee & Sims, 2024; Hopewell, 2019).

From a world-systems theory perspective, China occupies an ambiguous yet dynamic position straddling the core and semi-periphery. While it increasingly exhibits core-like economic influence, its strategic alliances with countries in the Global South reflect a deliberate positioning to redefine the terms of global economic integration (Wallerstein, 2004; Babones, 2018). Rather than merely seeking accession to existing core structures, China, through BRICS+, has facilitated institutional innovation—such as currency-swap agreements, development financing independent of the IMF, and support for local currency trade—that challenge the structural dependencies of the periphery (Liu & Papa, 2022).

China's expansive role in financing energy, digital infrastructure, and food security initiatives across BRICS+ members illustrates its capacity to act as a counter-hegemonic force, reshaping the semi-periphery into a zone of autonomous development rather than passive extraction (Ren, Li, Wang, & Zhang, 2020). Simultaneously, this leadership is not without tensions. Critics point to potential neo-dependency patterns where China replaces Western dominance with its own forms of asymmetry (Bond & Garcia, 2015). Nonetheless, China's emphasis on mutual benefit, technology transfer, and infrastructure connectivity resonates strongly with world-systems perspectives that advocate for restructuring rather than reinforcing global hierarchies.

By foregrounding solidarity-based development and enabling South-South linkages, China's leadership within BRICS+ disrupts the unidirectional logic of globalization. It offers a complex but compelling model in which peripheral agency is not absorbed by the core but rather reoriented through multipolar institutional mechanisms. As such, BRICS+ becomes a transformative platform—anchored by

China—for challenging capitalist world-system hierarchies and promoting plural centers of economic power.

Despite the promising outcomes presented above, BRICS+ initiatives face critical internal and external challenges that may constrain their transformative potential. The next section engages with these limitations.

4. CHALLENGES AND CRITIQUES

Despite BRICS+'s ambition to challenge global economic asymmetries through South-South cooperation, the bloc faces serious internal contradictions and external resistance that undermine its coherence and transformative potential. Initiatives like the NDB, CRA, and BRICS Grain Exchange signal institutional innovation but remain hindered by China's overrepresentation, intra-bloc disputes, transparency concerns, elite capture, and systemic geopolitical pressures. This section critically interrogates these challenges and their implications for BRICS+'s egalitarian claims, drawing on world-systems theory to show how new forms of hierarchy risk emerging within a supposedly post-hegemonic framework.

4.1. China's Dominance and Internal Tensions

China's disproportionate role within BRICS+—contributing over 40% to the NDB's $16 billion capital base and spearheading Belt and Road Initiative (BRI) alignments—illustrates both its leadership and the structural imbalances within the coalition (NDB, 2023; Chin, 2024). This dominance is reflected in voting rights, agenda-setting power, and project prioritization—raising concerns of institutional imbalance. Without mechanisms such as rotating leadership or weighted veto rights for smaller members, China's preeminence risks alienating countries like India and Brazil, potentially undermining bloc cohesion and legitimacy (Roberts et al., 2017). Flagship projects such as the $1 billion Ethiopia-Djibouti railway and Nigeria's $800 million Lekki Deep Sea Port, often jointly funded by the NDB and BRI-linked banks, highlight Beijing's centrality in infrastructure-led development (AfDB, 2023; Reuters, 2024). At the 2024 Kazan Summit, China proposed a $2 billion digital infrastructure fund via the NDB and expanded e-Yuan transactions to 15% of intra-BRICS trade (Lukyanov et al., 2024; Ren, Li, Wang, & Zhang, 2020). While these initiatives strengthen BRICS+'s global relevance, they also provoke concern among members like India and Brazil regarding asymmetric influence (Humphrey & Chen, 2020).

Diverging national agendas exacerbate intra-bloc tensions. India champions digital innovation, exemplified by the 300 million-user UPI system, while Russia prioritizes energy exports amid sanctions-induced constraints (Bloomberg, 2025a). Brazil advocates stronger NDB support for green energy transitions, yet Chinese-led project prioritization often sidelines these aspirations (Abdenur & Folly, 2015). The CRA has disbursed only $2 billion since its inception in 2015, primarily due to governance gridlock between China and India (Bradlow & Masamba, 2023; Reuters, 2024). Such divergences risk reproducing hierarchical patterns within a bloc that seeks to dismantle them, echoing Wallerstein's notion of core-like behavior within the semi-periphery (Wallerstein, 2004).

4.2. Transparency and Elite Capture

Institutional opacity and elite co-optation undermine BRICS+'s legitimacy. The NDB's project appraisal and selection mechanisms fall short of World Bank transparency standards, with limited public access to project documentation or environmental/social assessments (NDB, 2022). South Africa's $425 million rail infrastructure contract, although initially expected to benefit nearly 200,000 households, was terminated due to corruption allegations and procurement irregularities involving politically connected firms (Bloomberg, 2025b).

Similarly, Nigeria's $652 million road infrastructure project—funded via China Exim Bank—faced criticism for prioritizing urban trade corridors over rural connectivity, while pushing the country's debt burden to over $5 billion to Chinese lenders (Reuters, 2025). Egypt's $500 million wind energy initiative, despite its clean energy potential, experienced regulatory bottlenecks and delays that hindered equitable energy access (The Jerusalem Post, 2025).

Elite capture continues to distort developmental intent. In Algeria, the recently announced 3.2 GW solar development plan has raised concerns over state-controlled monopolization, with minimal inclusion of small-scale or community actors (Mercom India, 2025; Energy Capital & Power, 2025). While BRICS+ projects have generated over 1.5 million jobs across Africa, the distribution of these benefits remains uneven, often favoring urban elites and reinforcing structural inequalities—thus conflicting with the bloc's foundational principles of equitable development (AfDB, 2018).

4.3. Western Opposition and Geopolitical Pressures

BRICS+ also contends with significant geopolitical headwinds, particularly from Western powers. The United States, under the renewed leadership of President Trump, introduced tariff threats in 2024 targeting BRICS+ economies—proposing a 25% levy on Chinese goods and a 10% duty on Indian exports—jeopardizing nearly $500 billion in trade flows (Reuters, 2024; Lukyanov et al., 2024). These measures, which have since evolved through multiple adjustments in response to shifting trade negotiations and geopolitical dynamics, underscore the ongoing volatility in global trade policies. Sanctions imposed on Russia and Iran—key actors within the BRICS+ framework—have intensified since 2022, complicating the operationalization of the proposed BRICS Grain Exchange. While the 2024 Kazan Declaration endorsed the initiative to establish a BRICS Grain Exchange aimed at developing a fair agricultural trading system, the project has faced challenges due to geopolitical tensions and limited enthusiasm from other BRICS members (Clark & Liu, 2024). Russia, the world's largest wheat exporter, has been a primary advocate for the exchange, proposing its creation to facilitate trade among BRICS nations (Reuters, 2024a).

CRA, designed to provide financial support to BRICS countries during balance-of-payments crises, remains structurally linked to the IMF. Only 30% of a member country's quota can be accessed without an IMF program, which undermines BRICS+'s claim to financial sovereignty (Fernandes, 2024).

Moreover, Western-led institutions like the IMF and World Bank continue to attract debt-strained economies by offering competitive lending terms. For instance, Nigeria secured a $2.25 billion loan from the World Bank in 2024 to support economic reforms and poverty alleviation (Reuters, 2024b). Additionally, Nigeria fully repaid a $3.4 billion emergency loan from the IMF in 2025, reaffirming its continued engagement with Western financial institutions (Reuters, 2025a). These dynamics perpetuate core-periphery dependencies within the global order that BRICS+ seeks to transcend (Wallerstein, 2004).

4.4. Implementation Challenges

Operational constraints present another major challenge for BRICS+ initiatives. The Grain Exchange—intended to de-dollarize 20% of trade in wheat, maize, and soybeans—faces significant obstacles, including regulatory misalignment and logistics fragmentation across member states (Ye, 2023; Hofman & Srinivas, 2024). Sanctions on Russian agricultural exports further delay the platform's $5 billion cost-saving potential for African food importers (Lukyanov et al., 2024). Infrastructure projects also encounter execution issues. Ethiopia's $300 million solar initiative powers 100,000 homes but is hindered by outdated grid infrastructure (NDB, 2023; Chin, 2024). Egypt's wind project and Algeria's solar proposal face bureaucratic delays, with the latter still awaiting NDB membership approval (AfDB, 2023).

Debt sustainability remains a persistent concern. Nigeria's $652 million project, while improving urban mobility, exacerbates fiscal pressures, pushing debt levels to 30% of GDP and threatening long-term repayment capacity (Reuters, 2025). Broader challenges such as global financial volatility and conflict-related instability further constrain the bloc's ability to deliver inclusive and durable outcomes.

4.5. Theoretical Implications

This study contributes to the theoretical understanding of global economic governance by reinterpreting the BRICS+ framework through the lens of world-systems theory and critical international political economy. Rather than viewing BRICS+ merely as a geopolitical coalition or an emerging market bloc, this chapter conceptualizes it as a semi-peripheral intervention that disrupts hegemonic norms of financial governance from within the capitalist world-system.

By analyzing case studies from India, Brazil, South Africa, Ethiopia, Egypt, and Nigeria, the study highlights how semi-peripheral and peripheral states are leveraging BRICS+ institutions to gain autonomy over development financing, trade, and digital infrastructure. This case-based insight enriches world-systems theory by offering a typology of *semi-peripheral agency* that goes beyond resistance or alignment with core powers. BRICS+ does not reject global capitalism outright; instead, it constructs a "pragmatic alternative" that reconfigures financial flows without replicating IMF-style conditionalities.

Through mechanisms like the New Development Bank and the BRICS Grain Exchange, the bloc has introduced a distinct form of *developmental* multilateralism grounded in South-South cooperation. Unlike Bretton Woods institutions that impose top-down austerity, BRICS+ favors local currency trade, infrastructure investment, and knowledge exchange. This model of *alternative institutionalism* challenges liberal institutionalism's universalism and opens space for plural pathways to development—an area underexplored in mainstream global governance literature.

The study also identifies a shift in structural power relations: BRICS+ enables selected peripheral economies to move toward *functional semi-core* positions by accessing capital, technology, and markets without passing through core-state gatekeepers. This reframes dependency not as inevitable, but as historically constructed and reversible under conditions of regional coordination. The inclusion of Africa-centric case studies (Ethiopia, Nigeria, Algeria) foregrounds a recalibration of the periphery's role, extending world-systems theory into empirical application.

Finally, the analysis highlights BRICS+ as an epistemic project. The bloc's discourse around multipolarity, sovereignty, and post-Western governance embodies what scholars like Santos (2014) term *epistemologies of the South*. In this regard, BRICS+ is not merely a technical experiment in financial reform, but also a normative challenge to the monopoly of Western development thought. The promotion of non-dollar trade, decentralized technologies, and culturally situated policies reflects an emergent *normative pluralism* in global economic governance.

5. CONCLUSION AND POLICY RECOMMENDATIONS

BRICS+ stands as a bold counterforce to global economic inequalities, harnessing South-South cooperation to challenge the Western-led financial system. Through innovative mechanisms like the NDB, CRA, and the proposed BRICS Grain Exchange, it has empowered peripheral economies, particularly in Africa. This study contributes to the literature by analyzing BRICS+'s role in reducing global economic inequalities through a world-systems theory lens, offering an alternative to Western-centric financial analyses and filling a gap in understanding South-South cooperation as a transformative force in global economic governance. Yet, internal divisions, transparency gaps, and Western resistance pose significant hurdles. This chapter reflects on BRICS+'s achievements, critiques its limitations, and offers policy recommendations to strengthen its mission. Viewed through world-systems theory, BRICS+'s journey reveals both its potential to reshape global equity and the complexities of navigating a multipolar world.

This study advances the theoretical debate on semi-peripheral agency by offering case-based and theoretically grounded analysis of how BRICS+ initiatives—particularly the NDB, CRA, and UPI—function as instruments of developmental autonomy. Unlike mainstream global finance studies that focus predominantly on core-periphery dynamics within IMF-World Bank frameworks, this chapter offers a South-South alternative grounded in world-systems theory. By connecting financial instruments to shifts in structural power relations, the analysis contributes a new typology of counter-hegemonic financial strategies emerging from the semi-periphery.

5.1. Reflecting on Achievements

BRICS+ has made tangible progress in reducing economic disparities. The NDB's $7.5 billion investment portfolio in 2023 supported infrastructure development across member countries, contributing to significant employment generation and improved access to essential services (NDB, 2023). In South Africa, a $1.2 billion transport network project enhanced rural market connectivity, while Ethiopia's $300 million solar initiative expanded energy access to thousands of off-grid homes. Meanwhile, Brazil's $500 million bioenergy project supported sustainable rural development and job creation through sugarcane-based ethanol production (Cardoso, Shikida, & Finco, 2017). Beyond Africa, India's Unified Payments Interface (UPI) has integrated 300 million users into the formal economy, enabling inclusive digital finance and increasing income generation among marginalized communities (Abdenur & Folly,

2015). Initiatives like the proposed BRICS Grain Exchange aim to further reduce dollar dependency and improve food security across crisis-prone regions.

China's leadership has been a driving force, with its 40% NDB contribution and BRI synergies amplifying impact. Ethiopia's $1 billion railway and Nigeria's $800 million port have spurred regional trade, while the e-Yuan's 15% adoption in BRICS trade post-Kazan 2024 advances de-dollarization (Chin, 2024). These efforts disrupt core-periphery hierarchies, redistributing resources to empower the global South, as world-systems theory envisions (Wallerstein, 2004). BRICS+'s ability to finance projects without Western conditionalities marks a paradigm shift, offering peripheral nations greater sovereignty.

5.2. Assessing Challenges

Despite these strides, BRICS+ grapples with significant obstacles. China's dominance, while catalytic, breeds unease among members like India and Brazil, who seek equitable influence. The CRA's mere $2 billion disbursement since 2015 reflects governance disputes that stifle its potential. Transparency remains a weak point: the NDB's opaque project selection, coupled with corruption allegations in South Africa's transport project, undermines trust. In Nigeria, a 30% GDP debt burden from NDB loans raises sustainability concerns, while Egypt's bureaucratic delays limit energy access.

Western opposition further complicates BRICS+'s path. US tariff threats in 2024 and sanctions on Russia disrupt the Grain Exchange's wheat trade, while the CRA's reliance on IMF approval for large loans reinforces core dominance. Implementation hurdles, such as logistical barriers for the Grain Exchange and Ethiopia's grid limitations, curb scalability. These challenges highlight a paradox: BRICS+ seeks to dismantle global inequalities but risks creating new ones through China's influence and elite capture, echoing core-periphery tensions (Wallerstein, 2004).

5.3. Policy Recommendations

To realize its equitable vision, BRICS+ must address these challenges strategically. First, the NDB should enhance transparency by publishing project evaluations and engaging local communities, building on South Africa's 2023 audit model. Second, governance must be rebalanced. Empowering India and Brazil with greater NDB and CRA roles—perhaps through rotating leadership—can mitigate China's dominance and foster unity. Additionally, the NDB and CRA would benefit from codifying internal governance reforms: such as proportional voting thresholds, independent oversight committees, and civil society consultation processes. These institutional checks would reduce elite capture and reinforce participatory development governance, aligning BRICS+ more closely with its founding egalitarian principles (Grabel, 2017). Third, implementation requires bold action. A $500 million investment in trade infrastructure could streamline the Grain Exchange, ensuring its 2026 launch, while NDB debt caps at 20% of GDP can safeguard African economies like Nigeria. Finally, BRICS+ should pursue pragmatic diplomacy, partnering with the Asian Infrastructure Investment Bank (AIIB) for co-financed projects and leveraging Brazil's neutrality to negotiate sanction relief for Russia.

Only by embedding accountability, equity, and structural redistribution at the heart of its governance model can BRICS+ realize its transformative promise—not merely as a reaction to Western dominance, but as an independent paradigm of global financial justice.

5.4. Envisioning the Future

BRICS+ is poised to redefine global development, but its success hinges on balancing ambition with pragmatism. By prioritizing transparency, equity, and resilience, it can amplify the impact of initiatives like UPI, NDB projects, and the Grain Exchange. As Wallerstein's world-systems theory suggests, true structural change requires more than economic diversification—it demands institutional realignment and epistemic rethinking. BRICS+ remains at the cusp of this transformation. With reforms, it can lead a new era of global equity, proving that South-South cooperation can transform the lives of billions.

REFERENCES

Abdenur, A. E., & Folly, M. (2015). The New Development Bank and the institutionalization of the BRICS. *R/evolutions. Global Trends & Regional Issues, 3*(1), 66–92.

ABP. (2023, December 20). *UPI transactions grow in 2023: 118% in rural and semi-urban regions in India: Survey*. https://news.abplive.com/business/upi-transactions-grow-in-2023-118-in-rural-and-semi-urban-regions-in-india-digital-payments-digital-india-survey-1651378

Acharya, A. (2017). After liberal hegemony: The advent of a multiplex world order. *Ethics & International Affairs, 31*(3), 271–285. DOI: 10.1017/S089267941700020X

African Development Bank (AfDB). (2018). *African economic outlook 2018*. https://www.afdb.org/fileadmin/uploads/afdb/Documents/Publications/African_Economic_Outlook_2018_-_EN.pdf

African Development Bank (AfDB). (2023). African. *Economic Outlook, 2023*, •••. https://www.afdb.org/sites/default/files/documents/publications/afdb23-01_aeo_main_english_0602.pdf

African Development Bank (AfDB). (2024, May 7). *Ethiopia - Distributed renewable energy agriculture modalities (DREAM) programme - Project summary note*. African Development Bank. https://www.afdb.org/en/documents/ethiopia-distributed-renewable-energy-agriculture-modalities-dream-programme-project-summary-note

African Development Bank (AfDB). (2025, April 8). *Nigeria's food and agriculture revolution takes off backed by the African Development Bank*. African Development Bank. https://www.afdb.org/en/news-and-events/press-releases/nigerias-food-and-agriculture-revolution-takes-backed-african-development-bank-82711

Aggarwal, P. (2020). On de-risking and de-dollarizing intra-BRICS trade via smart contracts. *BRICS Journal of Economics, 4*(1), 54–69. DOI: 10.38050/2712-7508-2020-1-4-6

Armijo, L. E. (2007). The BRICs Countries (Brazil, Russia, India, and China) as Analytical Category: Mirage or Insight? *Asian Perspective, 31*(4), 7–42.

Armijo, L. E., & Roberts, C. (2014). The emerging powers and global governance: Why the BRICS matter. In Looney, R. E. (Ed.), *Handbook of emerging economies* (pp. 503–524). Routledge.

Arrighi, G. (1994). *The long twentieth century: Money, power and the origins of our times*. Verso Press.

Babb, S., & Kentikelenis, A. E. (2021). Markets everywhere: The Washington Consensus and the sociology of global institutional change. *Annual Review of Sociology*, *47*, 521–541.

Babones, S. (2018). *The new authoritarianism: Trump, populism, and the tyranny of experts*. Polity Press.

Banya, N., & Anders, T. (2024, September 2). *S. Africa's Transnet reports wider loss after pipeline lawsuit provision*. Reuters. https://www.reuters.com/business/autos-transportation/south-africas-transnet-reports-higher-loss-latest-financial-year-2024-09-02/

Bastanifar, I., Khan, K. H., & Koch, H. (2025). Understanding BRICSIZATION through an economic geopolitical model. *Journal of Open Innovation*, *11*(1), 100440. DOI: 10.1016/j.joitmc.2024.100440

Batista, P. N., Jr. (2023, November 13). *BRICS financial and monetary initiatives – NDB, CRA, and a possible new currency*. Grupo de Estudos sobre os BRICS (GEBRICS). https://sites.usp.br/gebrics/brics-financial-and-monetary-initiatives-ndb-cra-and-a-possible-new-currency-by-paulo-nogueira-batista-jr/

Bloomberg. (2025a, March 27). *Russia playing the long game to protect energy exports* [Video]. https://www.bloomberg.com/news/videos/2025-03-27/russia-playing-the-long-game-to-protect-energy-exports-video

Bloomberg. (2025b, April 16). *South African court ends $425 million rail pact in anti-graft push*. https://www.bloomberg.com/news/articles/2025-04-16/s-africa-court-ends-425-million-rail-pact-in-anti-graft-push

Bond, P. (2013). Sub-imperialism as lubricant of neoliberalism: South African "deputy sheriff" duty within BRICS. *Third World Quarterly*, *34*(2), 251–270. DOI: 10.1080/01436597.2013.775783

Bond, P., & Garcia, A. (2015). *BRICS: An anti-capitalist critique*. Pluto Press.

Business Today Egypt. (2024, June 11). *Egypt to obtain $1B loan from NDB by end of 2024 | FinMin*. Business Today Egypt. https://www.businesstodayegypt.com/Article/1/4708/Egypt-to-obtain-1B-loan-from-NDB-by-end-of

Cardin, A. (2025, May 9). *Brazil's inequality drop in 2024 stands out but still trails regional peers*. Rio Times Online. https://www.riotimesonline.com/brazils-inequality-drop-in-2024-stands-out-but-still-trails-regional-peers/

Cardoso, B. F., Shikida, P. F. A., & Finco, A. (2017). Development of Brazilian biodiesel sector from the perspective of stakeholders. *Energies, 10*(3), 399. DOI: 10.3390/en10030399

Chancel, L., Piketty, T., Saez, E., & Zucman, G. (2022). *World Inequality Report 2022*. World Inequality Lab. Retrieved April 7, 2025, from https://wir2022.wid.world

Chase-Dunn, C., & Hall, T. D. (1997). *Rise and demise: Comparing world-systems.* Westview Press.

Chin, G. T. (2014). The BRICS-led development bank: Purpose and politics beyond the G20. *Global Policy, 5*(3), 366–373.

Clark, N., & Liu, Z. Z. (2024, October 31). *Why expanded BRICS is backing a Russia-initiated grain exchange*. Council on Foreign Relations. https://www.cfr.org/blog/why-expanded-brics-backing-russia-initiated-grain-exchange

Cox, R. W. (1987). *Production, power, and world order: Social forces in the making of history*. Columbia University Press.

Degye, G., Abule, M., & Lamessa, T. (2024, August). *Policy Working Paper No. 25/2024*. Ethiopian Economics Association.

Dos Santos, T. (1970). The structure of dependence. *The American Economic Review, 60*(2), 231–236.

Energy Capital & Power. (2025, January 1). *Top 5 solar projects to watch in Algeria.* https://energycapitalpower.com/top-5-solar-projects-to-watch-in-algeria/

Escobar, A. (2011). *Encountering development: The making and unmaking of the Third World* (2nd ed.). Princeton University Press.

Fearnside, P. M. (2016). Environmental and social impacts of hydroelectric dams in Brazilian Amazonia: Implications for the aluminum industry. *World Development, 77*, 48–65. DOI: 10.1016/j.worlddev.2015.08.015

Fernandes, M. (2024, August 6). *BRICS and the IMF debt traps: What can the Contingent Reserve Arrangement do for the Global South?* Valdai Discussion Club. https://valdaiclub.com/a/highlights/brics-and-the-imf-debt-traps/

Gallagher, K. P. (2018). Reforming global economic governance as if development mattered. *Development and Change, 49*(6), 1605–1615.

Grabel, I. (2017). *When things don't fall apart: Global financial governance and developmental finance in an age of productive incoherence*. MIT Press.

Gramsci, A. (1971). *Selections from the prison notebooks of Antonio Gramsci* (Hoare, Q., & Smith, G. N., Eds. & Trans.). International Publishers.

Hochberg, M. (2020, October 20). *Algeria charts a path for renewable energy sector development.* Middle East Institute. https://www.mei.edu/publications/algeria-charts-path-renewable-energy-sector-development

Hofman, B., & Srinivas, P. S. (2024). New Development Bank's role in the global financial architecture. *Global Policy, 15*(2), 451–457.

Hopewell, K. (2013). New protagonists in global economic governance: Brazilian agribusiness at the WTO. *New Political Economy, 18*(4), 603–623.

Hopewell, K. (2017). The BRICS – Merely a fable? Emerging power alliances in global trade governance. *International Affairs, 93*(6), 1377–1396.

Hopewell, K. (2019). US-China conflict in global trade governance: The new politics of agricultural subsidies at the WTO. *Review of International Political Economy, 26*(2), 207–231.

Humphrey, C. (2020). *From drawing board to reality: The first four years of operations at the Asian Infrastructure Investment Bank and New Development Bank* (Working Paper). G-24 and Boston University Global Development Policy Center. https://www.g24.org/wp-content/uploads/2020/04/G-24-BU-GDP-Center-Paper-on-AIIB-and-NDB.pdf

Hurrell, A. (2018). Beyond the BRICS: Power, pluralism, and the future of global order. *Ethics & International Affairs, 32*(1), 89–101. DOI: 10.1017/S0892679418000126

International Energy Agency (IEA). (2023). *Ethiopia – Countries & Regions.* https://www.iea.org/countries/ethiopia

International Renewable Energy Agency (IRENA). (2023). *Planning and prospects for renewable power: North Africa.* https://www.irena.org/-/media/Files/IRENA/Agency/Publication/2023/Jan/IRENA_Planning_Prospects_NAfrica_2023.pdf

International Renewable Energy Agency (IRENA). (2023, September 4). *IRENA and AUDA-NEPAD join forces to advance regional interconnections in Africa.* https://www.irena.org/News/pressreleases/2023/Sep/IRENA-and-AUDA-NEPAD-Join-Forces-to-Advance-Regional-Interconnections-in-Africa

International Renewable Energy Agency (IRENA). (2024a). *Decentralised solar PV: A gender perspective.* https://www.irena.org/-/media/Files/IRENA/Agency/Publication/2024/Oct/IRENA_Decentralised_solar_PV_Gender_perspective_2024.pdf

Kahler, M. (2013). Rising powers and global governance: Negotiating change in a resilient status quo. *International Affairs*, *89*(3), 711–729.

Kentikelenis, A. E. (2017). Structural adjustment and health: A conceptual framework and evidence on pathways. *Social Science & Medicine*, *187*, 296–305. DOI: 10.1016/j.socscimed.2017.02.021 PMID: 28238540

Kentikelenis, A. E., Stubbs, T. H., & King, L. P. (2016). IMF conditionality and development policy space, 1985–2014. *Review of International Political Economy*, *23*(4), 543–582.

Lamarque, H., & Nugent, P. (2022). *Transport corridors in Africa: Synergy, slippage and sustainability*. Zed Books., DOI: 10.2307/j.ctv2x4kp3n

Lee, B. T. F., & Sims, J. P. (2024). Legitimacy through diversity: China's leadership in the BRICS+ expansion for global balance. *Fudan Journal of the Humanities and Social Sciences*. Advance online publication. DOI: 10.1007/s40647-024-00411-6

Liao, S., & McDowell, D. (2015). Redback rising: China's bilateral swap agreements and renminbi internationalization. *International Studies Quarterly*, *59*(3), 401–422.

Liu, Z., & Papa, M. (2022). Can BRICS de-dollarize the global financial system? Elements in the Economics of Emerging Markets. Cambridge University Press. https://doi.org/DOI: 10.1017/9781009029544

Lukyanov, F., Bhowmick, S., de Carvalho, G., Kugiel, P., Kudo, Y., & Niu, H. (2024, November 7). *The BRICS Summit 2024: An expanding alternative*. Council of Councils. https://www.cfr.org/councilofcouncils/global-memos/brics-summit-2024-expanding-alternative

Mercom India. (2025, March 24). *MENA weekly round-up: Algeria launches 3.2 GW solar projects*. https://mercomindia.com/mena-weekly-round-up-algeria-launches-3-2-gw-solar-projects

Milanovic, B. (2016). *Global inequality: A new approach for the age of globalization*. Harvard University Press., DOI: 10.2307/j.ctvjghwk4

Mittelman, J. H. (1996). Rethinking the "new regionalism" in the context of globalization. *Global Governance*, *2*(2), 189–213.

Mthembu, P. (2019). South Africa and BRICS in a multipolar world: Towards a diffusion of power and ideas? *Africa Insight*, *48*(4), 39–55. https://www.ajol.info/index.php/ai/article/view/186468

Narlikar, A. (2010). New powers in the club: The challenges of global trade governance. *International Affairs*, *86*(3), 717–728.

New Development Bank (NDB). (2022). *General strategy for 2022–2026.* https://www.ndb.int/wp-content/uploads/2022/07/NDB_StrategyDocument_eVersion_07.pdf

New Development Bank (NDB). (2023). *Annual report 2023: Investing in sustainable infrastructure.*

O'Neill, J. (2001). *Building Better Global Economic BRICs.* Goldman Sachs Global Economics Paper No: 66.

Overbeek, H. (2016). Will the BRICS transform the global economic order? In Changzheng, D., & Hongyu, W. (Eds.), *The Belt and Road Initiative and international society* (pp. 89–95). University of International Business and Economics Press.

Oxfam International. (2023). *Survival of the richest: How we must tax the super-rich now to fight inequality.* Retrieved April 5, 2025, from https://www.oxfam.org/en/research/survival-richest

Press Information Bureau (PIB). (2024, December 1). *UPI: Revolutionizing digital payments in India.* https://pib.gov.in/PressReleseDetailm.aspx?PRID=2079544&lang=1&reg=3

Press Information Bureau (PIB). (2025, March 24). *Advancing cashless India: Incentives for UPI small merchant transactions.* https://pib.gov.in/PressReleasePage.aspx?PRID=2114335

Ren, Y., Li, Z., Wang, Y., & Zhang, T. (2020). Development and prospect of food security cooperation in the BRICS countries. *Sustainability, 12*(5), 2125. DOI: 10.3390/su12052125

Reuters. (2024, August 31). BRICS New Development Bank authorizes Algeria to join. https://www.reuters.com/article/world/brics-new-development-bank-authorizes-algeria-to-join-idUSKBN3K006V/

Reuters. (2024a, October 24). *BRICS leaders tout joint finance, trade projects at Russian summit.* https://www.reuters.com/markets/commodities/russias-putin-outlines-brics-grain-exchange-proposal-2024-10-23/

Reuters. (2024b, June 13). *World Bank approves Nigeria's $2.25 billion loan request.* https://www.reuters.com/world/africa/world-bank-approves-nigerias-225-billion-loan-request-2024-06-13/

Reuters. (2025, May 6). *Nigeria approves $652 million China Exim Bank road finance package.* https://www.reuters.com/world/africa/nigeria-approves-652-million-china-exim-bank-road-finance-package-2025-05-06/

Reuters. (2025a, May 8). *IMF says Nigeria repays $3.4 billion COVID-19 funding.* https://www.reuters.com/world/africa/imf-says-nigeria-repays-34-billion-covid-19-funding-2025-05-08/

Roberts, C., Armijo, L. E., & Katada, S. N. (2017). *The BRICS and collective financial statecraft.* Oxford University Press.

Routh, A. (2024, August). *The role of nonbanks and fintechs in boosting India's UPI person-to-merchant transactions.* Payments System Research Briefing, Federal Reserve Bank of Kansas City, 1–6.

Sakai, P., Afionis, S., Favretto, N., Stringer, L. C., Ward, C., Sakai, M., Weirich Neto, P. H., Rocha, C. H., Alberti Gomes, J., de Souza, N. M., & Afzal, N. (2020). Understanding the implications of alternative bioenergy crops to support smallholder farmers in Brazil. *Sustainability, 12*(5), 2146. DOI: 10.3390/su12052146

Santos, B. de S. (2014). *Epistemologies of the South: Justice against epistemicide* (1st ed.). Routledge.

Shaw, T. M. (2015). African agency? Africa, South Africa and the BRICS. *International Politics, 52*(2), 255–268.

Soni, N. (2024, December 2). *Domestic UPI frauds: Finance Ministry presented data in LokSabha.* CyberPeace Foundation. https://www.cyberpeace.org/resources/blogs/domestic-upi-frauds-finance-ministry-presented-data-in-loksabha

Statista. (2024, May 2). Official renewable energy capacity target in Algeria 2030, by energy source. https://www.statista.com/statistics/1282572/official-renewable-energy-capacity-target-in-algeria-by-energy-source/

Statista. (2025, March 21). *BRICS and G7 countries' share of the world's total gross domestic product (GDP) in purchasing power parity (PPP) from 2000 to 2024.* Statista Research Department. https://www.statista.com/statistics/1412425/gdp-ppp-share-world-gdp-g7-brics/

Stephen, M. D. (2012). Rising regional powers and international institutions: The foreign policy orientations of India, Brazil and South Africa. *Global Society, 26*(3), 289–309.

Stiglitz, J. E. (2002). *Globalization and its discontents.* W. W. Norton & Company.

Stuenkel, O. (2015). *The BRICS and the Future of Global Order.* Polity Press.

Sulla, V., Zikhali, P., & Cuevas, P. F. (2022). *Inequality in Southern Africa: An assessment of the Southern African Customs Union.* World Bank Group. https://documents.worldbank.org/curated/en/099125303072236903

Swarajya Magazine. (2024, May 2). *India's income inequality eases in 2022–23, but wealth gap persists: Report*. https://swarajyamag.com/news-brief/indias-income-inequality-eases-in-2022-23-but-wealth-gap-persist-report

Takouleu, J. M. (2024, March 25). *Development of solar energy: A new turning point for Algeria*. Africa Energy Portal. https://africa-energy-portal.org/blogs/development-solar-energy-new-turning-point-algeria

The Jerusalem Post. (2025, March 21). *Egypt signs agreement for wind power project in Gulf of Suez*. https://www.jpost.com/business-and-innovation/article-846992

Times of India. (2024, June 30). *Inequality declined between 2011–12 & 2022–23: Government data*. https://timesofindia.indiatimes.com/india/inequality-declined-between-2011-12-2022-23-government-data/articleshow/110826780.cms

Tooze, A. (2021). *Shutdown: How Covid shook the world's economy*. Viking.

United Nations Conference on Trade and Development (UNCTAD). (2024). *Economic Development in Africa Report 2024: Unlocking Africa's Trade Potential – Boosting Regional Markets and Reducing Risks*. https://unctad.org/publication/economic-development-africa-report-2024

United Nations Economic Commission for Africa (UNECA). (2024, December 5). *Unlocking Africa's trade potential with cutting-edge data tools*. https://www.uneca.org/stories/unlocking-africa%27s-trade-potential-with-cutting-edge-data-tools

Vishwakarma, J. (2025, January 28). *UPI's share in India's digital payments jumps to 83%, RBI report says*. Indian Startup News. https://indianstartupnews.com/news/upi-share-in-indias-digital-payments-jumps-to-83-percent-rbi-report-says-8661582

Wallerstein, I. (2004). *World-systems analysis: An introduction*. Duke University Press.

World Bank. International Energy Agency (IEA), International Renewable Energy Agency (IRENA), United Nations Statistics Division (UNSD), & World Health Organization (WHO). (2024). *Tracking SDG 7: The energy progress report 2024* (English). World Bank Group. https://documents.worldbank.org/curated/en/099031225175211404

World Bank. (2025). *World Development Indicators*. Retrieved April 6, 2025, from https://databank.worldbank.org/source/world-development-indicators

Xin, G., Khan, H., & Ling, X. (2024). The impact of BRICS trade facilitation on China's import and export trade in agricultural products. *Frontiers in Sustainable Food Systems*, *8*, 1397350. DOI: 10.3389/fsufs.2024.1397350

Yang, X. A. (2019). Theorizing the BRICS. In Xing, L. (Ed.), *The international political economy of the BRICS* (pp. 37–56). Routledge.

Ye, F. (2023). The New Development Bank and the structure of the multilateral development financial system. *Review of Development Economics*, *27*(3), 1957–1972. DOI: 10.1111/rode.12995

KEY TERMS AND DEFINITIONS

BRICS+: An expanded geopolitical and economic grouping that builds upon the original BRICS (Brazil, Russia, India, China, South Africa) by incorporating additional emerging economies. BRICS+ aims to promote a multipolar world order through South-South cooperation, alternative development financing, and non-Western institutional frameworks.

Contingent Reserve Arrangement (CRA): A financial safety net created by BRICS to provide liquidity support during balance-of-payments crises. While intended as an alternative to the IMF, its operational link to IMF programs limits its autonomy.

Core-Periphery Structure: A concept from world-systems theory that categorizes countries into "core" (dominant), "semi-periphery" (intermediate), and "periphery" (dependent). BRICS+ seeks to shift peripheral and semi-peripheral countries toward greater economic agency and structural autonomy.

De-dollarization: The strategic reduction of reliance on the US dollar in international trade and finance. BRICS+ initiatives promoting trade in local currencies and the creation of the BRICS Grain Exchange aim to foster monetary sovereignty among emerging economies.

Developmental Sovereignty: The capacity of states to pursue independent development paths without external imposition. BRICS+ institutions like the NDB claim to uphold this principle by avoiding policy conditionalities.

Elite Capture: The process by which political or economic elites manipulate public institutions and resources for their own benefit. This remains a challenge within BRICS+ projects, where uneven benefit distribution can contradict inclusive development goals.

Institutional Innovation: The creation of new rules, mechanisms, or organizations that challenge existing global governance norms. BRICS+ exemplifies this through initiatives like the NDB, CRA, and efforts to create alternative trade platforms.

Multipolarity: A global order characterized by the diffusion of power among several influential states or blocs, as opposed to unipolar or bipolar dominance. BRICS+ advocates for institutional multipolarity through parallel governance mechanisms.

New Development Bank (NDB): A multilateral development bank established by BRICS countries in 2014 to finance infrastructure and sustainable development projects. Unlike traditional lenders, the NDB emphasizes respect for national sovereignty and minimal conditionalities.

South-South Cooperation: A form of international collaboration among countries of the Global South to share knowledge, technology, and development strategies. Within BRICS+, this concept is key to promoting alternative pathways to development beyond Western-led models.

Chapter 7
Demographic Factors Affecting Financial Risk Tolerance of Investors in Türkiye in Times of COVID-19 Pandemic

Lokman Dal
https://orcid.org/0000-0002-8932-8744
Independent Researcher, Turkey

Nuray Girginer
https://orcid.org/0000-0003-1228-5800
Eskisehir Osmangazi University, Turkey

ABSTRACT

This study examines the Financial Risk Tolerance (FRT) of domestic individual investors who invested in Borsa Istanbul (BIST) shares in Türkiye during the Covid-19 Pandemic in terms of their demographics. Data was collected from 761 individual investors via an online survey. The Financial Risk Tolerance Scale developed by Grable & Lytton (1999) was used to measure investors' FRT. Independent Sample t-Tests and One-Way ANOVA Tests were used for analyzing the data. A significant relationship was determined in terms of Risk Comfort and Experience component in individuals under and over the age of 40. No significant difference was found in terms of marital status, number of children, educational status and household income variables. FRTs of individuals who invested for less than 1 year differed

DOI: 10.4018/979-8-3373-1529-4.ch007

from the other investment periods. The research findings are expected to attract the attention of financial decision makers/experts, portfolio managers, financial institutions, policy makers and researchers.

INTRODUCTION

Investor behavior has a dynamic feature that is affected by small and large-scale facts and events that occur at different times. The specific or general situations that individuals experience can affect their desire and appetite to invest depending on the magnitude of the event and the degree of importance it holds for them. Sometimes individual or family-related facts and events, and sometimes events that concern the country or the world, can be decisive in investment decisions. Crises experienced in the world are at the forefront of events that affect individuals' investment behavior. Many crises of different sizes that have occurred in history have been characterized as systemic and non-systemic crises according to their areas of impact. Non-systemic crises are crises that only cause various negative effects (economic, political, strategic, social, etc.) on a specific sector/sectors and country/countries. Accordingly, events such as the Ebolavirus Outbreak, the 1999 Marmara Earthquake, etc. that occurred in the recent past can be given as examples of non-systemic crises. Systemic crises, on the other hand, have an impact on all sectors and/or countries and the damage they leave is much greater than non-systemic crises. World War II and the Asian Crisis can be given as examples of systemic crises. One of these systemic crises is the Covid-19 Pandemic, which has recently affected the entire world.

There are numerous empirical findings regarding the damages inflicted on national economies and global markets by the Covid-19 outbreak, the fourth global pandemic in the last century, at both the micro and macro levels. However, despite the fact that the Pandemic is one of the largest systemic shocks in world history in the last century, the impact of this systemic shock, especially on financial markets and investors, is among the subjects that have not been studied sufficiently in terms of quantity and quality. The Covid-19 Pandemic is a good representative case study for examining systemic shocks. Many national and global events in history, such as the Covid-19 Pandemic, have shown that individuals may change their behavior when they are under uncertainty and risk (Eichengreen et al., 2001; Cristian, 2012; Bashir et al., 2013; Hoffmann et al., 2013; Guillemette & Finke, 2014; Schooley & Worden, 2016; Necker & Ziegelmeyer, 2016; Chiang & Xiao, 2017).

The financial risk tolerance and financial preferences of individual investors, who are the building blocks of the global financial system, affect their savings, consumption and investment decisions. Financial Risk Tolerance is a concept related to the level of financial risk readiness of individuals. While some individuals take higher levels of risk in their financial decisions, others can accept lower levels of risk. Some individuals may tend to ignore the risk and remain indifferent. Financial Risk Tolerance, which is based on the explanation of this reactional difference in individuals, is among the important research topics of behavioral finance. Grable (2000) defines Financial Risk Tolerance as *"the maximum amount of uncertainty that someone is willing to accept when making a financial decision, reaches into almost every part of economic and social life"* (p. 625). Economic preferences that can change suddenly in crisis environments can affect individuals' financial risk tolerances in a chain reaction and can damage national or global economies. For example, the risk aversion that occurs in individuals after a global crisis may lead them to consume less and avoid risky investments; the resulting falling asset prices may exacerbate the economic downturn and slow down the recovery (Angrisani et al., 2020). Kohút et al. (2022) state that it is a known fact that demographic characteristics and personality traits are decisive in predicting happiness, but the roles of these factors may weaken under the adverse conditions created by the Covid-19 Pandemic and more situational factors may be on the agenda. It is evaluated that determining the demographic factors that cause changes in individuals' risk taking can provide financial decision makers with an idea about whether these factors will affect long-term economic growth and whether short- or long-term structural policies are needed in this context.

Developing countries have an important place among the actors that demand resources from international financial markets. Despite their fragile economic structures, developing countries are increasingly included in investment portfolios due to their above-average growth rates and the significant return opportunities they offer to developed country investors. In this context, it is important for policy makers who want to increase the depth of the country's capital markets to analyze how investor behavior differs (especially in the period of exposure to systemic risk).

It is known that there are many factors underlying the differences in individuals' approaches to risk. These factors can be listed as the individual's demographics, psychological states and personality traits. However, it has been observed that national and global events that may cause risk tolerance to differ over time also affect risk attitudes. Before the Covid-19 Pandemic, individuals' financial risk tolerances were investigated in the context of these variables, and the current situations of individuals in different sample groups in the normal period were revealed. In previous studies investigating the relationship between individuals' demographics and financial risk tolerance, it has been found that men are mostly more tolerant than women (Bajtelsmit & Bernasek, 1996; Grable, 2000; Faff, 2008; Sulaiman, 2012; Dawson & Henley, 2015; Shusha, 2017; Thanki & Baser, 2019), single individuals are mostly more tolerant than married individuals (Lee & Hanna, 1991; Guiso et al., 1996; Grable et al., 1998; Gutter et al., 1999; Joo & Grable, 2004, Anbar &

Eker, 2010; Dohmen et al., 2011), younger individuals are more tolerant than older individuals (Xiao et al., 2000; Hallahan et al., 2003; Yao et al., 2004; Levin et al., 2007; Weller et al., 2011; Paulsen et al., 2012; Bonsang & Dohmen, 2015), individuals with fewer children are more tolerant than those with many children (Riley & Russon, 1995; Jianakoplos & Bernasek, 1998; Chaulk et al., 2003; Van de Venter, 2006; Faff, 2008). Similarly, there is evidence that individuals with higher levels of education are more tolerant than those with lower levels of education (Riley & Chow, 1992; Hawley & Fujii, 1993; Grable & Lytton, 1999b; Sung & Hanna, 1996; Fan & Xiao, 2006; Van de Venter, 2006; Sulaiman, 2012; Reddy & Mahapatra, 2017), individuals with higher household incomes are more tolerant than those with lower incomes (Yook & Everett, 2003; Chang et al., 2004; Watson & McNaughton, 2007; Weber et al., 2013; Farrell, 2014; Ansari & Phatak, 2016; Sutejo et al., 2018), and professional/self-employed individuals are more tolerant than other individuals (Grable, 2000; Sulaiman, 2012).

It is a matter of curiosity whether the demographic factors that affected investors' financial risk tolerance before the Covid-19 Pandemic and summarized in the previous paragraph have changed during the Covid-19 period. When the studies conducted during and after the Covid-19 period are examined (Fan et al., 2020; Guenther et al., 2021; Volk et al., 2021; Heo et al., 2021; Heo et al., 2021a; Ullah et al., 2021; Kohút et al., 2022; Omanovic & Zaimovic, 2024; Battaglia et al., 2025; Tingley; 2025), it is seen that the studies were mostly conducted on the financial risk tolerances of individuals in developed countries. Although there were many studies on the financial risk tolerance of individuals before the Covid-19 Pandemic, it is seen that there are very limited number of studies investigating the demographic factors affecting the financial risk tolerance of individuals in the developing countries category during the Covid-19 Pandemic.

The purpose of this study is to determine the demographic factors affecting the financial risk tolerance of investors in developing countries where economic vulnerability is high and recovery and rehabilitation are late or difficult in the face of systemic shocks such as the Covid-19 Pandemic. Therefore, this research aims to determine the factors affecting the financial risk tolerance of individual portfolio investors and to analyze how these factors differ in periods when markets are exposed to systemic shocks.

Analyzing investor behavior in the face of systemic shocks is important in order to respond proactively to changing investor needs in similar systemic shocks that may occur in the future (Dal, 2023). At the same time, determining the underlying reasons for investors' risk-averse behavior during the Pandemic and encouraging them to reinvest by offering them alternative investment options in the context of these factors also has important and unique contributions in terms of making the economic recovery more sustainable and remaining more resilient to future shocks.

LITERATURE REVIEW

Since the beginning of the Covid-19 Pandemic, there have been very limited studies on financial risk tolerances in the context of investors' demographics. The studies conducted in the literature and the results found are summarized as follows:

Fan et al. (2020) determined that women were less tolerant to risk than men during the Pandemic period, in line with the data obtained before the Pandemic period. Bu et al. (2020) conducted a panel data analysis on risk behavior before and after the outbreak of the Coronavirus Pandemic in Wuhan, China, which was ground zero of the pandemic. They examined the exposure to the pandemic that subjects would experience in different cities and provinces of China to magnify the effect of the pandemic on their risk-taking vulnerability. As a result of the study, they determined that the subjects' wealth allocation to hypothetical risky investments decreased monotonically according to their degree of exposure to the pandemic. At the same time, they determined that the subjects shifted to significantly lower overall risk preferences regardless of their degree of exposure to the pandemic. They noted that higher levels of exposure to the pandemic led to a decrease in subjects' belief in their own luck and sense of control, and that this led to more pessimistic thoughts about economic and social issues. They found that short-term changes in individuals' risk-taking may be due to changes in beliefs and optimism rather than general risk preferences. Guenther et al (2021) found that, consistent with the pre-Covid-19 era, risk tolerance was higher in men than women during the UK lockdown and decreased with age. Heo et al. (2021) conducted research on the change in individuals' financial risk tolerance in parallel with the increase in the first Covid-19 cases in the USA. In this context, they collected data from a large investor and consumer base in the period April 2019-May 2020. They divided the period in question into 5 separate sub-periods and examined the changes in financial risk tolerance in each period. As a result of the research, they determined a general decrease in individuals' financial risk tolerance during the first peak of Covid-19 and with the declaration of the Pandemic. They concluded that Covid-19 caused the greatest decrease in financial risk tolerance in individuals aged 25 and under, and that it disproportionately affected young people in the research sample. Volk et al. (2021) conducted research on how demographics and personality may interact with the Pandemic in coping with Covid-19. In this context, they collected data from 516 North American youth. As a result of the research, they determined that personality has an indirect mediating role between income, age, gender, and having children variables and Covid-19 coping behaviors. Heo et al. (2021a) state that the role of demographics and behavioral factors in understanding financial risk tolerance is inconsistent in times of social and economic crises. Accordingly, their research results showed that the education variable was significant for financial decision makers before the Covid-19 Pandemic, but it was not significant after the Covid-19 Pandemic. Ullah et al. (2021) compared the pre- and post-Pandemic financial risk tolerance of 18.913 Financial Decision Makers from Pakistan between April 1, 2019 and July 31, 2020. They divided the sample participating in the study into 4 clusters during the said time period. As a result of the research, they concluded that there were two different clusters in terms of financial risk-taking behaviors. They determined that the first of these clusters consists of individuals with low risk tolerance, mostly women, low household income and very little capital investment. They concluded that the other cluster consists of individuals with more financial knowledge and a high propensity to take financial risks, mostly married men. They also determined that there was a downward movement in financial risk tolerance after the declaration of the Covid-19 Pandemic. Kohút et al. (2022) investigated the relationship between demographics, personality traits and some other variables of individuals and their past, present and future life satisfaction during the Covid-19 Pandemic. For this purpose, they collected data from 1020 Slovak adults at the beginning of the second wave of the Pandemic in Slovakia and in early November 2020, when strict quarantine measures were implemented. In the survey form they used, they asked the participants about their demographic characteristics such as their age, gender, education level, relationship status and religious affiliation. As a result of the research, they determined that being in a relationship, regardless of marriage status, had a positive effect on life satisfaction during the Covid-19 Pandemic. Rahman et al. (2023) investigated the impact of career experience of CEOs of public companies during the Covid-19 period on their investment behavior and risk tolerance, and examined the ability of CEOs to allocate financial assets and maintain solvency. As a result of the research, they determined a significant positive relationship between the career experiences of CEOs during the Covid-19 period and their capacity to allocate financial assets effectively. On the other hand, they concluded that Covid-19 had negative effects in terms of company solvency. Hochman et al. (2024) investigated the impact of the Covid-19 pandemic on risk-seeking behavior. They collected data from 1643 participants via an online survey at seven time points before the pandemic, four time points with restrictions, and two time points without restrictions during the pandemic. As a result of the research, they determined that there was a significant decrease in financial risk taking during the pandemic, the most significant decrease occurred in the first wave, and after the restrictions were lifted, risk tolerance gradually started to increase but did not reach the level before the pandemic. In their research, they concluded that emotional and subjective factors had an effect on risk tolerance. Mineyama & Tokuoka (2024) investigated financial risk tolerance in Covid-19 exposure in the context of age and gender variables. In their research using a survey on households in Japan, they determined that individuals with a high risk of contracting Covid-19 had higher risk tolerance. On the other hand, they found that Covid-19 vaccines compensate for the increase in risk tolerance due to the risk of death for individuals with high mortality rates. Sameera & S (2024) investigated how the Covid-19 Pandemic has changed the confidence and choice-making processes of investors in Telangana, India. In their study, which investigated demographic variables such as age, income brackets and employment type, they determined that investor confidence decreased significantly with the first outbreak of the pandemic, especially among young investors and those operating in the private sector, and that increased market volatility and economic uncertainty caused investors to turn to more cautious and risk-averse methods. They also argued that there were signs of significant changes in asset movement during the pandemic period, as investors valued liquidity and security over high-risk investments. The research results showed that despite a limited increase in investor confidence following the Covid-19 Pandemic, investors generally remained cautious against risk. Lal et al. (2024) conducted a study to analyze the role of hyperbolic discounting in causing panic selling behavior of investors during the Covid-19 financial crisis. They collected data from 121,293 active investors provided by the collaboration between Hiroshima University and Rakuten Securities Inc. Using mean comparison tests and probit regression method, they concluded that hyperbolic discounting plays a central role in triggering investors' panic selling behavior. They determined that panic selling behavior is affected by age, male gender, low education level, financial literacy, household income, household assets, risk aversion and overconfidence in financial information. Omanovic & Zaimovic (2024) examined the factors affecting financial risk tolerance and portfolio allocation among highly educated working-age adults (aged 18-64) in Bosnia and Herzegovina, and investigated how the Covid-19 Pandemic and the Russian invasion of Ukraine affected these financial decisions. They used purposive and snowball sampling techniques in their research, and collected data through Computer-Assisted Web Interviewing (CAWI). They collected data from a total of 507 people between May 1 and July 7, 2022. They used multinomial logistic regression in their research, which includes subjective and objective measures of risk tolerance. Considering various sociodemographic and psychological risk-taking factors, they concluded that risk attitudes, together with investment knowledge and experience, are the primary determinants of financial risk tolerance, while sociodemographic variables have minimal effects. They also concluded that the recent financial turmoil resulting from the Covid-19 Pandemic and the Russian invasion of Ukraine significantly affected individuals' subjective risk tolerance, while having no impact on objective risk tolerance. Battaglia et al. (2025) investigated whether there was a decrease in the financial risk tolerance (FRT) of individuals in Italy, the first Western country affected by the Covid-19 outbreak. In this context, they collected data from 2,167 people through an online survey between April 1 and May 30, 2020. In the study, they used three separate regression models, considering the mortality rate, infection and frequency rates. As a result of the research, they concluded that, in line with previous studies, older individuals have a decrease in financial risk tolerance, male individuals are more prone to risk, and married individuals are less tolerant of risk. They also found that education level had a slightly negative effect on investment risk, one of the components of financial risk tolerance, while occupational instability, low income, and stock market inexperience were associated with lower risk tolerance. They concluded that the Covid-19 Pandemic made individuals more risk averse. Tingley (2025) examined the impact of gender and marital status on financial risk tolerance along with generational differences before and during the Russia-China Crisis and the Covid-19 Pandemic. For this purpose, they used FinaMetrica investor data from 2012 to 2020 and created four generations (Silent Generation, Baby Boomers, Generation X, Generation Y) from a total of 47,466 financial risk tolerance surveys. In his analyses using linear regression analysis, he concluded that, in summary, single investors from four different generations reacted negatively during the Covid-19 Pandemic, but the Russia-China Crisis had a positive impact, while investors from the Silent Generation and Baby Boomers reduced their financial risk tolerance during the Covid-19 Pandemic, but there was no significant change in their financial risk tolerance during the Russia-China Crisis. On the other hand, it was determined that female investors within the Y generation reacted negatively to the Russia-China Crisis, but the Covid-19 outbreak did not have a significant impact.

It has been determined that recovery and economic rehabilitation after the Covid-19 Pandemic are more difficult and that there are very limited studies investigating the financial risk tolerance of individuals in developing country economies in terms of demographics. However, the studies in the literature on the relationship between demographic factors and financial risk tolerance in the period before the Covid-19 Pandemic and the results found are summarized in Table 1.

Table 1. Studies in the Literature on the Relationship Between Demographic Factors and Financial Risk Tolerance

Literature	Demographic Factors		Financial Risk Tolerance	
			High	Low
Bajtelsmit & Bernasek (1996) Embrey & Fox (1997) Grable (2000) Hariharan et al. (2000) Olsen & Cox (2001) Yao et al. (2004) Fehr-Duda et al. (2006) Faff (2008) Anbar ve Eker (2010) Ryack (2011) Sulaiman (2012) Weber et al. (2013) Thanki (2015) Dawson & Henly (2015) Ansari & Phatak (2016) Shusha (2017) Thanki & Baser (2019)	Gender	Male	X	
		Female		X
Baker & Haslem (1974) Lee & Hanna (1991) Lazzarone (1996) Sung & Hanna (1996) Guiso et al. (1996) Grable et al. (1998) Gutter et al. (1999) Hartog et al. (2002) Joo & Grable (2004) Hallahan et al. (2004) Yao et al. (2004) Anbar & Eker (2010) Dohmen et al. (2011) Sulaiman (2012) Thanki (2015) Thanki & Baser (2019)	Marital Status	Single	X	
		Married		X
Grable (2000) Hallahan et al. (2003) Van de Venter (2006) Watson & McNaughton (2007)		Single		X
		Married	X	
Riley & Russon (1995) Jianakoplos & Bernasek (1998) Chaulk et al. (2003) Van de Venter (2006) Faff (2008)	Number of Children	Few	X	
		Many		X

continued on following page

Table 1. Continued

Literature	Demographic Factors		Financial Risk Tolerance	
			High	Low
Grable (2000) Xiao et al. (2000) Hallahan et al. (2003) Chaulk et al. (2003) Yao et al. (2004) Levin et al. (2007) Faff et al. (2009) Anbar & Eker (2010) Weller et al. (2011) Paulsen et al. (2012) Sulaiman (2012) Bonsang & Dohmen (2015) Thanki & Baser (2019)	Age	Younger	X	
		Older		X
Wang & Hanna (1997) Hallahan et al. (2004) Grable et al. (2006) Van de Venter et al. (2012) Gibson et al. (2013)		Younger		X
		Older	X	
Riley & Chow (1992) Hawley & Fujii (1993) Sung & Hanna (1996) Grable & Lytton (1999) Grable & Joo (1999) Grable & Lytton (1999a) Grable (2000) Chang et al. (2004) Hallahan et al. (2004) Yao et al. (2004) Fan & Xiao (2006) Van de Venter (2006) Christiansen et al. (2006) Al-Ajmi (2008) Dohmen et al. (2011) Sulaiman (2012) Shusha (2017) Reddy & Mahapatra (2017)	Educational Status	Higher	X	
		Lower		X
Grable (2000) Sulaiman (2012)	Occupation	Professional Employee	X	
		Unprofessional Employee		X
Sulaiman (2012)		Self Employed	X	
		Employed in Someone Else's Business		X

continued on following page

Table 1. Continued

Literature	Demographic Factors		Financial Risk Tolerance	
			High	Low
Riley & Chow (1992) Sung & Hanna (1996) Grable et al. (1998) Grable (2000) Yook & Everett (2003) Chaulk et al. (2003) Grable et al. (2004) Chang et al. (2004) Hallahan et al. (2004) Fan & Xiao (2006) Watson & McNaughton (2007) Anbar & Eker (2010) Sulaiman (2012) Weber et al. (2013) Farrell (2014) Thanki (2015) Ansari & Phatak (2016) Sutejo et al. (2018)	Household Income	Higher	X	
		Lower		X

(Source: Original)

Gaps in the Literature

It is known that developed economies have recovered more quickly and sustainably from global shocks such as the Covid-19 Pandemic compared to other categories of countries. However, since the fragility of developing or underdeveloped economies such as Türkiye is high, achieving economic rehabilitation can take a long time. It is possible to stop the stock market abandonment that started with the crisis, to transfer savings back to the stock market, and to make the stock market attractive to investors again. In such economic crises, it is important to gain information and experience about the demographics of investors that affect their financial risk tolerance.

Individuals' financial preferences and risk tolerances can be affected over time by personality, demographics, social and economic conditions. Before the Covid-19 Pandemic, individuals' financial risk tolerances were investigated in the context of the variables in question, and the current situations of individuals in different sample groups in the normal period were revealed. It is observed that there are limited number of studies investigating the demographic factors affecting the financial risk tolerances of individuals in developing country economies during the Covid-19 Pandemic period, where recovery and economic rehabilitation after the Pandemic are more difficult.

This study was conducted to determine the demographic factors affecting the financial risk tolerance of stock investors in global shocks such as the Covid-19 Pandemic and to provide a forecast of the financial risk tolerance of stock market investors in countries with high economic fragility and where recovery may take time in the event of a possible future shock.

CONCEPTUAL FRAMEWORK AND THEORETICAL FOUNDATION

Financial Risk Tolerance is based on Prospect Theory. Prospect Theory tries to explain the issues that Expected Utility Theory is inconsistent in explaining and inadequate in describing, together with the reasons; it rejects the assumptions that individuals act rationally in their investment decisions and try to maximize their wealth by providing evidence (Kahneman & Tversky, 1979). It does not characterize the behavior of individuals; it describes and predicts it (Thaler, 1985). It argues that individuals tend to take risks when certain losses are expected and to accept a certain gain when absolute gains are expected (Statman, 1995). However, it is based on a simple assumption that the sadness experienced by a unit of loss is greater than the happiness of a unit of gain.

Financial risk is the possibility of losing movable and immovable properties that have material and moral value for individuals or institutions, regardless of the concept of time (Dal, 2023). The continuity of such a risk has led to individuals and institutions having different levels of risk definition, risk perception and risk tolerance. These differences have been a subject of curiosity for many scientists and researchers throughout history.

Financial Risk Tolerance, examined in the context of investor behavior, is the desire of an individual to make a decision without knowing the consequences, to engage in a potentially costly financial behavior (Semenov & Kuznetcov, 2015). It is defined as the amount of risk believed and accepted and the attitude towards risk (Hamurcu & Hamurcu, 2016). Financial Risk Tolerance (FRT) refers to the willingness of retail investors to accept adverse changes in investment value or an outcome that is negatively different from what was expected (Kannadhasan et al., 2016). It is the investor's readiness to take risks to achieve the investment objective (Rai et al., 2021).

Risk tolerance, which is an individual's attitude toward accepting risk, is an important concept that has implications for both financial service providers and consumers. For consumers, risk tolerance is a factor that can determine the appropriate mix of assets in a portfolio that is optimal in terms of risk and return according to the individual's needs (Hallahan et al., 2004). It has a great impact on an individual's future wealth because it is directly related to their portfolio selection decision (Ricciardi & Rice, 2014).

According to Gondaliya & Dhinaiya (2016), the maximum amount of uncertainty an investor can take when investing is called the risk tolerance level of that investor and successful investment decisions are made by those who have a comprehensive understanding of financial risk tolerance.

Risk tolerance is important because it affects the portfolio decisions that households make to achieve their long-term economic goals. Risk tolerance based on rational and conscious assessment can pave the way for the formation of appropriate portfolios and returns. Otherwise, serious financial problems may be inevitable (Yao & Hanna, 2005). For example, having a high financial risk tolerance for short-term investments may disrupt the household's goals.

It is critical to be aware of clients' circumstances and preferences, including investment objectives and financial risk tolerance levels. Financial advisors are required to be aware of these circumstances and preferences when providing appropriate investment advice to their investors (Van de Venter et al., 2012). Understanding financial risk tolerance behavior in the context of developing countries is vital for policy formulation and implementation towards the development of financial markets (Heenkenda, 2015).

Investigating whether risk tolerance levels differ for each type of employee is important in order to implement actions that attract the more risk tolerant sector to participate in the capital market. The logic behind this is that a country needs more risk tolerant people to stimulate the economy towards higher economic growth (Heenkenda, 2015).

METHODOLOGY

Instruments

In this study, 7 questions were asked to determine the demographic characteristics of stock investors in parallel with the purpose and conceptual framework of the research.

Questions asked in terms of demographic characteristics are listed below:

- Gender,
- Marital status,
- Number of children,
- Age,
- Educational status,

- Household income,
- Investment period.

The Financial Risk Tolerance Scale developed by Grable & Lytton (1999) was used to measure investors' financial risk tolerance. The Financial Risk Tolerance Scale consists of a total of 13 questions aimed at measuring 3 different factors. Of these 13 questions;

- 5 questions are aimed at determining the Risk Comfort and Experience factor,
- 5 questions are aimed at determining the Investment Risk factor,
- 3 questions are aimed at determining the Speculative Risk factor.

The scores obtained from the responses given by the investors to determine their financial risk tolerance were calculated by adding them. Each investor's financial risk tolerance score was evaluated according to the risk components and reference score ranges recorded by Grable & Lytton (1999). The minimum score that can be obtained from the responses given to the questions in the Financial Risk Tolerance performance is 13 and the maximum score can be 47.

From the scores obtained;

- 18 or less are rated as Low Risk Tolerance (Risk Group-1),
- 19-22 points are rated as Below Average Risk Tolerance (Risk Group-2),
- 23-28 points are rated as Average/Moderate Risk Tolerance (Risk Group-3),
- 29-32 points are rated as Above Average Risk Tolerance (Risk Group-4),
- 33 or more are rated as High Risk Tolerance (Risk Group-5).

Validity and Reliability

The original Financial Risk Tolerance Scale used in this study had a Cronbach's Alpha coefficient of 0.750 (Grable & Lytton, 1999b). Apart from the aforementioned scale, there is also a single-question Survey of Consumer Finance (SCF) in the literature to measure investors' Financial Risk Tolerance. The reason for using the scale developed by Grable & Lytton (1999) in this study is that it consists of general questions that can be answered even by people with no prior financial knowledge (Wasiuzzaman & Edalat, 2015), has a higher explanatory power than the Survey of Consumer Finance (SCF) (Grable & Lytton, 2001; Gilliam et al., 2010), and is widely accepted and used in Turkish and foreign literature (Grable et al., 2004; Orçun, 2015; Kübilay, 2015; Wasiuzzaman & Edalat, 2016; Pyles et al., 2016; Hüner, 2016; Marinelli et al., 2017; Thanki & Baser, 2019; Deger, 2019, Lawrenson, 2020; Öztop & Kuyu, 2020; Yao & Rabbani, 2021). Hanna & Chen

(1997) argued that the Survey of Consumer Finances (SCF) does not reflect pure risk preferences, Hanna, Gutter & Fan (2001) argued that the single-item SCF question is not related to the concept of risk tolerance in economic theory and Grable & Lytton (2001) warned researchers and practitioners to use the SCF with caution. Financial Risk Tolerance Scale was adapted to Turkish in line with the purpose of the research and the questions in the scale content were revised by taking expert opinion. Cronbach's Alpha coefficient of the scale adapted to Turkish in line with the purpose of the research was calculated as 0,569.

Sampling, Data Collection and Sample Characteristics

The data underlying the research was collected in March 2022. Central Registry Agency-Data Analysis Platform[2] statistics were used to determine the population. As of the date in question, it was determined that the number of domestic individual investors in Borsa Istanbul (BIST) shares was 2,338,598 people (https://www.vap.org.tr, Access Date: 30.09.2022). It has been observed that there are different approaches in the literature regarding the determination of the appropriate sample size. Stevens (1996) states that there should be 15 participants for each variable in the study. In the table developed by Yazıcıoğlu & Erdoğan (2004), it is stated that in order to provide an estimate for a population of over 1,000,000 people with a 95% confidence level and 5% sampling error, data should be collected from at least 384 people. Tabachnick & Fidell (2007) argue that in addition to 8 participants for each variable, there should be 50 more people. In order to increase the reliability of the research and to eliminate the risks that may arise from the differences in the approach in question, the sample size was determined as 750 people, and as a result, data was collected from 761 individual investors. The research was conducted with a 95% confidence level.

There are two main methods for measuring risk tolerance (Hanna, Gutter & Fan, 2001). These are:

- Assessing risky behavior and
- Asking questions about risk tolerance using a survey technique.

In this study, online survey method was preferred due to limitations such as accessibility to sources, money, time etc. in data collection. An online survey form was created via Google Forms application. After the form was created, the survey link was shared via social media channels. Since Türkiye was chosen as an example for data collection, support was received from individuals with a large follower base, especially on social media (X (Formerly Twitter), Facebook, WhatsApp) and stock investors (Borsa Istanbul-BIST), in line with the principle of "representativeness". In this context, the survey link was shared online via social media with people with a large number of followers to collect data. The "Simple Random Sampling" method was used to collect data.

Participants were presented with an information text before filling out the survey. In the text, participants were informed that the survey was for stock investors (Borsa Istanbul-BIST) and were asked to end the survey without answering if they were not BIST investors.

The research covers the demographic factors affecting the financial risk tolerances of domestic individual portfolio investors investing in Borsa Istanbul (BIST) shares in Türkiye, which is a developing country, during the Covid-19 Pandemic period. Foreign individual portfolio investors and institutional investors were excluded from the scope due to limitations such as access to sources, money, time, etc. in data collection. Due to the same limitations, other micro/macro-economic conditions and variables that may affect investors' financial risk tolerances in the relevant period were excluded from the scope.

It is assumed that all individuals from whom data was collected within the scope of the research are Borsa Istanbul (BIST) stock investors, that they participated in the survey of their own free will, that they understood the questions/statements addressed to them in the survey and gave realistic, accurate and sincere answers, and that they represent the population.

Demographics of the Sample

The frequency distribution of demographic characteristics of the participants is shown in Table 2.

Table 2. Frequency Table of Demographic Characteristics

		Frequency	Percentage (%)
Gender	Male	679	89,2
	Female	82	10,8
Marital Status	Married	547	71,9
	Single	214	28,1
Number of Children	No Children	275	36,1
	1	197	25,9
	2	243	31,9
	3 or More	46	6,0

continued on following page

Table 2. Continued

		Frequency	Percentage (%)
Age	25 or Less	41	5,4
	25–40	371	48,8
	40–55	290	38,1
	55 or More	59	7,8
Educational Status	Primary Education	7	,9
	High School	66	8,7
	Associate Degree/College	55	7,2
	Bachelor's Degree	441	58,0
	Postgraduate	192	25,2
Household Income[3]	5.000 TL[4] or Less	53	7,0
	5.000 TL–10.000 TL	213	28,0
	10.000 TL–15.000 TL	214	28,1
	15.000 TL–20.000 TL	126	16,6
	20.000 TL–25.000 TL	57	7,5
	25.000 TL or More	98	12,9
Investment Periods	1 Year or Less	64	8,4
	1 Year –3 Years	295	38,8
	3 Years–5 Years	115	15,1
	5 Years or More	287	37,7

n=761

When Table 2 is examined;

In terms of gender variable, it is understood that 679 of the 761 individuals participating in the research were male, which constitutes 89.2% of the sample. This situation confirms the fact that female investors are less tolerant than male investors, in parallel with other studies in the literature. In terms of the marital status variable, it is noteworthy that 547 of the 761 individuals participating in the study were married, making up 71.9% of the sample. In summary, it is possible to say that the vast majority of individuals investing in shares are married men.

It is observed that 63.8% of the investors participating in the research have at least 1 child, 86.9% are between the ages of 25-55, which is considered as "adults", 83.2% are at least a university graduate, and 56.1% have a household income between 5,000 TL and 15,000 TL during the period when the research was conducted.

In terms of investment period, it is understood that 91.6% of individuals have been investing for at least 1 year.

It is evaluated that the demographic findings reported in Table 2 can provide perspective to researchers in terms of revealing and understanding the profile of domestic individual portfolio investors in Türkiye.

Financial Risk Tolerance Group Characteristics of the Sample

Within the scope of the research, the scores obtained from the responses of the participants to the Financial Risk Tolerance scale were collected and the risk tolerance score of each investor was calculated. Risk tolerance scores were evaluated according to the risk groups determined by Grable & Lytton (1999:3). The risk groups that investors are included in according to the total scores are shown in Table 3.

Table 3. Financial Risk Tolerance Groups of the Investors

		Frequency	Percentage (%)
Risk Group-1	Low Risk Tolerance (Conservative Investor)	10	1,3
Risk Group-2	Below Average Risk Tolerance	38	5,0
Risk Group-3	Average/Moderate Risk Tolerance	259	34,0
Risk Group-4	Above Average Risk Tolerance	282	37,1
Risk Group-5	High Risk Tolerance (Aggressive Investor)	172	22,6

n=761

When Table 3 is examined, it is seen that 34% of investors had an Average/Moderate Risk Tolerance (Risk Group-3) during the Covid-19 outbreak, while 59.7% had an Above Average (Risk Group-4) and High (Risk Group-5) Risk Tolerance. On the other hand, 6.3% of the sample had a Below Average (Risk Group-2) and Low (Risk Group-1) Risk Tolerance.

Data Analysis

Within the scope of the research, data collected from domestic investors were scanned for missing, incorrect data and extreme values. The equality of variances was assessed using the Levene Test (Field, 2005). In order to determine the types of analysis to be used, the Shapiro-Wilk Normality Test was applied to the data set. It was determined that the skewness and kurtosis values in the data set were between +1.5 and -1.5, in other words, the data were normally distributed (Tabachnick & Fidell, 2013). As a result, parametric tests were found to be applicable.

Data were analyzed using SPSS 22 package program, and descriptive and inferential statistics were reported. Within the scope of the research, tests for differences between demographics and financial risk tolerance were conducted at a significance level of $p < .05$.

Of the 761 investors who participated in the study, 679 were male and 82 were female. The proportion of women in the sample was 10.8%. Since the difference between the two groups was quite large, parametric tests could not be applied for the gender demographic variable. In order to test the significance of the difference between other independent variables and financial risk tolerance, the following questions were asked to investors:

- Independent Sample t-Test was used in the analysis of questions with two answer choices,
- One Way Analysis of Variance (One Way ANOVA) was used in the analysis of questions with more than two answer choices.

As a result of the One-Way ANOVA Test, Tukey HSD Test was performed as a Post-Hoc test to determine between which groups there was a significant difference (Tabachnick & Fidell, 2019).

RESULTS

As a result of the Independent Sample t-Tests conducted to determine whether there is a significant difference between the marital status of the investors participating in the research and the general average of their financial risk tolerance during the Covid-19 period, their financial risk tolerance components and the risk groups they are included in, no statistically significant difference was determined in the context of all variables.

As a result of the One-Way ANOVA Tests conducted to determine whether there is a significant difference between the number of children of investors and the general average of their financial risk tolerance during the Covid-19 period, their financial risk tolerance components and the risk groups they are included in, no statistically significant difference was determined in the context of all variables.

Of the 761 investors who participated in the study, 41 were younger than 25, and 59 were older than 55. Since the numerical difference between the two different groups was large, the group of 41 people who were younger than 25 was combined with the upper group, and the group of 59 people who were 55 and older was combined with the lower group. As a result of the combination, 40 years of age was taken as the median. The new frequency table consisting of two different age groups is shown in Table 4.

Table 4. Revised Frequency Table of Investors' Age Groups

		Frequency	Percentage (%)
Age Groups	Less than 40	412	54,1
	40 or More	349	45,9

n=761

As a result of the Independent Sample t-Tests conducted to determine whether there is a significant difference between the age groups obtained in Table 4 and the general average of financial risk tolerances during the Covid-19 period, financial risk tolerance components and the risk groups they are included in, no significant difference was determined in terms of the general average of financial risk tolerances and the risk groups they are included in. However, a statistically significant difference was determined between the age groups of individuals and the Risk Comfort and Experience component of financial risk tolerance. The test results are shown in Table 5.

Table 5. Independent Samples t-Test Results for Risk Comfort and Experience of Investors According to Age Groups

Group Statistics				Levene's Test Statistics		t- Test Statistics		
Age Groups	N	Mean	SD	F	Sig.	t	df	Sig. (p*)
Less than 40	412	2,20	,433	,196	,658	2,663	738,875	**,008**
40 or More	349	2,12	,432					

n=761, *p>0,05

According to Table 5, the scores of investors less than 40 years of age (Mean: 2.20, SD= .433) are significantly higher than those of investors 40 or more age (Mean: 2.12, SD= .432). Accordingly, it is understood that the Risk Comfort and Experience of investors less than 40 years of age are relatively higher than those of investors 40 or more age.

No statistically significant difference was determined between the age variable and other financial risk tolerance components (Speculative Risk, Investment Risk).

As a result of One-Way ANOVA Tests conducted to determine whether there is a significant difference between the household income of the investors, their educational status, and the general average of their financial risk tolerance during the Covid-19 period, their financial risk tolerance components and the risk groups they are included in, no statistically significant difference was determined in the context of all variables.

As a result of ANOVA tests conducted to determine whether there is a significant difference between the investment periods and financial risk tolerance general scores of the participants, it was determined that there was a significant difference in terms of two variables. Tukey HSD Test was conducted to determine between which groups the difference occurred. The results of the analyses are shown in Table 6.

Table 6. Results of ANOVA and Tukey HSD Tests on Individuals' Financial Risk Tolerance General Scores According to Investment Periods

ANOVA Test Statistics					
	Sum of Squares	df	Mean Square	F	Sig. (p*)
Between Groups	181,242	3	60,414	3,369	**,018**
Within Groups	13575,252	757	17,933		
Total	13756,494	760			

Tukey HSD Test Statistics				
Investment Period	Investment Period	Mean Difference	Std. Error	Sig. (p*)
Less Than 1 Year	1 Year –3 Years	-1,59502*	,58395	**,033**
	3 Years –5 Years	-1,80136*	,66041	**,033**
	5 Years or More	-1,81457*	,58539	**,011**

n=761, *p>0,05

According to Table 6;

- There is a significant difference in financial risk tolerance general scores between investors with an investment period of less than 1 year and investors with an investment period of 1 year-3 years,
- There is a significant difference between investors with an investment period of less than 1 year and investors with an investment period of 3 years-5 years,
- There is a significant difference between investors with an investment period of less than 1 year and investors with an investment period of 5 years or more, according to investment periods.

A significant difference was determined in terms of the investment periods of the individuals participating in the research and the Speculative Risk and Investment Risk components of financial risk tolerance, and the ANOVA and Tukey Test results regarding the significant difference with Speculative Risk are shown in Table 7.

Table 7. Results of ANOVA and Tukey HSD Tests According to Investment Periods in Terms of Speculative Risk Averages of Individuals

ANOVA Test Statistics					
	Sum of Squares	df	Mean Square	F	Sig. (p*)
Between Groups	3,169	3	1,056	3,046	**,028**
Within Groups	262,491	757	,347		
Total	265,660	760			

Tukey HSD Test Statistics				
Investment Period	Investment Period	Mean Difference	Std. Error	Sig. (p*)
Less Than 1 Year	1 Year –3 Years	-,21289*	,08120	**,044**
	3 Years –5 Years	-,21603	,09183	,087
	5 Years or More	-,24466*	,08140	**,015**

n=761, *p>0,05

According to Table 7;

- There is a significant difference between investors with less than 1 year of investment period and investors with 1 year-3 years of investment period,
- There is a significant difference between investors with less than 1 year of investment period and investors with 5 years or more investment period in terms of Speculative Risk component according to investment periods.

A significant difference was determined according to investment periods in terms of Investment Risk, one of the components of financial risk tolerance. The ANOVA and Tukey HSD Test results regarding the difference are shown in Table 8.

Table 8. Results of ANOVA and Tukey HSD Tests According to Investment Periods in Terms of Investment Risk Averages of Individuals

ANOVA Test Statistics					
	Sum of Squares	df	Mean Square	F	Sig. (p*)
Between Groups	1,546	3	,515	3,592	**,013**
Within Groups	108,622	757	,143		
Total	110,169	760			

Tukey HSD Test Statistics				
Investment Period	Investment Period	Mean Difference	Std. Error	Sig. (p*)
Less Than 1 Year	1 Year –3 Years	-,15695*	,05223	**,015**
	3 Years –5 Years	-18000*	,05907	**,013**
	5 Years or More	-,15296*	,05236	**,019**

n=761, *p>0,05

According to Table 8;

- There is a significant difference in the investment risk component between investors with an investment period of less than 1 year and investors with an investment period of 1 year-3 years,
- There is a significant difference between investors with an investment period of less than 1 year and investors with an investment period of 3 years-5 years,
- There is a significant difference between investors with an investment period of less than 1 year and investors with 5 years or more investment period, according to investment periods.

No significant difference was determined as a result of ANOVA Tests conducted to determine whether there is a significant difference between individuals' investment periods and the other financial risk tolerance component, Risk Comfort and Experience. Similarly, no significant difference was determined in terms of two variables as a result of ANOVA Tests conducted to determine whether there is a significant difference between investors' investment periods and the risk groups they are included in.

DISCUSSION

In the research, it is evaluated that the ratio of male investors making portfolio investments in Borsa Istanbul (BIST) in Türkiye is relatively higher than that of female investors, which is parallel to many studies in the literature. This situation leaves unanswered the question of whether there is a significant and positive relationship between the gender of investors in Türkiye and their financial risk tolerance during the Covid-19 Pandemic. It is thought that encouraging women investors to invest in portfolios by policy makers and other financial actors could be a milestone in strengthening national capital.

No significant and positive relationship was found between marital status, number of children, household income, education level and financial risk tolerance.

Although no significant and positive relationship was found between the demographics of investors and their age groups and financial risk tolerance during the Covid-19 Pandemic, a statistically significant difference was determined between Risk Comfort and Experience, which are among the financial risk tolerance components. The scores of investors younger than 40 years old (Mean: 2.20, SD= .433) are significantly higher than those of investors aged 40 or more (Mean: 2.12, SD= .432). Accordingly, the fact that Risk Comfort and Experience of investors younger than 40 years old are relatively higher than those of investors aged 40 or more is similar to the results of many studies investigating the relationship between this variable and financial risk tolerance (Grable, 2000; Xiao et al., 2000; Hallahan et al., 2003;

Chaulk et al., 2003; Yao et al., 2004; Levin et al., 2007; Faff et al., 2009; Anbar & Eker, 2010; Weller et al., 2011; Paulsen et al., 2012; Sulaiman, 2012; Thanki & Baser, 2019, Fan et al., 2020). The higher Risk Comfort and Experience averages of investors under 40 years of age can be explained by the fact that the number of single people among these people is relatively higher, they have less responsibility compared to married investors, and they feel comfortable investing because of their average life expectancy. It is considered that individuals 40 or more years old do not feel as comfortable in terms of risk taking and experience as those less than 40 yaers old due to their marital status, number of children, monthly expenses, previous investment experience, being under relatively more responsibility, and their average life expectancy starting to decrease.

A significant and positive relationship was determined between the investment periods of investors and their financial risk tolerances in the Covid-19 Pandemic (p= .018 and p>0.05). It was determined that the financial risk tolerances of individuals with investment periods of less than 1 year differed from those with investment periods of 1 Year–3 Years (p= .033 and p>0.05), 3 Years–5 Years (p= .033 and p>0.05) and 5 years or more (p= .011 and p>0.05). It is evaluated that past investment experiences, losses and gains, opportunities and other experiences are effective in this differentiation.

The financial risk tolerance components with significant and positive relationships in terms of investment periods are Speculative Risk (p= .028 and p>0.05) and Investment Risk (p= .013 and p>0.05). A significant difference was determined in terms of Speculative Risk component between investors with investment periods of less than 1 year and those with investment periods of 1 year-3 years (p= .044 and p>0.05) and between 5 years or more investment periods (p= .015 and p>0.05). On the other hand, it was determined that the Investment Risks of individuals with investment periods of less than 1 year and with investment period of 1 Year–3 Years (p= .015 and p>0.05), 3 Years–5 Years (p= .013 and p>0.05) and with 5 years or more investment periods (p= .019 and p>0.05) differed.

The results of this study conducted during the Covid-19 Pandemic period, compared to studies conducted before the Pandemic, confirm that male investors can take more risks than female investors in terms of gender variable. It is seen that the proportional difference between the number of female and male investors in Türkiye is relatively higher than the rates obtained in many studies in the literature. In terms of marital status variable, it has been reported in many studies that singles can take higher risks than married people. In this differentiation, it is a fact explained in the literature that married individuals are members of a social institution for which they are responsible, other than themselves. However, it is noteworthy that no differentiation was determined in terms of the marital status variable in this study. The same applies to the number of children variable in this study. In terms of the age variable, many studies in the literature have reported that younger investors have higher financial risk tolerance than older investors. However, there are also studies supporting the opposite (See Table 1). This study suggests that the lack of a difference in the financial risk tolerance of individuals in terms of age, and the difference in the Risk Comfort and Experience dimension between individuals more and less than 40 years of age may be a reflection of different findings in the literature. Many studies in the literature have found that there is a positive correlation between individuals' education levels, household income and financial risk tolerance. The fact that such a difference could not be determined for both variables during the Covid-19 Pandemic period among investors in Türkiye differs from many studies in the literature. The fact that the difference in financial risk tolerances of investors in terms of investment periods before the Covid-19 Pandemic continues during the Covid-19 Pandemic period is consistent with the literature.

CONCLUSION

This research provides insights for researchers, finance experts and policy makers to examine the demographic factors affecting the financial risk tolerance of domestic individual investors in developing countries such as Türkiye, which are economically vulnerable and have a late recovery, in the face of possible future global shocks such as the Covid-19 Pandemic.

The research results provide findings that there has been an increase in the financial risk tolerance of domestic individual portfolio investors in Türkiye during the Covid-19 Pandemic compared to the normal period. In this context, it is recommended that the factors affecting the increased risk tolerance and reported in this study be examined by investment strategists, investment consultants, portfolio managers, financial institutions and organizations.

When compared with the sample results of other studies conducted in Türkiye (Kübilay, 2015; Orçun, 2015), it was determined that the financial risk tolerances of the sample covered in this study increased proportionally during the Covid-19 Pandemic period. In other words, the financial risk tolerances of individual portfolio investors in Türkiye increased during the Pandemic period compared to pre-pandemic period. Therefore, it is evaluated that if systemic risks such as the Covid-19 Pandemic occur again in the future, stock investors may increase their financial risk tolerance by taking advantage of the declines in stock market indices.

The financial preferences and risk tolerances of individual investors have a dynamic structure. For this reason, it is evaluated that in global shock periods, an up-to-date consideration of individuals' shock exposure, some demographics that change over time (household income, number of children, etc.) and risk tolerances can provide a competitive advantage to financial institutions and organizations.

It is evaluated that the study can provide ideas to investment advisors, portfolio managers and brokerage firms in terms of predicting investor behavior in possible future global shocks such as the Covid-19 Pandemic and in this context, offering them refined investment options compatible with their risk tolerances.

It is considered that conducting similar studies on different sample groups (e.g. traders/brokers, investment firms) and using different research techniques will contribute positively to the literature. Another issue suggested by researchers is conducting similar studies to examine other social and psychological factors that may affect investors' financial risk tolerance and financial preferences.

REFERENCES

Al-Ajmi, J. Y. (2008). Risk tolerance of individual investors in an emerging market. *International Research Journal of Finance and Economics, 17*(1), 15–26.

Anbar, A., & Eker, M. (2010). An empirical investigation for determining of the relation between personal financial risk tolerance and demographic characteristic. *Ege Academic Review, 10*(2), 503–522.

Angrisani, M., Cipriani, M., Guarino, A., Kendall, R., & Pina, J. O. Z. (2020). Risk preferences at the time of COVID-19: An experiment with professional traders and students, *Federal Reserve Bank of New York Staff Reports*, No. 927.

Ansari, S., & Phatak, Y. (2016). A study of assessment of financial risk tolerance and preferred investment avenues of investors, *Prestige International Journal of Management and Research*, 9(2/1), 1-7.

Bajtelsmit, V. L., & Bernasek, A. (1996). Why do women invest differently than men? *Financial Counseling and Planning, 7*, 1–10. DOI: 10.2139/ssrn.2238

Baker, H. K., & Haslem, J. A. (1974). The impact of investor socio-economic characteristics on risk and return preferences. *Journal of Business Research, 2*(1), 469–476.

Bashir, T., Uppal, S. T., Hanif, K., Yaseen, S. M., & Saraj, K. (2013). Financial risk tolerant attitude: Empirical evidence from Pakistan. *European Scientific Journal, 9*(19), 200–209.

Battaglia, F., Cervellati, E. M., Salerno, D., Stella, G. P., & Vannoni, V. (2025). How the COVID-19 pandemic changed Italians' financial risk tolerance. *Qualitative Research in Financial Markets, 17*(2), 415–431. DOI: 10.1108/QRFM-01-2024-0019

Bonsang, E., & Dohmen, T. (2015). Risk attitude and cognitive aging. *Journal of Economic Behavior & Organization, 112*, 112–126. DOI: 10.1016/j.jebo.2015.01.004

Bu, D., Hanspal, T., Lao, Y., & Liu, Y. (2020). Risk taking during a global crisis: Evidence from Wuhan. *Covid Economics, 5*, 106–146.

Chang, C., DeVaney, S. A., & Chiremba, S. T. (2004). Determinants of subjective and objective risk tolerance. *Journal of Personal Finance, 3*, 53–67.

Chaulk, B., Johnson, P. J., & Bulcroft, R. (2003). Effects of marriage and children on financial risk tolerance: A synthesis of family development and prospect theory. *Journal of Family and Economic Issues, 24*, 257–279. DOI: 10.1023/A:1025495221519

Chiang, T. F., & Xiao, J. J. (2017). Household characteristics and the change of financial risk tolerance during the financial crisis in the United States. *International Journal of Consumer Studies, 41*(5), 484–493. DOI: 10.1111/ijcs.12356

Christiansen, C., Joensen, J. S., & Rangvid, J. (2006). Gender marriage the decision to invest in stocks bonds: Do single women invest more in less risky assets? *(D-CAF Working Paper No. 18)*, School of Economics and Management, University of Aarhus, Denmark.

Cristian, P. (2012). Risk tolerance analysis: Romanian case before and during financial turmoil, Romania. *Economia e Sociologia, 5*(2a), 11–23.

Dal, L. (2023). *The factors affecting financial risk tolerance of investors in Turkey according to A/B personality traits in times of Covid-19 pandemic*, [Doctoral dissertation, Eskisehir Osmangazi University]. National Thesis Center of the Council of Higher Education database. Data Analysis Platform (Veri Analiz Platformu-VAP) at https://www.vap.org.tr

Dawson, C., & Henley, A. (2015). Gender, risk, and venture creation intentions. *Journal of Small Business Management, 53*(2), 501–515. DOI: 10.1111/jsbm.12080

Deger, M. N. (2019). *Factors affecting individual pension system participants' financial risk tolerance: An application on Mersin University staff,* [Masters Degree dissertatiton, Mersin University]. National Thesis Center of the Council of Higher Education database.

Dohmen, T., Falk, A., Huffman, D., Sunde, U., Schupp, J., & Wagner, G. G. (2011). Individual risk attitudes: Measurement, determinants, and behavioral consequences. *Journal of the European Economic Association, 9*(3), 522–550. DOI: 10.1111/j.1542-4774.2011.01015.x

Eichengreen, B., Hale, G., & Mody, A. (2001). Flight to quality: investor risk tolerance and the spread of emerging market crises. In *International financial contagion* (pp. 129–155). Springer US., DOI: 10.1007/978-1-4757-3314-3_6

Embrey, L. L., & Fox, J. J. (1997). Gender differences in the investment decision-making process. *Financial Counseling and Planning, 8*(2), 33–40.

Faff, R. (2008). On the linkage between financial risk tolerance and risk aversion. *Journal of Financial Research, 31*(1), 1–23. DOI: 10.1111/j.1475-6803.2008.00229.x

Faff, R., Hallahan, T., & McKenzie, M. (2009). Nonlinear linkages between financial risk tolerance and demographic characteristics. *Applied Economics Letters, 16*(13), 1329–1332. DOI: 10.1080/13504850701381123

Fan, J. X., & Xiao, J. J. (2006). Cross-cultural differences in risk tolerance: A comparison between Chinese and Americans. *Journal of Personal Finance*, *5*(3), 54–75.

Fan, Y., Orhun, A. Y., & Turjeman, D. (2020). *Heterogeneous actions, beliefs, constraints and risk tolerance during the COVID-19 pandemic (No. w27211)*. National Bureau of Economic Research., DOI: 10.3386/w27211

Farrell, J. (2014). Demographic and socioeconomic factors of investors. In *Investor Behavior: The Psychology of Financial Planning and Investing*, 117-134, DOI: DOI: 10.1002/9781118813454.ch7

Fehr-Duda, H., De Gennaro, M., & Schubert, R. (2006). Gender, financial risk, and probability weights. *Theory and Decision*, *60*, 283–313. DOI: 10.1007/s11238-005-4590-0

Gibson, R. J., Michayluk, D., & Van de Venter, G. (2013). Financial risk tolerance: An analysis of unexplored factors. *Financial Services Review*, *22*(1), 23–50.

Gilliam, J., Chatterjee, S., & Grable, J. (2010). Measuring the perception of financial risk tolerance: A tale of two measures. *Financial Counseling and Planning*, *21*(2).

Gondaliya, V., & Dhinaiya, G. (2016). Assessing financial risk tolerance: Do demographic, socioeconomic and attitudinal factors work. *International Journal of Marketing & Financial Management*, *4*(5), 32–38.

Grable, J., Lytton, R., & O'neill, B. (2004). Projection bias and financial risk tolerance. *Journal of Behavioral Finance*, *5*(3), 142–147. DOI: 10.1207/s15427579jpfm0503_2

Grable, J., & Lytton, R. H. (1999a). Financial risk tolerance revisited: The development of a risk assessment instrument. *Financial Services Review*, *8*(3), 163–181. DOI: 10.1016/S1057-0810(99)00041-4

Grable, J., Lytton, R. H., O'neill, B., Joo, S. H., & Klock, D. (2006). Risk tolerance, projection bias, vividness, and equity prices. *Journal of Investing*, *15*(2), 68–74.

Grable, J. E. (2000). Financial risk tolerance and additional factors that affect risk taking in everyday money matters. *Journal of Business and Psychology*, *14*, 625–630. DOI: 10.1023/A:1022994314982

Grable, J. E., & Joo, S. H. (1999). Factors related to risk tolerance: A further examination. *Consumer Interests Annual*, *45*(1), 53–58.

Grable, J. E., & Lytton, R. H. (1999b). Assessing financial risk tolerance: Do demographic, socioeconomic, and attitudinal factors work? *Family Relations and Human Development/Family Economics and Resource Management Biennial*, 3(1), 80-88.

Grable, J. E., & Lytton, R. H. (2001). Assessing the concurrent validity of the SCF risk tolerance question. *Financial Counseling and Planning*, *12*(2), 43–53.

Grable, J. E., Lytton, R. H., & Kratzer, C. Y. (1998). Determinants of defined contribution plan employee participation: A403 (b) perspective. *Consumer Interests Annual*, *44*, 109–114.

Guenther, B., Galizzi, M. M., & Sanders, J. G. (2021). Heterogeneity in risk-taking during the COVID-19 pandemic: Evidence from the UK lockdown. *Frontiers in Psychology*, *12*, 1–15. DOI: 10.3389/fpsyg.2021.643653 PMID: 33868115

Guillemette, M., & Finke, M. (2014). Do large swings in equity values change risk tolerance? *Journal of Financial Planning*, *27*(6), 44–50.

Guiso, L., Jappelli, T., & Terlizzese, D. (1996). Income risk, borrowing constraints, and portfolio choice. *The American Economic Review*, *86*(1), 158–172.

Gutter, M. S., Fox, J. J., & Montalto, C. P. (1999). Racial differences in investor decision making. *Financial Services Review*, *8*(3), 149–162. DOI: 10.1016/S1057-0810(99)00040-2

Hallahan, T., Faff, R., & McKenzie, M. (2003). An exploratory investigation of the relation between risk tolerance scores and demographic characteristics. *Journal of Multinational Financial Management*, *13*(4-5), 483–502. DOI: 10.1016/S1042-444X(03)00022-7

Hallahan, T. A., Faff, R. W., & McKenzie, M. D. (2004). An empirical investigation of personal financial risk tolerance. *Financial Services Review-Greenwich*, *13*(1), 57–78.

Hamurcu, Ç., & Hamurcu, H. D. Y. (2016). Financial risk tolerance and burnout relation: Information and communication technology (ICT) sector study. *Aksaray Üniversitesi İktisadi ve İdari Bilimler Fakültesi Dergisi*, *8*(2), 95–101.

Hanna, S. D., Gutter, M. S., & Fan, J. X. (2001). A measure of risk tolerance based on economic theory. *Financial Counseling and Planning*, *12*(2), 53–60.

Hariharan, G., Chapman, K. S., & Domian, D. L. (2000). Risk tolerance and asset allocation for investors nearing retirement. *Financial Services Review*, *9*(2), 159–170. DOI: 10.1016/S1057-0810(00)00063-9 PMID: 12500326

Hartog, J., Ferrer-i-Carbonell, A., & Jonker, N. (2002). Linking measured risk aversion to individual characteristics. *Kyklos*, *55*(1), 3–26. DOI: 10.1111/1467-6435.00175

Hawley, C. B., & Fujii, E. T. (1993). An empirical analysis of preferences for financial risk: Further evidence on the Friedman–Savage model. *Journal of Post Keynesian Economics*, *16*(2), 197–204. DOI: 10.1080/01603477.1993.11489978

Heenkenda, S. (2015). Determination of financial risk tolerance among different household sectors in Sri Lanka. *Asian Journal of Empirical Research*, *5*(11), 206–220.

Heo, W., Grable, J. E., & Rabbani, A. G. (2021). A test of the association between the initial surge in COVID-19 cases and subsequent changes in financial risk tolerance. *Review of Behavioral Finance*, *13*(1), 3–19. DOI: 10.1108/RBF-06-2020-0121

Heo, W., Rabbani, A., & Grable, J. E. (2021a). An evaluation of the effect of the COVID-19 pandemic on the risk tolerance of financial decision makers. *Finance Research Letters*, *41*. Advance online publication. DOI: 10.1016/j.frl.2020.101842 PMID: 36568732

Hochman, G., Ofir, M., & Ayal, S. (2024). Financial risk tolerance during a major negative life experience: The case of the COVID-19 Pandemic. DOI: DOI: 10.21203/rs.3.rs-4742565/v1

Hoffmann, A. O., Post, T., & Pennings, J. M. (2013). Individual investor perceptions and behavior during the financial crisis. *Journal of Banking & Finance*, *37*(1), 60–74. DOI: 10.1016/j.jbankfin.2012.08.007

Hüner, E. G. (2016). *Effects of anger and anxiety traits on financial risk tolerance of novices and experts,* [Masters Degree dissertatiton, Middle East Technical University]. National Thesis Center of the Council of Higher Education database.

Jianakoplos, N. A., & Bernasek, A. (1998). Are women more risk averse? *Economic Inquiry*, *36*(4), 620–630. DOI: 10.1111/j.1465-7295.1998.tb01740.x

Joo, S. H., & Grable, J. E. (2004). An exploratory framework of the determinants of financial satisfaction. *Journal of Family and Economic Issues*, *25*, 25–50. DOI: 10.1023/B:JEEI.0000016722.37994.9f

Kahneman, D., & Tversky, A. (1979). Prospect theory: An analysis of decision under risk. *Econometrica*, *47*, 263–291.

Kannadhasan, M., Aramvalarthan, S., Mitra, S. K., & Goyal, V. (2016). Relationship between biopsychosocial factors and financial risk tolerance: An empirical study. *Vikalpa*, *41*(2), 117–131. DOI: 10.1177/0256090916642685

Kohút, M., Srol, J., & Vladimíra, C. (2022). How are you holding up? Personality, cognitive and social predictors of a perceived shift in subjective well-being during COVID-19 pandemic. *Personality and Individual Differences, 186*, 1–8. DOI: 10.1016/j.paid.2021.111349 PMID: 34690396

Kübilay, B. (2015). *Investor bias in terms of investment psychology, financial risk tolerance and financial personality: A field survey on individual investors,* [Doctoral dissertatiton, Muğla Sıtkı Koçman University]. National Thesis Center of the Council of Higher Education database.

Lal, S., Nguyen, T. X. T., Bawalle, A. A., Khan, M. S. R., & Kadoya, Y. (2024). Unraveling investor behavior: The role of hyperbolic discounting in panic selling behavior on the global COVID-19 financial crisis. *Behavioral Sciences (Basel, Switzerland), 14*(9), 795. DOI: 10.3390/bs14090795 PMID: 39336010

Lawrenson, J. (2020). *Modelling financial risk tolerance of female South African investors,* [Doctoral dissertation, North-West University]. Boloka Institutional Repository.

Lazzarone, B. G. (1996). The economic well-being of rural nevada elders, *Proceedings of the 1996 Conference of the Western Region Home Management Family Economics Educators*, 67-74.

Lee, H. K., & Hanna, S. (1991). Wealth and stock ownership, In *Proceedings of the Association for Financial Counseling and Planning Education*, 126-140.

Levin, I. P., Hart, S. S., Weller, J. A., & Harshman, L. A. (2007). Stability of choices in a risky decision-making task: A 3-year longitudinal study with children and adults. *Journal of Behavioral Decision Making, 20*(3), 241–252. DOI: 10.1002/bdm.552

Marinelli, N., Mazzoli, C., & Palmucci, F. (2017). Mind the gap: Inconsistencies between subjective and objective financial risk tolerance. *Journal of Behavioral Finance, 18*(2), 219–230. DOI: 10.1080/15427560.2017.1308944

Mineyama, T., & Tokuoka, K. (2024). Does the COVID-19 pandemic change individuals' risk preference? *Journal of Risk and Uncertainty, 68*(2), 163–182. DOI: 10.1007/s11166-024-09427-5

Necker, S., & Ziegelmeyer, M. (2016). Household risk taking after the financial crisis. *The Quarterly Review of Economics and Finance, 59*, 141–160. DOI: 10.1016/j.qref.2015.03.006

Olsen, R. A., & Cox, C. M. (2001). The influence of gender on the perception and response to investment risk: The case of professional investors. *The Journal of Psychology and Financial Markets, 2*(1), 29–36. DOI: 10.1207/S15327760JPFM0201_3

Omanovic, A., & Zaimovic, A. (2024). The determinants of financial risk tolerance and portfolio allocation: Have the Covid-19 pandemic and the Ukraine war affected our risk tolerance? *Borsa Istanbul Review*, *24*(6), 1381–1392. DOI: 10.1016/j.bir.2024.11.001

Orçun, Ç. (2015). *An investigation of individual investor's financial risk perception,* [Doctoral dissertatiton, Dokuz Eylül University]. National Thesis Center of the Council of Higher Education database.

Öztop, A. O., & Kuyu, E. (2020). Influence of socio-demographic characteristics, financial literacy and mood on financial risk tolerance. *Journal of Business Economics and Finance*, *9*(3), 209–222.

Paulsen, D. J., Platt, M. L., Huettel, S. A., & Brannon, E. M. (2012). From risk-seeking to risk-averse: The development of economic risk preference from childhood to adulthood. *Frontiers in Psychology*, *3*, 313. DOI: 10.3389/fpsyg.2012.00313 PMID: 22973247

Pyles, M. K., Li, Y., Wu, S., & Dolvin, S. D. (2016). Cultural influences on risk tolerance and portfolio creation. *Journal of Behavioral and Experimental Finance*, *9*, 43–55. DOI: 10.1016/j.jbef.2016.01.001

Rahman, M. J., Zhu, H., & Beiyi, S. (2023). Is COVID-19 a turning point? Evidence from CEOs' investment behavior and risk tolerance. *International Journal of Emerging Markets*. Advance online publication. DOI: 10.1108/IJOEM-02-2023-0264

Rai, K., Gupta, A., & Tyagi, A. (2021). Personality traits leads to investor's financial risk tolerance: A structural equation modelling approach. *Management and Labour Studies*, *46*(4), 422–437. DOI: 10.1177/0258042X211018

Reddy, K. S., & Mahapatra, M. S. (2017). Risk tolerance, personal financial knowledge and demographic characteristics evidence from India. *Journal of Developing Areas*, *51*(3), 51–62. DOI: 10.1353/jda.2017.0060

Ricciardi, V., & Rice, D. (2014). Risk perception and risk tolerance. *Investor Behavior: The Psychology of Financial Planning and Investing*, 325-345, DOI: .DOI: 10.1002/9781118813454.ch18

Riley, N. F., & Russon, M. G. (1995). Individual asset allocation and indicators of perceived client risk tolerance. *Journal of Financial and Strategic Decisions*, *8*(1), 65–70.

Riley, W., & Chow, K. V. (1992). Asset allocation and individual risk aversion. *Financial Analysts Journal*, *48*(6), 32–37. DOI: 10.2469/faj.v48.n6.32

Ryack, K. (2011). The impact of family relationships and financial education on financial risk tolerance. *Financial Services Review*, *20*(3), 181–193.

Sameera, V. V. L. & S, L. T. D. (2024). Impact of Covid-19 on portfolio management of investors in Telangana. *Proceedings of the 4th Indian International Conference on Industrial Engineering and Operations Management,* DOI: DOI: 10.46254/IN04.20240118

Schooley, D. K., & Worden, D. D. (2016). Perceived and realized risk tolerance: Changes during the 2008 financial crisis. *Financial Counseling and Planning*, *27*(2), 265–276. DOI: 10.1891/1052-3073.27.2.265

Semenov, A. S., & Kuznetcov, V. S. (2015). Assessment of level of risk in decision-making in terms of career exploitation. *International Journal of Economics and Financial Issues*, *5*(3), 165–172.

Shusha, A. A. (2017). Does financial literacy moderate the relationship among demographic characteristics and financial risk tolerance? Evidence from Egypt, *Australasian Accounting. Business and Finance Journal*, *11*(3), 67–86. DOI: 10.14453/aabfj.v11i3.6

Statman, M. (1995). Behavioral finance versus standard finance, In *AIMR Conference Proceedings*, 7, 14-22, CFA Institute.

Stevens, J. (1996). Applied multivariate statistics for the social sciences, 3rd Edition. Mahwah, Lawrence Erlbaum, New Jersey.

Sulaiman, E. K. (2012). An empirical analysis of financial risk tolerance and demographic features of individual investors, *2nd Annual International Conference on Accounting and Finance (AF 2012). Procedia Economics and Finance*, *2*, 109–115. DOI: 10.1016/S2212-5671(12)00070-6

Sung, J., & Hanna, S. D. (1996). Factors related to risk tolerance. *Financial Counseling and Planning*, *7*, 11–20.

Sutejo, B. S., Pranata, Y. K. N., & Mahadwartha, P. A. (2018). Demography factors, financial risk tolerance, and retail investors. *Advances in Social Science, Education and Humanities Research, 186*, 80–83.

Tabachnick, B. G., & Fidell, L. (2019). *Using multivariate statistics* (7th ed.). Pearson.

Tabachnick, B. G., & Fidell, L. S. (2007). *Using multivariate statistics* (5th ed.). Pearson Education.

Tabachnick, B. G., & Fidell, L. S. (2013). *Using multivariate statistics* (6th ed.). Pearson Education.

Thaler, R. (1985). Mental accounting and consumer choice. *Marketing Science*, *4*(3), 199–214.

Thanki, H. (2015). Risk tolerance dependant on what? Demographics or personality type: Findings from an empirical research. *Journal of Marketing and Consumer Research*, *6*, 48–56.

Thanki, H., & Baser, N. (2019). Interactive impact of demographic variables and personality type on risk tolerance. *Emerging Economy Studies*, *5*(1), 42–54. DOI: 10.1177/2394901519825924

Tingley, H. D. (2025). *The impact of economic shocks on financial risk tolerance using panel data analysis,* [Doctoral dissertation, Manchester Metropolitan University]. Manchester Metropolitan University's Research Repository (e-space).

Ullah, M., Rashdi, U. S., & Shaikh, S. (2021). COVID-19 outbreak and risk tolerance of financial decision makers. *International Journal of Management*, *12*(2), 433–440.

Van de Venter, G. (2006). Financial planners' perceptions of risk tolerance. *2006 Financial Management Association's (FMA) Annual Conference*, 1-31, Salt Lake City, Utah, USA.

Van de Venter, G., Michayluk, D., & Davey, G. (2012). A longitudinal study of financial risk tolerance. *Journal of Economic Psychology*, *33*(4), 794–800. DOI: 10.1016/j.joep.2012.03.001

Volk, A. A., Brazil, K. J., Franklin-Luther, P., Dane, A. V., & Vaillancourt, T. (2021). The influence of demographics and personality on COVID-19 coping in young adults. *Personality and Individual Differences*, *168*. Advance online publication. DOI: 10.1016/j.paid.2020.110398 PMID: 32952250

Wang, H., & Hanna, S. (1997). Does risk tolerance decrease with age. *Financial Counseling and Planning*, *8*(2), 27–31.

Wasiuzzaman, S., & Edalat, S. (2016). Personality, risk tolerance and social network use: An exploratory study. *Managerial Finance*, *42*(6), 536–552. DOI: 10.1108/MF-05-2015-0159

Watson, J., & McNaughton, M. (2007). Gender differences in risk aversion and expected retirement benefits. *Financial Analysts Journal*, *63*(4), 52–62. DOI: 10.2469/faj.v63.n4.4749

Weber, M., Weber, E. U., & Nosić, A. (2013). Who takes risks when and why: Determinants of changes in investor risk taking. *Review of Finance*, *17*(3), 847–883. DOI: 10.1093/rof/rfs024

Weller, J. A., Levin, I. P., & Denburg, N. L. (2011). Trajectory of risky decision making for potential gains and losses from ages 5 to 85. *Journal of Behavioral Decision Making*, *24*(4), 331–344. DOI: 10.1002/bdm.690

Xiao, J. J., Alhabeeb, M. J., Hong, G. S., & Haynes, G. W. (2000). Risk tolerance of family business owners. *Consumer Interests Annual*, *46*, 140–146.

Yao, R., & Hanna, S. D. (2005). The effect of gender and marital status on financial risk tolerance. *Journal of Personal Finance*, *4*(1), 66–85.

Yao, R., Hanna, S. D., & Lindamood, S. (2004). Changes in financial risk tolerance, 1983-2001. *Financial Services Review*, *13*(4), 249–266.

Yao, Z., & Rabbani, A. G. (2021). Association between investment risk tolerance and portfolio risk: The role of confidence level. *Journal of Behavioral and Experimental Finance*, *30*. Advance online publication. DOI: 10.1016/j.jbef.2021.100482

Yazıcıoğlu, Y., & Erdoğan, S. (2004). *SPSS uygulamalı bilimsel araştırma yöntemleri*. Detay Yayıncılık.

Yook, K. C., & Everett, R. (2003). Assessing risk tolerance: Questioning the questionnaire method. *Journal of Financial Planning*, *16*(8), 48–55.

KEY TERMS AND DEFINITIONS

Behavioral Finance: A finance theory that supports the thesis that individuals cannot always act rationally when making financial decisions, and is based on the view that individuals affect markets by engaging in irrational behaviors such as herd behavior, representativeness fallacy, overconfidence, loss aversion, and framing effect.

Covid-19: A highly contagious disease caused by the SARS-CoV-2 virus, which is known to have emerged in Wuhan, China, in the late of 2019 and then spread throughout the world, causing a pandemic. It starts with high fever, cough, and shortness of breath, and becomes fatal with severe pneumonia, respiratory and kidney failure.

Demography: Statistical information consisting of data such as gender, age, marital status, employment, education level, birth/death rates obtained to describe the characteristics of a population or sample.

Financial Risk Tolerance: Maximum amount of risk that risk-hungry investors can take after satisfying their appetite.

Financial Risk: The possibility of losing movable and immovable assets that have tangible and intangible value for individuals or institutions, regardless of the concept of time.

Investor Behavior: Attitudes such as risk taking, risk avoidance, fear, panic, excitement, greed, regret, etc. that are effective in individuals' investment decisions and are put into action as a result of their mental processes.

Prospect Theory: A behavioral finance theory that is essentially profit-oriented and based on the principle that individuals avoid loss, uncertainty and risk, and always prefer certain and definite options to others.

Risk: The absolute or probable existence of a threat that has different meanings and criteria for every living being on earth and that, if realized, could directly or indirectly affect the living space of the living being to a certain extent.

ENDNOTES

[1] This study was derived from the doctoral thesis titled "The Factors Affecting Financial Risk Tolerance Of Investors in Turkey According to A/B Personality Traits in Times of Covid-19 Pandemic" completed by Dr. Lokman Dal under the supervision of Prof.Dr. Nuray Girginer on 22.06.2023.

[2] Data Analysis Platform is an online data service provided by the Central Registry Agency that reports data on all securities traded in the capital markets in Türkiye (Borsa Istanbul companies, number of domestic and foreign investors, portfolio values, etc.), constantly updates this data.

[3] The reason why household monthly income ranges are quite low compared to today's economic conditions is that the research was conducted in October 2021. As of October 2021, when the data for the research was collected, the gross minimum wage in Türkiye was 3,577.50 TL and the net minimum wage was 2,825.90 TL. Source: https://www.aile.gov.tr/asgari-ucret/asgari-ucret-2021/ , Access Date: 12.05.2025).

[4] Turkish Lira.

Chapter 8
An Evaluation on the Global Innovation Index: A Club Convergence Approach

Öznur Taşdöken
https://orcid.org/0000-0001-7381-4361
Antalya Chamber of Commerce and Industry, Turkey

ABSTRACT

This study analyzes club convergence among countries based on global innovation and income levels by considering global innovation index values for 123 countries between 2011 and 2024. The club convergence approach developed by Phillips and Sul (2007) is used for this analysis. Unlike traditional convergence tests, this approach considers factors with heterogeneity in its analysis. This study evaluates the convergence of countries into similar innovation clubs by considering their global innovation index values over different periods. Based on the analysis results, it can be concluded that the developments in countries' innovations at the global scale are not homogeneous and that countries belong to different convergence clubs. This situation indicates that the developments in countries' innovations at the global scale are heterogeneous. The heterogeneity in the development of innovation in countries also demonstrates structural differences in the economic development and technological progress of countries, even among those with the same income level.

1. INTRODUCTION

Economic variables such as economic inequality, income, total factor productivity and quality of human capital, knowledge and technology investments and research, market and commercial development among countries and regions have

DOI: 10.4018/979-8-3373-1529-4.ch008

an impact on the economy of a country. Changes in these economic variables vary among countries over time and cause technological inequalities to increase among countries. These differences cause economic growth rates and technological development levels to differ among countries.

There are numerous studies in the literature that examine economic differences among countries. The theoretical evaluations and empirical research findings from these studies show that technological developments play a significant role in shaping economic development and economic growth (Ahmad et al., 2024; Ahmad et al., 2023). Considering the important role of technological progress in shaping economic development and growth, changes in macroeconomic dynamics also provide insights into regional economic development and regional growth expectations.

Technological developments contribute to sustainable economic growth in countries (Romer, 1990), to changes in the social structure, and to an increase in the level of welfare (Acemoğlu and Johnson, 2023). However, while technological advancements create new opportunities for countries, they also lead to the emergence of new challenges. One of the most significant of these challenges is the increasing inequality between countries and regions. In order to eliminate these inequalities, various policies are being developed by many international and national public institutions. However, during the implementation of these policies, countries face numerous legal barriers.

Using countries' technological transformation in a way that increases economic and social benefits, limits risks, and builds inclusive prosperity poses challenges for public policy. Therefore, decisions and policies made by international organizations help eliminate the difficulties in implementing public policies across countries. To examine the impact of technological developments on policies in different countries, this study considers the research question: *"Is it necessary to reshape national and global institutions and policies with new approaches and regulations to adapt to the new dynamics brought by the digital age?"* Based on this question, the study evaluates the role of institutional policies in countries' technological advancements. Accordingly, Section 6 provides an assessment of how technological changes affect institutional structures by referring to relevant studies in the literature.

In recent years, technological advancements have had profound impacts on global economies. The rapid development and diffusion of new technologies significantly affect markets, economic growth, and income distribution. In this context, this study explores the research question: *"How does the development of new technologies affect markets, economic growth, income distribution, and club convergence expectations among countries on a global scale based on their level of economic income?"* The study examines the effects of new technologies on economic systems and analyzes how these effects are shaped. Accordingly, in Section 4, a theoretical and empirical analysis is conducted to investigate club formations among countries based on their levels of economic income.

Economic inequality and technological advancements are two significant factors deeply influencing the dynamics of the global economy. The economic disparities between developed and developing countries determine not only their internal dynamics but also their competitive positions on the international stage. The speed of emergence and the diffusion capacity of technological innovations have a profound impact on expectations of economic convergence. However, these impacts often vary depending on countries' access to and capacity for technology adoption. Within this context, this study analyzes the factors influencing technological convergence among countries, taking into account the research question: *'How do technological developments in developed and developing economies affect expectations of economic convergence between these countries?'* Thus, the study's five chapters explore the dual impact of technological advancements on societal and economic dynamics. Consequently, the differences between countries regarding how technology realizes its dual role of potentially exacerbating inequalities while supporting inclusivity and resilience are examined

In this study, the panel club convergence approach will be used to analyze innovation convergence among countries. In this approach, the global innovation index(GII) value will be utilized to examine the observed distribution differences between countries, and log-t tests will be applied to test for convergence and to track the formation of clubs. Along with this analysis, it is expected that the convergence in the GII for each country within similar clubs will be due to similar changes in variables such as human capital, research and development investments, institutions, knowledge, and technology.In this context, the following research questions have been formulated to analyze the objective of the study, taking into consideration relevant studies in the literature:

> Q1: Is there a need to reshape national and global institutions and policies with new approaches and regulations in order to adapt to the new dynamics brought about by the digital age?
> Q2: How do the development of new technologies affect markets, economic growth, income distribution, and club convergence expectations based on countries' income levels on a global scale?
> Q3: How do technological developments in developed and developing economies influence expectations of economic convergence between these countries?

These questions, prepared for the club convergence approach which dynamically examines differences and similarities among countries help the research systematically interpret the phenomenon under investigation. Moreover, the research questions, multilayered structures, not only by questioning whether general convergence exists, but also by identifying which countries are part of which clubs and which factors are decisive in the formation of these clubs.

The continuation of the paper is as follows: Chapter 2 provides a brief review of studies on global innovation. Chapter 3 explains the data used in the study and the club convergence approach. Chapter 4 analyzes the impact of technological advancements on the economy. Chapter 5 examines the formation of innovation clubs among countries. Chapter 6 offers an evaluation of new technological developments and institutional regulations. Chapter 7 presents the conclusion.

2. STUDIES CONDUCTED ON THE GLOBAL INNOVATION INDEX

Various econometric approaches have been used to analyze the innovation relationship between countries using the GII. In the study by Bate et al. (2023), a multiple linear regression analysis and variance analysis (ANOVA) based on per capita income were performed using the GII for 63 countries. The analysis revealed that the changes in countries' innovation were among the main factors contributing to their economic growth. In the study by Vukoszavlyev (2019), variables such as GDP per capita measured in purchasing power parity, unemployment rate, life expectancy, crude death rate, and Human Development Index (HDI) were used to explore the connection between innovation and geographical regions' variability in the innovation index across 126 countries. Non-parametric hypothesis tests, post-hoc tests, and linear regression approaches were applied. The research found that there were differences between countries when considering the GII value. In the study by Yıldırım et al. (2024), the artificial neural network (ANN) model was used to predict the GII score for 125 countries between 2013 and 2025. The analysis concluded that the ANN model was sufficient for calculating the GII score of countries. In the study by Nasir & Zhang (2024), the relationship between innovation inputs, outputs, and efficiency was analyzed using a panel data set for 105 countries between 2013 and 2021. Regression and panel quantile regression approaches, along with the panel-corrected standard errors approach, were used in the analysis. The analysis found that having input and output indices had a positive impact on the GII. Furthermore, according to the results of the quantile regression approach, there is a clear and consistent correlation between the input, output, and efficiency of innovation at higher quantile values. In the study by Oturakci (2023), the relationship between the factors used in calculating the GII was analyzed using the canonical correlation approach for the years 2013-2020. The analysis concluded that human capital (69.2%), Research and Development (R&D) (68.7%), and creative outputs (98.8%) explained the GII. In the study by Gogodze (2016), the relationships between the components of innovation were investigated using GII values for the years 2011-2015. The research found that the management of institutional capital was an important indicator for innovation development in non-low-income countries. In the study by Huarng & Yu (2022), fuzzy set qualitative comparative analysis (fsQCA) and structural qualitative analysis were used for the 2020 GII data. The findings from the analysis suggest that positive/negative changes in all factors (except for market development) used in the calculation of the GII tend to make the GII positive/negative. In the study by Yu et al. (2021), the GII data for the years 2016-2020 were analyzed using the fuzzy set/Qualitative Comparative Analysis (fsQCA) approach. The results of the analysis indicate that there is a causal combination among the factors of the GII. In the study by Coutinho & Au-Yong-Oliveira (2024), an analysis was conducted to evaluate the factors affecting the innovation ecosystem performance of 64 countries using the GII data for 2022. The analysis concluded that human capital and research, business development, education, R&D investment, innovation partnerships, ecological sustainability, and knowledge absorption are significant factors impacting GII performance. In the study by Barrios et al. (2019), a convergence analysis was conducted across European regions using innovation data for the years 2002-2012. The analysis found that there were seven convergence clubs among European regions. In the study by Crespo & Crespo (2016), fuzzy-set qualitative comparative analysis was used to analyze GII data for high- and low-income countries. Five input factors of GII (human capital and research, infrastructure, market development, and business development) were used in the analysis. The results of the analysis indicated that causal combinations of conditions in these factors lead to high innovation performance in both high- and low-income countries. Additionally, in low-income countries, the conditions alone were not sufficient to predict high innovation performance. However, in high-income countries, human capital and research conditions alone were found to be sufficient to achieve better innovation performance.

There are many studies in the literature related to the GII. However, these studies generally analyze the variables used to calculate the GII or the relationships between countries using different econometric approaches. Therefore, this study uses GII data for 123 countries between 2011 and 2024. This study will apply the convergence approach to country panel time series data in accordance with the methodology of Phillips and Sul (2007). Thus, based on the findings, the underlying reasons for the innovation differences between countries and regions will be investigated. Consequently, the results are expected to contribute to the relevant research.

3. ECONOMETRIC METHODOLOGY AND DATASET

This section of the study analyzes the formation of clusters among countries using the GII. The analysis considers the dataset used, countries, GII, and the club convergence approach.

3.1. Data Set Used In The Study

Various indices have been developed to measure countries' levels of innovation and to conduct comparative analyses among them. One such index is the GII, which was first published in 2007 through a collaboration between the World Intellectual Property Organization (WIPO), Cornell University, and INSEAD. This index ranks countries' innovation capacities on a global scale by taking into account numerous variables such as Research and Development (R&D) expenditures, patent applications, quality of higher education, and information and communication technology infrastructure (Dutta et al., 2017, p. 48). Each year, the index provides the global innovation rankings of approximately 130 countries.

The calculation of the GII is based on more than 80 indicators grouped under seven dimensions within two main categories. The first main category is the Innovation Input Sub-Index. This category is further divided into: Institutions (political environment, regulatory framework, business environment), Human capital and research (education level, higher education, R&D investments), Infrastructure (information and communication technologies, general infrastructure, environmental sustainability), Market sophistication (credit availability, investment environment, trade competition), and Business sophistication (knowledge workers, innovative firms, university-industry collaborations) (Dutta et al., 2024).

The second main category is the Innovation Output Sub-Index, which is divided into: Knowledge and technology outputs (patent applications, scientific publications, high-tech exports) and Creative outputs (designs, trademark applications, products of cultural and creative industries). Considering the factors used in the calculation of the index, the development of innovation is examined comparatively across many countries and over different years on a global scale (Dutta et al., 2024). In this context, the GII is one of the most frequently used indices in the economics literature for comparing innovation across countries.

To conduct a club convergence analysis of countries based on the GII, countries were classified according to the income groups provided in the 2024 GII report. One of the main reasons for making this distinction in the analysis is the variation in parameters used in the calculation of the GII—such as institutional structure, level of economic development, and the quality of human capital—across countries.

Categorizing countries by income level when constructing the dataset enhances the reliability of the findings obtained from the econometric estimations.

The differences in innovation levels and investments aimed at fostering innovation among countries primarily stem from variations in their income levels. The study considers both the GII values and income levels for 123 countries over the period from 2011 to 2024. The countries included in the analysis are presented in Table 1, and the analysis was conducted using the Stata software.

Table 1. Countries Used in Analysis

High Income Group			**Upper Middle Income Group**	
ABD	Ireland	Uruguay	Albania	Indonesia
Australia	Hong Kong	Poland	Argentina	Jamaica
Austria	Hungary	Portugal	Armenia	Russian
Bahrain	Iceland	Qatar	Belarus	South Africa
Belgium	Israel	Romania	Bosnia and Herzegovina	Serbia
Brunei Darussalam	Italy	Saudi Arabia	Botswana	Thailand
Canada	Japan	Singapore	Brazil	Türkiye
Chile	Kuwait	Slovakia	Bulgaria	
Croatia	Latvia	Slovenia	China	
Cyprus	Lithuania	Spain	Colombia	
Czech Republic	Luxembourg	Sweden	Dominican Republic	
Denmark	Malta	Switzerland	El Salvador	
Estonia	Netherlands	Trinidad and Tobago	Georgia	
Finland	New Zealand	United Arab Emirates	Malaysia	
France	Norway	United Kingdom	Mexico	
Germany	Oman		Montenegro	
Greece	Panama		Peru	
Lower Middle And Low Income Group				
Algeria	Ghana	Nepal	Cameroon	Tunisia
Bangladesh	Iran	Pakistan	Ecuador	Mozambique
Benin	Kazakhstan	Philippines	Ukraine	Lebanon
Bolivia	Kenya	Ethiopia	Cambodia	Madagascar
Burkina Faso	Uganda	Rwanda	Viet Nam	Togo
Guinea	Honduras	Niger	Côte d'Ivoire	Morocco
Malawi	India	Nigeria	Namibia	Mongolia
Yemen	Guatemala	Nicaragua	Costa Rica	Mali

continued on following page

Table 1. Continued

High Income Group			Upper Middle Income Group	
Zambia	Kyrgyzstan	Sri Lanka	Senegal	Tajikistan
Zimbabwe	Jordan	Paraguay	Egypt	Azerbaijan

Resource: Dutta et al., (2024)

To observe the formation of clubs among countries based on differences in innovation development between developed and developing countries, and the innovation rankings according to income levels, the log t test developed by Phillips & Sul (2007) is employed to test for convergence. In the analyses, the dataset is organized based on the countries with the lowest GII and innovation values by income level, taking the year 2024 into account. In the analysis, the null hypothesis of the convergence test is formulated as "convergence exists".

3.2. Club Convergence Approach

The convergence approach is based on the assumption that differences in economic performance between countries or regions may diminish over time, meaning that these countries or regions tend to converge economically in the long run. Within the framework of the neoclassical growth theory, this approach suggests that key indicators such as per capita income, productivity, human capital, and innovation in developed and developing countries will converge to similar levels over time. The classical convergence hypothesis predicts that all countries will reach a single equilibrium level in the long term, assuming that they possess similar structural conditions.

In the economics literature, various theories of economic growth have been developed based on different assumptions. One such theory, the neoclassical growth model, was developed by Solow (1956) under the assumption of diminishing returns to capital. According to this model, countries with lower capital per worker are expected to grow at a faster rate than countries with higher levels of capital, due to higher marginal returns. In other words, developing countries tend to converge over time to the per capita capital levels of developed countries. This process is defined in the literature as β-convergence and is based on the principle of diminishing returns, one of the fundamental assumptions of the neoclassical growth model. Within this framework, long-term growth reaches a steady-state level determined by exogenous technological progress and the rate of labor force growth.

Another type of convergence, known as σ-convergence, analyzes whether income distribution among countries or regions becomes more homogeneous over time. This approach focuses on observing whether absolute income disparities are narrowing and provides important insights for assessing the effects of economic integration processes (Furceri, 2005;Monfort, 2008). However, while these theoretical approaches offer an important framework for explaining observed growth differences among countries, they do not account for structural characteristics, institutional differences, and socio-cultural heterogeneity. Moreover, the convergence approach is widely used as a significant econometric tool for analyzing differences in economic development among countries, evaluating the effectiveness of regional policies, and developing sustainable growth strategies.

In recent years, convergence analyses have extended to include multidimensional development indicators such as innovation capacity, education level, health indicators, and environmental performance. In this context, panel data analyses, dynamic models, and particularly the log-t test method developed by Phillips and Sul (2007) are frequently used for the empirical testing of convergence. The club convergence approach developed by Phillips and Sul (2007, 2009) reveals that countries with similar structural characteristics may form sub-groups within themselves and converge toward different equilibrium levels, thus addressing a significant gap in the literature.

The fundamental basis of the club convergence approach developed by Phillips and Sul (2007, 2009) is the recognition that there are both temporal and cross-sectional differences among countries in indicators such as technological progress, human capital accumulation, and institutional development. Taking this heterogeneity into account, the model calculates the degree to which each economy deviates from or aligns with the overall growth trend through time-varying factor loadings. Within this framework, the log t regression test can be used to statistically test the presence of intra-club convergence in panel data sets.

From an economic perspective, this approach emphasizes that developing countries may follow distinct growth paths and that it should not be expected for these countries to grow at the same pacc or with the same structural characteristics as developed economies. Studies in the literature and growth models developed based on different assumptions show that factors such as technological capacity, institutional structure, human capital accumulation, and sensitivity to external shocks are fundamental determinants of countries' long-term growth trends (Acemoglu, 2009).

This study investigates the formation of clubs in the GII among countries. To analyze the convergence of global innovation across countries, the approach developed by Phillips & Sul (2007, 2009), which is based on the log t test, has been employed. The primary reason for using this approach in the study is its distinction from the existing convergence theories in the literature. According to the studies by Apergis & Cooray (2014:787), Tomal (2022:2025), and Belloc & Molina (2023:2809), these differences are as follows:

- The club convergence approach does not rely on assumptions regarding the stability of the trend in the panel common component or the stationarity of the variables.
- This approach eliminates the biased parameter problem that arises from β-convergence among variables.
- The club convergence method serves as an asymptotic cointegration test that is not affected by small sample issues.
- The results obtained from the club convergence analysis are based on a general form of a nonlinear and time-varying factor model.
- The club convergence approach is a suitable econometric tool for short time series analyses and general cluster convergence analyses. Furthermore, it is not dependent on the stationarity properties of the variables. Therefore, stationarity tests for the variables were not conducted in this study.
- In a panel dataset, countries converging toward the same equilibrium are determined endogenously along with other countries.

Considering the advantages of the log t test developed by Phillips & Sul (2007, 2009), it can be said that this approach is appropriate for investigating the clustering of countries in the GII based on innovation development in different regions and the increases in underlying factors contributing to this development.

Club convergence among countries in a panel time series variable is tested using the method developed by Phillips & Sul (2007, 2009). In this test, a factor model is initially used. In this model, the time-varying common factor equation for X_{it} in country i at time t is given as follows:

$$X_{it} = \delta_{it}\mu_t \tag{1}$$

Equation 1: The parameter X_{it} represents GII in country i at time t, and the parameter aaa is δ_{it} time-varying factor loading that represents convergence to the common factor μ_t.The parameter δ_{it}examines the degree of convergence by identifying any amount of convergence in the factor loadings. It also measures the idiosyncratic distance between $X_{it}$and μ_t. The equation $X_{it} = \delta_{it}\mu_t$ indicates that the GII for each country depends on the factors used in its calculation. The factor loadings δ_{it}allow for testing convergence by examining whether they converge to t → ∞ common constant δ over time. However, in this case, country-specific differences are eliminated over time. Therefore, in their study Phillips & Sul (2007) propose modeling the non-stationary transitional behavior of the factor loadings,

$$h_{it} = \frac{X_{it}}{N^{-1}\sum_{i=1}^{N} X_{it}} = \frac{\delta_{it}}{N^{-1}\sum_{i=1}^{N} \delta_{it}} \tag{2}$$

Equation 2: The parameter N represents the number of countries. The variable h_{it} is the relative transition path term and provides the potential individual trajectory for each country iii relative to the panel average. To form the null hypothesis of convergence, Phillips & Sul (2009) propose a semi-parametric model for the time-varying parameter δ_{it}.

$$\delta_{it} = \delta_i + \sigma_i S_{it} L(t)^{-1} t^{-\alpha} \tag{3}$$

Equation 3: When the parameter δ_{it} is fixed, $\sigma_i > 0$ is the standart deviation of horizontal sections h_{it}. It is i.i.d.(0,1) throught S_{it} but weakly dependent on t, and L(t) is a slowly varying function that tends to infinity as t approaches infinity.

L(t) function is logarithm of t; moreover, the S_{it} parameter adds country-specific and time-varying components to the model; additionally, the magnitude of á will determine the scope, the nature of any convergence or deviation (δ_{it}).In this context, the null hypothesis of convergence and the alternative hypothesis of divergence or club convergence for all $\alpha \geq 0$, $\delta_{it} = \delta_i$ is not rejected. In this framework, Phillips and Sul (2007) have proven that it is possible to test these hypotheses using the following 'log t' regression model. To do this;

$$\log\left(\frac{H_1}{H_t}\right) - 2\log L(t) = \hat{\alpha} + \hat{b}\log t + \hat{u}_t \tag{4}$$

$t = [rT], [rT] + 1, \ldots, t$, r > 0 ve H_1/H_t is the variance ratio of cross-sections. The extent of convergence within groups (i.e., club convergence and club formation) can be analyzed using log (t) regressions. Considering the appropriate coefficient $\hat{b} = 2.\hat{\alpha}$ in log (t), $\hat{t}_b = < -1.65$ tests the convergence hypothesis by rejecting the null value at the 5% significance level (Phillips & Sul, 2007; 2009).

4. EFFECTS OF TECHNOLOGICAL DEVELOPMENTS ON THE ECONOMY

There are many different growth models in the economics literature. These models are based on the works of numerous economists such as Adam Smith (1776), David Ricardo (1817), Thomas Malthus (1798), Solow (1956), Joseph Schumpeter (1934), Harrod (1939) and Domar (1946), Lucas (1988), Romer (1986), Arrow (1962), and Sheshinski (1967). These theories generally focus on factors such as firms' competitive behavior, the dynamics of economic equilibrium, diminishing returns, the accumulation of physical and human capital, per capita income, population growth rate, knowledge and experience accumulation, technological developments, education, division of labor, and specialization, all of which form the foundations of growth theories (Acemoglu, 2009).

In the Neoclassical growth model, one of the economic growth theories, Solow (1956) considered technology as an external factor. However, in the new growth models developed through the works of Lucas (1988) and Romer (1986), technological developments, the quality of human capital, and research and development activities are considered internal factors in the production function. In other words, in the more recent economic growth theories, technological developments and knowledge accumulation are accepted as one of the key dynamics of economic growth in countries (Conte, 2006).

The increase in technological developments that began in the 1880s, along with the rise in capital accumulation and specialization, forms the foundation of the economic growth of many countries (Ahmad et al., 2024; Ahmad et al., 2023). The development of information and communication technologies, the use of artificial intelligence in the production process, the shift to automation in production, and the use of robotic processes have led to profound changes in economic structures. In other words, the acceleration of technological developments in countries has also led to changes in income distribution in the production process, the emergence of new sectors, increased competitiveness, the formation of new markets, a rise in demand for skilled labor, improvements in labor productivity, the development of financial systems (Cai & Song, 2022), and increases in total factor productivity and efficiency (Chen & Zhou, 2024).

The log t test developed by Phillips & Sul (2007) is used to analyze whether convergence exists in the GII based on income levels between developed and developing countries. This analysis provides important insights into understanding the economic convergence processes that change over different time periods among countries classified by income groups. Additionally, it offers valuable information on how global innovation clubs may vary according to countries' levels of development and how these changes can be utilized by policymakers. The results of the analysis are presented in Table 2.

Table 2. Global Innovation Value by Income Level for All Countries Club Convergence Estimation Results

Countries	Number of Countries	Countries	tƃ	Log(t)	Inference
High Income Group	49	All Countries	-0.8984	-39.3587	No Convergence
Upper Middle Income Group	24	All Countries	-0.8543	-10.6582	No Convergence
Lower Middle And Low Income Group	50	All Countries	-1.4033	-7.9721	No Convergence

Resource: Prepared by the author.

Table 2 provides the results of the log t regression estimation for the GII based on income levels: high income group, upper middle income group, and lower middle and low income group, for the entire sample set. The respective Log(t) statistics values are found as -39.3587, -10.6582, and -7.9721. Since these values are less than the critical value of -1.65, the null hypothesis is rejected at the 5% significance level. According to this finding, there is no general convergence in the GII across the countries used in the analysis based on income levels. In other words, considering the results of the log t test estimation, there is no convergence in innovation among the countries analyzed based on income levels.

This finding indicates that there are structural and economic differences among countries with different income levels. Therefore, it can be said that these countries are unlikely to reach a single economic equilibrium. However, the absence of overall convergence among these countries does not rule out the possibility of club convergence. Accordingly, the analysis examines the likelihood of clubs for each country by considering a clustering algorithm among the countries.

Table 3. Global Innovation Index By Economic İncome Level Of High-İncome Countries Club Convergence Results

Club	**Number of Countries**	**Countries**	**tƀ**	**Log(t)**	**Inference**
Convergene	49	All Countries	-0.8984	-39.3587	No Convergence
İnitial convergence club					
Club 1	29	Ireland, Luxembourg, Iceland, Australia, New Zealand, Cyprus, Spain, Malta, Czech Republic, Portugal, Saudi Arabia, Slovenia, Lithuania, Hungary, Poland, Latvia, Croatia, Greece, Slovak Republic, Romania, Qatar, Chile, Uruguay, Kuwait, Bahrain, Oman, Panama, Brunei Darussalam, Trinidad and Tobago	-0.037	-0.381	Club convergence
Club 2	7	Netherlands, Denmark, Hong Kong, Norway, Belgium, Italy, United Arab Emirates	0.105	0.967	Club convergence
Club 3	4	Canada, Israel, Estonia, Austria	0.642	1.416	Club convergence
Club 4	6	Singapore, United Kingdom, Finland, Germany, France, Japan	0.47	1.554	Club convergence
Clup 5	3	Switzerland, Sweden, ABD	0.137	1.512	Club convergence
Merge of Clubs					
Club			**tƀ**	**Log(t)**	**Inference**
Club 1+2		-	-0.399	-6.476	No merge
Club 2+3		-	-0.204	-1.647	Merge
Club 3+4		-	-0.251	-3.496	No merge
Club 4+5		-	-0.309	-4.020	No merge
Final Clubs after Merge					
Club			**tƀ**	**Log(t)**	**Inference**
Club 1	29	Ireland, Luxembourg, Iceland, Australia, New Zealand, Cyprus, Spain, Malta, Czech Republic, Portugal, Saudi Arabia, Slovenia, Lithuania, Hungary, Poland, Latvia, Croatia, Greece, Slovak Republic, Romania, Qatar, Chile, Uruguay, Kuwait, Bahrain, Oman, Panama, Brunei Darussalam, Trinidad and Tobago	-0.037	-0.381	Club convergence
Club 2	11	Netherlands, Denmark, Canada, Israel, Estonia, Austria, Hong Kong, Norway, Belgium, Italy, United Arab Emirates	-0.204	-1.647	Club convergence
Club 3	6	Singapore, United Kingdom, Finland, Germany, France, Japan	0.47	1.554	Club convergence
Club 4	3	Switzerland, Sweden, ABD	0.137	1.512	Club convergence

Resource: Prepared by the author.

Considering Table 3, it is observed that different clubs have been formed. Accordingly, Club 1 consists of twenty-nine countries, Club 2 of seven countries, Club 3 of four countries, Club 4 of six countries, and Club 5 of twenty-three countries. The log(t) statistic values for these clubs are as follows: Club 1: -0.381, Club 2: -0.967, Club 3: 1.416, Club 4: 1.554, and Club 5: 1.512. Since the log(t) values are greater than the critical value, we accept the null hypothesis of no convergence at the 5% significance level. In other words, this indicates that there is convergence in global innovation based on income level among the countries within these clubs. In this context, the clubs that satisfy the convergence hypothesis also provide insights into whether smaller clubs can potentially be merged with larger ones.

After the merging of the clubs, the results show that Club 1 consists of twenty-nine countries, Club 2 of eleven countries, Club 3 of six countries, and Club 4 of three countries. The log(t) statistic values for these clubs are as follows: Club 1: -0.381, Club 2: -0.647, Club 3: 1.554, and Club 4: 1.512. The results indicate that the clubs have significantly merged with one another. Furthermore, it shows that developed countries are clustered into four distinct clubs.

The convergence of countries into similar clubs also indicates the presence of common dynamics among them. For example, the fact that the ABD, Sweden, and Switzerland are in the same club can be attributed to factors such as high capital accumulation, advanced education systems, R&D investments, and active involvement of the private sector in these countries. Increasing investments in human capital and R&D expenditures aimed at enhancing countries' innovation ecosystems not only support this convergence (Sudolska & Łapińska, 2020), but also contribute to the generation and development of new ideas (Oturakci, 2023). Considering the results obtained, the inclusion of the ABD, Sweden, and Switzerland in the same club also highlights their significant contributions to technological advancements and the development of global innovation policies.

Table 4. Global Innovation Index By Economic İncome Level Of Middle-İncome Countries Club Convergence Results

Club	Number of Countries	Countries	tɓ	Log(t)	Inference
Convergene	24	All Countries	-0.8543	-10.6582	No Convergence
İnitial convergence club					
Club 1	6	Armenia, Montenegro, South Africa, Botswana, Dominican republic, El Salvador	1.46	5.18	Club convergence
Club 2	6	Georgia, Peru, Jamaica, Bosnia & Herzegovina, Albania, Belarus	0.603	2.257	Club convergence

continued on following page

Table 4. Continued

Club	Number of Countries	Countries	tƃ	Log(t)	Inference
Club 3	5	Serbia, Indonesia, Mexico, Colombia, Argentina	0.332	0.603	Club convergence
Club 4	7	China, Malaysia, Turkey, Bulgaria, Thailand, Brazil, Russian Federation	0.030	0.174	Club convergence
Merge of Clubs					
Club			**tƃ**	**Log(t)**	**Inference**
Club 1+2		-	1.132	5.552	Merge
Club 2+3		-	-0.185	-0.354	Merge
Club 3+4		-	-0.997	-14.26	Not Merge
Final Clubs after Merge					
Club			**tƃ**	**Log(t)**	**Inference**
Club 1	17	Serbia, Indonesia, Georgia, Mexico, Colombia, Armenia, Montenegro, South Africa, Peru, Argentina, Jamaica, Bosnia & Herzegovina, Albania, Belarus, Botswana, Dominican republic, El Salvador	0.283	0.920	Club convergence
Club 2	7	China, Malaysia, Turkey, Bulgaria, Thailand, Brazil, Russian Federation	0.030	0.174	Club convergence

Resource: Prepared by the author.

Considering Table 4, it is observed that different countries have formed into a single club. Accordingly, Club 1 consists of six countries, Club 2 of six countries, Club 3 of five countries, and Club 4 of seven countries.

The log(t) statistic values for these clubs are as follows: Club 1: 5.18, Club 2: 2.257, Club 3: 0.603, and Club 4: 0.174. All of these log(t) values are greater than the critical value. In this context, the statistical significance among these countries indicates that the null hypothesis is accepted. This shows that there is convergence in global innovation based on income levels among these countries. Furthermore, the application of the convergence hypothesis across these clubs also provides insights into whether smaller clubs can potentially be merged with larger ones.

After the merging of the clubs, the results show that Club 1 consists of seventeen countries and Club 2 of seven countries. The log(t) statistic values for these clubs are 0.920 for Club 1 and 0.174 for Club 2. The results indicate that the clubs have significantly merged with one another. Furthermore, it shows that developing countries are clustered into two distinct clubs.

Table 5. Global Innovation Index by economic income level of countries in the Lower Middle and Low Income Group Club Convergence Results

Club	Number of Countries	Countries	tБ	Log(t)	Inference
Convergene	50	All Countries	-1.4033	-7.9721	No Convergence
İnitial convergence club					
Club 1	27	Rwanda, Ukraine, Jordan, Senegal, Kenya, Costa Rica, Kyrgyzstan, Ghana, Cambodia, Bangladesh, Kazakhstan, Tajikistan, Nepal, Côte d'Ivoire, Nigeria, Honduras, Paraguay, Algeria, Azerbaijan, Zambia, Zimbabwe, Benin, Namibia, Ecuador, Cameroon, Guatemala, Nicaragua	0.307	1.555	Club convergence
Club 2	11	Morocco, Mozambique, Mongolia, Ethiopia, Mali, Niger, Egypt, Sri Lanka, Pakistan, Lebanon, Bolivia	0.668	2.154	Club convergence
Club 3	10	Guinea, Yemen, Madagascar, Viet Nam, Philippines, Togo, Uganda, Iran, Burkina Faso, Tunisia	-0.386	-0.667	Club convergence
Club 4	2	Malawi, India	-6.225	-2.959	No Club convergence
Merge of Clubs					
Club			**tБ**	**Log(t)**	**Inference**
Club 1+2	-	-	-0.529	-3.534	No Merge
Club 2+3	-	-	-0.775	-2.724	No Merge
Club 3+4	-	-	-1.070	-2.048	No Merge
Final Clubs after Merge					
Club	-	-	**tБ**	**Log(t)**	**Inference**
Club 1	-	-	-0.529	-3.534	No Club convergence
Club 2	-	-	-0.775	-2.724	No Club convergence

Resource: Prepared by the author.

Considering Table 5, it is observed that different countries have formed into separate clubs. Accordingly, Club 1 consists of six countries, Club 2 of six countries, Club 3 of five countries, and Club 4 of seven countries. The log(t) statistic values for these clubs are as follows: Club 1: 5.18, Club 2: 2.257, Club 3: 0.603, and Club 4: 0.174. All of these values are greater than the critical value. The statistical significance among these countries indicates that the null hypothesis is accepted. This demonstrates the presence of club convergence in global innovation based on income levels among these countries. Furthermore, the application of the convergence hypothesis across these clubs also provides insights into whether smaller clubs can potentially be merged with larger ones. In this regard, when we consider the results after the merging of clubs, no distinct clubs are formed among these countries.

The GII convergence analysis based on countries' income levels contributes to a better understanding of the human and physical investments made to enhance innovation. In this regard, our results do not support the convergence hypothesis when all countries are considered collectively. The primary reason for this is that countries do not move toward a single long-term equilibrium, due to their differing economic and institutional structures. In other words, the structural and institutional heterogeneity among countries prevents them from converging toward a single steady state in innovation indicators. However, the results of the analysis reveal that countries exhibit club convergence in terms of the GII when grouped by income level. Assessments among countries with varying levels of development and income show that even among those with similar income levels, there are notable differences in institutional capacity, human capital, and R&D investments (Kijek et al., 2022).

This indicates a clear divergence in terms of GII performance among countries and shows that countries with similar structural characteristics tend to be part of the same convergence clubs—thereby displaying parallel trends in innovation investment. On the other hand, a distinct heterogeneity in innovation structures is observed among countries belonging to different clubs, depending on income level. Within this framework, the main economic conclusions that can be drawn from the analysis are as follows:

- While new technologies support economic growth on a global scale, they also appear to exacerbate structural and economic inequalities among countries (Acemoglu and Johnson, 2023; Biyase et al., 2023).
- It has been identified that technological developments are not equally distributed among countries in different clubs, leading to structural divergence.
- It is understood that developing countries need to strengthen their investments aimed at enhancing innovation and technological production capacity. In this context, the effective diffusion of advanced technologies from developed countries to others emerges as a critical policy need.
- Technological developments and innovative capacity vary among countries depending on income level, and this disparity leads to asymmetric outcomes in the diffusion and economic effects of technology (Carayannis & Grigoroudis, 2016). In other words, new technological advancements highlight significant differences between countries in terms of boosting innovation capacity, developing, and disseminating new technologies. Therefore, while technological progress and structural transformation enhance market integration and economic growth (Hall and Rosenberg, 2010), they also cause global innovation imbalances among countries. This situation affects

sustainable global competitiveness among countries (Veselica, 2019: p. 441) and has implications for their economic growth (Islam, 2025).

Developing countries face significant structural and institutional barriers in the process of integrating into the global innovation system. Convergence analyses of the Global Innovation Index (GII) based on income levels reveal that these countries generally do not move toward a single long-term innovation equilibrium. However, they may exhibit partial convergence within subgroups (clubs) that share similar structural and economic characteristics. At the core of this divergence lie factors such as unequal access to technological advancements, inadequate institutional capacity, shortage of skilled labor, and underinvestment in infrastructure.

In this context, based on the findings of the analysis, differences in countries' economic performance, levels of integration into global technology, domestic political shocks, and social conflicts directly affect their ability to transition from their current innovation clubs to more advanced ones. Considering that the observed innovation-based divergence among countries stems not only from income levels but also from structural and environmental factors, it is of critical importance to strengthen strategic, institutional, and financial investments in order for countries to access structures with higher innovation capacity.

From a policymaking perspective, the results of the club convergence approach contribute to the development of country-specific policies. In other words, instead of implementing one-size-fits-all policies for economic growth and development, it allows for the formulation of differentiated development strategies tailored to groups of countries that share similar structural and dynamic characteristics. Furthermore, rather than evaluating developing countries as a homogeneous group, analyzing them by further disaggregation enables the design of more targeted and effective economic policies.

5. FORMATION OF INNOVATION CLUBS ACROSS COUNTRIES

In economic literature, economic growth theories have been developed by considering different assumptions. One of these theories is the neoclassical growth model. According to the assumption of diminishing returns to capital in the neoclassical growth model by Solow (1956), countries with less capital per worker are expected to have higher growth rates compared to countries with higher return rates. In other words, developing countries have lower labor-capital accumulation and are expected to converge over time with developed countries that have higher labor-capital accumulation. This theory is known as the convergence hypothesis. According to this theory, income inequality between developed and developing countries will gradually diminish, and the growth potential of developing countries will be higher.

The convergence hypothesis initially emerged with the prediction that income disparities between developed and developing countries would converge over time. However, in economic literature, the issue of whether convergence occurs between countries has been explored by using various macroeconomic variables. In other words, club convergence between countries has also been investigated by many researchers in areas such as health, education expenditures, foreign trade, tourism, energy consumption (Ulucak & Apergis, 2018: 21), and household consumption expenditures (Taşdöken & Kahyaoğlu, 2022). In these studies, it can be stated that convergence between countries with different levels of development occurs mainly among countries with similar macroeconomic structures and institutional characteristics (Baumol, 1986).

Considering the heterogeneous institutional structures of countries, the convergence hypothesis has been combined with the club clustering approach (Du, 2017). Thus, countries with different levels of development, but with similar characteristics in terms of economic structure, education expenditures, the quality of human capital, income levels, and factor endowments, are expected to converge toward similar equilibria. In other words, clusters or clubs are formed based on different characteristics such as macroeconomic structure, education expenditures, and the quality of human capital of countries with varying levels of development. While these clubs exhibit homogeneity within themselves, they show heterogeneity with respect to other clubs.

Analyzing the formation of clusters in innovation among countries on a global scale provides information about the level of development in innovation specific to each cluster by considering factors such as technological developments, the quality of human capital, knowledge, inputs, and outputs. In this context, to monitor club formation in the differences, in innovation development between developed and developing countries, an analysis is conducted using the log t-test developed by Phillips & Sul (2007) to test whether convergence occurs.

Table 6. Global Innovation Value Of All Countries Club Convergence Estimation Results

Countries	Number of Countries	Countries	tβ	Log(t)	Inference
High Income Group	49	All Countries	- 1.3463	- 13.9326	No Convergence
Upper Middle Income Group	24	All Countries	-2.473	-38.416	No Convergence
Lower Middle And Low Income Group	50	All Countries	- 2.4544	- 14.4143	No Convergence

Resource: Prepared by the author.

Table 6 provides the GII log t regression estimation results for the high-income group, upper-middle-income group, and lower-middle and low-income groups for the entire sample. The Log(t) statistic values are found to be -13.9326, -38.416, and -14.4143, respectively. Since these values are smaller than the critical value of -1.65, the null hypothesis is rejected at the 5% significance level. According to this finding, there is no general convergence in the GII among the countries used in the analysis. In other words, considering the log t test results, the innovation indices of all countries do not converge towards a common equilibrium level. These results indicate structural and economic differences between countries with varying income levels. it can be said that these countries will not reach a single economic equilibrium. However, the lack of convergence between these countries does not rule out the possibility of club convergence among them. Thus, in the analysis, clustering algorithms are considered between countries, and the likelihood of clubs for each country is examined.

Table 7. Global Innovation Index of High Income Countries Club Convergence Model Estimation Results

Club	Number of Countries	Countries	tβ	Log(t)	Inference
Convergene	49	All Countries	- 1.3463	- 13.932	No Convergence
İnitial convergence club					
Club 1	2	ABD, Switzerland	0.332	1.898	Club convergence
Club 2	10	United Arab Emirates, Estonia, Israel, Canada, Japan, France, Germany, United Kingdom, Singapore, Sweden	0.006	0.011	Club convergence
Club 3	3	Denmark, Netherlands, Finland	0.343	0.854	Club convergence

continued on following page

Table 7. Continued

Club	Number of Countries	Countries	tb	Log(t)	Inference
Club 4	9	Cyprus, Italy, Belgium, Australia, Iceland, Luxembourg, Ireland, Hong Kong, Austria	0.889	8.375	Club convergence
Clup 5	3	Lithuania, Malta, Norway	0.048	0.457	Club convergence
Clup 6	5	Hungary, Portugal, Czech Republic, Spain, New Zealand	0.312	1.285	Club convergence
Clup 7	7	Brunei Darussalam, Qatar, Greece, Croatia, Latvia, Poland, Slovenia	0.154	0.471	Club convergence
Clup 8	2	Saudi Arabia, Slovak Republic	0.047	0.023	Club convergence
Clup 9	2	Chile, Romania	-2.097	-0.761	Club convergence
Clup 10	2	Oman, Bahrain	1.272	1.581	Club convergence
Clup 11	2	Trinidad and Tobago, Panama	0.757	1.737	Club convergence
Clup 12	2	Kuwait, Uruguay (**Not convergent Group**)	-10.193	-4.735	No Club convergence
Merge of Clubs					
Club			**tb**	**Log(t)**	**Inference**
Club 1+2		-	-0.55	-2.995	No merge
Club 2+3		-	-0.189	-0.586	merge
Club 3+4		-	-1.067	-15.901	No merge
Club 4+5		-	0.083	0.791	merge
Club 5+6		-	0.053	0.648	merge
Club 6+7		-	-0.14	-0.534	merge
Club 7+8		-	0.017	0.091	merge
Club 8+9		-	-0.531	-0.358	merge
Club 9+10		-	-1.703	-8.793	No merge
Club 10+11		-	-0.311	-0.575	merge
Club 11+12		-	-0.821	-2.231	No merge
Final Clubs after Merge					
Club			**tb**	**Log(t)**	**Inference**
Club 1	2	ABD, Switzerland	0.332	1.898	Club convergence
Club 2	13	United Arab Emirates, Estonia, Israel, Canada, Japan, France, Denmark, Germany, Netherlands, Finland, United Kingdom, Singapore, Sweden	-0.189	-0.586	Club convergence

continued on following page

Table 7. Continued

Club	Number of Countries	Countries	tɓ	Log(t)	Inference
Club 3	12	Lithuania, Malta, Cyprus, Italy, Belgium, Australia, Iceland, Luxembourg, Norway, Ireland, Hong Kong, Austria	0.083	0.791	Club convergence
Club 4	14	Brunei Darussalam, Qatar, Saudi Arabia, Slovak Republic, Greece, Croatia, Latvia, Poland, Hungary, Slovenia, Portugal, Czech Republic, Spain, New Zealand	-0.28	-1.52	Club convergence
Club 5	2	Chile, Romania	-2.097	-0.761	Club convergence
Club 6	4	Trinidad and Tobago, Panama, Oman, Bahrain	-0.311	-0.575	Club convergence
Group 7	2	Kuwait, Uruguay (**Not convergent Group)**	-10.193	-4.735	No Club convergence
Club	**Number of Countries**	**Countries**	**tɓ**	**Log(t)**	**Inference**
Convergence	49	All Countries	-1.3463	-13.932	No Convergence
İnitial convergence club					
Club 1	2	ABD, Switzerland	0.332	1.898	Club convergence
Club 2	10	United Arab Emirates, Estonia, Israel, Canada, Japan, France, Germany, United Kingdom, Singapore, Sweden	0.006	0.011	Club convergence
Club 3	3	Denmark, Netherlands, Finland	0.343	0.854	Club convergence
Club 4	9	Malawi, India Cyprus, Italy, Belgium, Australia, Iceland, Luxembourg, Ireland, Hong Kong, Austria	0.889	8.375	Club convergence
Club 5	3	Lithuania, Malta, Norway	0.048	0.457	Club convergence
Club 6	5	Hungary, Portugal, Czech Republic, Spain, New Zealand	0.312	1.285	Club convergence
Club 7	7	Brunei Darussalam, Qatar, Greece, Croatia, Latvia, Poland, Slovenia	0.154	0.471	Club convergence
Club 8	2	Saudi Arabia, Slovak Republic	0.047	0.023	Club convergence
Club 9	2	Chile, Romania	-2.097	-0.761	Club convergence
Club 10	2	Oman, Bahrain	1.272	1.581	Club convergence
Club 11	2	Trinidad and Tobago, Panama	0.757	1.737	Club convergence
Club 12	2	Kuwait, Uruguay (not convergent Group)	-10.193	-4.735	No Club convergence
Merge of Clubs					
Club			**tɓ**	**Log(t)**	**Inference**

continued on following page

Table 7. Continued

Club	Number of Countries	Countries	tƃ	Log(t)	Inference
Club 1+2	-	-	-0.55	-2.995	No merge
Club 2+3	-	-	-0.189	-0.586	merge
Club 3+4	-	-	-1.067	-15.901	No merge
Club 4+5	-	-	0.083	0.791	merge
Club 5+6	-	-	0.053	0.648	merge
Club 6+7	-	-	-0.14	-0.534	merge
Club 7+8	-	-	0.017	0.091	merge
Club 8+9	-	-	-0.531	-0.358	merge
Club 9+10	-	-	-1.703	-8.793	No merge
Club 10+11	-	-	-0.311	-0.575	merge
Club 11+12	-	-	-0.821	-2.231	No merge
Final Clubs after Merge					
Club	-	-	**tƃ**	**Log(t)**	**Inference**
Club 1	2	ABD, Switzerland	0.332	1.898	Club convergence
Club 2	13	United Arab Emirates, Estonia, Israel, Canada, Japan, France, Denmark, Germany, Netherlands, Finland, United Kingdom, Singapore, Sweden	-0.189	-0.586	Club convergence
Club 3	12	Lithuania, Malta, Cyprus, Italy, Belgium, Australia, Iceland, Luxembourg, Norway, Ireland, Hong Kong, Austria	0.083	0.791	Club convergence
Club 4	14	Brunei Darussalam, Qatar, Saudi Arabia, Slovak Republic, Greece, Croatia, Latvia, Poland, Hungary, Slovenia, Portugal, Czech Republic, Spain, New Zealand	-0.28	-1.52	Club convergence
Club 5	2	Chile, Romania	-2.097	-0.761	Club convergence
Club 6	4	Trinidad and Tobago, Panama, Oman, Bahrain	-0.311	-0.575	Club convergence
Group 7	2	Kuwait , Uruguay (Not convergent Group)	-10.193	-4.735	No Club Convergence

Resource: Prepared by the author.

Considering Table 7, it is observed that different clubs have formed. Accordingly, Club 1 consists of three countries, Club 2 of thirteen countries, Club 3 of twenty-two countries, Club 4 of twenty-six countries, Club 5 of twenty-two countries, Club 6 of twenty-three countries, Club 7 of eight countries, Club 8 of four countries, Club 9 of two countries, and the Not Convergent Group 10 consists of one country.

For these clubs, the log(t) statistic values are as follows: Club 1 – 4.760, Club 2 – -0.586, Club 3: -1.632, Club 4: -0.455, Club 5: -1.144, Club 6: 0.605, Club 7: -0.477, Club 8: 3.686, and Club 9: -0.53. Among these, the log(t) statistic values of Club 1, Club 2, Club 3, Club 4, Club 5, Club 6, Club 7, Club 8, and Club 9 are greater than the critical value. The statistical significance indicates that the null hypothesis is accepted. This implies that there is convergence in innovation among the countries within these clubs. Its application among clubs that fulfil the convergence hypothesis also shows whether smaller clubs can be merged with larger clubs.

Following the merging of the clubs, the results show that Club 1 consists of two countries, Club 2 of thirteen countries, Club 3 of twelve countries, Club 4 of fourteen countries, Club 5 of twenty-two countries, Club 6 of four countries, and Club 7 of two countries. The log(t) statistic values for these clubs are as follows: Club 1: 1.898, Club 2: -0.586, Club 3: 0.791, Club 4: -1.52, Club 5: 0.761, Club 6: -0.575, and Club 7: -4.735. The results indicate that the clubs have significantly merged with one another. Additionally, it is observed that developing countries are clustered into six clubs, and there is a distinct group that includes Kuwait and Uruguay.

In general, developed countries are at the center of the global innovation system, and they play a significant role in advancing the innovation ecosystem worldwide through technological progress, R&D expenditures, high-tech production, strong university-industry collaborations, effective intellectual property protection mechanisms, innovative policy implementations, and patent applications. However, considering the obtained results, it is observed that the level of investment in the factors contributing to the development of innovation varies among developed countries.

Table 8. Global Innovation Index in the Middle Income Club Convergence Model Estimation Results

Club	Number of Countries	Countries	tb	Log(t)	Inference
Convergene	24	All Countries	-2.473	-38.416	No Convergence
İnitial convergence club					
Club 1	4	Thailand, Bulgaria, Turkey, Malaysia	0.686	3.533	Club convergence
Club 2	10	South Africa, Montenegro, Armenia, Colombia, Russian Federation, Georgia, Mexico, Indonesia, Serbia, Brazil	0.097	0.345	Club convergence
Club 3	5	Belarus, Bosnia & Herzegovina, Jamaica, Argentina, Peru	0.572	2.325	Club convergence
Club 4	3	El Salvador, Dominican republic, Albania	2.424	1.393	Club convergence

continued on following page

Table 8. Continued

Club	Number of Countries	Countries	tб	Log(t)	Inference
Clup 5 Not convergent Group	2	Botswana, China	- 2.769	- 17.115	No Club convergence
Merge of Clubs					
Club			**tб**	**Log(t)**	**Inference**
Club 1+2	-	-	- 1.693	- 15.536	No merge
Club 2+3	-	-	- 0.507	-2.618	No merge
Club 3+4	-	-	- 2.808	-9.403	No merge
Club 4+5	-	-	- 2.958	- 28.944	No merge
Final Clubs after Merge					
Club	-	-	**tб**	**Log(t)**	**Inference**
Club 1	-	-	- 1.693	- 15.536	No Club convergence
Club 2	-	-	- 0.507	-2.618	No Club convergence
Club 3	-	-	- 2.808	-9.403	No Club convergence

Resource: Prepared by the author.

Considering Table 8, it is observed that different clubs have formed. Accordingly, Club 1 consists of three countries, Club 2 of thirteen countries, Club 3 of twenty-two countries, Club 4 of twenty-six countries, Club 5 of twenty-two countries, Club 6 of twenty-three countries, Club 7 of eight countries, Club 8 of four countries, Club 9 of two countries, and the Not Convergent Group 10 consists of one country.

For these clubs, the log(t) statistic values are as follows: Club 1: 4.760, Club 2: -0.586, Club 3: -1.632, Club 4: -0.455, Club 5: -1.144, Club 6: 0.605, Club 7: -0.477, Club 8: 3.686, and Club 9: -0.53. The log(t) statistic values for Club 1 through Club 9 are greater than the critical value. In this context, the statistical significance indicates that the null hypothesis is accepted. In other words, there is club convergence in innovation among the countries within these clubs. However, when we consider the results after the merging of clubs, no new clubs are formed among these countries.

Upper-middle-income countries have developed various strategies to enhance their innovation performance. While China and Malaysia stand out with their investments in technology and education (Zhang et al., 2012), Turkey is making efforts to improve creative outputs and the protection of intellectual property rights (Bural, 2025). However, improvements are still needed in areas such as the employment of a qualified workforce in these countries.

Significant investments have been made and policies developed in these countries to foster innovation. These countries contribute to the advancement of innovation particularly through industrial transformation, digitalization, and public policies, while also working to enhance their global competitiveness. This increasing R&D investments (Pegkas et al., 2019), strengthening intellectual property protection systems (Neves et al., 2021; Hammami, 2021), implementing legal regulations (Rowthorn et al., 2016), improving infrastructure performance (Hussain et al., 2024), and promoting international collaborations will accelerate the diffusion of information technology. As a result, these efforts will contribute to ensuring sustainability in the development of innovation.

Table 9. The Lower Middle and Low Income Group Global Innovation Index Club Convergence Model Estimation Results

Club	**Number of Countries**	**Countries**	**tб**	**Log(t)**	**Inference**
Convergene	50	All Countries	-2.4544	-14.4143	No Convergence
İnitial convergence club					
Club 1	2	Viet Nam, India	1.504	0.697	Club convergence
Club 2	7	Ghana, Costa Rica, Mongolia, Morocco, Iran, Ukraine, Philippines	0.781	1.709	Club convergence
Club 3	2	Tunisia, Jordan	-1.206	-0.645	Club convergence
Club 4	7	Nicaragua, Zimbabwe, Nigeria, Bangladesh, Senegal, Egypt, Kazakhstan	0.208	0.369	Club convergence
Clup 5	2	Azerbaijan, Paraguay	3.472	1.094	Club convergence
Clup 6	11	Togo, Madagascar, Nepal, Ecuador, Rwanda, Cambodia, Namibia, Kyrgyzstan, Kenya, Pakistan, Sri Lanka	0.247	0.773	Club convergence
Clup 7	16	Niger, Mali, Ethiopia, Burkina Faso, Mozambique, Cameroon, Guatemala, Uganda, Benin, Zambia, Algeria, Honduras, Côte d'Ivoire, Tajikistan, Bolivia, Lebanon	-0.64	-1.174	Club convergence
Clup 8	2	Malawi, Yemen	-1.682	-0.530	Club convergence
Clup 9	1	Guinea (Not convergent Group)	-	-	-
Merge of Clubs					
Club			**tб**	**Log(t)**	**Inference**
Club 1+2		-	-0.18	-0.612	merge

continued on following page

Table 9. Continued

Club	Number of Countries	Countries	tƃ	Log(t)	Inference
Club 2+3		-	0.662	1.461	merge
Club 3+4		-	-0.327	-0.915	merge
Club 4+5		-	0.269	0.493	merge
Club 5+6		-	-0.062	-0.230	merge
Club 6+7		-	-1.527	-6.703	No merge
Club 7+8		-	-1.974	-3.992	No merge
Club 8+9		-	-4.331	-1.707	No merge
Final Clubs after Merge					
Club			**tƃ**	**Log(t)**	**Inference**
Club 1	11	Ghana, Tunisia, Jordan, Costa Rica, Mongolia, Morocco, Iran, Ukraine, Philippines, Viet Nam, India	-0.36	-1.280	Club convergence
Club 2	20	Nicaragua, Togo, Zimbabwe, Nigeria, Madagascar, Nepal, Bangladesh, Ecuador, Rwanda, Cambodia, Namibia, Kyrgyzstan, Kenya, Azerbaijan, Paraguay, Pakistan, Senegal, Sri Lanka, Egypt, Kazakhstan	0.198	0.443	Club convergence
Club 3	16	Niger, Mali, Ethiopia, Burkina Faso, Mozambique, Cameroon, Guatemala, Uganda, Benin, Zambia, Algeria, Honduras, Côte d'Ivoire, Tajikistan, Bolivia, Lebanon	-0.64	-1.174	Club convergence
Club 4	2	Malawi, Yemen	-1.682	-0.53	Club convergence
Group 5	1	Guinea (**Not convergent**)	-	-	-

Resource: Prepared by the author.

Considering Table 9, it is observed that different clubs have merged. Accordingly, Club 1 consists of three countries, Club 2 of thirteen countries, Club 3 of twenty-two countries, Club 4 of twenty-six countries, Club 5 of twenty-two countries, Club 6 of twenty-three countries, Club 7 of eight countries, Club 8 of four countries, Club 9 of two countries, and the Not Convergent Group 10 consists of one country.

The log(t) statistic values for these clubs are as follows: Club 1: 4.760, Club 2: -0.586, Club 3: -1.632, Club 4: -0.455, Club 5: -1.144, Club 6: 0.605, Club 7: -0.477, Club 8: 3.686, and Club 9: -0.53. The log(t) values for Clubs 1, Clubs 2, Clubs 3, Clubs 4, Clubs 5, Clubs 6, Clubs 7, Clubs 8 and Clubs 9 are greater than the critical value. The statistical significance indicates that the null hypothesis is accepted. This shows that there is convergence in innovation among the countries within these clubs.

After combining the clubs, our results are as follows: club 1 includes eleven countries, club 2 includes twenty countries, club 3 includes sixteen countries, club 4 includes two countries, and group 5 is singular. The log(t) statistic values for club 1 are -1.280, for club 2 they are 0.443, for club 3 they are 1.174, and for club 4 they are 0.53. These results indicate significant clustering among the clubs. Additionally, they show that developing countries are clustered into four clubs, forming one group. In other words, countries that make significant investments in strengthening educational systems, digital infrastructure, and enhancing R&D activities are in the same club.

Considering the results we obtained, structural barriers in low-to-middle-income countries, such as lack of financing (He et al., 2024), shortage of a skilled workforce, inadequate education systems, deficiencies in digital and physical infrastructure, limited access to information and technology, insufficient institutional structures, and an unstable political environment, constitute the greatest obstacles to the development of innovation in these countries. In this context, these countries need to work on developing a sustainable and inclusive innovation ecosystem. These efforts should focus on strengthening education systems to enhance the quality of human capital (Falk & Hagsten, 2021; Suarez-Villa & Hasnath, 1993), increasing investments in digital and physical infrastructure (Hussain et al., 2024), promoting R&D activities (Pegkas et al., 2019; Lucas, 1988), improving institutional structures, and developing institutional capital (Gogodze, 2016). Furthermore, efforts should be made to develop their innovation capacities through international collaborations and knowledge sharing. It can be said that the development of innovation in these countries will also contribute to achieving long-term economic growth objectives.

Considering the innovation convergence among developed and developing countries, it can be said that there is heterogeneity in the innovation development levels among country clubs. In other words, investments in factors such as institutional developments, human capital investments and research, infrastructure, market sophistication, business sophistication, knowledge and technology outputs, and creative outputs vary among country clubs. Therefore, the convergence of clubs among these countries or their presence in the same club indicates that they share similar conditions and that there is a classification among countries. The basis for the classification of innovation development between countries primarily lies in the fact that developing countries started their industrialization process later and did not invest enough in developing their own technologies. Secondly, it can be said that the very high levels of information and technology production, technological capacities, and technology investments in developed countries contribute to this classification. Thirdly, changes in countries' innovation levels are fundamentally based on their income levels (Bate et al., 2023).

There is no general convergence of GII between developed and developing countries. However, convergence has occurred within the clubs that include these country groups. This situation is caused by factors such as similar technological developments, R&D investments, the presence of high-tech sectors, faster dissemination of technological knowledge, industrial property rights, and the development of digital infrastructure, leading to a convergence of countries towards similar innovation levels. In other words, for the changes in GII between countries to contribute to club convergence, factors that influence innovation development, such as strengthening the institutional capacities and technological infrastructures of countries and increasing R&D investments, must be enhanced. Among developed countries, developments in innovation exhibit harmonized performance indicators. In other words, since the income levels of developed countries are generally similar, the expenditures made to enhance innovation are also similar. However, innovation developments in developing countries show significant differences. Therefore, the inequalities in innovation investments and developments among countries form the basis for the creation of country clubs.

Considering the findings obtained, it is evident that income levels, institutional structures, technological infrastructure, and human capital investments play a decisive role in enhancing innovation capacity in developing countries. In particular, the diffusion of innovation in developing countries holds strategic importance not only for economic development but also for long-term sustainable growth and global competitiveness. In this context, in developing countries:

- Human capital, one of the fundamental components of innovation, is often qualitatively insufficient in developing countries. Therefore, policies should be developed to improve the quality of human capital.
- Necessary infrastructure development efforts should be undertaken to support technological advancement.
- R&D investments need to be increased.
- Developing countries face limitations in direct access to technology. Thus, bilateral R&D projects, technology transfer agreements, and academic networks with developed countries should be established.

Achieving higher levels of innovation within the scope of the GII in developing countries is possible not only through technical investments but also through strategic planning, effective governance, regional cooperation, and long-term political commitment. The diffusion of innovation will strengthen these countries' positions in global competitiveness and play a decisive role in achieving sustainable development goals.

6. NEW TECHNOLOGICAL DEVELOPMENTS AND INSTITUTIONAL REGULATIONS

In every period of human history, studies have been carried out to differentiate people's needs and to meet these needs. These studies have been described as innovation. These efforts have been categorized as innovation. While innovation was initially used to find solutions to technical issues and problems, over time, it evolved into inventions that relied on systematic knowledge, utilizing engineering and mathematics to achieve consistent results. This situation has revealed the necessity of making policies and legal regulations to protect innovative ideas developed by institutions over time.

The Industrial Revolution, which began in England between 1750 and 1830 and is one of the most significant turning points in human history, profoundly transformed economic systems, social structures, institutions, and daily life (Kraus et al., 2021). With the Industrial Revolution, the transition from manual labor to mechanization began. This created a new demand for labor, accelerated rural-to-urban migration, altered the structure of labor markets, and played a significant role in changing the social and cultural structure. Technological advancements have continued from the Industrial Revolution to the present day, and these technological advances have also caused changes in social structures, institutions, and economic factors. In particular, technological progress has led to the emergence of inequalities between countries and, over time, an increase in these inequalities (Acemoğlu and Johnson, 2023).

Policies should be developed for the advancement of technological innovations and the protection of these technologies. However, challenges are faced in public/private sector policies and the implementation process of these policies due to the development of technological innovations. In this context, national and international institutions and policies need to be reorganized to adapt to new technological changes and to ensure (or increase) the sustainable global competitiveness of countries. Specifically, institutional and legal regulations required for the integration of technological innovations in public institutions and the private sector need to be made. When preparing these regulations, the GII value of each country can be taken into account. In other words, the institutions (political environment, regulatory framework, business environment), human capital and research (education level, higher education, R&D investments), infrastructure (information and communication technologies, general infrastructure, sustainable environment), market sophistication (credit facilities, investment environment, trade competition), and business sophistication (knowledge workers, innovative firms, university-industry collaborations) factors used to calculate GII values provide detailed information for each country. Moreover, these factors also give the global ranking of each country's innovation value (Dutta et al., 2024). Therefore, this will contribute to the development of policy approaches and roadmaps for innovation for each country. In this way, policies to be implemented based on changes in the factors contributing to technological progress in developed and developing countries will be tailored to the structure of each country (Crespo & Crespo, 2016).

There are many factors that influence the development of innovation at a global scale. These factors include the lack of innovation policies (Bittar & Di Serio, 2024; Zecchini, 2020), the quality of human capital (Falk & Hagsten, 2021; Suarez-Villa & Hasnath, 1993), R&D policies (Pegkas et al., 2019), intellectual property (Neves et al., 2021; Hammami, 2021), knowledge sharing by businesses (Iqbal et al., 2025), legal regulations (Rowthorn et al., 2016), and infrastructure performance (Hussain et al., 2024). Considering the institutional and economic structure of countries, measures should be taken to increase innovation capacity. These precautions:

- Innovation strategies should be defined, and necessary legal regulations should be implemented.
- Financial support and access to R&D investments, which are key factors in the development of innovation, should be facilitated. In other words, financial incentives should be provided through tools such as tax reductions, direct grants, and government-supported venture capital funds to increase R&D spending by the public and private sectors.
- Education policies should be supported by curriculum reforms, particularly in STEM (Science, Technology, Engineering, Mathematics) fields, to improve the quality of human capital. In particular, efforts should be made in developing countries to increase literacy rates and ensure women complete their education.
- Efforts should be made to continuously develop individuals' qualifications through lifelong learning programs.
- To protect innovation, commercialize innovative ideas, and support entrepreneurship, national and international intellectual property systems should be restructured with a focus on flexibility, inclusivity, and digital alignment. In particular, in developing countries, newly established national intellectual property systems should examine advanced intellectual property systems, such as those in the USA, Germany, and Japan, as best practice examples (Neves et al., 2021).
- Legal regulations to protect intellectual property rights should be prepared in developed and developing countries, and awareness-raising training in this area should be provided.
- In developing countries, efforts should be made to establish open innovation platforms to facilitate the flow of information between companies, universities, and research centers.

- Legal regulations should be made to update intellectual property laws, simplify patent and trademark application processes, and ease commercialization processes to foster innovation.
- In particular, investments should be made to strengthen physical and digital infrastructure investments, such as internet infrastructure, research laboratories, and digital data centers, to enhance innovation in developing countries.

Efforts to develop innovation in countries should be carried out gradually and over time. In other words, these efforts require a multifaceted approach in the process of developing and implementing innovation policies, and effectively managing each factor forms the foundation of innovation advancements. In this context, the implementation of these policies will contribute to both the economic growth of countries and the quantitative/qualitative increase in innovation.

7. CONCLUSION

This study analyzes club convergence among countries based on global innovation and income levels by considering GII values for 123 countries between 2011 and 2024. The club convergence approach developed by Phillips and Sul (2007) is used for this analysis. Unlike traditional convergence tests, this approach considers factors with heterogeneity in its analysis. In this context, this study evaluates the convergence of countries into similar innovation clubs by considering their GII values over different time periods. Based on the results of the analysis, it can be concluded that the developments in countries' innovations at the global scale are not homogeneous and that countries belong to different convergence clubs. This situation indicates that the developments in countries' innovations at the global scale are heterogeneous. The heterogeneity in the developments of innovation in countries also demonstrates that there are structural differences in the economic development and technological progress of countries, even among those with the same income level. In other words, policymakers need to develop policies for innovation development by considering factors such as the countries' economic structure, institutional differences, innovation infrastructure, innovation expenditures, education systems, and the quality of human capital

According to our results, the formation of clubs among countries differs both in GII values and in terms of GII value of income levels. Changes in factors affecting the formation of clusters among countries and the development of technology are also important factors in the change of cluster formation. Therefore, changes in factors such as the quality of human capital underlying technological advancement, countries' GDP values, growth rates, the quality of institutions, and R&D investments demonstrate that countries within the same club are converging towards each other. This situation shows that there is heterogeneity among countries in innovation. Furthermore, considering the obtained findings, it supports the hypothesis that these countries do not converge to a single equilibrium, thus confirming Baumol's convergence hypothesis.

In order for countries to pass to the different clubs, their scores in the GII need to increase. In this case, investments need to be increased in three different categories for the development of innovation in countries. These categories are;

- **Institutional Differences**: Efforts to improve indicators such as the rule of law, property rights, institutional capacity, and the implementation of legal regulations—especially in developing countries—will contribute significantly to enhancing innovation.
- **Innovation Infrastructure**: Increasing R&D expenditures, enhancing support for the commercialization of innovations, and promoting innovative ideas and social entrepreneurship will contribute to the development of innovation in these countries. In other words, the expenditures made by countries to foster innovation not only boost their economic growth but also strengthen their global competitiveness.
- **Education System and Human Capital**: Increasing education expenditures and providing high-quality education in higher education institutions will contribute to enhancing the quality of human capital.

Policymakers should develop country-specific policies to foster innovation by taking into account the structural and economic differences of each country. For this, a detailed analysis of each country is necessary. In this context, it is expected that the results obtained from this study will contribute to researchers working on the subject in the future.

REFERENCES

Acemoglu, D. (2009). *Introduction to modern economic growth* (Vol. 4, Issue 1). Prınceton Unıversty Press.

Acemoğlu, D., ve Johnson S. (2023). İktisadar ve Teknoloji, Doğan Kitapevi

Ahmad, N., Nguyen, D. K., & Tian, X. L. (2024). Assessing the impact of the sharing economy and technological innovation on sustainable development: An empirical investigation of the United Kingdom. *Technological Forecasting and Social Change, 209*(February 2023), 123743. https://doi.org/DOI: 10.1016/j.techfore.2024.123743

Ahmad, N., Youjin, L., Žiković, S., & Belyaeva, Z. (2023). The effects of technological innovation on sustainable development and environmental degradation: Evidence from China. *Technology in Society, 72*(December 2022). https://doi.org/DOI: 10.1016/j.techsoc.2022.102184

Apergis, N., & Cooray, A. (2014). Convergence in sovereign debt ratios across heavily indebted EU countries: Evidence from club convergence. *Applied Economics Letters, 21*(11), 786–788. DOI: 10.1080/13504851.2014.889798

Barrios, C., Flores, E., & Martínez, M. Á. (2019). Club convergence in innovation activity across European regions. *Papers in Regional Science, 98*(4), 1545–1565. DOI: 10.1111/pirs.12429

Bate, A. F., Wachira, E. W., & Danka, S. (2023). The determinants of innovation performance: An income-based cross-country comparative analysis using the Global Innovation Index (GII). *Journal of Innovation and Entrepreneurship, 12*(1). Advance online publication. DOI: 10.1186/s13731-023-00283-2

Baumol, W. (1986). Productivity Growth, Convergence, and Welfare: What the Long-run Data Show. *The American Economic Review, 76*(5), 1072–1085. DOI: 10.2307/1816469

Belloc, I., & Molina, J. A. (2023). The ecological footprint in Africa: Identifying convergence clubs from 1970 to 2018. *Applied Economics Letters, 30*(19), 2808–2813. DOI: 10.1080/13504851.2022.2107984

Bittar, A. de V., & Di Serio, L. C. (2024). Do innovation policies support micro and small enterprises to overcome barriers? *Innovation & Management Review, 21*(2), 137–152. DOI: 10.1108/INMR-12-2021-0234

Biyase, M., Zwane, T., Mncayi, P., & Maleka, M. (2023). Do Technological Innovation and Financial Development Affect Inequality? Evidence from BRICS Countries. *International Journal of Financial Studies, 11*(1). Advance online publication. DOI: 10.3390/ijfs11010043

Bural, D. (2025). Protecting intellectual property rights in Türkiye: Navigating legal and cultural dimensions. *Crime, Law, and Social Change, 83*(1), 1–17. DOI: 10.1007/s10611-024-10195-1

Cai, X., & Song, X. (2022). The nexus between digital finance and carbon emissions: Evidence from China. *Frontiers in Psychology, 13*. Advance online publication. DOI: 10.3389/fpsyg.2022.997692 PMID: 36275290

Carayannis, E. G., & Grigoroudis, E. (2016). Using multiobjective mathematical programming to link national competitiveness, productivity, and innovation. *Annals of Operations Research, 247*(2), 635–655. DOI: 10.1007/s10479-015-1873-x

Chen, T., & Zhou, S. (2024). The impact of digital economy on the upgrading of manufacturing structure. *PLoS ONE, 19*(7 July), 107503. https://doi.org/DOI: 10.1371/journal.pone.0307184

Conte, A. (2006). The evolution of the Literature on technological change over time: A survey. In *Papers on Entrepreneurship*. Growth and Public Policy.

Coutinho, E. M. O., & Au-Yong-Oliveira, M. (2024). Innovation's performance: A transnational analysis based on the Global Innovation Index. *Administrative Sciences, 14*(2). Advance online publication. DOI: 10.3390/admsci14020032

Crespo, N. F., & Crespo, C. F. (2016). Global innovation index: Moving beyond the absolute value of ranking with a fuzzy-set analysis. *Journal of Business Research, 69*(11), 5265–5271. DOI: 10.1016/j.jbusres.2016.04.123

Du, K. (2017). Econometric Convergence Test and Club Clustering Using Stata. *The Stata Journal, 17*(4), 882–900. DOI: 10.1177/1536867X1801700407

Dutta, S., Lanvin, B., León, L. R., & Wunsch-Vincent, S. (2024). Global innovation index 2024 unlocking the promise of social entrepreneurship. In *WIPO* (Vol. 15, Issue 1).

Dutta, S., Lavin, B., & Wunsch-Vincet, S. (2017). The global innovation index 2017, ınnovatıon feeding the world. In *Cornell University* (Vol. 3). INSEAD, and the World Intellectual Property Organization.

Falk, M., & Hagsten, E. (2021). Innovation intensity and skills in firms across five European countries. *Eurasian Business Review*, *11*(3), 371–394. DOI: 10.1007/s40821-021-00188-8

Furceri, D. (2005). b and r-convergence : A mathematical relation of causality. *Economics Letters*, *89*(89), 212–215. DOI: 10.1016/j.econlet.2005.05.026

Gogodze, J. (2016). Mechanisms and functions within a national innovation system. *Journal of Technology Management & Innovation*, *11*(4), 12–21. DOI: 10.4067/S0718-27242016000400003

Hall, B. H., & Rosenberg, N. (Eds.). (2010). *Handbook of the Economics of Innovation* (Vol. 1). Elsevier., Available online https://www.sciencedirect.com/handbook/handbook-of-the-economics-of-innovation/vol/1/suppl/C

Hammami, S. (2021). The effect of intellectual property protection on innovation: Empirical analysis of developing countries panel. *African Journal of Science, Technology, Innovation and Development*, *13*(4), 397–405. DOI: 10.1080/20421338.2020.1824608

He, F., Hu, L. J., & Chen, L. (2024). The effect of financial development on ındustrial green technology ınnovation efficiency: Experience analysis from 288 cities in China. *Sustainability (Switzerland)*, *16*(13). Advance online publication. DOI: 10.3390/su16135619

Huarng, K. H., & Yu, T. H. K. (2022). Analysis of global ınnovation ındex by structural qualitative association. *Technological Forecasting and Social Change*, *182*(March), 121850. DOI: 10.1016/j.techfore.2022.121850

Hussain, H., Jun, W., & Radulescu, M. (2024). Innovation performance in the digital divide context: Nexus of digital infrastructure, digital innovation, and E-knowledge. *Journal of the Knowledge Economy*, •••, 3772–3792. DOI: 10.1007/s13132-024-02058-w

Iqbal, S., Bashir, M., Bureš, V., Zanker, M., Ullah, S., & Rizwan, A. (2025). Impact of knowledge sharing and innovation on performance of organization: Evidence from the pharmaceutical industry of Pakistan. *Cogent Business & Management*, *12*(1). Advance online publication. DOI: 10.1080/23311975.2025.2471536

Islam, H. (2025). Dynamic effects of uncertainty, risks, R&D, and innovation on global economic growth. *Innovation and Green Development*, *4*(2), 100225. DOI: 10.1016/j.igd.2025.100225

Kijek, T., Kijek, A., & Matras-Bolibok, A. (2022). Club convergence in R&D expenditure across European regions. *Sustainability (Switzerland)*, *14*(2), 1–17. DOI: 10.3390/su14020832

Kraus, S., Jones, P., Kailer, N., Weinmann, A., Chaparro-Banegas, N., & Roig-Tierno, N. (2021). Digital Transformation: An overview of the current state of the art of research. *SAGE Open*, *11*(3). Advance online publication. DOI: 10.1177/21582440211047576

Lucas, R. E. (1988). On the mechanics of economic development. *Journal of Monetary Economics*, *22*(1), 3–42. DOI: 10.1016/0304-3932(88)90168-7

Nasir, M. H., & Zhang, S. (2024). Evaluating innovative factors of the global innovation index: A panel data approach. *Innovation and Green Development*, *3*(1), 100096. DOI: 10.1016/j.igd.2023.100096

Neves, P. C., Afonso, O., Silva, D., & Sochirca, E. (2021). The link between intellectual property rights, innovation, and growth: A meta-analysis. *Economic Modelling, 97*(June 2019), 196–209. https://doi.org/DOI: 10.1016/j.econmod.2021.01.019

Monfort, B. P. (2008). Convergence of EU regions measures and evolution. In *European Union Regional Policy*.

Oturakci, M. (2023). Comprehensive analysis of the global innovation index: Statistical and strategic approach. *Technology Analysis and Strategic Management*, *35*(6), 676–688. DOI: 10.1080/09537325.2021.1980209

Pegkas, P., Staikouras, C., & Tsamadias, C. (2019). Does research and development expenditure impact innovation? Evidence from the European Union countries. *Journal of Policy Modeling*, *41*(5), 1005–1025. DOI: 10.1016/j.jpolmod.2019.07.001

Phillips, P., & Sul, D. (2007). Transition modeling and econometric convergence tests. *Econometrica*, *75*(6), 1771–1855.

Phıllıps, P., & Sul, D. (2009). Economic Transition and Growth. *Journal of Applied Econometrics, 24*(22 April), 1153–1185. DOI: 10.1002/jae

Romer, P. M. (1986). Increasing Returns and Long-Run Growth. *Journal of Political Economy*, *94*(5), 1002–1037.

Romer, P. M. (1990). Endogenous technological change. *Journal of Political Economy*, *98*(5), 71–102.

Rowthorn, V., Plum, A. J., & Zervos, J. (2016). Legal and regulatory barriers to reverse innovation. *Annals of Global Health*, *82*(6), 991–1000. DOI: 10.1016/j.aogh.2016.10.013

Solow, R. M. (1956). A Contribution to the theory of economic growth. *The Quarterly Journal of Economics*, *70*(1), 65–94. DOI: 10.5897/jeif2013.0518

Suarez-Villa, L., & Hasnath, S. A. (1993). The effect of infrastructure on invention, İnnovation capacity and the dynamics of public construction investment. *Technological Forecasting and Social Change*, *44*(4), 333–358. DOI: 10.1016/0040-1625(93)90040-e

Sudolska, A., & Łapińska, J. (2020). Exploring determinants of innovation capability in manufacturing companies operating in Poland. *Sustainability (Switzerland)*, *12*(17), 1–20. DOI: 10.3390/su12177101

Taşdöken, Ö., & Kahyaoğlu, H. (2022). Davranışsal makroekonomi çerçevesinde hane halkı borçluluk düzeyinin analizi. *Selçuk Üniversitesi Sosyal Bilimler Meslek Yüksekokulu Dergisi*, *25*, 156–174. DOI: 10.29249/selcuksbmyd.1061507

Tomal, M. (2022). Testing for overall and cluster convergence of housing rents using robust methodology: Evidence from Polish provincial capitals. [). Springer Berlin Heidelberg. https://doi.org/10.1007/s00181-021-02080-w]. *Empirical Economics*, *62*(4). Advance online publication.

Ulucak, R., & Apergis, N. (2018). Does convergence really matter for the environment? An application based on club convergence and on the ecological footprint concept for the EU countries. *Environmental Science and Policy*, *80*(June 2017), 21–27. DOI: 10.1016/j.envsci.2017.11.002

Veselica, R. (2019). The impact od digital ınnovation on natıonal competitiveness. In *The main directions in tax system'S reform in the Azerbaijan Republic* (p. 441). Issue March., https://www.researchgate.net/publication/341735109

Vukoszavlyev, S. (2019). The connenction between global innovation index and economic well-being indexes. *Applied Studies in Agribusiness and Commerce*, *13*(3–4), 87–92. DOI: 10.19041/apstract/2019/3-4/11

Yıldırım, R., Ukelge, M., Sarac, E., & Oturakci, M. (2024). A novel approach for predicting global innovation index scores. *International Journal of Applied Management Science.*, *16*, 239–260. DOI: 10.1504/IJAMS.2024.140047

Yu, T. H. K., Huarng, K. H., & Huang, D. H. (2021). Causal complexity analysis of the Global Innovation Index. *Journal of Business Research*, *137*(August), 39–45. DOI: 10.1016/j.jbusres.2021.08.013

Zecchini, S. (2020). Pitfalls in innovation policy making. *Journal of the International Council for Small Business*, *1*(1), 36–41. DOI: 10.1080/26437015.2020.1714360

Zhang, R., Sun, K., Delgado, M. S., & Kumbhakar, S. C. (2012). Productivity in China's high technology industry: Regional heterogeneity and R & D. *Technological Forecasting and Social Change*, *79*(1), 127–141. DOI: 10.1016/j.techfore.2011.08.005

KEY TERMS AND DEFINITIONS

Club Convergence: This is an approach used to test for the presence of convergence, utilizing the log t test developed by Phillips & Sul (2007).

Digital Infrastructure Investments: These refer to investments in factors such as high-speed internet access, data security, software infrastructure, and digital platforms.

Economic Growth: Economic growth can be described as the increase in a country's capacity to produce goods and services over time.

Global Innovation Index: This is an international index that measures a country's innovation capacity and performance.

Human Capital Investments: Human capital refers to individuals' qualities such as knowledge, skills, abilities, and health. The development of these attributes in individuals contributes significantly to economic growth. As human capital improves, the quality of the labor force increases, which in turn enhances the productivity and innovation capacity of businesses.

Innovation: Innovation is defined as the process of creating and implementing new ideas, products, services, or processes.

R&D Expenditures: These expenditures, carried out by various institutions such as the private sector, public sector, and universities, are key drivers of technological progress and the industrial transformation of businesses. Investments in R&D also contribute to increasing countries' competitiveness and productivity.

Chapter 9
Technology and CSR: Comparative Insights From Public, Private, and Foreign Banks in India

G. Mookambigai
https://orcid.org/0009-0003-2757-4135
Sathyabama Institute of Science and Technology, India

R. Thamilselvan
https://orcid.org/0000-0002-8999-0498
Sathyabama Institute of Science and Technology, India

ABSTRACT

This chapter examines the role of technology in meeting corporate social responsibility (CSR) compliance in the Indian public, private and foreign banks. They compare how technology brings value to CSR projects by fostering economic inclusion and building resilience in times of crisis, using digital tools. Problems of digital divides, as well as of organizational and time resources, prevent the equal realization of CSR, while digital technologies make information about the outward dimensions of CSR visible. Research highlights the sectoral differences and provides a practical guide for better utilization of technology in CSR. It underlines the importance of inclusive policies and cooperation frameworks that can support sustainable economic growth and responsible banking activities.

INTRODUCTION

Technology, therefore, becomes a force of disruption that changes the way in which we approach economic inclusion and resiliency, particularly in times of financial, social and environmental crisis. However, as economies grew increasingly

DOI: 10.4018/979-8-3373-1529-4.ch009

digital, the promise of technology to combat systemic inequalities only grew. The backbone of the economy, CSR in banking is driven by technology – a country like India, which struggles with financial inclusion, has encountered this, and we all have not been able to leave our mark on any organization. The public sector, private sector, and foreign banks follow a variety of practices for effective implementation of the rules, against which adoption will be different in their use of technology. It relieves some of their responsibilities.

Regulations are driving the banking industry. Regulatory environments lead the banks. The CSR provision in the Companies Act 2013 requires all companies, including banks, to utilize a minimum of 2% average net profits on CSR expenditure. Government bodies, including PSBs, prefer to align with government practices on CSR initiatives because the government also enforces these. At the same time, even non-shareholder banks (both private and foreign) are also getting involved with corporate social responsibility initiatives as well as innovative attempts at achieving a positive footprint on society through community engagements. However, the technology and CSR lens has altered how economic banks are promoting inclusion, but there are still issues of power imbalances as well as access inequities; infrastructure lack (deficit) affecting digital illiteracy (Angelini & Nieri, 2022).

Public sector banks, with their vast network, especially in small towns, and also as a government arm, are driving the movement, using technology to take the financial inclusion drive to the masses. Inclusive access to finance for the marginalized has also been possible because of digital payment systems, Aadhaar-based banking and mobile banking services. Several PSBs have been toying with CSR activities on digital literacy, rural banking and micro finance, involving weaker sections with the formal economy. This is read quite a challenge, but not easy to implement in remote locations where banking infrastructure, and digital technologies in general, are limited (see Akanfe et al., 2025; Johnson, 2024).

The banks in the private sector are mainly technology- and efficiency-driven and have made CSR an integral part of their business strategies. Digital financial services, fin-tech partnerships, and mobile banking apps are increasing, with no access to banking. Private banks conduct CSR activities and invest in skill development, entrepreneurship, and financial literacy for weaker sections. However, their CSR policy is focused primarily on urban and semi-urban areas, and rural India is really left out of this outreach. Additionally, in some cases, the limited impetus to only profit maximization would effectively limit the level of future sustainable CSR activities (Parthiban et al., 2018; Saxena, 2016).

Banks are able to benefit from varying modes of operation as they adopt existing global corporate social responsibility (CSR) best practices with an emphasis on sustainability and environmental initiatives, and digital financial empowerment has also been rolled out. These banks leverage technology to drive CSR in green banking, financial literacy and social impact investing. Many such projects often support SDGs, which in turn strengthen India's broader economic and environmental concerns. However, foreign banks would have to grapple with the complexity of the Indian phenomenon- the meeting point of local regulation, CSR, which means something and bilateral relations (Gbaf News, 2019; Kumar & Gokhru, 2023).

While technology enables us to enhance CSR initiatives, there are still obstacles that exist. Impact/implications – Low-income and rural populations are primary beneficiaries of tech-based CSR, but digital exclusion constrains the scope. Cheap digital tools, the digital illiterate and inadequate access to the internet exacerbate financial inequality and retard the emergence of a growing, inclusive economy. In addition, the distribution of resources in the banking industry segments also determines the level at which technology is used in the transformation process (Pérez-Escolar & Canet, 2022; Raihan et al., 2024).

Understanding the opportunities and barriers towards technology in CSR will be the key to facilitating the generalization of corporate sustainable finance. The comparison of CSR practices between public and private or foreign banks can provide exciting, actionable best practices, gaps, and ways forward for improvement (Raihan et al., 2024). The financial industry has a transformative potential to tackle economic inequality. The present chapter is an attempt to analyze some of these dimensions in depth and provide strategic implications for strengthening the technology-based CSR intervention process in India's banking sector.

BACKGROUND

The corporate social responsibility (CSR) initiatives have significantly transformed. The banking industry sector would be such a stabilizing device by the sustained coherence of the economy, as it has to assume quite an enormous role in bridging the financial-market gap of not only other sectors, but also for various dimensions within its segment itself. In the Indian banking sector, CSR has become more of a constraint (the law's rule, the bank branch manager's corporate ethics) from the newly emerged socially responsible approach in regulations. The latter, by the way, all Indian companies incorporated under the Companies Act 2013 (and this includes banks) have to set aside a percentage of their profit for social work as Corporate Social Responsibility(CSR). The push of ad hoc legislative prescriptions, but only concerning banking and not to technical application with financial reality other (Angelini & Nieri, 2022). Created some more CSR.

PSBs played a potent role in pioneering financial programmes and mass-oriented coverage, mainly achieved through the operative guidance of the government policies. PMJDY, DBT, and digital banking systems are the initiatives that have brought that promise to the poor sections. These banks and lenders have leveraged tech models such as Biometrics, mobile banking, and digital education projects to provide improved access and efficiency in delivering financial services. Nonetheless, there are obstacles to access, such as inadequate infrastructure, low literacy levels or slow adoption of modern financial technologies that inhibit the expansion of accessibility (Johnson & Joy, 2024; Raihan et al., 2024). These players are using technology models such as biometric authentication, mobile banking, and digital education to endeavour to make the delivery of financial services increasingly accessible and efficient. Nonetheless, there are several impediments to broadening access, including inadequate infrastructure and low literacy, lowering the speed of diffusion of new financial technology (Johnson & Joyi, 2024; Raihan et al., 2024).

Having a market-driven economy, private banks have focused their CSR contribution on strategic investments that are in sync with the business objectives. Many have gone on to work for fin-tech companies developing powerful tools to enhance digital transactions, micro-lending and financial literacy. Skill development, entrepreneurship encouragement and sustainable economic solutions are pretty typical in their CSR projects. Their tech-savvy, sometimes, can enable them to launch slick digital banking products. However, the extent of their outreach being urban-centric and CSR models being profit-centric are questions that still linger.

Foreign players in banking have a global view of CSR and emphasize sustainability, ethical banking, and digital empowerment. As a result, they've introduced innovative green banking, AI-supported financial literacy and economic impact investments. Despite being technologically advanced, foreign banks are confronted with a restrictive environment and regulations, which limit their CSR activities and, pertinently in the hinterland, demand for localized modus operandi in the practice of CSR (Sharda, Swamy, & Singh, 2014; Siddeswara, 2020).

This expansion has been further accelerated by the recent explosion of fin-tech, again changing the banking industry's views on CSR. Blockchain, AI (Artificial Intelligence), and mobile banking have also brought better efficiencies in financial services, as well as greater transparency and traceability in CSR initiatives. Despite the progress, this is also worrying with respect to the digital divide, cyber insecurity and the ethics of tech in social development. The emerging trend of the study of influencer marketing is also gradually attracting attention in terms of its morality and ethics, in particular, the mental health that surrounds those who influence (Mahdi, Bouaziz, & Abbes, 2023; Priyadarshana, Rao, & Rao, 2024; Wylde et al., 2023).

This chapter undertakes a comparative analysis of CSR practices of public, private, and foreign banks in India to demonstrate that technology could help promote economic inclusion. This article underscores that despite the immense promises of tech-enabled CSR, we need to consider digital divides, regulatory hurdles, and good implementable models to make sure that the underprivileged are not our last thought.

The background section concludes by creating a basis upon which CSR, technology, and banking intersect in the Indian scenario, thus premising the arrangement of the following series of comparatives, observations, and policies.

THEORETICAL FRAMEWORK: TECHNOLOGY, CSR, AND ECONOMIC INCLUSION

Promoting economic inclusion is essential for sustainable development and implies that all individuals and communities have equal rights to make use of and benefit from financial services. However, there are two undetermined forces, corporate social responsibility (CSR) and technology, that are pressing on whether economic gaps and wage gaps will bridge or widen. Discontinuities and cross-fertilization between these domains and their potential to innovate financial inclusion are investigated with this theoretical large-frame approach.

Role of CSR in Mitigating Inequalities

Voluntary CSR as a commitment to do well (and help), in response to corporate contributions to ill CSR prompts business attitudes, with a view to correcting economic imbalance: it was the motives of profit-driven business that Firms engage in CSR to:

- Socio-economic Factors induce education and skill development, ensuring the preferential employment of the marginalized.
- Offer to invest in microfinance initiatives and entrepreneurship programs in the less fortunate sectors of the community and hclp promote financial inclusion.
- One that fosters sustainability through environmentally conscious business practices that empower local communities.
- Implement equitable labour policies that promote fair labour practices, fair wages, and diversity and inclusion (D&I).
- Promote a fair supply chain, abolish labour exploitation , and realize economic equity.

CSR alleviates social inequalities, which increases the economic inclusion of disadvantaged groups by addressing these dimensions.

Technology as a Driver of Inclusion and Inequality

Its technological thrust, specifically for digital innovation, automation and AI, has revolutionized economies. It provides opportunities for earning a living, but also poses the risk of widening inequality:

Positive Impacts:

- **The digital inclusion** increases access to financial services, education , and healthcare for marginalized populations
- **Employment creation**: Creates new job opportunities in the digital economy.
- **Increased productivity**: Promotes efficiency among industries, bringing economic growth and elevated living standards.

Negative Impacts:

Human Displacement by Automation: AI could lead to the loss of many low-skilled jobs due to robotics, increasing unemployment in vulnerable communities.

Digital divide: Lack of access to technology can alienate people without internet access or digital competence.

Data Discrimination: In hiring processes and financial services, algorithmic biases can perpetuate social inequalities.

Conceptualizing the Interplay Between CSR and Technology

CSR and technology are intrinsically tied to defining economic inclusion. Using CSR strategies, businesses can leverage the positive benefits of technology inclusion and mitigate its negative externalities. This interaction can be conceptualized via:

Tech-Driven CSR Initiatives:

- Investments in digital literacy programs by companies to fill skill gaps
- Supporting accessible tech solutions for people with disabilities

Ethical Technology Development:

- Enforcing AI ethics and fairness policies to avoid bias in algorithmic decisions.
- This hopes to promote open-source technological solutions to drive grass-roots innovations, particularly in a crisis.

Inclusive Business Models:

- Supporting social enterprises that utilize technology as a means for economic inclusion.
- Alleviating remote work opportunities for underprivileged populations.

Regulatory and Policy Support:

- Philosophers, Socio-economists and Industrialists are pushing CSR-related tech policy legislation.
- Creating public-private partnerships to scale tech-driven CSR initiatives.

CSR begin to tackle this issue. The convergence between CSR and technology offers an opportunity for economic inclusion. There is the potential for disruptive innovation, but the technological challenges that have emerged in making such innovations beneficial to society now must be matched with responsible corporate strategies to level the playing field for all. CSR can take a corrective angle that makes economic profit not a gap-widening tool but a tool to trigger inclusive involvement in a knowledge economy, based on innovation and digitization. With CSR, ethical tech companies can be both competitive in the market and grow the economy in a way that is good for everyone and long-term sustainable.

CONCEPTUAL FRAMEWORK

Business inclusion, technology, CSR, and the banking sector of India. It also investigates the technology-enabled CSR initiatives that can bridge the poverty divide and build the resilience of a nation in public, private and foreign banks. To sum up, the framework integrates relevant theoretical lenses with practical elements to allow a structured insight into CSR replication over different bank models.

Technological Innovation in CSR: The impact of the fin-tech revolution on CSR practices.

Regulatory and Institutional Framework: Policies like the Companies Act, 2013, and RBI guidelines impact CSR compliance and technology incorporation in banking.

Banking Sectoral Differences: Public, private, and foreign banks offer distinct approaches to technology deployment to pursue CSR compliance.

Challenges and Barriers: Digital literacy gaps, infrastructural constraints, cybersecurity challenges and regulatory compliance hurdles.

Sustainability and Impact: The topic focused on sustainability and the impact of Technology in Driving Corporate Social Responsibility (CSR)

By applying this framework, the study constructs a framework for assessing the role of technology in CSR implementation through the banking sector to prepare strategic recommendations for enhancing digital financial inclusion.

CSR COMPLIANCE IN INDIAN BANKING: AN OVERVIEW

The Indian banking sector is also a major player in carrying forward corporate social responsibility (CSR) works and initiatives to promote economic inclusion, financial literacy, and social welfare. With the kind of reach and resources that few other industries enjoy, banks are in the perfect position to address social inequalities via targeted CSR activities. This section is devoted to the introduction of CSR in Indian Banking, regarding the regulatory framework, specificity of public and private banks and CSR (domestic and foreign) activities carried out by the sector (Angelini & Nieri, 2022).

Legal framework of corporate social responsibility (CSR) The Companies Act, 2013 provides legal basis for CSR in India and mandated that banks including those 'whose net worth is INR 5 billion or more, or turnover is INR 10 billion or more,' need to spend at least tow Percent accumulated profits made over three years preceding the financial year on undertaken activities of CSR. It was a significant departure from the world of voluntary philanthropy, and it represented an effort to make sure companies were doing good for society.

As per Section 135 of the Act, every company (Including holding and subsidiary) which has a net worth of five million rupees or more, or turned over one thousand crore rupees OR a net profit of 5 Crs, is required to abide by the CSR regulation.

The companies referred to above shall constitute a Corporate social responsibility committee of the board consisting of three or more directors, of which at least one director shall be an independent director and such committee shall formulate and recommend to the board, a Corporate social responsibility Policy which shall indicate the activities to be undertaken by the company as specified in Schedule VII, monitor the Corporate social responsibility Policy of the company from time to time and also disclose the company's expenditure, if any, on such activities incorporated in the Board's Report.

As per section 135 of the Act, where every company, private limited or public which have, in the immediately preceding financial year, a net worth of Rs.500 crore or more; or a turnover of Rs.1000 crore or more; or a net profit of Rs.5 crores or more; the company constitued CSR committee and in every financial years company shall spend, in every financial year, at least 2% of the average net profits of the company made during the three immediately preceding financial years for CSR and if not spent such amount, the board shall in its report mad under section 134, specify the of not such amount in such prescribed manner, as may be prescribed, the date of the commencement of the Act i.e. 22nd January, 2014.

Eradicating extreme hunger, poverty and malnutrition, promoting preventive health care and sanitation including contribution to the Swach Bharat Kosh set-up by the Central Government for the promotion of sanitation and making available safe drinking water; -Promoting education, including special education and employment enhancing vocation skills especially among children, women, elderly, and the differently abled and livelihood enhancement projects; -Ensuring environmental sustainability, ecological balance, protection of flora and fauna, animal welfare, agroforestry, conservation of natural resources and maintaining quality of soil, air and water, including cess contribution to the Clean Ganga Fund set-up by the Central Government for rejuvenation of river Ganga; The generated by Ministry of Corporate Affairs/ Govt. of India Page 8 of 8 -Protection of national heritage, art and culture including restoration of buildings and sites of historical importance and works of art; setting up public libraries; promotion and development of traditional arts and handicrafts; -Measures for the benefit of armed forces veterans, war widows and their dependents; -Training to promote rural sports, nationally recognized sports, Paralympic sports and Olympic sports; -Contribution to the Prime Minister's National Relief Fund or any other fund set up by the Central Government for socio-economic development and relief and welfare of the Scheduled Castes, the Scheduled Tribes, other backward classes, minorities and women; and -the fund mentioning (retail, wholesale, distribution, production, inequality) permalink embed save parent the words are referring to those as well, there is no mention that some communities living in the same areas can't access basic necessities either. CSR isn't just for tech giants. As banks are the lifeline of any economy, they also come under CSR and have done a lot of work in financial literacy, rural development, scholarships, digital inclusion programmes, etc. SBI has moved on to education, skill and health, while HDFC group has a "Parivartan" programme for rural economic development. Failure to comply with CSR duties would entail a fine of 50,000- 25 lakh. Directors and officers of the company may also be held guilty and, in extreme cases, even imprisoned (for a term not exceeding three years as per the amendments brought in by the Companies (Amendment) Act, 2019). Mandatory CSR regulations have been framed in order to facilitate the development model of turning profits of corporate economic reforms into societal wellbeing. Compliance is gnarly for most businesses; the CSR movement is waiting in the wings. However, the same cannot be said of corporate entities (like banks and others), which consider CSR as a route to sustainable growth and a means of filling voids in the local economy for the betterment of society.

What should have been done from the beginning is that CSR programmes must be aligned with the development agenda of the nation as well as global frameworks such as the UN Sustainable Development Goals (SDGs). For example, in SDG5 about gender equality, there is so much that Indian banks are lagging behind, and worse still, the farther you go up the ladder. But if banks like OCBC rock up for this gender balance journey with some part of their brain left at the door and history-backpack of structural biases stuffed in their bag, resorting to intentional measures to promote women and international talent into decision-making levels then I guess, as Singha & Sivarethinamohan (2022) suggest, can be placed under close scrutiny.

The CSR initiatives put up by the bank should be in line with the national development agenda and essentially include enabling policy-finance inclusion promoted by RBI, as well as sustainable banking. Additionally, it has to write its Corporate Social Responsibility activities in its annual report along with the amounts spent and projects implemented by the bank, and it must also ensure that it meets all of its legal requirements.

TECHNOLOGY AND CSR IMPLEMENTATION

Of all the CSR tech solutions to make, in the Indian banking context, because people come out to justify every CSR thing. Given this backdrop, how are banks trying to use digital platforms and technology to help them improve their CSR efforts? However, the implementation of CSR is confronted by challenges in the use of technology that must be resolved in order to accomplish inclusive and sustainable development (Joseph & Jeslina, 2019; Mishra, 2022).

Banks can utilize digital platforms as novel mechanisms to manage and monitor their CSR initiatives efficiently. A typical research field in this domain is combining the mobile applications, web pages, and social media actions of numerous banks to advertise their CSR activities and share and monitor them, such as features to donate by customers to CSR causes, like education, healthcare, rural development projects, etc, as a part of their mobile banking apps. In addition, blockchain technology is also reviewed to enhance the transparency and accountability of the allocation and utilization mechanism of CSR redistribution funds (Financial Express, 2024).

Banks also leverage analytic data and artificial intelligence (AI) in order to identify the business field that requires CSR intervention. Could banks even detect economic distress and allocate CSR money cleverly by reading their customers' data and investment behaviours? For instance, machine learning algorithms can be utilized to identify communities that may benefit from financial literacy programs or microfinance assistance (Nooribakhsh et al., 2024).

That way, we can lift out of the reach of many CSR initiatives, people, places and ways that we may not be able to reach ourselves." One of its main benefits is the ability to access and serve hitherto underserved populations, notably in remote locations, where the brick-and-mortar banking infrastructure is scarce. Webinars, e-learning content and virtual workshops regarding digital finance literacy support wider access to programs and knowledge, which is no longer managed through traditional gateways (Atanasov et al., 2023; Potocan, 2021).

This is in addition to growing investments in digital banking applications as a means to enhance financial inclusion. This has also led to mobile banking, biometric authentication, and digital payment systems by public and private sector rural banks, leading to greater banking penetration. Aadhaar-based payment systems and the Unified Payments Interface (UPI) have helped social welfare programs and direct benefit transfers, ensuring that payments reach individuals for whom they are earmarked and bypassing intermediaries (World Bank Group, 2016; EY India, 2025).

According to Tams et al. (2016), the online enabling platforms in relation to crowdfunding and donation-based CSR interventions are one of the significant impacts. These CSR (corporate social responsibility)-driven crowdfunding portals on the websites of some of the Indian banks let their customers, employees and others participate in social causes such as education, healthcare, and environmental conservation. Digital fundraising campaigns are a great way to take CSR outreach to new heights as people and organizations come forward to be a part of the same.

Contrary to the various religions, there are a number of issues which hinder the effective implementation of technology-based corporate social responsibility. The digital divide is a significant issue. A large portion of Indian society, especially in rural India, is deprived of being accessible to stable internet access, digital literacy or mobile control disturbances, which restrict it from enjoying the benefits of technology-driven CSR programmes.

Lastly, cybersecurity and data privacy are also issues. With banks migrating to digital channels to push CSR programmes online, securing financial transactions and personal user details has gained focus. Cyber threats, fraud, and other risks are threats to digital CSR initiatives, and they call for robust cybersecurity plans and regulatory monitoring (Thakur, 2024).

Aside from digital mediums and data analysis, new immersive technologies like AR and VR are also becoming disruptive assets for CSR-run health and education projects. They can potentially extend access to emotional and mental health interventions by offering captivating and personalized therapeutic contexts. As Singha and Singha (2024a) point out, virtual and augmented reality not only enable exposure therapy and the treatment of trauma: They offer the option to provide care at a distance, keeping personal life private and undisturbed.

There are also barriers, including resistance to change and insufficient IT infrastructure at banks. The majority of traditional banks have remnants of old systems that are not entirely compatible with modern-day digital services. The field staff and CSR teams also require training on how to use the new technological tools for planning and implementation.

To overcome these challenges, banks will need to invest in digital literacy programs, enhance their cybersecurity frameworks and revamp their technological infrastructure. Socially responsible actions are also cutting across fields and the community, as CSR in the banking industry has been exploring CSR goals.

Leveraging technology for improved outreach, while managing the operational nuances for better results, opens the door for a better CSR program.

COMPARATIVE ANALYSIS: PUBLIC, PRIVATE, AND FOREIGN BANKS

The relative approach was applied to evaluate CSR adherence by the public sector, private sector, and foreign banks of India. The research methodology used both qualitative and quantitative methods, including content analysis of banks' CSR reports, financial statements, and mandatory reporting documents. In addition, first-hand information was collected through interviews with top management and local CSR officers, as well as from a questionnaire administered to different stakeholders participating in CSR activities.

Some other indicators that rank companies include spending on CSR, investment focus, technology adoption in total CSR activities and compliance with the CSR acts and rules, among others. This study also considered social impact as an indicator of financial inclusion, and then the use of a cost-benefit analysis to compare financial analysis. These variables provide background on CSR activity in industry and reveal optimal practices of CSR in this study.

Key Findings on CSR Compliance Across Sectors

1. **Public Sector Banks (PSBs)** among Public Banks CSR Compliance Public sector banks are highly compliant with CSR regulations as mandated by the government. CSR projects of these 25 included one in the area of financial inclusion and two each in rural development and education. PSBs played a significant role in the Pradhan Mantri Jan Dhan Yojana and the government's skill development programme. However, implementation was commonly ineffective as it fell victim to bureaucratic obstacles and poor integration of technology.

2. **Private Sector Banks:** Private banks are focusing more on strategic innovation in CSR. These programmes are typically anchored around brand positioning and the corporates' CSR (corporate social responsibility) values and concentrate on entrepreneurship, digital literacy and environmental sustainability initiatives. Private banks continued to tap technology while trying to reach the bottom of the pyramid through CSR initiatives such as mobile-based banking, financial education tools based on artificial intelligence, and transparency on blockchain.
3. **Foreign Banks:** Making significant contribution to CSR: Foreign banks have shown partial compliance towards CSR, mainly in areas of specific social impact initiatives, which contribute to global sustainable efforts. Their CSR programmes were primarily focused on environmental protection, women's empowerment, and corporate giving. They do that through some of the most advanced technology that foreign banks have depended upon to allow for it. Their outreach was limited, however, because they have fewer branches in India.

Technology's Role in Shaping Sectoral Differences

The Enabler of CSR in the Banking Industry Technology was one of the key discriminators across the three banking sectors, with respect to the implementation of CSR. State-owned banks continued to be hamstrung by legacy systems and regulatory red tape, but private and foreign banks deployed cutting-edge technology to address this opportunity and impact.

None of the public banks has a high reliance on the digital mode of CSR engagement, and all are dependent on the direct funding method and face-to-face outreach programme.

Popularise the use of fin-tech for CSR projects (e.g. mobile wallet-based financial literacy campaigns, AI-based customer engagement for social and digital crowdfunding portals.

. It features international best practices in technology-enabled CSR, like the ones that concern Blockchain Fund Transparency and full automation of sustainability projects involving the removal of IoT devices monitoring the environment.

In summary, the comparative analysis reveals that all three banking sectors in India are involved in CSR activities. Still, their CSR practices vary considerably in relation to legislation, strategic approach and technology adoption. The endeavours can be accentuated by enhanced collaboration among the government and private players and greater digitization in the public sector banks to make the CSR initiatives more meaningful and bring a much larger domain of society within the ambit of the reach of CSR.

TECHNOLOGY-INDUCED INEQUALITIES IN CSR

However, embedding technology in CSR work, on the one hand, provides possibilities in terms of innovation, scalability, and effectiveness, but, on the other, it presents challenges that can reinforce or even amplify social injustices that already exist. For banks, digital technologies offer tremendous opportunities to magnify the impact and success of CSR activities. Yet, if developed and implemented exclusively, these efforts may inadvertently exacerbate inequalities. A key concern is the continued digital divide, which has affected rural and low-income communities more than others for too long. Such communities typically struggle with poor plumbing, unclear access to clean drinking water, and limited access to reliable internet, situations that prevent their active participation and thus preclude benefits from technology-based CSR programs.

Public sector banks are relatively more focused on financial inclusion and rural development, and also have infrastructure-related constraints that discourage high-tech CSR initiatives. Their CSR initiatives are often centred around core community development initiatives like financial education and the building of capacity. However, their beneficiaries – themselves – are usually doubly disadvantaged by geography for traditional banking as well as e-learning platforms, apps, and other digital banking tools due to a lack of digital literacy.

On the other hand, private/foreign banks, with an extensive presence in urban / semi-urban areas, have better financial and technological infrastructure. This gives them the opportunity to include cutting-edge innovation like AI-powered analytics, mobile CSR apps, blockchain-powered transparency tools, and digital monitoring capabilities into CSR programmes. Indeed, these advances in CSR will benefit from their ability to help urban dwellers. Still, conversely, they are not necessarily informed that services need to respond to the daily routines of poor householders in low-density and underserved rural regions.

Further, the over-emphasis on online elements – such as AI-enabled chatbots, digital financial literacy portal, and automated learning modules – may inadvertently exclude the low-literacy and tech-dumb populace. CSRs will not resonate with programmes or with the people that need them the most without hybrid digital and in-person engagement and localized outreach.

Resource gaps among banks exacerbate this technological asymmetry. Though the public sector banks have a greater penetration, they tend to be suppressed by financial and infrastructure constraints, thereby stifling their capability to take on the most advanced technologies. On the other hand, private banks – equipped with deeper pockets and exposure to the innovation ecosystem – are forging ahead with their CSR blueprints through new tools such as predictive analytics, AI-powered automated donation platforms and digital dashboards for real-time impact analysis.

Divide by foreign banks getting wider. In many cases, foreign banks exacerbate the trend, as they roll out CSR initiatives that take the lead from best practices in the world and trends classified as high-end, blockchain, IoT, and the like, which seldom reach the rural level.

This is likely to contribute to a further widening of the technological and economic gap between rural and urban beneficiaries through well-intentioned but ill-considered CSR activities. Digital interventions can get overly urban-focused, discounting the very communities that CSR is trying to enable. Without this type of contextual tailoring, such programmes can appear inclusive while actually acting to exclude.

To address the issue, a two-pronged approach is required. Banks must use technology as a facilitator of, not substitute for, local connection. Second, they have to invest in digital literacy, build rural infrastructure, and adopt hybrid CSR models that combine online tools and offline support systems. Public-private and global bank partnerships to facilitate sharing of experiences, pooling of resources, and joint action toward a more inclusive delivery of CSR are key.

CSR programs also need to address internal imbalances—gender and workplace dynamics among them. Singha and Sivarethinamohan (2021) find that gender discrimination and lack of supervisory encouragement are common among women in Indian banks who play essential roles in creating organizational harmony. Solving such structural challenges is more than bird-proofing technology. It requires a new kind of office culture, one in which the work is stripped of all convenience and any ambiguity about whether the work day is done.

Incorporating philosophical traditions such as Ubuntu, focusing on empathy, shared humanity, and common-sense wellbeing, offers productive pathways toward reimagining diversity and inclusion. As Singha and Sivarethinamohan (2022a) have pointed out, Ubuntu-based management approaches can have an impact on the organizational climate in terms of promoting gender equity and fostering inclusive environments, especially in the banking sector.

In summary, technology has the potential to revolutionize CSR in the banking sector, but it also presents issues around digital divide, resource disparity and cultural insensitivity. In order to ensure that impact isn't spread too thin, or CSR become an exercise in tokenism, banks need to develop joined-up initiatives that are both technologically advanced and socially focused. Only then will CSR work as a social actor for fair economic inclusion and strong communities.

PATHWAYS FOR ECONOMIC INCLUSION AND RESILIENCE

Building on the former suggestions, the time is ripe to pave strategic paths that enhance economic inclusion and resilience, as part of Corporate Social Responsibility (CSR). For that, banks need to recast their CSR blueprints, powered by new-age digital technologies that are more inclusive. Drawing from the example in chapter 1, one promising approach is the use of FinTech applications (including mobile banking, digital payments, control, and transparency enabled by blockchain and related technologies). These tools can complement CSR outreach, track fund utilization more effectively, monitor social impact in real-time and promote contributing interaction with the beneficiaries. By incorporating such advancements, banks can help make CSR initiatives not just more effective and transparent, but also fairer and more accessible to those at the bottom of the pyramid.

There is no getting around the fact that investing in digital literacy and infrastructure readiness is a key part of closing the digital divide. Banks can support digital financial literacy programs to reach marginalized sections of society, which can raise the level of cooperation between them and local government agencies, NGOs, and academic institutions around technology-based CSR. The promotion of the internet connection and the creation of digital service points in rural and disadvantaged areas, among others, will further Mikelet participation and accessibility to CO devices (Pérez-Escolar & Canet, 2022).

Social responsibility decision-making also needs to be jammed with AI and big data. They can harness local socio-economic and environmental data to pinpoint areas most in need of intervention. Such tools may be used to help guide strategic CSR giving by linking charitable activity to local needs and facilitating adaptive, region-specific responses. Impact assessments powered by AI give banks instant feedback, allowing them to tweak and fine-tune their CSR actions from time to time (Podile, 2024).

Policymakers can play a fundamental role in ensuring that CSR is helpful, not a hindrance, to sustainable economic inclusion. Regulatory models should be created to promote the adoption of technology for CSR. Incentives, whether tax incentives, subsidies, or the form of official recognition, must be offered to the banks to encourage them to roll out digital infrastructure, especially in underserved areas.

Increased transparency to be realized through stringent CSR reporting regulations is as important. If public disclosure of CSR projects, particularly with technological interventions, is standardized, then it would help to ensure accountability and good practices within the sector. Furthermore, policies need to promote cooperation between the public, private, and foreign banks in which joint CSR projects can be carried out. Building spaces for joint action that enable financial institutions to pool resources, exchange technology, and align strategies can enormously enhance the scale and effectiveness of CSR.

Multi-stakeholder engagement is imperative—local bakeries. Already, banking programs that match corporate social responsibility (CSR) initiatives with the economic needs of individual communities are emerging with support from local banks, community organizations and technology providers. CSR collaborations may come together to address systemic issues such as financial exclusion, digital illiteracy and climate risk. These partnerships would leverage multiple expertise to create robust and replicable CSR initiatives.

A blending of digital outreach and physical fieldwork must be the next phase in the CSR's contributions to impact and resilience. Although mobile apps and AI-driven platforms enable financial education, they need to be supplemented with on-the-ground programs like community centres and in-person coaching, particularly for the less privileged, like the elderly, who may not have access to digital technology (Atanasov et al., 2023).

Additionally, CSR initiatives need to be coherent with national objectives and global best practices, including the United Nations Sustainable Development Goals (SDGs). Aligning CSR strategies with the SDGs serves as a platform for sustainability and reflects the concrete, positive effects of technology-innovated CSR in driving lasting economic stability and social justice (Shayan et al., 2022).

The prospects of AI and CSR integration should rise on the ethical design that area leaves on empathy, diversity, cognition and social responsibility. As Singha and Singha (2023) argue, inclusion, mindfulness, and emotional engagement are necessary to co-build AI systems with sustainable and equitable gains. The impact of CSR can be vastly enhanced by applying AI to sectors such as education, creative arts, mental health, and rural empowerment.

In conclusion, technology-based CSR can only be effective if it combines shared governance, broad policy-making and innovative implementation pathways. By embracing digital inequality head-on and facilitating co-creation with a broad base of stakeholders, and by harnessing cutting-edge IT, the Indian banking industry can be a potent force in promoting a more inclusive, more resilient and more sovereign economy. To bring such vision to reality, a comprehensive framework should be adopted that combines infrastructure and policy inclusiveness with the continuous adoption of new technology.

Table 1. DEMOGRAPHIC PROFILE OF MOBILE BANKING USERS IN INDIA

Age Group	Percentage (%)
Below 25	17.70%
26–35	42.95%
36–45	26.56%
46 and above	12.79%

Putranto (2020) studied the factors of consumer behaviour for mobile banking services, focusing on Mobile Banking Technology Acceptance and its user Demographics. The user distribution among Nigerian banks that had activated mobile technology showed that 26–35 is the age category with the highest proportion of Mobile banking users, which account for 42.95%, thus indicating young working class professionals are at the forefront in adaptation and usage. This generation is considered to be digitally savvy, financially active and familiar with the mobile-centric finance ecosystem.

36–45 age range, which consists of about a quarter (26.56%), already utilizes mobile banking to a great extent and shows that the technology is becoming more popular among mid-career persons as well. In contrast, the proportion of users under 25 years is only 17.70% in the Sample. Despite being digitally literate, their limited income and financial dependence or non-bank participation could be the reason for lower involvement. The 46+ category is the smallest percentage of users at 12.79%. It may be a result of lower digital skills levels, as well as having most likely become too used to debits from conventional banks.

These results highlight the need for focused CSR and DFS inclusion strategies. Initiatives focused on promoting the use of mobile health applications among older adults and young people need to focus on providing digital literacy training, increasing awareness, and creating user-friendly platforms for these populations.

Table 2. OCCUPATION

Occupation	Percentage (%)
Students	25.24%
Salaried Employees	44.26%
Business Owners	15.74%
Others	14.75%

As echoed in Putranto (2020), a large proportion of mobile banking users are employed as salaried employees (44.26%), revealing that formal sector employment has an essential bearing on digital financial services uptake. Students are one of the largest groups (25.24%), probably due to more exposure to digital technology. They also tend to have potentially higher purchasing power, at least those who obtain an education in an urban area—SMEs (15.74%). The increase in confidence that entrepreneurs have for financial transactions using mobile platforms is evident in the response of business owners, which is growing year on year.

These findings indicate that banks' CSR programmes must design tailor-made packages for minority groups, among which are enterprise owners and informal sector workers. Approaches could involve providing easy-to-use, multilingual interfaces and innovative micro-loan products in order to increase financial inclusion and digital economy participation.

Table 3. EDUCATION LEVEL

Education Level	Percentage (%)
Undergraduate	45.08%
Postgraduate and above	54.92%

Putranto (2020) highlights that a large number of people using mobile banking in India have a higher level of education, with 54.92% a postgraduate degree and more than half, which is equal to 45.08%, are undergraduate graduates. This indicates a positive relationship between the level of education and mobile banking usage, as those with a higher educational background are likely to be more confident in digital technologies and have trust in online financial channels.

For equitable digital access to be developed, banks and CSR programs need to invest in understanding the nature of such initiatives, paying attention to offline users who lack formal education. Interventions of this type can be used to reduce the technology divide and encourage more inclusive digital finance participation.

In general, the results suggest that young, well-educated, and salaried people mainly use mobile banking in India. However, there are still people in this stage of digital transformation who fall behind, such as older persons, workers in the informal sector, and those with less education. Accordingly, CSR interventions designed to promote financial inclusion must be adapted for these underserved groups, focusing specifically on rural and poorer communities that will enable the benefits of digital banking adoption across a broad segment of those who need it most.

RECOMMENDATIONS AND SOLUTIONS

It is vital for the swift execution of CSR among Indian banking natives that we take a significant amount and assign it to digital infrastructure. Public institutions and technology partners must work hand in hand with banks, who should carry the torch of expanding the reach of internet connectivity, rooted in creating easy access to digital services, undoubtedly in rural, unbanked areas. For outreach to marginalized groups, inclusive approaches should involve the creation of digital kiosks, mobile banking units and internet-enabled community centres. With multi-language support, voice-assisted features, and minimalist mobile applications that are built for low-tech users, they will have to follow the above-mentioned design principles. Integrating financial literacy into CSR is therefore also central to efforts to address the digital divide. Strategic moves include organizing local community programs and workshops together with NGO staples, schools to promote digital banking, financial planning and cybersecurity education; creating target marketing campaigns to appeal to vulnerable consumer groups; and broadcasting highly empowering content specialized for the needs of minority populations.

An identical robust regulatory framework is also essential. Regulators will have to enforce strict CSR reporting norms on funds allocation and utilization, and the audit process apprising its impact. Additionally, a single, interoperable digital compliance system will also increase transparency and public accountability. Moreover, policy incentives, e.g. tax rebates and monetary rewards, would help banks actively participate in digital inclusion-based CSR initiatives. More collaboration among public, private and even foreign banks, like pooling resources and sharing learning from such programs, can extend the benefits of these programs. For CSR to be viable, it requires four essential pillars: a clear theoretical foundation in the concept of corporate social responsibility; suitable strategies and instruments for implementation; business interactions with civil society and public–private partnership (PPP) at the state level. The process does not require isolation by banks, but collaboration with local authorities, government entities, fin techs and non-profits working in areas of financial exclusion, education, environmental sustainability and healthcare.

For instance, enabling fin-tech solutions like mobile payments and microfinancing to be built onto a blockchain ecosystem for CSR tracking will give a remarkable boost to financial inclusion and drive profound socio-economic change in the long run. With the help of technologies such as artificial intelligence (AI) and big data analytics, a bank is able to map socio-economic data in order to identify community needs, based on which the bank can design CSR intervention programs suitably. The use of AI-powered chatbots can help improve public engagement through live updates on CSR initiatives, and blockchain technology is likely to be used for improved transparency and accountability, which will reduce the chances of funds being misrouted. This hybrid model of CSR delivery combines the efficiency of digital tools with the accessibility and trust developed through face-to-face interaction to drive maximum impact. In addition, solutions that combine online and brick-and-mortar coaching centres help to bridge the digital divide for thousands more who do not have online access.

And maintaining CSR efforts at lasting levels means effective corporate incubators. Positive psychology interventions (Singha and Singha 2024), such as stress management techniques, strategies to support work-life balance, and health workplace relationships programs, do strengthen employee engagement and wellbeing, which is vital for the overall sustainability of the organization. Singha (2024) outlines neuro leadership training and resilience-building initiatives that also help in creating psychological safety alongside adaptability to be on top of their nerves. India is a land where mindfulness was seeded more than 2500 years back by Siddhartha. Thus, Indian roots have always been strong in incorporating age-old contemplative methods into daily lives. India-based mindfulness-based interventions (MBIs) offer practical secular tools that are transformative in Corporate wellness and leadership development. These interventions have shown effectiveness in Indian as well as Western contexts and are especially congruent with CSR-driven human capital development (Singha & Singha, 2024b).

In the end, adopting technology in CSR isn't about change; it's about adoption. Banking sector must empower sustainable CSR practices for feasible economic recovery through digitization, financial literacy embedding in public, compering regulatory oversight in letter spirit and transaction/compliance handling along with adoption of AI / Big Data tools to promote equal opportunity nege reserving a future based on urban-sub-urban ventures where millions are deprived of structural inequalities. For example, innovation-led education models can be embedded within CSR, such as digital learning hubs, online financial education or higher educational institution partnerships, to contribute towards a skilled future-ready workforce and socio-economic empowerment. Echoing the points of Singha and Singha (2024c), adaptive learning environments that venerate critical thought, problem-solving capabilities, and cross-cultural competencies are inherent in contributing substantially to this new era of digital economy.

In addition, half of all the CSR practices are based on cross-functional collaboration and public-private partnerships that limit banking operations for the promotion of social welfare. Singha and Singha (2024d), pairing academia, industry, local communities and public agencies are essential to solve complex socio-environmental problems. These collaborations produce hands-on educational opportunities, promote collaborative capacities, and involve students in initiatives focused on sustainability literacy, economic advancement and equity. Correctly applied, these cross-disciplinary CSR frameworks place financial institutions as one of the main protagonists in a new world of greater financial inclusion and sustainable development.

FUTURE RESEARCH DIRECTIONS

Emerging technologies such as blockchain technology, artificial intelligence (AI) and machine learning have become more and more popular to apply CSR in banks, and future researchers are recommended to explore further the changing role of emerging technologies. Studying how such technologies enhance transparency, efficiency and accountability in CSR projects might provide essential lessons for policymakers and banks.

Comparisons between CSR practices and ICT in bank industries of different levels of development status (developing and developed economies) are another area where such research would add to our knowledge of global best practice adoption of technology. Future studies may further investigate the differences in CSR strategies of banks in different countries, considering differences in regulatory context, economic environment and technological infrastructure across countries.

Longitudinal investigations Long-term consequences (economic inclusion, financial literacy, impact on society) of technology-enabled CSR effect, mediation, moderated mediation, and moderated moderation effects can be studied across time. Longitudinal case studies of these practices can provide insights into the models of CSR that are sustainable and effective, depending on the sector in question.

Bank-fintech partnerships continue to grow in prevalence, and future research might explore how digital financial services facilitate CSR growth. Research regarding mobile banking, micro-finance remedies, and AI-driven financial technologies might help write a playbook for inclusively doing economic development in areas where marginalized people live.

Concomitant with the rise of reliance on technology, future research should explore the efficacy of a hybrid model in this context (i.e., a model endowed with the combination of digital and offline interventions).

Subsequent research could also investigate policy innovations that will enhance the effectiveness and compliance with CSR. For government departments and FIs, the learnings are in terms of how to adapt the regulatory landscape to facilitate and incentivize an inclusive technology-led CSR project.

Knowing how customers, employees, regulators, and communities react to and engage with CSR initiatives in the banking industry can add to an understanding of how CSR policies could be tailored. CSR programming involving stakeholders is the key driver for banks in developing effective CSR programs that shareholders expect.

This will allow future research on the intersection of technology and CSR in banking, emerging trends and opportunities, comparative perspectives, durability of the long-term integration between technology and CSR, fin-tech integration, hybrid CSR models, legislative/regulatory framework innovations, and stakeholder engagement under increasing technological disruption. The purpose of going beyond is for an increased awareness, new and additional to the bank system, to achieve better corporate responsibility practices that may well be sustainable, not unlikely acceptable and doubtless inclusive.

DISCUSSION

In India's banking sector, there is tremendous transformative potential for integrating technology into CSR strategies, and hence, there are some major challenges, too. The chapter fills a significant literature gap by discussing how technology tools interface CSR compliance, financial inclusion and institutional diversity in public sector banks (PSB), new private sector banks (NBS) and foreign banks. Naturally, comparative work is key as the priorities of organizations operating under each focus area differ and their abilities to implement interventions depend on what resources they allocate(*)(^).

Technology — through mobile banking, digital wallets and a suite of AI-driven analytics on digital platforms, etc., is changing the way CSR is performed in organizations by making it more transparent while increasing reach and aiding efficiency. In case of public sector banks, CSR activities are aligned with national development goals, leveraging technology to run mass media financial literacy programmes. Private banks concentrate on specific output-related categories such as education, skilling, and innovations by using partnerships with fintechs. Foreign banks, capable of mobilizing the community to a small extent, have implemented global best practices such as blockchain tracking, but also carried out AI-powered responsibility programs.

Yet the digital divide, further compounded by inadequate infrastructure and low digital literacy, continues to stand as a significant roadblock — especially for rural and underserved areas. Public banks generally have inefficient and obsolete legacy systems, private banks may put their profitability above the welfare of all citizens, while foreign banks are not there in such numbers to ensure equitable outreach on CSR initiatives. This discrepancy must be addressed through highly focused regulatory and collaboration initiatives to ensure that innovation does not compromise access.

What makes this even worse is that sectoral focus varies vastly — public banks are tackling gov-mandated work on rural development and women borrowers, private banks invest in high-growth scale-up digital education and skilling activities, foreign banks align with global sustainability agendas. This further emphasizes the creation of synergetic platforms and a comprehensive CSR policy framework to harmonize efforts across different types of institutions.

The technology paradox: the dialectic of solutions and exclusion. The fact that technology can both solve problems and be a source of exclusion itself highlights the need for context-sensitive CSR. Scaling up inclusive services with public banks necessitates novel partnerships and regulatory backing. Still, we need confirmation that private banks will not allow fiscal favourites to detract from the social bottom line. Foreign banks should tailor their CSR strategies to for the Indian economic and social diversity. Open source solutions and the capabilities of interbank data sharing could lead to a more equitable financial ecosystem.

It is essential to have sustainable CSR, too, in line with cultural diversity. In the same way that Singha and Singha (2023a) assert, Singha and Singh assert that" Institutional resilience is developed by more inclusive environments across race, gender, ability-based differences, religion and how we perceive cultural backgrounds. As a result, leadership must implement more inclusive policies that foster access, equity, and representation. When incorporated into CSR frameworks, these values enhance employee engagement, spur innovation and create a more cohesive connection between corporate goals and social progress beyond the balance sheet.

Addiction at Workplace: A people-centred CSR approach also comprises treating addiction as a workplace health issue. As seen from the work of Singha and Kanna (2025), addiction is not just behavioural but also neurobiological, genetic, and influenced by environmental factors. The Multidimensional Addiction Behaviour Scale (MABS) is a holistic measure of behaviour type that may guide future CSR initiatives to channel evidence-based, empathetic efforts towards the areas most likely to foster wellbeing and recovery. Singha and Yogesh (n.d.) argue that validation of such instruments is stringent, and only those which pass rigorous validation tests are considered relevant in organizational contexts.

Therefore, cultural sensitivity in CSR is akin to the lessons we take away from educational realms. Singha et al. Sound pedagogical principles (Thorpe 2023) demonstrate that the incorporation of religious and cultural elements into curricula can advance intercultural understanding—a position with equal relevance to workplace ephemera. Recognizing spiritual diversity and creating an environment where people can comfortably bring their whole selves to work can enhance both inclusive CSR and preserving the hygiene of employees.

Internal CSR problem in Hiring is Perception bias. Singha and Singha (2023b) elaborate on structured interviews, transparency and strategies to prevent bias in fair hiring. For example, in digitally transformed environments where inclusion has to be hard-coded into the design of algorithms (Singha, 2024a), diversity hiring would be an essential aspect that could provide a dual benefit — improve the public face of corporate reputation and lead toward long-term sustainability.

Several studies suggest that human resource management (HRM) serves as a strategic actor to anchor sustainability in organizational culture. Singha (2024b) similarly illustrates that HR should be involved in setting metrics, incentives, and recognition programs to hire, train and develop a more sustainable leadership. It turns HR into a micro-level enabler of responsible innovation.

Positive psychology is what sustainable organizations are built on. In the work of Singha (2024c), efforts to foster autonomy, trust and a focus on individual strengths translate directly into increased levels of employee engagement and wellbeing. These attributes are critical to resilient, inclusive businesses; qualities that are particularly important during a time of rapid workforce disruption. Similarly, empathy and transparency (Singha 2024d) are the values which can inspire digital leadership to work against gender disparities and unity.

One of them is mentorship, which is currently developing in the continued liberation of inclusive leadership, as Singha (2024e) states, culturally responsive coaching results in empathetic leaders and diverse leadership pipelines. This helps in diversity and institutional change that is transformational. As an example of participation in inter-faith dialogue, corporate actions could align to contribute towards counter-pillarisation (Singha, 2024f), thereby repositioning the corporation as a means of social cohesion(mapping stakeholders) in the larger social-scape.

Finally, CSR in India needs to acknowledge the religious and cultural identities that confound trust among formal institutions. The value in creating inclusive educational spaces drives the sense of belonging and involvement (Singha & Singha, 2023c). Designing culturally relevant programs in CSR around such principles, with offerings like digital literacy training and microloans, can help build trust and adoption among these underrepresented groups. Dignity, Accountability and Equal Treatment within a Culturally Competent CSR Framework

Another vital dimension of a CSR strategy is the internal users. Resilience, along with positive psychological informed practices such as stress management, work-life balance and significant workplace relationships, fosters ethical workplace cultures (Singha & Singha, 2024e). This dual CSR focus, both internal and external, helps shape responsible employers as well as sustainable finance institutions in a rapidly changing world.

All in all, there is substantial potential for technology for CSR in the Indian banking sector, yet it faces challenges of digital exclusion, institutional disparity, and cultural misalignment. These gaps underscore the importance of cross-sector partnerships, inclusive design, and community-rooted programs. Further, suppose innovation is embedded with a lens of equity and cultural relevance. In that case, CSR can transition from being an enabler of social compliance to becoming a dominant stakeholder instrument for resilience, justice, and inclusive development.

CONCLUSION

The present chapter looks into the association of technology with corporate social responsibility (CSR) in the Indian banking industry (public, private, foreign banks). It has showcased the transformative role that technology can play in enhancing CSR compliance, advancing economic inclusion, and improving resilience in times of economic, social and environmental shocks. However, some implications regarding the already established impacts of technology, digital isolation, and limited resources restraining practical CSR activities in various banking sectors were also present.

However, public sector banks are under compulsion from the government that provides for their budget to provide banking for the unserved and underserved, which is an important role that they play in financial inclusion. But this is the same group that is suffering from an ageing technology legacy. The shareholders' side of public sector banks is enriched by owning their liquidation assets. Alternatively, with respect to the inventive incentives of CSR practice in the private bank sectors, foreign rivals equate to a social goal. However, community engagement at a local level demanded by CSR activities is difficult for foreign banks with only a nodding acquaintance with the country in which they are allowed to operate.

However, these differences aside, technology has been the most significant enabler for CSR initiatives for banks- enabling them to expand their reach, increase transparency and improve impact assessment. When used inclusively, digital platforms, fin-tech products, and AI-enabled approaches could help close economic divides. But that will require collaboration between policymakers, regulators and the financial industry to ensure that technology becomes an equalizer, not a divider. In order for CSR to be supportive of sustainable economic development, the digital divide and technology infrastructure in rural areas need to be reduced, and participation in all groups must be fostered.

Moving forward, the banking industry must consider a more complete (and inclusive) view of CSR, one that recognizes the balance between technology and access. Industry partnership, cooperation, fixing, and aligning their CSR programs with the national development plan and sustainable world can help reduce economic disparities. It is also a good idea for future studies to keep investigating how such technology will mature its role in the CSR space, how beneficiaries can continue to benefit from these digital interventions in the long run and how to couple effective, evidence-based policy frameworks that would facilitate inclusive financial and broader social progress.

Technology is a powerful facilitator when it comes to promoting CSR within the banking industry. It's good, but the rich should redistribute their proportions towards all society groups for viable long-term economic inclusion. The Indian banking sector can play a significant role in reducing financial and non-financial inequalities in the wake of the ongoing global crises by bridging the sectoral gap and making effective use of digital innovations.

REFERENCES

Akanfe, O., Bhatt, P., & Lawong, D. A. (2025). Technology advancements shaping the financial inclusion landscape: Present interventions, the emergence of artificial intelligence and future directions. *Information Systems Frontiers*. Advance online publication. DOI: 10.1007/s10796-025-10597-z

Angelini, A., & Nieri, F. (2022). Corporate Social Responsibility in the Banking Industry: An Overview. In *International series in advanced management studies* (pp. 57–75). https://doi.org/DOI: 10.1007/978-3-031-12027-5_4

Atanasov, A., Chipriyanova, G., & Krasteva-Hristova, R. (2023). Integration of Digital Technologies in Corporate Social Responsibility (CSR) activities: A systematic literature review and bibliometric analysis. *Journal of Risk and Financial Management*, *16*(8), 373. DOI: 10.3390/jrfm16080373

Financial Express. (2024, September 11). The impact of digital transformation on CSR: Trends, challenges, and future outlook. *Financial Express*. https://www.financialexpress.com/business/industry-the-impact-of-digital-transformation-on-csr-trends-challenges-and-future-outlook-3608335/

Gbaf News. (2019, February 8). UN's sustainable development goals: The critical role of banks in creating a sustainable future. *Global Banking and Finance*. https://www.globalbankingandfinance.com/uns-sustainable-development-goals-the-critical-role-of-banks-in-creating-a-sustainable-future

India, E. Y. (2025, January 10). India's transformative digital infrastructure, innovative policies, and enhanced financial literacy are unlocking new pathways to true financial inclusion. *EY*. https://www.ey.com/en_in/insights/financial-services/how-can-india-drive-financial-inclusion-through-technology-and-literacy

Johnson, M. (2024). Empowering Financial Inclusion: The crucial role of public sector banks in implementing Pradhan Mantri Jan-Dhan Yojana (PMJDY). *International Journal for Research in Applied Science and Engineering Technology*, *12*(4), 3681–3684. DOI: 10.22214/ijraset.2024.60726

Johnson, M., & Joy, V. S. (2024). Empowering financial inclusion: The crucial role of public sector banks in implementing Pradhan Mantri Jan-Dhan Yojana (PMJDY). *International Journal for Research in Applied Science and Engineering Technology*, *12*(4), 3681.

Joseph, S., & Jeslina, R. (2019). DigitizationDigitization as a tool for CSR implementation in the Indian banking industry: A study on SBI. *International Journal of Research and Analytical Reviews*, *6*(1). IJRAR19VP011.pdf

Kumar, M., & Gokhru, A. (2023). A comparison of CSR practices of selected Indian and foreign banks. *International Journal of Management. Public Policy Research, 2*(1), 71.

Mahdi, I. B. S., Bouaziz, M., & Abbes, M. B. (2023). The moderating effect of fin-tech on the relationship between CSR and banks' financial stability: Baron and Kenny's approach analysis. *EuroMed Journal of Business*. Advance online publication. DOI: 10.1108/emjb-03-2023-0082

Mishra, K. (2022). A comparative study on corporate social responsibility (CSR) practices in public & private sector banks of India. *International Research Journal of Modernization in Engineering, Technology and Science, 4*(8) fin_irjmets1660652664.pdf

Nooribakhsh, M., Fernández-Diego, M., González-Ladrón-De-Guevara, F., & Mollamotalebi, M. (2024). Community detection in social networks using machine learning: A systematic mapping study. *Knowledge and Information Systems, 66*(12), 7205–7259. DOI: 10.1007/s10115-024-02201-8

Parthiban, R., Aiswarya, S. S., & Dinesh Kumar, R. (2018). CSR practices: Public and private sector banks in India. *International Journal of Interdisciplinary Research and Innovations, 6*(4), 566–573.

Pérez-Escolar, M., & Canet, F. (2022). Research on vulnerable people and digital inclusion: Toward a consolidated taxonomical framework. *Universal Access in the Information Society, 22*(3), 1059–1072. DOI: 10.1007/s10209-022-00867-x PMID: 35125988

Pérez-Escolar, M., & Canet, F. (2022). Research on vulnerable people and digital inclusion: Toward a consolidated taxonomical framework. *Universal Access in the Information Society, 22*(3), 1059–1072. DOI: 10.1007/s10209-022-00867-x PMID: 35125988

Podile, V. (2024). Artificial intelligence and corporate social responsibility: Synergies, challenges, and future directions. *International Journal of Advanced Multidisciplinary Research and Studies, 4*(6), 95–99. 10.126180467

Potocan, V. (2021). Technology and corporate social responsibility. *Sustainability, 13*(15), 8658. DOI: 10.3390/su13158658

Priyadarshana, D., Rao, T. R., & Rao, M. S. (2024). AI and blockchain technology for secure and transparent financial transactions. *International Journal of Science and Research Archive, 13*(1), 2013–2019. DOI: 10.30574/ijsra.2024.13.1.1845

Putranto, I. A. (2020). Acceptance technology factors of mobile banking usage based on UTAUT2 model. *Jurnal Riset Akuntansi dan Bisnis Airlangga, 5*(2), 920–937. http://dx.doi.org/DOI: 10.31093/jraba.v5i2.234

Raihan, M. M., Subroto, S., Chowdhury, N., Koch, K., Ruttan, E., & Turin, T. C. (2024). *Dimensions and barriers for digital (in)equity and digital divide: a systematic integrative review.* Digital Transformation and Society., DOI: 10.1108/dts-04-2024-0054

Saxena, S. (2016). A comparative study of corporate social responsibility (CSR) of private and public sector banks. *World Wide Journal of Multidisciplinary Research and Development*, *2*(1), 21–23.

Sharda, G., Swamy, N., & Singh, C. (2014). *Impact of foreign banks on the Indian economy* (Working Paper No. 451). Indian Institute of Management Bangalore

Shayan, N. F., Mohabbati-Kalejahi, N., Alavi, S., & Zahid, M. A. (2022). Sustainable Development Goals (SDGs) as a framework for Corporate Social Responsibility (CSR). *Sustainability*, *14*(3), 1222. DOI: 10.3390/su14031222

Siddeswara, N. (2020). Indian rural banking and finance: A study on progress and challenges. *International Journal of Applied Research*, *6*(3), 531–533.

Singha, R. (2024). Stress, Resilience, and Brain Performance. In Saluja, S., Kukreja, J., & Sharma, S. (Eds.), *Building Organizational Resilience With Neuroleadership* (pp. 14–29). IGI Global Scientific Publishing., DOI: 10.4018/979-8-3693-1785-3.ch002

Singha, R., & Kanna, S. Y. (2025). Neuroeconomic insights on addiction: Integrating the Multidimensional Addiction Behaviour Scale for treatment, prevention, and holistic wellbeing. In Reddy, K. (Ed.), *Behavioral economics and neuroeconomics of health and healthcare* (pp. 181–212). IGI Global., DOI: 10.4018/979-8-3693-6055-2.ch009

Singha, R., & Singha, S. (2023). Economic sustainability, mindfulness, and diversity in the age of artificial intelligence and machine learning. In *Machine Intelligence* (pp. 273–285). Taylor & Francis., https://www.taylorfrancis.com/chapters/edit/10.1201/9781003424550-15/economic-sustainability-mindfulness-diversity-age-artificial-intelligence-machine-learning-ranjit-singha-surjit-singha

Singha, R., & Singha, S. (2023b). The Role of Perception in Recruitment Processes. In Even, A., & Christiansen, B. (Eds.), *Enhancing Employee Engagement and Productivity in the Post-Pandemic Multigenerational Workforce* (pp. 275–296). IGI Global Scientific Publishing., DOI: 10.4018/978-1-6684-9172-0.ch014

Singha, R., & Singha, S. (2023c). Faith and culture in education: Fostering inclusive environments. In DeHart, J. (Ed.), *The Role of Faith and Religious Diversity in Educational Practices* (pp. 149–172). IGI Global., DOI: 10.4018/978-1-6684-9184-3.ch007

Singha, R., & Singha, S. (2024). Positive interventions at work: Enhancing employee wellbeing and organizational sustainability. In Baykal, E. (Ed.), *Fostering organizational sustainability with positive psychology* (pp. 151–179). IGI Global., DOI: 10.4018/979-8-3693-1524-8.ch007

Singha, R., & Singha, S. (2024a). Mental health treatment: Exploring the potential of augmented reality and virtual reality. In Hiran, K., Doshi, R., & Patel, M. (Eds.), *Applications of virtual and augmented reality for health and wellbeing* (pp. 91–110). IGI Global., DOI: 10.4018/979-8-3693-1123-3.ch006

Singha, R., & Singha, S. (2024b). Mindfulness-based interventions: Applications in Western and Indian psychology. In Sathiyaseelan, A., & Balasundaram, S. (Eds.), *Global applications of Indian psychology: Therapeutic and strategic models* (pp. 192–212). IGI Global., DOI: 10.4018/978-1-6684-9778-4.ch011

Singha, R., & Singha, S. (2024c). Educational innovation transforming higher education for workforce readiness. In Christiansen, B., & Even, A. (Eds.), *Advancing student employability through higher education* (pp. 37–55). IGI Global., DOI: 10.4018/979-8-3693-0517-1.ch003

Singha, R., & Singha, S. (2024e). Positive Interventions at Work: Enhancing Employee Wellbeing and Organizational Sustainability. In Baykal, E. (Ed.), *Fostering Organizational Sustainability With Positive Psychology* (pp. 151–179). IGI Global Scientific Publishing., DOI: 10.4018/979-8-3693-1524-8.ch007

Singha, R., & Yogesh, K. S. (2025a). Qualitative Instrumentation Field Tests and Expert Panel Reviews: A Focus on the Multidimensional Addiction Behaviour Scale (MABS) for Dissertation Research. In R. Throne (Ed.), *Qualitative Research Methods for Dissertation Research* (pp. 547-580). IGI Global Scientific Publishing. https://doi.org/DOI: 10.4018/979-8-3693-3069-2.ch020

Singha, S. (2024). Inclusive Responses to Diversity-Driven Populism. In Chacko Chennattuserry, J., Deshpande, M., & Hong, P. (Eds.), *Encyclopedia of New Populism and Responses in the 21st Century*. Springer., DOI: 10.1007/978-981-16-9859-0_446-1

Singha, S. (2024a). Unveiling Gender Dynamics in Digital Capitalism: Navigating the Path to Social Gender Equality. In Topçu, Ç. (Ed.), *Digital Capitalism in the New Media Era* (pp. 161–186). IGI Global Scientific Publishing., DOI: 10.4018/979-8-3693-1182-0.ch009

Singha, S. (2024b). Fostering a Culture of Sustainability Through Human Resources Practices. In Popescu, C., Martínez-Falcó, J., Marco-Lajara, B., Sánchez-García, E., & Millán-Tudela, L. (Eds.), *Building Sustainable Human Resources Management Practices for Businesses* (pp. 107–124). IGI Global Scientific Publishing., DOI: 10.4018/979-8-3693-1994-9.ch007

Singha, S. (2024c). Enhancing workplace positivity: Strategies for cultivating a flourishing organizational culture. In Baykal, E. (Ed.), *Fostering organizational sustainability with positive psychology* (pp. 54–83). IGI Global., DOI: 10.4018/979-8-3693-1524-8.ch003

Singha, S. (2024d). Cultivating inclusive leadership: Navigating organizational culture in the digital era. In Darwish, D. (Ed.), *Effective technology for gender equity in business and organizations* (pp. 139–166). IGI Global., DOI: 10.4018/979-8-3693-3435-5.ch005

Singha, S. (2024e). Unveiling the synergy: Inclusive coaching practices in leadership. In Wefald, A. (Ed.), *Navigating the coaching and leadership landscape: Strategies and insights for success* (pp. 189–210). IGI Global., DOI: 10.4018/979-8-3693-5242-7.ch010

Singha, S., & Singha, R. (2023a). Understanding diversity: The power of differences. In Even, A., & Christiansen, B. (Eds.), *Enhancing employee engagement and productivity in the post-pandemic multigenerational workforce* (pp. 297–313). IGI Global., DOI: 10.4018/978-1-6684-9172-0.ch015

Singha, S., & Singha, R. (2024d). Cross-disciplinary collaborations and partnerships for sustainability education: Including community-based learning, industry partnerships, and international collaborations. In Goi, C. (Ed.), *Teaching and learning for a sustainable future: Innovative strategies and best practices* (pp. 17–37). IGI Global., DOI: 10.4018/978-1-6684-9859-0.ch002

Singha, S., Singha, R., & Ruben, V. M. (2023). Explorations of the links between multiculturalism and religious diversity. In DeHart, J. (Ed.), *The role of faith and religious diversity in educational practices* (pp. 120–148). IGI Global Scientific Publishing., DOI: 10.4018/978-1-6684-9184-3.ch006

Singha, S., & Sivarethinamohan, R. (2021). The role of women in the formation of organizational climates in various workspaces in Bengaluru, India. *Journal of International Women's Studies*, *22*(6), 13. https://vc.bridgew.edu/jiws/vol22/iss6/13

Singha, S., & Sivarethinamohan, R. (2022). Social inclusion, equality, leadership, and diversity to attain Sustainable Development Goal 5 in the Indian banking industry. *Journal of International Women's Studies*, *23*(5), 9. https://vc.bridgew.edu/jiws/vol23/iss5/9

Singha, S., & Sivarethinamohan, R. (2022a). Formation of positive organizational climate: Integration of Ubuntu diversity management in banks. *Journal of International Women's Studies*, *24*(4), 10. https://vc.bridgew.edu/jiws/vol24/iss4/10

Thakur, M. (2024). Cybersecurity threats and countermeasures in the digital age. *Journal of Applied Science and Education*, *4*(1). Advance online publication. DOI: 10.54060/a2zjournals.jase.42

World Bank Group. (2016). Digital Financial Inclusion. In the *World Bank*. https://www.worldbank.org/en/topic/financialinclusion/publication/digital-financial-inclusion

Wylde, V., Prakash, E., Hewage, C., & Platts, J. (2023). Ethical challenges in the use of digital technologies: AI and big data. In *Advanced sciences and technologies for security applications* (pp. 33–58). https://doi.org/DOI: 10.1007/978-3-031-09691-4_3

KEY TERMS AND DEFINITIONS

Corporate Social Responsibility (CSR): The voluntary and legal business activities that integrate social, environmental, and ethical concerns into a company's business practices. In India, CSR compliance is governed by Section 135 of the Companies Act, 2013, which mandates that eligible companies (including banks) must spend a certain proportion of their average net profits in a financial year towards socially relevant projects, including health, education &environmental sustainability and rural development.

Economic Inclusion: Economic inclusion is the process of ensuring equal access to economic opportunities, resources, and financial services for all individuals, particularly marginalized and disadvantaged groups. In the banking sector, economic inclusion involves expanding financial literacy, microfinance, and credit accessibility to underserved populations, thereby fostering equitable economic participation.

Financial Crisis: A financial crisis is when financial institutions, markets, or economies experience a severe disruption, often leading to liquidity shortages, declining asset values, and economic recessions. Monetary crises can arise due to systemic banking failures, stock market crashes, sovereign debt defaults, or external financial shocks, significantly affecting businesses and consumers.

Foreign Banks in India: Foreign banks in India are financial institutions headquartered outside India but operating within the country under the regulatory framework of the Reserve Bank of India (RBI). These banks provide financial services, foreign exchange transactions, and international banking solutions while adhering to Indian banking norms and compliance requirements. Examples include Citibank, HSBC, and Standard Chartered.

Private Sector Banks: Private sector banks are private organizations wherein the majority of the equity is held by private shareholders, either individual investors or corporations. Such banks are essentially commercial in their operations, and the RBI closely monitors these banks to ensure that they remain profitable, provide good banking services to customers, and focus on continuous technological improvements of standards. In India, HDFC Bank, ICICI Bank, and Axis Bank are examples of sorts.

Public Sector Banks (PSBs): These are state-owned banks where the Indian government directly has a 50% or more ownership. These banks work under the rules and regulations laid down by the Reserve Bank of India (RBI). They are an essential part of financial inclusion, rural banking, and priority sector lending. These might include the State Bank of India (SBI), Punjab National Bank (PUB) and Bank of Baroda.

Technology and Inequality: Technology and inequality refer to the disparities arising from unequal access to digital tools, internet connectivity, and financial technology, leading to economic and social imbalances. While technological advancements can drive economic growth, they can also widen income gaps, exclude underprivileged communities from financial services, and create disparities in job opportunities and education accessibility.

Compilation of References

Abbasi, T., & Abbasi, S. A. (2010). Biomass energy and the environmental impacts associated with its production and utilization. *Renewable & Sustainable Energy Reviews, 14*(3), 919–937.

Abdenur, A. E., & Folly, M. (2015). The New Development Bank and the institutionalization of the BRICS. *R/evolutions. Global Trends & Regional Issues, 3*(1), 66–92.

ABP. (2023, December 20). *UPI transactions grow in 2023: 118% in rural and semi-urban regions in India: Survey.* https://news.abplive.com/business/upi-transactions-grow-in-2023-118-in-rural-and-semi-urban-regions-in-india-digital-payments-digital-india-survey-1651378

Acemoglu, D. (2009). *Introduction to modern economic growth* (Vol. 4, Issue 1). Prınceton Unıversty Press.

Acemoğlu, D., ve Johnson S. (2023). İktisadar ve Teknoloji, Doğan Kitapevi

Acharya, A. (2017). After liberal hegemony: The advent of a multiplex world order. *Ethics & International Affairs, 31*(3), 271–285. DOI: 10.1017/S089267941700020X

Açımuz, B. (2022). Devletin yükümlülüklerine, sorumluluğuna ve yargıcın yetkilerine yaklaşımda dönüştürücü etkileri bakımından sistemik iklim davaları. *Yeditepe Üniversitesi Hukuk Fakültesi Dergisi, 19*(2), 343–428.

Ackermann, T., & Söder, L. (2002). An overview of wind energy-status 2002. *Renewable & Sustainable Energy Reviews, 6*(1-2), 67–127.

African Development Bank (AfDB). (2018). *African economic outlook 2018.* https://www.afdb.org/fileadmin/uploads/afdb/Documents/Publications/African_Economic_Outlook_2018_-_EN.pdf

African Development Bank (AfDB). (2023). African. *Economic Outlook, 2023,* •••. https://www.afdb.org/sites/default/files/documents/publications/afdb23-01_aeo_main_english_0602.pdf

African Development Bank (AfDB). (2024, May 7). *Ethiopia - Distributed renewable energy agriculture modalities (DREAM) programme - Project summary note*. African Development Bank. https://www.afdb.org/en/documents/ethiopia-distributed-renewable-energy-agriculture-modalities-dream-programme-project-summary-note

African Development Bank (AfDB). (2025, April 8). *Nigeria's food and agriculture revolution takes off backed by the African Development Bank*. African Development Bank. https://www.afdb.org/en/news-and-events/press-releases/nigerias-food-and-agriculture-revolution-takes-backed-african-development-bank-82711

Aggarwal, P. (2020). On de-risking and de-dollarizing intra-BRICS trade via smart contracts. *BRICS Journal of Economics*, *4*(1), 54–69. DOI: 10.38050/2712-7508-2020-1-4-6

Agrawal, M., Goyal, A., Akhtar, A., & Abbas, H. (2024). Green bond: A government initiative towards sustainable finance. In *Issues of Sustainability in AI and New-Age Thematic Investing*. IGI Global., DOI: 10.4018/979-8-3693-3282-5.ch008

Ahmad, N., Nguyen, D. K., & Tian, X. L. (2024). Assessing the impact of the sharing economy and technological innovation on sustainable development: An empirical investigation of the United Kingdom. *Technological Forecasting and Social Change, 209*(February 2023), 123743. https://doi.org/DOI: 10.1016/j.techfore.2024.123743

Ahmad, N., Youjin, L., Žiković, S., & Belyaeva, Z. (2023). The effects of technological innovation on sustainable development and environmental degradation: Evidence from China. *Technology in Society, 72*(December 2022). https://doi.org/DOI: 10.1016/j.techsoc.2022.102184

Ahmed, K., Shahbaz, M., Qasim, A., & Long, W. (2015). The linkages between deforestation, energy and growth for environmental degradation in Pakistan. *Ecological Indicators*, *49*, 95–103.

Ajanaku, B. A., & Collins, A. R. (2021). Economic growth and deforestation in African countries: Is the environmental Kuznets curve hypothesis applicable? *Forest Policy and Economics*, *129*, 102488.

Akanfe, O., Bhatt, P., & Lawong, D. A. (2025). Technology advancements shaping the financial inclusion landscape: Present interventions, the emergence of artificial intelligence and future directions. *Information Systems Frontiers*. Advance online publication. DOI: 10.1007/s10796-025-10597-z

Akbostancı, E., Türüt Aşık, S., & Tunç, G. İ. (2006). "İmalat Sanayi ve Kirlilik: Bir Kirli Endüstri Sığınağı Olarak Türkiye". *Ankara Üniversitesi Siyasal Bilgiler Fakültesi Dergisi. Cilt*, *60*(1), 1–28.

Akyıldız, B. (2008). Çevresel Etkinlik Analizi: Kuznets Eğrisi Yaklaşımı. Yüksek Lisans Tezi. Dokuz Eylül Üniversitesi. Sosyal Bilimler Enstitüsü. 1-225

Al-Ajmi, J. Y. (2008). Risk tolerance of individual investors in an emerging market. *International Research Journal of Finance and Economics, 17*(1), 15–26.

Alakbarov, N., Gündüz, M., & Şaşmaz, M. (2024). Exploring the link between economic growth, energy consumption, and environmental pollution in G20. *Natural Resources Forum*, 1–17. DOI: 10.1111/1477-8947.12440

Ali, N., Phoungthong, K., Techato, K., Ali, W., Abbas, S., Dhanraj, J. A., & Khan, A. (2022). FDI, Green Innovation and Environmental Quality Nexus: New Insights from BRICS Economies. *Sustainability, 14*(4). Advance online publication. DOI: 10.3390/su14042181

Alola, A. A., Akadiri, S. S., & Usman, O. (2020). Domestic material consumption and greenhouse gas emissions in the EU-28 countries: Implications for environmental sustainability targets. *Sustainable Development, 29*(2), 388–397. DOI: 10.1002/sd.2154

Amin, N., Shabbir, M. S., Pan, Y., & Asif, M. (2025). Beyond Growth: The Triple Green Strategy (Green Energy, Green Innovation, and Green Finance) for Sustainable Emissions Reduction in BRICS Countries. *Sustainable Development*. Advance online publication. DOI: 10.1002/sd.3411

Amin, N., Sharif, A., Shabbir, M. S., & Pan, Y. (2025). Evaluating the impact of natural resource rents, R&D expenditures, green finance and energy efficiency on carbon emissions in BRICS economies: Greening the path to carbon neutrality in the post-COP 27 era. *Technology in Society, 81*. Advance online publication. DOI: 10.1016/j.techsoc.2025.102826

Amin, N., Sharif, A., Tayyab, M., & Pan, Y. (2024). Green Technological Advances and Resource Rents as Levers for Carbon Reduction in BRICS: Implications for SDGs 7, 8, 9, 12, and 13. *Sustainable Development*. Advance online publication. DOI: 10.1002/sd.3294

Amorocho-Daza, H., Sušnik, J., van der Zaag, P., & Slinger, J. H. (2025). A model-based policy analysis framework for social-ecological systems: Integrating uncertainty and participation in system dynamics modelling. *Ecological Modelling, 499*, 110943. DOI: 10.1016/j.ecolmodel.2024.110943

Anbar, A., & Eker, M. (2010). An empirical investigation for determining of the relation between personal financial risk tolerance and demographic characteristic. *Ege Academic Review, 10*(2), 503–522.

Andrée, B., Chamorro, A., Spencer, P., Koomen, E., & Dogo, H. (2019). Revisiting the relation between economic growth and the environment; a global assessment of deforestation, pollution and carbon emission. *Renewable and Sustainable Energy, 114*, 109221. DOI: 10.1016/j.rser.2019.06.028

Andreoni, V., & Galmarini, S. (2012). Decoupling economic growth from carbon dioxide emissions: A decomposition analysis of Italian energy consumption. *Energy, 44*(1), 682–691. DOI: 10.1016/j.energy.2012.05.024

Angelini, A., & Nieri, F. (2022). Corporate Social Responsibility in the Banking Industry: An Overview. In *International series in advanced management studies* (pp. 57–75). https://doi.org/DOI: 10.1007/978-3-031-12027-5_4

Angrisani, M., Cipriani, M., Guarino, A., Kendall, R., & Pina, J. O. Z. (2020). Risk preferences at the time of COVID-19: An experiment with professional traders and students, *Federal Reserve Bank of New York Staff Reports*, No. 927.

Ansari, S., & Phatak, Y. (2016). A study of assessment of financial risk tolerance and preferred investment avenues of investors, *Prestige International Journal of Management and Research*, 9(2/1), 1-7.

Apergis, N., & Cooray, A. (2014). Convergence in sovereign debt ratios across heavily indebted EU countries: Evidence from club convergence. *Applied Economics Letters, 21*(11), 786–788. DOI: 10.1080/13504851.2014.889798

Arı, F. (2023). Başlıca enerji kaynakları ve çevresel etkilerinin değerlendirilmesi. *Dicle Üniversitesi İktisadi ve İdari Bilimler Fakültesi Dergisi, 13*(26), 697–718.

Armijo, L. E. (2007). The BRICs Countries (Brazil, Russia, India, and China) as Analytical Category: Mirage or Insight? *Asian Perspective, 31*(4), 7–42.

Armijo, L. E., & Roberts, C. (2014). The emerging powers and global governance: Why the BRICS matter. In Looney, R. E. (Ed.), *Handbook of emerging economies* (pp. 503–524). Routledge.

Arrighi, G. (1994). *The long twentieth century: Money, power and the origins of our times.* Verso Press.

Arruda Filho, M. T. d., Torres, P. H. C., & Jacobi, P. R. (2024). A systematic review of the literature on climate justice: A comparison between the Global North and South. *Sustainability, 16*, 9888. DOI: 10.3390/su16229888

Arslan, S., Darıcı, M., & Karahan, Ç. (2001). Türkiye'nin jeotermal enerji potansiyeli. *Jeotermal Enerji Semineri,* 21-27.

Asan, Ü. (1995). Global iklim değişimi ve Türkiye ormanlarında karbon birikimi. *Istanbul Üniversitesi Orman Fakültesi Dergisi*, *45*(1-2), 23–38.

Atanasov, A., Chipriyanova, G., & Krasteva-Hristova, R. (2023). Integration of Digital Technologies in Corporate Social Responsibility (CSR) activities: A systematic literature review and bibliometric analysis. *Journal of Risk and Financial Management*, *16*(8), 373. DOI: 10.3390/jrfm16080373

Atvur, S., Gülal, A. G. G., & Oğuz, C. U. (2023). İklim krizi ve ekolojik bağlamda devletin rolünü yeniden düşünmek. *Politik Ekonomik Kuram, 7*(Özel Sayı), 44-57.

Aydoğdu, M. H. (2024). İklim Değişikliği: Sorunlar ve Bunlar Yönetilebilir Mi? *Ssd Journal*, *9*(46), 79–91.

Babb, S., & Kentikelenis, A. E. (2021). Markets everywhere: The Washington Consensus and the sociology of global institutional change. *Annual Review of Sociology*, *47*, 521–541.

Babones, S. (2018). *The new authoritarianism: Trump, populism, and the tyranny of experts*. Polity Press.

Bahturidze, Z., Vasilyeva, N., Shahoud, Z., & Pogodin, S. (2024). Inclusion as a Driver for the Implementation of SDG 30 by the BRICS Countries. *Springer Geography*, (Part F2388), 135–147. DOI: 10.1007/978-3-031-50407-5_11

Bai, X., Hasan, S., Andersen, L. S., Bjørn, A., Kilkiş, Ş., & Ospina, D. (2024). Translating Earth system boundaries for cities and businesses. *Nature Sustainability*, *7*, 108–119. DOI: 10.1038/s41893-023-01255-w

Bajtelsmit, V. L., & Bernasek, A. (1996). Why do women invest differently than men? *Financial Counseling and Planning*, *7*, 1–10. DOI: 10.2139/ssrn.2238

Baker, H. K., & Haslem, J. A. (1974). The impact of investor socio-economic characteristics on risk and return preferences. *Journal of Business Research*, *2*(1), 469–476.

Banya, N., & Anders, T. (2024, September 2). *S. Africa's Transnet reports wider loss after pipeline lawsuit provision.* Reuters. https://www.reuters.com/business/autos-transportation/south-africas-transnet-reports-higher-loss-latest-financial-year-2024-09-02/

Barbier, E. (2001). The Economics of Tropical Deforestation and Land Use: An Introduction to the Special Issue. *Land Economics*, *77*(2), 155–171. DOI: 10.2307/3147087

Barrios, C., Flores, E., & Martínez, M. Á. (2019). Club convergence in innovation activity across European regions. *Papers in Regional Science*, *98*(4), 1545–1565. DOI: 10.1111/pirs.12429

Başar, S., & Temurlenk, M. S. (2007). Çevreye Uyarlanmiş Kuznets Eğrisi: Türkiye Üzerine Bir Uygulama. *Atatürk Üniversitesi İktisadi ve İdari Bilimler Dergisi, 21*(1), 1–12.

Bashir, T., Uppal, S. T., Hanif, K., Yaseen, S. M., & Saraj, K. (2013). Financial risk tolerant attitude: Empirical evidence from Pakistan. *European Scientific Journal, 9*(19), 200–209.

Başoğlu, A. (2014). Küresel iklim değişikliğinin ekonomik etkileri. *Sosyal Bilimler Dergisi, 7*, 175–196.

Bastanifar, I., Khan, K. H., & Koch, H. (2025). Understanding BRICSIZATION through an economic geopolitical model. *Journal of Open Innovation, 11*(1), 100440. DOI: 10.1016/j.joitmc.2024.100440

Bate, A. F., Wachira, E. W., & Danka, S. (2023). The determinants of innovation performance: An income-based cross-country comparative analysis using the Global Innovation Index (GII). *Journal of Innovation and Entrepreneurship, 12*(1). Advance online publication. DOI: 10.1186/s13731-023-00283-2

Batista, P. N., Jr. (2023, November 13). *BRICS financial and monetary initiatives – NDB, CRA, and a possible new currency*. Grupo de Estudos sobre os BRICS (GEBRICS). https://sites.usp.br/gebrics/brics-financial-and-monetary-initiatives-ndb-cra-and-a-possible-new-currency-by-paulo-nogueira-batista-jr/

Battaglia, F., Cervellati, E. M., Salerno, D., Stella, G. P., & Vannoni, V. (2025). How the COVID-19 pandemic changed Italians' financial risk tolerance. *Qualitative Research in Financial Markets, 17*(2), 415–431. DOI: 10.1108/QRFM-01-2024-0019

Baumol, W. (1986). Productivity Growth, Convergence, and Welfare: What the Long-run Data Show. *The American Economic Review, 76*(5), 1072–1085. DOI: 10.2307/1816469

Baxtiyarovich, A. R., & Vaxobovich, M. M. (2025). The Impact Of Clımate Change On Human Health. *Yangı O 'Zbekıston. YANGI TADQIQOTLAR JURNALI, 2*(4), 267–268.

Belloc, I., & Molina, J. A. (2023). The ecological footprint in Africa: Identifying convergence clubs from 1970 to 2018. *Applied Economics Letters, 30*(19), 2808–2813. DOI: 10.1080/13504851.2022.2107984

Berger, J., & Liebe, U. (2025). Effective climate action must address both social inequality and inequality aversion. *npj. Climate Action, 4*(1), 1–6. DOI: 10.1038/s44168-025-00208-7

Beşballı, S. G. (2023). Çevre sorunları çerçevesinde küresel iklim değişikliği. *Artvin Çoruh Üniversitesi Uluslararası Sosyal Bilimler Dergisi, 9*(2), 500–521. DOI: 10.22466/acusbd.1388179

Bhattarai, M., & Hammig, M. (2001). Institutions and the Environmental Kuznets Curve for Deforestation: A Crosscountry Analysis for Latin America, Africa and Asia. *World Development, 29*(6), 995–1010.

Biely, K., & Chakori, S. (2025). Sustainability transition theories: Perpetuating or breaking with the status quo. *Sustainable Development, 33*(1), 52–68. DOI: 10.1002/sd.3101

Bittar, A. de V., & Di Serio, L. C. (2024). Do innovation policies support micro and small enterprises to overcome barriers? *Innovation & Management Review, 21*(2), 137–152. DOI: 10.1108/INMR-12-2021-0234

Biyase, M., Zwane, T., Mncayi, P., & Maleka, M. (2023). Do Technological Innovation and Financial Development Affect Inequality? Evidence from BRICS Countries. *International Journal of Financial Studies, 11*(1). Advance online publication. DOI: 10.3390/ijfs11010043

Bloomberg. (2025a, March 27). *Russia playing the long game to protect energy exports* [Video]. https://www.bloomberg.com/news/videos/2025-03-27/russia-playing-the-long-game-to-protect-energy-exports-video

Bloomberg. (2025b, April 16). *South African court ends $425 million rail pact in anti-graft push.* https://www.bloomberg.com/news/articles/2025-04-16/s-africa-court-ends-425-million-rail-pact-in-anti-graft-push

Bond, P. (2013). Sub-imperialism as lubricant of neoliberalism: South African "deputy sheriff" duty within BRICS. *Third World Quarterly, 34*(2), 251–270. DOI: 10.1080/01436597.2013.775783

Bond, P., & Garcia, A. (2015). *BRICS: An anti-capitalist critique.* Pluto Press.

Bonsang, E., & Dohmen, T. (2015). Risk attitude and cognitive aging. *Journal of Economic Behavior & Organization, 112*, 112–126. DOI: 10.1016/j.jebo.2015.01.004

Bozkurt, S., & Tür, R. (2015). *Dünyada ve Türkiyede hidroelektrik enerji, gelişimi ve genel değerlendirme. 4.* Su Yapıları Sempozyumu Kitabı.

Breusch, T., & Pagan, A. (1980). The Lagrange Multiplier Test its Applications to Model Specification in Econometrics. *The Review of Economic Studies,* •••, 239–253.

Bu, D., Hanspal, T., Lao, Y., & Liu, Y. (2020). Risk taking during a global crisis: Evidence from Wuhan. *Covid Economics, 5*, 106–146.

Buitenzorgy, M., & Mol, A. (2010). Does Democracy Lead to a Better Environment? Deforestation and the Democratic Transition Peak. *Environmental and Resource Economics, 48*, 59–70.

Bulut, Ü. (2021). Environmental sustainability in Turkey: An environmental Kuznets curve estimation for ecological footprint. *International Journal of Sustainable Development and World Ecology, 28*(3), 227–237. DOI: 10.1080/13504509.2020.1793425

Bural, D. (2025). Protecting intellectual property rights in Türkiye: Navigating legal and cultural dimensions. *Crime, Law, and Social Change, 83*(1), 1–17. DOI: 10.1007/s10611-024-10195-1

Business Today Egypt. (2024, June 11). *Egypt to obtain $1B loan from NDB by end of 2024 | FinMin*. Business Today Egypt. https://www.businesstodayegypt.com/Article/1/4708/Egypt-to-obtain-1B-loan-from-NDB-by-end-of

Caglar, A. E., Yavuz, E., & Mert, M.. (2022). The ecological footprint facing asymmetric natural resources challenges: Evidence from the USA. *Environmental Science and Pollution Research International, 29*, 10521–10534. DOI: 10.1007/s11356-021-16406-9

Çağlar, E. M., & Mert, M. (2017). Türkiye'de Çevresel Kuznets Hipotezi ve Yenilenebilir Enerji Tüketiminin Karbon Salımı Üzerine Etkisi: Yapısal Kırılmalı Eşbütünleşme Yaklaşımı. *Yönetim ve Ekonomi Dergisi, 24*(1), 21–38.

Cai, X., & Song, X. (2022). The nexus between digital finance and carbon emissions: Evidence from China. *Frontiers in Psychology, 13*. Advance online publication. DOI: 10.3389/fpsyg.2022.997692 PMID: 36275290

Çakır, G. (2012). Sürdürülebilir kalkınma adına iklim değişikliğinin küresel ölçekte irdelenmesi. In *GreenAge Symposium, Mimar Sinan Fine Arts University, Faculty of Architecture* (pp. 448-457).

Caney, S. (2024). Climate justice and the moral relevance of the past. *Journal of Practical Ethics, 12*(1). Advance online publication. DOI: 10.3998/jpe.6269

Caporale, G. M., Gil-Alana, L., Plastun, A., & Makarenko, I. (2022). Persistence in ESG and conventional stock market indices. *Journal of Economics and Finance, 46*(4), 678–703. DOI: 10.1007/s12197-022-09580-0

Caravaggio, N. (2020). A global empirical re-assessment of the Environmental Kuznets curve for deforestation. *Forest Policy and Economics, 119*, 102282.

Carayannis, E. G., & Grigoroudis, E. (2016). Using multiobjective mathematical programming to link national competitiveness, productivity, and innovation. *Annals of Operations Research, 247*(2), 635–655. DOI: 10.1007/s10479-015-1873-x

Cardin, A. (2025, May 9). *Brazil's inequality drop in 2024 stands out but still trails regional peers.* Rio Times Online. https://www.riotimesonline.com/brazils-inequality-drop-in-2024-stands-out-but-still-trails-regional-peers/

Cardoso, B. F., Shikida, P. F. A., & Finco, A. (2017). Development of Brazilian biodiesel sector from the perspective of stakeholders. *Energies, 10*(3), 399. DOI: 10.3390/en10030399

Carman, J. P., Lu, D., Ballew, M., Low, J., Verner, M., & Rosenthal, S. A. (2025). Americans' support for climate justice. *Environmental Science & Policy, 163*, 103976. DOI: 10.1016/j.envsci.2024.103976

Carson, R. T. (2010). The Environmental Kuznets Curve: Seeking Empirical Regularity and Theoretical Structure. *Review of Environmental Economics and Policy, 4*(1), 3–23.

Cary, M., & Bekun, F. (2021). Democracy and deforestation: The role of spillover effects. *Forest Policy and Economics, 125*, 102398.

Çetin, M. Ş., Parlak, B., & Şenol, S. (2024). İklim krizi ve göçe ilişkin kavramsal değerlendirme. *Kent Akademisi Dergisi, 17*(1), 217–230.

Cetin, M., Ozturk, I., Sumerli Sarigul, S., Murshed, M., & Kilavuz, E. (2025). Nexus between technological innovation and environmental pollution in selected OECD countries. *Natural Resources Forum, 49*(1), 841–862. DOI: 10.1111/1477-8947.12458

Chancel, L., Piketty, T., Saez, E., & Zucman, G. (2022). *World Inequality Report 2022*. World Inequality Lab. Retrieved April 7, 2025, from https://wir2022.wid.world

Chancel, L. (2022). Global carbon inequality over 1990–2019. *Nature Sustainability, 5*, 931–938. DOI: 10.1038/s41893-022-00955-z

Chang, C., DeVaney, S. A., & Chiremba, S. T. (2004). Determinants of subjective and objective risk tolerance. *Journal of Personal Finance, 3*, 53–67.

Chase-Dunn, C., & Hall, T. D. (1997). *Rise and demise: Comparing world-systems.* Westview Press.

Chaulk, B., Johnson, P. J., & Bulcroft, R. (2003). Effects of marriage and children on financial risk tolerance: A synthesis of family development and prospect theory. *Journal of Family and Economic Issues, 24*, 257–279. DOI: 10.1023/A:1025495221519

Chen, J., Wang, P., Cui, L., Huang, S., & Song, M. (2018). Decomposition and decoupling analysis of CO2 emissions in OECD. *Applied Energy, 231*(1 December), 937-950. doi:DOI: 10.1016/j.apenergy.2018.09.179

Chen, T., & Zhou, S. (2024). The impact of digital economy on the upgrading of manufacturing structure. *PLoS ONE, 19*(7 July), 107503. https://doi.org/DOI: 10.1371/journal.pone.0307184

Chen, L., Li, K., Chen, S., Wang, X., & Tang, L. (2021). Industrial activity, energy structure, and environmental pollution in China. *Energy Economics*, *104*, 105633. DOI: 10.1016/j.eneco.2021.105633

Chiang, T. F., & Xiao, J. J. (2017). Household characteristics and the change of financial risk tolerance during the financial crisis in the United States. *International Journal of Consumer Studies*, *41*(5), 484–493. DOI: 10.1111/ijcs.12356

Chin, G. T. (2014). The BRICS-led development bank: Purpose and politics beyond the G20. *Global Policy*, *5*(3), 366–373.

Chishti, M. Z., & Sinha, A. (2022). Do the shocks in technological and financial innovation influence the environmental quality? Evidence from BRICS economies. *Technology in Society*, *68*. Advance online publication. DOI: 10.1016/j.techsoc.2021.101828

Christiansen, C., Joensen, J. S., & Rangvid, J. (2006). Gender marriage the decision to invest in stocks bonds: Do single women invest more in less risky assets? *(D-CAF Working Paper No. 18)*, School of Economics and Management, University of Aarhus, Denmark.

Çıtak, E., & Pala, P. B. K. (2016). Yenilenebilir enerjinin enerji güvenliğine etkisi. *Süleyman Demirel Üniversitesi Sosyal Bilimler Enstitüsü Dergisi*, (25), 79–102.

Clark, N., & Liu, Z. Z. (2024, October 31). *Why expanded BRICS is backing a Russia-initiated grain exchange*. Council on Foreign Relations. https://www.cfr.org/blog/why-expanded-brics-backing-russia-initiated-grain-exchange

Çoban, O., & Şahbaz Kılınç, N. (2016). Enerji kullanımının çevresel etkilerinin incelenmesi. *Marmara Coğrafya Dergisi*, (33), 589–606.

Conte, A. (2006). The evolution of the Literature on technological change over time: A survey. In *Papers on Entrepreneurship*. Growth and Public Policy.

Copeland, B. R., & Taylor, M. S. (2003). *Trade and the Environment*. Princeton University Press.

Coutinho, E. M. O., & Au-Yong-Oliveira, M. (2024). Innovation's performance: A transnational analysis based on the Global Innovation Index. *Administrative Sciences, 14*(2). Advance online publication. DOI: 10.3390/admsci14020032

Cox, R. W. (1987). *Production, power, and world order: Social forces in the making of history*. Columbia University Press.

Crespo, N. F., & Crespo, C. F. (2016). Global innovation index: Moving beyond the absolute value of ranking with a fuzzy-set analysis. *Journal of Business Research, 69*(11), 5265–5271. DOI: 10.1016/j.jbusres.2016.04.123

Cristian, P. (2012). Risk tolerance analysis: Romanian case before and during financial turmoil, Romania. *Economia e Sociologia, 5*(2a), 11–23.

Cropper, M., & Griffiths, C. (1994). The Interaction of Population Growth and Environmental Quality. *The American Economic Review, 84*(2), 250–254.

Çukurçayır, M. A., & Sağır, H. (2008). Enerji Sorunu, Çevre ve Alternatif Enerji Kaynakları. *Selçuk Üniversitesi Sosyal Bilimler Dergisi, 20*, 257–278.

Dal, L. (2023). *The factors affecting financial risk tolerance of investors in Turkey according to A/B personality traits in times of Covid-19 pandemic*, [Doctoral dissertation, Eskisehir Osmangazi University]. National Thesis Center of the Council of Higher Education database. Data Analysis Platform (Veri Analiz Platformu-VAP) at https://www.vap.org.tr

Damette, O., & Delacote, P. (2012). On the economic factors of deforestation: What can we learn from quantile analysis? *Economic Modelling, 29*(6), 2427–2434. DOI: 10.1016/j.econmod.2012.06.015

Davarcıoğlu, B. (2018). Küresel iklim değişikliği ve uyum çalışmaları: Türkiye açısından değerlendirilmesi. [MBD]. *Mesleki Bilimler Dergisi, 7*(2), 376–392.

Dawson, C., & Henley, A. (2015). Gender, risk, and venture creation intentions. *Journal of Small Business Management, 53*(2), 501–515. DOI: 10.1111/jsbm.12080

de Ridder, K., Schultz, F. C., & Pies, I. (2023). Procedural climate justice: Conceptualizing a polycentric solution to a global problem. *Ecological Economics, 214*, 107998. DOI: 10.1016/j.ecolecon.2023.107998

Deger, M. N. (2019). *Factors affecting individual pension system participants' financial risk tolerance: An application on Mersin University staff,* [Masters Degree dissertatiton, Mersin University]. National Thesis Center of the Council of Higher Education database.

Degye, G., Abule, M., & Lamessa, T. (2024, August). *Policy Working Paper No. 25/2024*. Ethiopian Economics Association.

Demirbaş, M., & Aydın, R. (2020). 21. Yüzyılın en büyük tehdidi: Küresel iklim değişikliği. *Ecological Life Sciences*, *15*(4), 163–179.

Dinçbaş, T. (2017). *Türkiye'de iklim değişikliği bağlamında temiz teknoloji edinimi: metalik olmayan mineral ürünler sektöründe bir uygulama* [Doktora Tezi]. Ankara Üniversitesi.

Dışkaya, S. K. (2017). Türkiye'nin enerji güvenliğinde yenilenebilir enerji etkisinin politik ekonomi perspektifi. *Marmara Üniversitesi Siyasal Bilimler Dergisi*, *5*(2), 129–150.

Dohmen, T., Falk, A., Huffman, D., Sunde, U., Schupp, J., & Wagner, G. G. (2011). Individual risk attitudes: Measurement, determinants, and behavioral consequences. *Journal of the European Economic Association*, *9*(3), 522–550. DOI: 10.1111/j.1542-4774.2011.01015.x

Dorman, D. R., & Ciplet, D. (2022). Sustainable energy for all? Assessing global distributive justice in the green climate fund's energy finance. *Global Environmental Politics*, *22*(1), 94–116. DOI: 10.1162/glep_a_00621

Dos Santos, T. (1970). The structure of dependence. *The American Economic Review*, *60*(2), 231–236.

Du, K. (2017). Econometric Convergence Test and Club Clustering Using Stata. *The Stata Journal*, *17*(4), 882–900. DOI: 10.1177/1536867X1801700407

Dumitrescu, E., & Hurlin, C. (2012). TEsting for Granger non-causality in heterogeneous panels. *Economic Modelling*, *29*, 1450–1460.

Duru, B. (2001). Viyana'dan kyoto'ya iklim değişikliği serüveni. *Mülkiye Dergisi*, *25*(230), 301–333.

Dutta, S., Lanvin, B., León, L. R., & Wunsch-Vincent, S. (2024). Global innovation index 2024 unlocking the promise of social entrepreneurship. In *WIPO* (Vol. 15, Issue 1).

Dutta, S., Lavin, B., & Wunsch-Vincet, S. (2017). The global innovation index 2017, ınnovatıon feeding the world. In *Cornell University* (Vol. 3). INSEAD, and the World Intellectual Property Organization.

Ediger, V. Ş. (2009). Türkiye'nin Sürdürülebilir Enerji Gelişimi. TÜBA. *Günce*, *39*, 18–25.

Eichengreen, B., Hale, G., & Mody, A. (2001). Flight to quality: investor risk tolerance and the spread of emerging market crises. In *International financial contagion* (pp. 129–155). Springer US., DOI: 10.1007/978-1-4757-3314-3_6

Embrey, L. L., & Fox, J. J. (1997). Gender differences in the investment decision-making process. *Financial Counseling and Planning*, *8*(2), 33–40.

Energy Capital & Power. (2025, January 1). *Top 5 solar projects to watch in Algeria.* https://energycapitalpower.com/top-5-solar-projects-to-watch-in-algeria/

Enke, B. (2024). Moral boundaries. *Annual Review of Economics*, *16*, 133–157. DOI: 10.1146/annurev-economics-091223-093730

Eregha, P. B., Nathaniel, S. P., & Vo, X. V. (2022). Economic growth, environmental regulations, energy use, and ecological footprint linkage in the Next-11 countries: Implications for environmental sustainability. *Energy & Environment*, *34*(5), 1327–1347. DOI: 10.1177/0958305X221084293

Escobar, A. (2011). *Encountering development: The making and unmaking of the Third World* (2nd ed.). Princeton University Press.

Esmaeili, A., & Nasrnia, F. (2014). Deforestation and the Environmental Kuznets Curve in Iran. *Small-scale Forestry*, *13*, 397–406.

Estrada, F., Lupi, V., Botzen, W. J. W., & Tol, R. S. J. (2025). Urban and non-urban contributions to the social cost of carbon. *Nature Communications*, *16*, 4193. DOI: 10.1038/s41467-025-59466-y

Eti, S., Yüksel, S., Dinçer, H., Kalkavan, H., Hacioglu, U., Mikhaylov, A., & Pinter, G. (2024). Assessment of technical and financial challenges for renewable energy project alternatives. *Cleaner Engineering and Technology*, *18*, 100719.

Fabre, A., Douenne, T., & Mattauch, L. (2025). Majority support for global redistributive and climate policies. *Nature Human Behaviour*. Advance online publication. DOI: 10.1038/s41562-025-02175-9

Faff, R. (2008). On the linkage between financial risk tolerance and risk aversion. *Journal of Financial Research*, *31*(1), 1–23. DOI: 10.1111/j.1475-6803.2008.00229.x

Faff, R., Hallahan, T., & McKenzie, M. (2009). Nonlinear linkages between financial risk tolerance and demographic characteristics. *Applied Economics Letters*, *16*(13), 1329–1332. DOI: 10.1080/13504850701381123

Falk, M., & Hagsten, E. (2021). Innovation intensity and skills in firms across five European countries. *Eurasian Business Review*, *11*(3), 371–394. DOI: 10.1007/s40821-021-00188-8

Fan, J. X., & Xiao, J. J. (2006). Cross-cultural differences in risk tolerance: A comparison between Chinese and Americans. *Journal of Personal Finance*, *5*(3), 54–75.

Fan, Y., Orhun, A. Y., & Turjeman, D. (2020). *Heterogeneous actions, beliefs, constraints and risk tolerance during the COVID-19 pandemic (No. w27211)*. National Bureau of Economic Research., DOI: 10.3386/w27211

FAOSTAT. (2025). Food and Agricultre Organization of the United Nations: https://www.fao.org/faostat/en/#data/QI retrieved from.

Farooq, U., Bhanja, N., Rather, S., & Dar, A. (2024). From pollution to prosperity: Using inverted N-shaped environmental Kuznets curve to predict India's environmental improvement milestones. *Journal of Cleaner Production*, *434*, 140175. DOI: 10.1016/j.jclepro.2023.140175

Farrell, J. (2014). Demographic and socioeconomic factors of investors. In *Investor Behavior: The Psychology of Financial Planning and Investing*, 117-134, DOI: DOI: 10.1002/9781118813454.ch7

Fearnside, P. M. (2016). Environmental and social impacts of hydroelectric dams in Brazilian Amazonia: Implications for the aluminum industry. *World Development*, *77*, 48–65. DOI: 10.1016/j.worlddev.2015.08.015

Fehr-Duda, H., De Gennaro, M., & Schubert, R. (2006). Gender, financial risk, and probability weights. *Theory and Decision*, *60*, 283–313. DOI: 10.1007/s11238-005-4590-0

Fernandes, M. (2024, August 6). *BRICS and the IMF debt traps: What can the Contingent Reserve Arrangement do for the Global South?* Valdai Discussion Club. https://valdaiclub.com/a/highlights/brics-and-the-imf-debt-traps/

Field, C. B., Campbell, J. E., & Lobell, D. B. (2008). Biomass energy: The scale of the potential resource. *Trends in Ecology & Evolution*, *23*(2), 65–72. PMID: 18215439

Financial Express. (2024, September 11). The impact of digital transformation on CSR: Trends, challenges, and future outlook. *Financial Express*. https://www.financialexpress.com/business/industry-the-impact-of-digital-transformation-on-csr-trends-challenges-and-future-outlook-3608335/

Follingstad, G. (2023). Tipping points for a seminal new era of climate resilience and climate justice. *Journal of Climate Resilience and Justice*, *1*, 3–7. DOI: 10.1162/crcj_e_00011

Fraser, N. (2010). *Scales of justice: Reimagining political space in a globalizing world*. Columbia University Press.

Furceri, D. (2005). b and r-convergence : A mathematical relation of causality. *Economics Letters*, *89*(89), 212–215. DOI: 10.1016/j.econlet.2005.05.026

Gallagher, K. P. (2018). Reforming global economic governance as if development mattered. *Development and Change*, *49*(6), 1605–1615.

Gbaf News. (2019, February 8). UN's sustainable development goals: The critical role of banks in creating a sustainable future. *Global Banking and Finance*. https://www.globalbankingandfinance.com/uns-sustainable-development-goals-the-critical-role-of-banks-in-creating-a-sustainable-future

Gibson, R. J., Michayluk, D., & Van de Venter, G. (2013). Financial risk tolerance: An analysis of unexplored factors. *Financial Services Review*, *22*(1), 23–50.

Gilliam, J., Chatterjee, S., & Grable, J. (2010). Measuring the perception of financial risk tolerance: A tale of two measures. *Financial Counseling and Planning*, *21*(2).

Global Forest Watch. (2025a) https://www.globalforestwatch.org/dashboards/country/TUR/?map=eyJjYW5Cb3VuZCI6dHJ1ZX0% D. retrieved from.

Global Forest Watch. (2025b) https://www.globalforestwatch.org/dashboards/country/USA/?map=eyJjYW5Cb3VuZCI6dHJ1ZX0%3D. retrieved from.

Global Forest Watch. (2025c). https://www.globalforestwatch.org/dashboards/country/DEU/?map=eyJjYW5Cb3VuZCI6dHJ1ZX0%3D. retrieved from.

Global Forest Watch. (2025d). https://www.globalforestwatch.org/dashboards/country/ARG/?map=eyJjYW5Cb3VuZCI6dHJ1ZX0%3D. retrieved from.

Global Forest Watch. (2025e). https://www.globalforestwatch.org/dashboards/country/AUS/?map=eyJjYW5Cb3VuZCI6dHJ1ZX0%3D. retrieved from.

Global Forest Watch. (2025f). https://www.globalforestwatch.org/dashboards/country/BRA/?map=eyJjYW5Cb3VuZCI6dHJ1ZX0%3D. retrieved from.

Global Forest Watch. (2025g). https://www.globalforestwatch.org/dashboards/country/CHN/?map=eyJjYW5Cb3VuZCI6dHJ1ZX0%3D. retrieved from.

Global Forest Watch. (2025h). https://www.globalforestwatch.org/dashboards/country/IDN/?map=eyJjYW5Cb3VuZCI6dHJ1ZX0%3D retrieved from.

Global Forest Watch. (2025i). https://www.globalforestwatch.org/dashboards/country/FRA/?map=eyJjYW5Cb3VuZCI6dHJ1ZX0%3D. retrieved from.

Global Forest Watch. (2025j). https://www.globalforestwatch.org/dashboards/country/ZAF/?map=eyJjYW5Cb3VuZCI6dHJ1ZX0%3D. retrieved from.

Global Forest Watch. (2025k). https://www.globalforestwatch.org/dashboards/country/KOR/?map=eyJjYW5Cb3VuZCI6dHJ1ZX0%3D. retrieved from.

Global Forest Watch. (2025l). https://www.globalforestwatch.org/dashboards/country/IND/?map=eyJjYW5Cb3VuZCI6dHJ1ZX0%3D. retrieved from.

Global Forest Watch. (2025m). https://www.globalforestwatch.org/dashboards/country/GBR/?map=eyJjYW5Cb3VuZCI6dHJ1ZX0%3D. retrieved from.

Global Forest Watch. (2025n). https://www.globalforestwatch.org/dashboards/country/ITA/?map=eyJjYW5Cb3VuZCI6dHJ1ZX0%3D. retrieved from.

Global Forest Watch. (2025o). https://www.globalforestwatch.org/dashboards/country/JPN/?map=eyJjYW5Cb3VuZCI6dHJ1ZX0%3D. retrieved from.

Global Forest Watch. (2025p). https://www.globalforestwatch.org/dashboards/country/CAN/?map=eyJjYW5Cb3VuZCI6dHJ1ZX0%3D. retrieved from.

Global Forest Watch. (2025r). https://www.globalforestwatch.org/dashboards/country/MEX/?map=eyJjYW5Cb3VuZCI6dHJ1ZX0%3D. retrieved from.

Global Forest Watch. (2025s). https://www.globalforestwatch.org/dashboards/country/RUS/?map=eyJjYW5Cb3VuZCI6dHJ1ZX0%3D. retrieved from.

Global Forest Watch. (2025t). Global Forest Watch: https://www.globalforestwatch.org/dashboards/country//?map=eyJjYW5Cb3VuZCI6dHJ1ZX0%3D retrieved from.

Gogodze, J. (2016). Mechanisms and functions within a national innovation system. *Journal of Technology Management & Innovation*, *11*(4), 12–21. DOI: 10.4067/S0718-27242016000400003

Gondaliya, V., & Dhinaiya, G. (2016). Assessing financial risk tolerance: Do demographic, socioeconomic and attitudinal factors work. *International Journal of Marketing & Financial Management*, *4*(5), 32–38.

Gorus, M. S., & Aslan, M. (2019). Impacts of economic indicators on environmental degradation: Evidence from MENA countries. *Renewable & Sustainable Energy Reviews*, *103*(April), 259–268.

Gosseries, A. (2023). *What is intergenerational justice?* Wiley.

Grabel, I. (2017). *When things don't fall apart: Global financial governance and developmental finance in an age of productive incoherence*. MIT Press.

Grable, J. E., & Lytton, R. H. (1999b). Assessing financial risk tolerance: Do demographic, socioeconomic, and attitudinal factors work? *Family Relations and Human Development/Family Economics and Resource Management Biennial*, 3(1), 80-88.

Grable, J. E. (2000). Financial risk tolerance and additional factors that affect risk taking in everyday money matters. *Journal of Business and Psychology, 14*, 625–630. DOI: 10.1023/A:1022994314982

Grable, J. E., & Joo, S. H. (1999). Factors related to risk tolerance: A further examination. *Consumer Interests Annual, 45*(1), 53–58.

Grable, J. E., & Lytton, R. H. (2001). Assessing the concurrent validity of the SCF risk tolerance question. *Financial Counseling and Planning, 12*(2), 43–53.

Grable, J. E., Lytton, R. H., & Kratzer, C. Y. (1998). Determinants of defined contribution plan employee participation: A403 (b) perspective. *Consumer Interests Annual, 44*, 109–114.

Grable, J., & Lytton, R. H. (1999a). Financial risk tolerance revisited: The development of a risk assessment instrument. *Financial Services Review, 8*(3), 163–181. DOI: 10.1016/S1057-0810(99)00041-4

Grable, J., Lytton, R. H., O'neill, B., Joo, S. H., & Klock, D. (2006). Risk tolerance, projection bias, vividness, and equity prices. *Journal of Investing, 15*(2), 68–74.

Grable, J., Lytton, R., & O'neill, B. (2004). Projection bias and financial risk tolerance. *Journal of Behavioral Finance, 5*(3), 142–147. DOI: 10.1207/s15427579jpfm0503_2

Gramsci, A. (1971). *Selections from the prison notebooks of Antonio Gramsci* (Hoare, Q., & Smith, G. N., Eds. & Trans.). International Publishers.

Grossman, G. M., & Krueger, A. B. (1991). *Environmental Impacts of a North American Free Trade Agreement (No. w3914)*. National Bureau of Economic Research.

Guang Wen, Z., Murshed, M., Siddik, A. B., Alam, M. S., Balsalobre-Lorente, D., & Mahmood, H. (2023). Achieving the objectives of the 2030 sustainable development goals agenda: Causalities between economic growth, environmental sustainability, financial development, and renewable energy consumption. *Sustainable Development, 31*(2), 680–697. DOI: 10.1002/sd.2411

Guenther, B., Galizzi, M. M., & Sanders, J. G. (2021). Heterogeneity in risk-taking during the COVID-19 pandemic: Evidence from the UK lockdown. *Frontiers in Psychology, 12*, 1–15. DOI: 10.3389/fpsyg.2021.643653 PMID: 33868115

Guillemette, M., & Finke, M. (2014). Do large swings in equity values change risk tolerance? *Journal of Financial Planning, 27*(6), 44–50.

Guiso, L., Jappelli, T., & Terlizzese, D. (1996). Income risk, borrowing constraints, and portfolio choice. *The American Economic Review, 86*(1), 158–172.

Güner, E. D., & Turan, E. S. (2017). Yenilenebilir enerji kaynaklarının küresel iklim değişikliği üzerine etkisi. *Doğal Afetler ve Çevre Dergisi*, *3*(1), 48–55.

Gupta, J., Bai, X., Liverman, D. M., Rockström, J., Qin, D., & Stewart-Koster, B. (2024a). A just world on a safe planet: A Lancet Planetary Health–Earth Commission report on Earth-system boundaries, translations, and transformations. *The Lancet Planetary Health Commission*, *8*, e813–e873. DOI: 10.1016/S2542-5196(24)00042-1

Gupta, J., Prodani, K., Bai, X., Gifford, L., Lenton, T. M., & Otto, I. (2024b). Earth system boundaries and Earth system justice: Sharing the ecospace. *Environmental Politics*, *33*(7), 1286–1305. DOI: 10.1080/09644016.2023.2234794

Gürdal Arslan, H., & Gürbüz, H. (2022). Current Validity of Environmental Kuznets Curve with Panel Data Methods. *Journal of Economics and Administrative Sciences*, *23*(4), 981–991. DOI: 10.37880/cumuiibf.1139068

Gürses, E. N., & Baysal, Y. B. (2024). The Role of Logistics in Partnership for the Goals: SDG 17. In *Effective Logistics for Sustainable Development Goals*. IGI Global., DOI: 10.4018/979-8-3693-7071-1.ch012

Gutter, M. S., Fox, J. J., & Montalto, C. P. (1999). Racial differences in investor decision making. *Financial Services Review*, *8*(3), 149–162. DOI: 10.1016/S1057-0810(99)00040-2

Hallahan, T. A., Faff, R. W., & McKenzie, M. D. (2004). An empirical investigation of personal financial risk tolerance. *Financial Services Review-Greenwich*, *13*(1), 57–78.

Hallahan, T., Faff, R., & McKenzie, M. (2003). An exploratory investigation of the relation between risk tolerance scores and demographic characteristics. *Journal of Multinational Financial Management*, *13*(4-5), 483–502. DOI: 10.1016/S1042-444X(03)00022-7

Hall, B. H., & Rosenberg, N. (Eds.). (2010). *Handbook of the Economics of Innovation* (Vol. 1). Elsevier., Available online https://www.sciencedirect.com/handbook/handbook-of-the-economics-of-innovation/vol/1/suppl/C

Hammami, S. (2021). The effect of intellectual property protection on innovation: Empirical analysis of developing countries panel. *African Journal of Science, Technology, Innovation and Development*, *13*(4), 397–405. DOI: 10.1080/20421338.2020.1824608

Hamurcu, Ç., & Hamurcu, H. D. Y. (2016). Financial risk tolerance and burnout relation: Information and communication technology (ICT) sector study. *Aksaray Üniversitesi İktisadi ve İdari Bilimler Fakültesi Dergisi*, *8*(2), 95–101.

Hanna, S. D., Gutter, M. S., & Fan, J. X. (2001). A measure of risk tolerance based on economic theory. *Financial Counseling and Planning*, *12*(2), 53–60.

Hariharan, G., Chapman, K. S., & Domian, D. L. (2000). Risk tolerance and asset allocation for investors nearing retirement. *Financial Services Review*, *9*(2), 159–170. DOI: 10.1016/S1057-0810(00)00063-9 PMID: 12500326

Hartog, J., Ferrer-i-Carbonell, A., & Jonker, N. (2002). Linking measured risk aversion to individual characteristics. *Kyklos*, *55*(1), 3–26. DOI: 10.1111/1467-6435.00175

Hawley, C. B., & Fujii, E. T. (1993). An empirical analysis of preferences for financial risk: Further evidence on the Friedman–Savage model. *Journal of Post Keynesian Economics*, *16*(2), 197–204. DOI: 10.1080/01603477.1993.11489978

Hayli, S. (2001). Rüzgâr enerjisinin önemi Dünya'da ve Türkiye'deki durumu. *Fırat Üniversitesi Sosyal Bilimler Dergisi*, *11*(1), 1–26.

Heenkenda, S. (2015). Determination of financial risk tolerance among different household sectors in Sri Lanka. *Asian Journal of Empirical Research*, *5*(11), 206–220.

He, F., Hu, L. J., & Chen, L. (2024). The effect of financial development on ındustrial green technology ınnovation efficiency: Experience analysis from 288 cities in China. *Sustainability (Switzerland)*, *16*(13). Advance online publication. DOI: 10.3390/su16135619

Heo, W., Grable, J. E., & Rabbani, A. G. (2021). A test of the association between the initial surge in COVID-19 cases and subsequent changes in financial risk tolerance. *Review of Behavioral Finance*, *13*(1), 3–19. DOI: 10.1108/RBF-06-2020-0121

Heo, W., Rabbani, A., & Grable, J. E. (2021a). An evaluation of the effect of the COVID-19 pandemic on the risk tolerance of financial decision makers. *Finance Research Letters*, *41*. Advance online publication. DOI: 10.1016/j.frl.2020.101842 PMID: 36568732

Hickel, J. (2020). Quantifying national responsibility for climate breakdown: An equality-based attribution approach for carbon dioxide emiss. ions in excess of the planetary boundary. *The Lancet. Planetary Health*, *4*(9), e399–e404.

Hieu, V. M., & Hai, N. T. (2023). The role of environmental, social, and governance responsibilities and economic development on achieving the SDGs: Evidence from BRICS countries. *Economic Research-Ekonomska Istrazivanja*, *36*(1), 1338–1360. DOI: 10.1080/1331677X.2022.2086598

Hochberg, M. (2020, October 20). *Algeria charts a path for renewable energy sector development*. Middle East Institute. https://www.mei.edu/publications/algeria-charts-path-renewable-energy-sector-development

Hochman, G., Ofir, M., & Ayal, S. (2024). Financial risk tolerance during a major negative life experience: The case of the COVID-19 Pandemic. DOI: DOI: 10.21203/rs.3.rs-4742565/v1

Hoffmann, A. O., Post, T., & Pennings, J. M. (2013). Individual investor perceptions and behavior during the financial crisis. *Journal of Banking & Finance*, *37*(1), 60–74. DOI: 10.1016/j.jbankfin.2012.08.007

Hofman, B., & Srinivas, P. S. (2024). New Development Bank's role in the global financial architecture. *Global Policy*, *15*(2), 451–457.

Hopewell, K. (2013). New protagonists in global economic governance: Brazilian agribusiness at the WTO. *New Political Economy*, *18*(4), 603–623.

Hopewell, K. (2017). The BRICS – Merely a fable? Emerging power alliances in global trade governance. *International Affairs*, *93*(6), 1377–1396.

Hopewell, K. (2019). US-China conflict in global trade governance: The new politics of agricultural subsidies at the WTO. *Review of International Political Economy*, *26*(2), 207–231.

Huarng, K. H., & Yu, T. H. K. (2022). Analysis of global ınnovation ındex by structural qualitative association. *Technological Forecasting and Social Change*, *182*(March), 121850. DOI: 10.1016/j.techfore.2022.121850

Humphrey, C. (2020). *From drawing board to reality: The first four years of operations at the Asian Infrastructure Investment Bank and New Development Bank* (Working Paper). G-24 and Boston University Global Development Policy Center. https://www.g24.org/wp-content/uploads/2020/04/G-24-BU-GDP-Center-Paper-on-AIIB-and-NDB.pdf

Hüner, E. G. (2016). *Effects of anger and anxiety traits on financial risk tolerance of novices and experts,* [Masters Degree dissertatiton, Middle East Technical University]. National Thesis Center of the Council of Higher Education database.

Hurrell, A. (2018). Beyond the BRICS: Power, pluralism, and the future of global order. *Ethics & International Affairs*, *32*(1), 89–101. DOI: 10.1017/S0892679418000126

Hussain, H., Jun, W., & Radulescu, M. (2024). Innovation performance in the digital divide context: Nexus of digital infrastructure, digital innovation, and E-knowledge. *Journal of the Knowledge Economy*, •••, 3772–3792. DOI: 10.1007/s13132-024-02058-w

Ignatov, A. A. (2021). Implementation of sdg 16: Russia's role and actions. *Vestnik RUDN. International Relations*, *21*(2), 372–387. DOI: 10.22363/2313-0660-2021-21-2-372-387

India, E. Y. (2025, January 10). India's transformative digital infrastructure, innovative policies, and enhanced financial literacy are unlocking new pathways to true financial inclusion. *EY*. https://www.ey.com/en_in/insights/financial-services/how-can-india-drive-financial-inclusion-through-technology-and-literacy

Intergovernmental Panel on Climate Change (IPCC). (2001). Climate Change 2001: Synthesis Report, https://www.ipcc.ch/site/assets/uploads/2018/05/SYR_TAR_full_report.pdf adresinden alındı. Erişim Tarihi:08.03.2025.

International Court of Justice. (2025). Obligations of states in respect of climate change. July 23, 2025. https://www.icj-cij.org/sites/default/files/case-related/187/187-20250723-sum-01-00-en.pdf

International Energy Agency (IEA). (2023). *Ethiopia – Countries & Regions*. https://www.iea.org/countries/ethiopia

International Renewable Energy Agency (IRENA). (2023). *Planning and prospects for renewable power: North Africa*. https://www.irena.org/-/media/Files/IRENA/Agency/Publication/2023/Jan/IRENA_Planning_Prospects_NAfrica_2023.pdf

International Renewable Energy Agency (IRENA). (2023, September 4). *IRENA and AUDA-NEPAD join forces to advance regional interconnections in Africa*. https://www.irena.org/News/pressreleases/2023/Sep/IRENA-and-AUDA-NEPAD-Join-Forces-to-Advance-Regional-Interconnections-in-Africa

International Renewable Energy Agency (IRENA). (2024a). *Decentralised solar PV: A gender perspective*. https://www.irena.org/-/media/Files/IRENA/Agency/Publication/2024/Oct/IRENA_Decentralised_solar_PV_Gender_perspective_2024.pdf

Iqbal, S., Bashir, M., Bureš, V., Zanker, M., Ullah, S., & Rizwan, A. (2025). Impact of knowledge sharing and innovation on performance of organization: Evidence from the pharmaceutical industry of Pakistan. *Cogent Business & Management*, *12*(1). Advance online publication. DOI: 10.1080/23311975.2025.2471536

Işık, C.. (2024). Renewable energy, climate policy uncertainty, industrial production, domestic exports/re-exports, and CO2 emissions in the USA: A SVAR approach. *Gondwana Research, 127*, 556–164.

Islam, H. (2025). Dynamic effects of uncertainty, risks, R&D, and innovation on global economic growth. *Innovation and Green Development*, *4*(2), 100225. DOI: 10.1016/j.igd.2025.100225

Islam, M. S. (2024). Rethinking climate justice: Insights from environmental sociology. *Climate (Basel)*, *12*, 203. DOI: 10.3390/cli12120203

Iwata, H., Okada, K., & Samreth, S. (2011). A note on the environmental Kuznets curve for CO2: A pooled mean group approach. *Applied Energy*, *88*(5), 1986–1996. DOI: 10.1016/j.apenergy.2010.11.005

Jafarizadeh, H., Yamini, E., Zolfaghari, S. M., Esmaeilion, F., Assad, M. E. H., & Soltani, M. (2024). Navigating challenges in large-scale renewable energy storage: Barriers, solutions, and innovations. *Energy Reports*, *12*, 2179–2192.

Jianakoplos, N. A., & Bernasek, A. (1998). Are women more risk averse? *Economic Inquiry*, *36*(4), 620–630. DOI: 10.1111/j.1465-7295.1998.tb01740.x

Jiang, J.-J., Ye, B., Zhou, N., & Zhang, X.-L. (2019). Decoupling analysis and environmental Kuznets curve modelling of provincial-level CO2 emissions and economic growth in China: A case study. *Journal of Cleaner Production, 212*(1 March), 1242-1255. doi:DOI: 10.1016/j.jclepro.2018.12.116

Jiang, T., He, X., Su, B., Havea, P. H., Wei, K., Kundzewicz, Z. W., & Liu, D. (2024). COP 28: Challenge of coping with climate crisis. *The Innovation*, *5*(1). PMID: 38239781

Johnson, M. (2024). Empowering Financial Inclusion: The crucial role of public sector banks in implementing Pradhan Mantri Jan-Dhan Yojana (PMJDY). *International Journal for Research in Applied Science and Engineering Technology*, *12*(4), 3681–3684. DOI: 10.22214/ijraset.2024.60726

Johnson, M., & Joy, V. S. (2024). Empowering financial inclusion: The crucial role of public sector banks in implementing Pradhan Mantri Jan-Dhan Yojana (PMJDY). *International Journal for Research in Applied Science and Engineering Technology*, *12*(4), 3681.

Jones, R., Reid, P., & Macmillan, A. (2024). An Indigenous climate justice policy analysis tool. *Climate Policy*, *24*(8), 1080–1095. DOI: 10.1080/14693062.2024.2362845

Joo, S. H., & Grable, J. E. (2004). An exploratory framework of the determinants of financial satisfaction. *Journal of Family and Economic Issues*, *25*, 25–50. DOI: 10.1023/B:JEEI.0000016722.37994.9f

Joseph, S., & Jeslina, R. (2019). DigitizationDigitization as a tool for CSR implementation in the Indian banking industry: A study on SBI. *International Journal of Research and Analytical Reviews, 6*(1). IJRAR19VP011.pdf

Joshi, P., & Beck, K. (2016). Environmental Kuznets curve for deforestation: evidence using GMM estimation for OECD and non-OECD regions. *iForest - Biogeosciences and Forestry, 10*(1), 196-203. doi:DOI: 10.3832/ifor2066-009

Kadıoğlu, M., & Sonu, B. H. (2007). Küresel Đklim Değişimi ve Türkiye. *Güncel Yayıncılık aş*, (110). https://eskisakarya.imo.org.tr/resimler/ekutuphane/pdf/3937.pdf

Kahler, M. (2013). Rising powers and global governance: Negotiating change in a resilient status quo. *International Affairs*, *89*(3), 711–729.

Kahneman, D., & Tversky, A. (1979). Prospect theory: An analysis of decision under risk. *Econometrica*, *47*, 263–291.

Kahraman, S., & Şenol, P. (2018). İklim Değişikliği: Küresel, Bölgesel ve Kentsel Etkileri. Akademia Sosyal Bilimler Dergisi353-370.

Kannadhasan, M., Aramvalarthan, S., Mitra, S. K., & Goyal, V. (2016). Relationship between biopsychosocial factors and financial risk tolerance: An empirical study. *Vikalpa*, *41*(2), 117–131. DOI: 10.1177/0256090916642685

Kaplan, Y. A. (2015). Overview of wind energy in the world and assessment of current wind energy policies in Turkey. *Renewable & Sustainable Energy Reviews*, *43*, 562–568.

Karahasan, B., & Pınar, M. (2022). The environmental Kuznets curve for Turkish provinces: A spatial panel data approach. *Environmental Science and Pollution Research International*, *29*, 25519–25531. DOI: 10.1007/s11356-021-17706-w PMID: 34843050

Kayan, A., & Küçük, A. (2022). Küresel iklim krizinin oluşmasında politik kararların etkisi. [DÜSBED]. *Dicle Üniversitesi Sosyal Bilimler Enstitüsü Dergisi*, *31*, 521–526.

Keleş, R., & Hamamcı, C. (1993). *Çevrebilim, İmge Kitabevi*. Baskı.

Kentikelenis, A. E. (2017). Structural adjustment and health: A conceptual framework and evidence on pathways. *Social Science & Medicine*, *187*, 296–305. DOI: 10.1016/j.socscimed.2017.02.021 PMID: 28238540

Kentikelenis, A. E., Stubbs, T. H., & King, L. P. (2016). IMF conditionality and development policy space, 1985–2014. *Review of International Political Economy, 23*(4), 543–582.

Khan, M. N., Jan, A. A., Asif, M., Lai, F.-W., Shad, M. K., & Shadab, S. (2023). Do domestic innovations promote trade openness? Empirical evidence from emerging economies. *Heliyon, 9*(12). Advance online publication. DOI: 10.1016/j.heliyon.2023.e22848 PMID: 38076083

Kijek, T., Kijek, A., & Matras-Bolibok, A. (2022). Club convergence in R&D expenditure across European regions. *Sustainability (Switzerland), 14*(2), 1–17. DOI: 10.3390/su14020832

Kılıç, C. (2009). Küresel iklim değişikliği çerçevesinde sürdürülebilir kalkınma çabaları ve Türkiye. *Cumhuriyet University Journal of Economics & Administrative Sciences/Cumhuriyet Üniversitesi İktisadi ve İdari Bilimler Dergisi, 10*(2).

Kiprizli, G. (2022). Through the Lenses of Morality and Responsibility: BRICS, Climate Change and Sustainable Development [Ahlak ve Sorumluluk Bakışıyla: BRICS, İklim Değişikliği ve Sürdürülebilir Kalkınma]. *Uluslararasi Iliskiler, 19*(75), 65–82. DOI: 10.33458/uidergisi.1164936

Kızmaz, Z. (2021). İklim değişikliğinin kırsal alandaki etkisi ve alternatif arayışlar: Sosyolojik bir yaklaşım. *Firat University Journal of Social Sciences, 31*(1), 431–453.

Koçak, H., & Bozyurt, O. (2024). Küresel iklim değişikliğine yönelik çözüm odaklı yaklaşımlar. *Journal of Social* [joshas]. *Humanıtıes And Admınıstratıve Scıences, 7*(47), 2468–2479.

Koç, E., & Kaya, K. (2015). Enerji kaynaklari–yenilenebilir enerji durumu. *Mühendis ve Makina, 56*(668), 36–47.

Kohút, M., Srol, J., & Vladimíra, C. (2022). How are you holding up? Personality, cognitive and social predictors of a perceived shift in subjective well-being during COVID-19 pandemic. *Personality and Individual Differences, 186*, 1–8. DOI: 10.1016/j.paid.2021.111349 PMID: 34690396

Koop, G., & Tole, L. (1999). Is there an evironmental Kuznets curve for deforestation? *Journal of Development Economics, 58*(1), 231–244.

Köseoğlu, P., & Erten, S. (2022). Paris Anlaşması'na Göre Çevre Eğitimi Nasıl Olmalıdır? *Dokuz Eylül Üniversitesi Buca Eğitim Fakültesi Dergisi*, (54), 1528–1544.

Koyuncu Çakmak, T. (2025). Green Industrial Policies and Sustainable Economy Approaches Ensuring Industrial Growth and Environmental Balance. In Meçik, O. (Ed.), *Macroeconomic Challenges to Structural Reform and Industrial Development* (pp. 447–462). IGI Global., DOI: 10.4018/979-8-3693-5508-4.ch017

Kraus, S., Jones, P., Kailer, N., Weinmann, A., Chaparro-Banegas, N., & Roig-Tierno, N. (2021). Digital Transformation: An overview of the current state of the art of research. *SAGE Open*, *11*(3). Advance online publication. DOI: 10.1177/21582440211047576

Krawczyk, F., & Braun, A. Ch. (2025). Models like heroes? Making Integrated Assessment Models (IAMs) ready for deep decarbonization and a socio-economic transformation. *Energy Research & Social Science*, *121*, 103959. DOI: 10.1016/j.erss.2025.103959

Kübilay, B. (2015). *Investor bias in terms of investment psychology, financial risk tolerance and financial personality: A field survey on individual investors,* [Doctoral dissertatiton, Muğla Sıtkı Koçman University]. National Thesis Center of the Council of Higher Education database.

Kukreti, M., Sehajpal, S., Tiwari, R., & Sood, K. (2024a). Driving global health and sustainable development goals with smart technology. In *Driving Global Health and Sustainable Development Goals With Smart Technology*. IGI Global., DOI: 10.4018/979-8-3373-0240-9

Kumar, M., & Gokhru, A. (2023). A comparison of CSR practices of selected Indian and foreign banks. *International Journal of Management. Public Policy Research*, *2*(1), 71.

Lal, S., Nguyen, T. X. T., Bawalle, A. A., Khan, M. S. R., & Kadoya, Y. (2024). Unraveling investor behavior: The role of hyperbolic discounting in panic selling behavior on the global COVID-19 financial crisis. *Behavioral Sciences (Basel, Switzerland)*, *14*(9), 795. DOI: 10.3390/bs14090795 PMID: 39336010

Lamarque, H., & Nugent, P. (2022). *Transport corridors in Africa: Synergy, slippage and sustainability*. Zed Books., DOI: 10.2307/j.ctv2x4kp3n

Lawrenson, J. (2020). *Modelling financial risk tolerance of female South African investors,* [Doctoral dissertation, North-West University]. Boloka Institutional Repository.

Lazzarone, B. G. (1996). The economic well-being of rural nevada elders, *Proceedings of the 1996 Conference of the Western Region Home Management Family Economics Educators*, 67-74.

Lee, B. T. F., & Sims, J. P. (2024). Legitimacy through diversity: China's leadership in the BRICS+ expansion for global balance. *Fudan Journal of the Humanities and Social Sciences*. Advance online publication. DOI: 10.1007/s40647-024-00411-6

Lee, H. K., & Hanna, S. (1991). Wealth and stock ownership, In *Proceedings of the Association for Financial Counseling and Planning Education*, 126-140.

Lettau, H., Lettau, K., & Molion, L. (1979). Amazonia's Hydrologic Cycle and the Role of Atmospheric Recycling in Assessing Deforestation Effects. s. 227-238. doi:DOI: 10.1175/1520-0493(1979)107<0227:AHCATR>2.0.CO;2

Leung, D. Y., & Yang, Y. (2012). Wind energy development and its environmental impact: A review. *Renewable & Sustainable Energy Reviews*, *16*(1), 1031–1039.

Levin, I. P., Hart, S. S., Weller, J. A., & Harshman, L. A. (2007). Stability of choices in a risky decision-making task: A 3-year longitudinal study with children and adults. *Journal of Behavioral Decision Making*, *20*(3), 241–252. DOI: 10.1002/bdm.552

Liao, S., & McDowell, D. (2015). Redback rising: China's bilateral swap agreements and renminbi internationalization. *International Studies Quarterly*, *59*(3), 401–422.

Li, T., Liu, Y., & Lv, A. (2024). Review of Research on the Present Situation of Development and Resource Potential of Wind and Solar Energy in China. *Energies*, *17*(16), 4158.

Liu, Z., & Papa, M. (2022). Can BRICS de-dollarize the global financial system? Elements in the Economics of Emerging Markets. Cambridge University Press. https://doi.org/DOI: 10.1017/9781009029544

Locatelli, B., Benra, F., Geneletti, D., Loft, L., Loos, J., & Schröter, B. (2025). Framing the relationship between justice and ecosystem services: A systematic review. *Ecosystem Services*, *74*, 101755. DOI: 10.1016/j.ecoser.2025.101755

Low, S., Brutschin, E., Baum, C. M., & Sovacool, B. K. (2025). Expert perspectives on incorporating justice considerations into integrated assessment modelling. *npj. Climate (Basel)*, *4*, 10. DOI: 10.1038/s44168-025-00218-5

Lucas, R. E. (1988). On the mechanics of economic development. *Journal of Monetary Economics*, *22*(1), 3–42. DOI: 10.1016/0304-3932(88)90168-7

Lukyanov, F., Bhowmick, S., de Carvalho, G., Kugiel, P., Kudo, Y., & Niu, H. (2024, November 7). *The BRICS Summit 2024: An expanding alternative*. Council of Councils. https://www.cfr.org/councilofcouncils/global-memos/brics-summit-2024-expanding-alternative

Madaleno, M., & Moutinho, V. (2018). Effects decomposition: Separation of carbon emissions decoupling and decoupling effort in aggregated EU-15. *Environment, Development and Sustainability*, *20*, 181–198. DOI: 10.1007/s10668-018-0238-4

Mahdi, I. B. S., Bouaziz, M., & Abbes, M. B. (2023). The moderating effect of fin-tech on the relationship between CSR and banks' financial stability: Baron and Kenny's approach analysis. *EuroMed Journal of Business*. Advance online publication. DOI: 10.1108/emjb-03-2023-0082

Maji, I. (2017). The link between trade openness and deforestation for environmental quality in Nigeria. *GeoJournal*, *82*, 131–138. DOI: 10.1007/s10708-015-9678-7

Malik, A., & Narayan Sah, A. (2024). Can stronger governance and institutional quality drive growth through inward foreign direct investments in BRICS nations? *Suid-Afrikaanse Tydskrif vir Ekonomiese en Bestuurswetenskappe*, *27*(1). Advance online publication. DOI: 10.4102/sajems.v27i1.5785

Mar'I, M., Seraj, M., & Tursoy, T. (2023). The Role of Fiscal Policy in G20 Countries in the Context of the Environmental Kuznets Curve Hypothesis. *Energies*, *15*, 2215. DOI: 10.3390/en16052215

Marinelli, N., Mazzoli, C., & Palmucci, F. (2017). Mind the gap: Inconsistencies between subjective and objective financial risk tolerance. *Journal of Behavioral Finance*, *18*(2), 219–230. DOI: 10.1080/15427560.2017.1308944

Mather, A., & Needle, C., & Fairbairn. (1999). Environmental Kuznets Curves and Forest Trends. *Geography (Sheffield, England)*, *84*(1), 55–65.

McBride, B., Hawkes, S., & Buse, K. (2019). Soft power and global health: The sustainable development goals (SDGs) era health agendas of the G7, G20 and BRICS. *BMC Public Health*, *19*(1). Advance online publication. DOI: 10.1186/s12889-019-7114-5 PMID: 31234831

McCauley, D., & Heffron, R. (2018). Just transition: Integrating climate, energy and environmental justice. *Energy Policy*, *119*, 1–7. DOI: 10.1016/j.enpol.2018.04.014

McManus, C., Baeta Neves, A. A., Finan, T. J., Pimentel, F., Pimentel, D., & Schleicher, R. T. (2024). The South-South Dimension in International Research Collaboration. *Anais da Academia Brasileira de Ciências*, *96*(3). Advance online publication. DOI: 10.1590/0001-3765202420230942 PMID: 39166652

Mercom India. (2025, March 24). *MENA weekly round-up: Algeria launches 3.2 GW solar projects*. https://mercomindia.com/mena-weekly-round-up-algeria-launches-3-2-gw-solar-projects

Milanovic, B. (2016). *Global inequality: A new approach for the age of globalization*. Harvard University Press., DOI: 10.2307/j.ctvjghwk4

Mineyama, T., & Tokuoka, K. (2024). Does the COVID-19 pandemic change individuals' risk preference? *Journal of Risk and Uncertainty*, *68*(2), 163–182. DOI: 10.1007/s11166-024-09427-5

Mishra, K. (2022). A comparative study on corporate social responsibility (CSR) practices in public & private sector banks of India. *International Research Journal of Modernization in Engineering, Technology and Science, 4*(8) fin_irjmets1660652664.pdf

Mittelman, J. H. (1996). Rethinking the "new regionalism" in the context of globalization. *Global Governance*, *2*(2), 189–213.

Molion, L. (1975). A Climatonomic Study of the Energy and Moisture Fluxes of the Amazonas Basin With Considerations of Deforestation Effects. *The University of Wisconsin - Madison ProQuest Dissertations & Theses*. https://www.proquest.com/openview/9457913a63ae525fc8641de0477982c7/1?cbl=18750&diss=y&pq-origsite=gscholar retrieved from.

Monfort, B. P. (2008). Convergence of EU regions measures and evolution. In *European Union Regional Policy*.

Morozkina, A., & Skryabina, V. (2021). BRICS and Partnerships for Sustainable Development: Prospects for Trade with Least Developed Countries. *International Organisations Research Journal*, *16*(1). Advance online publication. DOI: 10.17323/1996-7845-2021-01-04

Mthembu, P. (2019). South Africa and BRICS in a multipolar world: Towards a diffusion of power and ideas? *Africa Insight*, *48*(4), 39–55. https://www.ajol.info/index.php/ai/article/view/186468

Murakami, D., Shevchenko, P. V., Matsui, T., Arandjelović, A., & Myrvoll, T. A. (2025). Climate-economy projections under shared socioeconomic pathways and net-zero scenarios. *arXiv*. https://doi.org//arXiv.2504.11721DOI: 10.48550

Murat, G., & Şengül, B. (2024). Küresel İklim Değişikliğinin İşgücü Verimliliği ve İstihdam Üzerine Yansımaları: Bir Sosyal Politika Önlemi Olarak Yeşil İşler. *Mülkiye Dergisi*, *48*(3), 717–748.

Murshed, M., Rahman, M. A., & Alam, M. S.. (2021). The nexus between environmental regulations, economic growth, and environmental sustainability: Linking environmental patents to ecological footprint reduction in South Asia. *Environmental Science and Pollution Research International, 28*, 49967–49988. DOI: 10.1007/s11356-021-13381-z

Naqvi, A. (2021). Decoupling trends of emissions across EU regions and the role of environmental policies. *Journal of Cleaner Production, 323*(10 November), 129130. doi:DOI: 10.1016/j.jclepro.2021.129130

Narayan, P., Saboori, B., & Soleymani, A. (2016). Economic growth and carbon emissions. *Economic Modelling, 53*, 388–397. DOI: 10.1016/j.econmod.2015.10.027

Narlikar, A. (2010). New powers in the club: The challenges of global trade governance. *International Affairs, 86*(3), 717–728.

Nasir, M. H., & Zhang, S. (2024). Evaluating innovative factors of the global innovation index: A panel data approach. *Innovation and Green Development, 3*(1), 100096. DOI: 10.1016/j.igd.2023.100096

Necker, S., & Ziegelmeyer, M. (2016). Household risk taking after the financial crisis. *The Quarterly Review of Economics and Finance, 59*, 141–160. DOI: 10.1016/j.qref.2015.03.006

Neves, P. C., Afonso, O., Silva, D., & Sochirca, E. (2021). The link between intellectual property rights, innovation, and growth: A meta-analysis. *Economic Modelling, 97*(June 2019), 196–209. https://doi.org/DOI: 10.1016/j.econmod.2021.01.019

New Development Bank (NDB). (2022). *General strategy for 2022–2026*. https://www.ndb.int/wp-content/uploads/2022/07/NDB_StrategyDocument_eVersion_07.pdf

New Development Bank (NDB). (2023). *Annual report 2023: Investing in sustainable infrastructure*.

Nooribakhsh, M., Fernández-Diego, M., González-Ladrón-De-Guevara, F., & Mollamotalebi, M. (2024). Community detection in social networks using machine learning: A systematic mapping study. *Knowledge and Information Systems, 66*(12), 7205–7259. DOI: 10.1007/s10115-024-02201-8

O'Neill, J. (2001). *Building Better Global Economic BRICs*. Goldman Sachs Global Economics Paper No: 66.

Odei, S., Dunyo, S., & Anderson, H. (2025). Research and development, economic growth, CO2 emissions and environmental Kuznets curve. *Sustainable Futures : An Applied Journal of Technology, Environment and Society*, *9*, 100541. DOI: 10.1016/j.sftr.2025.100541

Ofori, E. K., & Appiah-Opoku, S. (2024). Sustainable Development Goals in BRICS and G7 countries: Increasing accomplishments through policy synergies in four dimensions. *Sustainable Development*, *32*(1), 287–306. DOI: 10.1002/sd.2653

Ogunbode, C. A., Doran, R., Ayanian, A. H., Park, J., Utsugi, A., & van den Broek, K. L. (2024). Climate justice beliefs related to climate action and policy support around the world. *Nature Climate Change*, *14*, 1144–1150. DOI: 10.1038/s41558-024-02168-y

Ogundari, K., Ademuwagun, A., & Ajao, O. (2017). Revisiting Environmental Kuznets Curve in Sub-Sahara Africa: Evidence from deforestation and all GHG emissions from agriculture. *International Journal of Social Economics*, *44*(2), 222–231. DOI: 10.1108/IJSE-02-2015-0034

Okeke-Uzodike, O. U. E. (2019). Sustainable women's entrepreneurship: A view from two BRICS nations. *Journal of International Women's Studies*, *20*(2), 340–358.

Olsen, R. A., & Cox, C. M. (2001). The influence of gender on the perception and response to investment risk: The case of professional investors. *The Journal of Psychology and Financial Markets*, *2*(1), 29–36. DOI: 10.1207/S15327760JPFM0201_3

Omanovic, A., & Zaimovic, A. (2024). The determinants of financial risk tolerance and portfolio allocation: Have the Covid-19 pandemic and the Ukraine war affected our risk tolerance? *Borsa Istanbul Review*, *24*(6), 1381–1392. DOI: 10.1016/j.bir.2024.11.001

Ongan, S., Işık, C., & Amin, A.. (2023). Are economic growth and environmental pollution a dilemma? *Environmental Science and Pollution Research International*, *30*, 49591–49604. DOI: 10.1007/s11356-023-25698-y

Orçun, Ç. (2015). *An investigation of individual investor's financial risk perception,* [Doctoral dissertatiton, Dokuz Eylül University]. National Thesis Center of the Council of Higher Education database.

Ostrom, E. (2009). A polycentric approach for coping with climate change. Available at *SSRN* 1934353.

Otto, F. (2024). The climate crisis is solvable, but human rights must trump profits. *Nature*, *630*, 551–553. DOI: 10.1038/d41586-024-01762-6

Otto, F. (2025). *Climate injustice: Why we need to fight global inequality to combat climate change*. Greystone.

Oturakci, M. (2023). Comprehensive analysis of the global innovation index: Statistical and strategic approach. *Technology Analysis and Strategic Management, 35*(6), 676–688. DOI: 10.1080/09537325.2021.1980209

Overbeek, H. (2016). Will the BRICS transform the global economic order? In Changzheng, D., & Hongyu, W. (Eds.), *The Belt and Road Initiative and international society* (pp. 89–95). University of International Business and Economics Press.

Owuor, S., Wamukota, C., Klagge, B., Greiner, C., & Nyandega, I. (2025). Unintended socio-economic transformations associated with large-scale renewable energy projects: the case of Menengai Geothermal Project in Kenya. *Review of Regional Research*. https://doi.org/DOI: 10.1007/s10037-025-00240-4

Oxfam International. (2023). *Survival of the richest: How we must tax the super-rich now to fight inequality*. Retrieved April 5, 2025, from https://www.oxfam.org/en/research/survival-richest

Özcan, E. S. (2013). Dünyada ve Türkiye'de Güneş Enerjisi. Tubitak Bilim ve Teknik Dergisi, 55-59.

Özokçu, S., & Özdemir, Ö. (2017). Economic growth, energy, and environmental Kuznets curve. *Renewable and Sustainable Energy, 72*, 639–647. DOI: 10.1016/j.rser.2017.01.059

Öztop, A. O., & Kuyu, E. (2020). Influence of socio-demographic characteristics, financial literacy and mood on financial risk tolerance. *Journal of Business Economics and Finance, 9*(3), 209–222.

Öztürk, K. (2002). Küresel iklim değişikliği ve Türkiye'ye olası etkileri. *Gazi Üniversitesi Gazi Eğitim Fakültesi Dergisi*, 22(1).

Öztürk, M., & Öztürk, A. (2019). BMİDÇS'den Paris Anlaşması'na: Birleşmiş Milletler'in iklim değişikliğiyle mücadele çabaları. *Ömer Halisdemir Üniversitesi İktisadi ve İdari Bilimler Fakültesi Dergisi,* 12(4), 527-541.

Panayotou, T. (1993). "Empirical tests and policy analysis of environmental degradation at different stages of economic development," ILO Working Papers 992927783402676, International Labour Organization.

Paris Agreement. (2015). https://unfccc.int/files/essential_background/convention/application/pdf/english_paris_agreement.pdf (Erişim Tarihi: 23.02.2025).

Parthiban, R., Aiswarya, S. S., & Dinesh Kumar, R. (2018). CSR practices: Public and private sector banks in India. *International Journal of Interdisciplinary Research and Innovations*, *6*(4), 566–573.

Pata, U. K. (2021). Linking renewable energy, globalization, agriculture, CO2 emissions and ecological footprint in BRIC countries: A sustainability perspective, *Renewable Energy*, Volume 173, 197-208, ISSN 0960-1481, DOI: <ALIGNMENT.qj></ALIGNMENT>10.1016/j.renene.2021.03.125

Paulsen, D. J., Platt, M. L., Huettel, S. A., & Brannon, E. M. (2012). From risk-seeking to risk-averse: The development of economic risk preference from childhood to adulthood. *Frontiers in Psychology*, *3*, 313. DOI: 10.3389/fpsyg.2012.00313 PMID: 22973247

Pegkas, P., Staikouras, C., & Tsamadias, C. (2019). Does research and development expenditure impact innovation? Evidence from the European Union countries. *Journal of Policy Modeling*, *41*(5), 1005–1025. DOI: 10.1016/j.jpolmod.2019.07.001

Pérez-Escolar, M., & Canet, F. (2022). Research on vulnerable people and digital inclusion: Toward a consolidated taxonomical framework. *Universal Access in the Information Society*, *22*(3), 1059–1072. DOI: 10.1007/s10209-022-00867-x PMID: 35125988

Pesaran, M. (2007). A Simple Panel Unit Root Test in The Presence of Cross-Section Dependence. *Journal of Applied Econometrics*, *22*, 265–312.

Pesaran, M., & Yamagata, T. (2008). Testing slope homogeneity in large panels. *Journal of Econometrics*, *142*, 50–93.

Phıllıps, P., & Sul, D. (2009). Economic Transition and Growth. *Journal of Applied Econometrics, 24*(22 April), 1153–1185. DOI: 10.1002/jae

Phillips, P., & Sul, D. (2007). Transition modeling and econometric convergence tests. *Econometrica*, *75*(6), 1771–1855.

Podile, V. (2024). Artificial intelligence and corporate social responsibility: Synergies, challenges, and future directions. *International Journal of Advanced Multidisciplinary Research and Studies*, *4*(6), 95–99. 10.126180467

Pollex, J. (2024). Climate justice and policy analysis: Still a reserved relationship. *npj. Climate Action*, *3*, 65. DOI: 10.1038/s44168-024-00146-w

Polomé, P., & Trotignon, J. (2016). Amazonian Deforestation, Environmental Kuznets Curve and Deforestation Policy: A Cointegration Approach. https://shs.hal.science/halshs-01274854/ retrieved from.

Potocan, V. (2021). Technology and corporate social responsibility. *Sustainability, 13*(15), 8658. DOI: 10.3390/su13158658

Press Information Bureau (PIB). (2024, December 1). *UPI: Revolutionizing digital payments in India.* https://pib.gov.in/PressReleseDetailm.aspx?PRID=2079544&lang=1&reg=3

Press Information Bureau (PIB). (2025, March 24). *Advancing cashless India: Incentives for UPI small merchant transactions.* https://pib.gov.in/PressReleasePage.aspx?PRID=2114335

Priyadarshana, D., Rao, T. R., & Rao, M. S. (2024). AI and blockchain technology for secure and transparent financial transactions. *International Journal of Science and Research Archive, 13*(1), 2013–2019. DOI: 10.30574/ijsra.2024.13.1.1845

Putranto, I. A. (2020). Acceptance technology factors of mobile banking usage based on UTAUT2 model. *Jurnal Riset Akuntansi dan Bisnis Airlangga, 5*(2), 920–937. http://dx.doi.org/DOI: 10.31093/jraba.v5i2.234

Pyles, M. K., Li, Y., Wu, S., & Dolvin, S. D. (2016). Cultural influences on risk tolerance and portfolio creation. *Journal of Behavioral and Experimental Finance, 9*, 43–55. DOI: 10.1016/j.jbef.2016.01.001

Rahman, M. J., Zhu, H., & Beiyi, S. (2023). Is COVID-19 a turning point? Evidence from CEOs' investment behavior and risk tolerance. *International Journal of Emerging Markets*. Advance online publication. DOI: 10.1108/IJOEM-02-2023-0264

Rahman, M. M., & Alam, K. (2022). Impact of industrialization and non-renewable energy on environmental pollution in Australia: Do renewable energy and financial development play a mitigating role? *Renewable Energy, 195*, 203–213.

Raihan, M. M., Subroto, S., Chowdhury, N., Koch, K., Ruttan, E., & Turin, T. C. (2024). *Dimensions and barriers for digital (in)equity and digital divide: a systematic integrative review*. Digital Transformation and Society., DOI: 10.1108/dts-04-2024-0054

Rai, K., Gupta, A., & Tyagi, A. (2021). Personality traits leads to investor's financial risk tolerance: A structural equation modelling approach. *Management and Labour Studies, 46*(4), 422–437. DOI: 10.1177/0258042X211018

Rao, C., & Yan, B. (2020). Study on the interactive influence between economic growth and environmental pollution. *Environmental Science and Pollution Research International, 27*, 39442–39465. DOI: 10.1007/s11356-020-10017-6

Rawls, J. (1999). *Theory of justice*. Harvard University Press.

Reddy, K. S., & Mahapatra, M. S. (2017). Risk tolerance, personal financial knowledge and demographic characteristics evidence from India. *Journal of Developing Areas*, *51*(3), 51–62. DOI: 10.1353/jda.2017.0060

Ren, Y., Li, Z., Wang, Y., & Zhang, T. (2020). Development and prospect of food security cooperation in the BRICS countries. *Sustainability*, *12*(5), 2125. DOI: 10.3390/su12052125

Reuters. (2024, August 31). BRICS New Development Bank authorizes Algeria to join. https://www.reuters.com/article/world/brics-new-development-bank-authorizes-algeria-to-join-idUSKBN3K006V/

Reuters. (2024a, October 24). *BRICS leaders tout joint finance, trade projects at Russian summit.* https://www.reuters.com/markets/commodities/russias-putin-outlines-brics-grain-exchange-proposal-2024-10-23/

Reuters. (2024b, June 13). *World Bank approves Nigeria's $2.25 billion loan request.* https://www.reuters.com/world/africa/world-bank-approves-nigerias-225-billion-loan-request-2024-06-13/

Reuters. (2025, May 6). *Nigeria approves $652 million China Exim Bank road finance package.* https://www.reuters.com/world/africa/nigeria-approves-652-million-china-exim-bank-road-finance-package-2025-05-06/

Reuters. (2025a, May 8). *IMF says Nigeria repays $3.4 billion COVID-19 funding.* https://www.reuters.com/world/africa/imf-says-nigeria-repays-34-billion-covid-19-funding-2025-05-08/

Reyhan, A. S., & Reyhan, H. (2016). Küresel ısınmanın nedenleri, sonuçları, çözümleri üzerine yeni değerlendirmeler. *Memleket Siyaset Yönetim*, *11*(26), 1–24.

Ricciardi, V., & Rice, D. (2014). Risk perception and risk tolerance. *Investor Behavior: The Psychology of Financial Planning and Investing*, 325-345, DOI: .DOI: 10.1002/9781118813454.ch18

Richardson, K., Steffen, W., Lucht, W., Bendtsen, J., Cornell, S. E., & Donges, J. F.. (2023). Earth beyond six of nine planetary boundaries. *Science Advances*, *9*(37), eadh2458. Advance online publication. DOI: 10.1126/sciadv.adh24

Riley, N. F., & Russon, M. G. (1995). Individual asset allocation and indicators of perceived client risk tolerance. *Journal of Financial and Strategic Decisions*, *8*(1), 65–70.

Riley, W., & Chow, K. V. (1992). Asset allocation and individual risk aversion. *Financial Analysts Journal*, *48*(6), 32–37. DOI: 10.2469/faj.v48.n6.32

Roberts, C., Armijo, L. E., & Katada, S. N. (2017). *The BRICS and collective financial statecraft*. Oxford University Press.

Rockström, J., Donges, J. F., Fetzer, I., Martin, M. A., Wang-Erlandsson, L., & Richardson, K. (2024b). Planetary Boundaries guide humanity's future on Earth. *Nature Reviews. Earth & Environment*, *5*, 773–788. DOI: 10.1038/s43017-024-00597-z

Rockström, J., Gupta, J., Qin, D., Lade, S. L., Abrams, J. F., & Andersen, L. S.. (2023). Safe and just Earth system boundaries. *Nature*, *619*, 102–111. DOI: 10.1038/s41586-023-06083-8

Rockström, J., Kotzé, L., Milutinović, S., Biermann, F., Brovkin, V., & Donges, J.. (2024a). The planetary commons: A new paradigm for safeguarding Earth-regulating systems in the Anthropocene. *Proceedings of the National Academy of Sciences of the United States of America*, *121*(5), e2301531121. DOI: 10.1073/pnas.2301531121

Rockström, J., Steffen, W., Noone, K., Persson, A., Stuart, I. I. I., Chapin, F., Lambin, E., & Lenton, T. M.. (2009). Planetary boundaries: Exploring the safe operating space for humanity. *Ecology and Society*, *14*(2), 32. https://www.ecologyandsociety.org/vol14/iss2/art32/

Romer, P. M. (1986). Increasing Returns and Long-Run Growth. *Journal of Political Economy*, *94*(5), 1002–1037.

Romer, P. M. (1990). Endogenous technological change. *Journal of Political Economy*, *98*(5), 71–102.

Routh, A. (2024, August). *The role of nonbanks and fintechs in boosting India's UPI person-to-merchant transactions*. Payments System Research Briefing, Federal Reserve Bank of Kansas City, 1 6.

Rout, S. K., Gupta, M., & Sahoo, M. (n.d.). The role of technological innovation and diffusion, energy consumption and financial development in affecting ecological footprint in BRICS: An empirical analysis. *Environmental Science and Pollution Research International*. Advance online publication. DOI: 10.1007/s11356-021-17734-6 PMID: 34841485

Rowthorn, V., Plum, A. J., & Zervos, J. (2016). Legal and regulatory barriers to reverse innovation. *Annals of Global Health*, *82*(6), 991–1000. DOI: 10.1016/j.aogh.2016.10.013

Ryack, K. (2011). The impact of family relationships and financial education on financial risk tolerance. *Financial Services Review*, *20*(3), 181–193.

Saatçi, M., & Dumrul, Y. (2011). Çevre Kirliliği Ve Ekonomik Büyüme İlişkisi: Çevresel Kuznets Eğrisinin Türk Ekonomisi İçin Yapısal Kırılmalı Eş-Bütünleşme Yöntemiyle Tahmini. *Erciyes Üniversitesi İktisadi ve İdari Bilimler Fakültesi Dergisi, 37*, 65–86.

Saba, C. S. (2025). Artificial intelligence (AI)-poverty-economic growth nexus in selected BRICS-Plus countries: Does the moderating role of governance matter? *AI & Society*. Advance online publication. DOI: 10.1007/s00146-025-02213-0

Saba, C. S., & Ngepah, N. (2024). The impact of artificial intelligence (AI) on employment and economic growth in BRICS: Does the moderating role of governance Matter? *Research in Globalization, 8*. Advance online publication. DOI: 10.1016/j.resglo.2024.100213

Sabir, S., & Gorus, M. S. (2019). The impact of globalization on ecological footprint: Empirical evidence from the South Asian countries. *Environmental Science and Pollution Research International, 26*, 33387–33398. DOI: 10.1007/s11356-019-06458-3

Sadorsky, P. (2014). The effect of urbanization on CO2 emissions in emerging economies. *Energy Economics, 41*(January), 147–153.

Sağır, H. (2025). Enerji Politikaları ve Paradigma Değişimi: İklim Değişikliği Bağlamında Dönüşüm. *Uluslararası Ekonomi ve Siyaset Bilimleri Akademik Araştırmalar Dergisi, 8*(20), 84–95.

Sahle, M., Lahoti, S. A., Lee, S. Y., Brundiers, K., van Riper, C. J., & Pohl, C.. (2025). Revisiting the sustainability science research agenda. *Sustainability Science, 20*, 1–19. DOI: 10.1007/s11625-024-01586-3

Sahoo, M., Bhujabal, P., Gupta, M., & Islam, M. K. (2024). Empowering BRICS economies: The crucial role of green finance, information and communication technology and innovation in sustainable development. *Sustainable Development, 32*(6), 7292–7308. DOI: 10.1002/sd.3083

Saidur, R., Rahim, N. A., Islam, M. R., & Solangi, K. H. (2011). Environmental impact of wind energy. *Renewable & Sustainable Energy Reviews, 15*(5), 2423–2430.

Sakai, P., Afionis, S., Favretto, N., Stringer, L. C., Ward, C., Sakai, M., Weirich Neto, P. H., Rocha, C. H., Alberti Gomes, J., de Souza, N. M., & Afzal, N. (2020). Understanding the implications of alternative bioenergy crops to support smallholder farmers in Brazil. *Sustainability, 12*(5), 2146. DOI: 10.3390/su12052146

Sakharov, A. (2021). BRICS' Contribution to the Global Transition to Sustainable Consumption and Production Patterns. *International Organisations Research Journal, 16*(1), 1–29. DOI: 10.17323/1996-7845-2021-01-01

Sakharov, A., & Dorokhina, K. (2023). BRICS Sustainable Development Index: The Results1 [Индекс устойчивого развития стран БРИКС: результаты1]. *International Organisations Research Journal, 18*(1). Advance online publication. DOI: 10.17323/1996-7845-2023-01-03

Saleh, H. M., & Hassan, A. I. (2024). The challenges of sustainable energy transition: A focus on renewable energy. *Applied Chemical Engineering, 7*(2), 2084.

Sameera, V. V. L. & S, L. T. D. (2024). Impact of Covid-19 on portfolio management of investors in Telangana. *Proceedings of the 4th Indian International Conference on Industrial Engineering and Operations Management,* DOI: DOI: 10.46254/IN04.20240118

Şanlı, F. B., Bayrakdar, S., & İncekara, B. (2017). Küresel iklim değişikliğinin etkileri ve bu etkileri önlemeye yönelik uluslararası girişimler. *Süleyman Demirel Üniversitesi İktisadi ve İdari Bilimler Fakültesi Dergisi, 22*(1), 201–212.

Santos, B. de S. (2014). *Epistemologies of the South: Justice against epistemicide* (1st ed.). Routledge.

Sarang, S., & Prabhakar, R. (2023). Capacity-Building for Successful Climate Justice Collaborations. *Journal of Climate Resilience and Justice, 1*, 93–106. DOI: 10.1162/crcj_a_00008

Saxena, S. (2016). A comparative study of corporate social responsibility (CSR) of private and public sector banks. *World Wide Journal of Multidisciplinary Research and Development, 2*(1), 21–23.

Schlosberg, D. (2013). Theorising environmental justice: The expanding sphere of a discourse. *Environmental Politics, 22*(1), 37–55. DOI: 10.1080/09644016.2013.755387

Schmid, N., & Lumsden, C. (2023). Sowing the seeds of change: Policy feedback and ratcheting up in South African energy policy. *Energy Policy, 178*, 113597. DOI: 10.1016/j.enpol.2023.113597

Schöngart, S., Nicholls, Z., Hoffmann, R., Pelz, S., & Schleussner, C.-F. (2025). High-income groups disproportionately contribute to climate extremes worldwide. *Nature Climate Change*. Advance online publication. DOI: 10.1038/s41558-025-02325-x

Schooley, D. K., & Worden, D. D. (2016). Perceived and realized risk tolerance: Changes during the 2008 financial crisis. *Financial Counseling and Planning, 27*(2), 265–276. DOI: 10.1891/1052-3073.27.2.265

Sehajpal, S., & Sidhu, N. K. (2024). Neuroscience, nursing, and financial innovation: A synergistic approach to optimized patient care and economic well-being. In *Neuromarketing's Role in Sustainable Finance*. IGI Global., DOI: 10.4018/979-8-3693-9117-4.ch008

Semenov, A. S., & Kuznetcov, V. S. (2015). Assessment of level of risk in decision-making in terms of career exploitation. *International Journal of Economics and Financial Issues*, *5*(3), 165–172.

Şen, Z. (2022). İklim değişikliği ve Türkiye. *Çevre Şehir ve İklim Dergisi,* 1(1), 1-19.

Sen, A. (1985). *Commodities and capabilities*. Oxford University Press.

Sen, A. (1995). *Inequality reexamined.* Oxford University Press.

Sen, A. (1999). *Development as freedom*. Knopf.

Sevim, C. (2011). Enerji Teknolojilerindeki Anlayış Model Değişimi ve Hızlı İklim Değişikliği. *Yaşar Üniversitesi E-Dergisi*, *6*(21), 3515–3522.

Shafik, N. (1994). Economic Development and Environmental Quality: An Econometric Analysis. *Oxford Economic Papers*, *46*, 757–773. DOI: 10.1093/oep/46. Supplement_1.757

Sharda, G., Swamy, N., & Singh, C. (2014). *Impact of foreign banks on the Indian economy* (Working Paper No. 451). Indian Institute of Management Bangalore
Shayan, N. F., Mohabbati-Kalejahi, N., Alavi, S., & Zahid, M. A. (2022). Sustainable Development Goals (SDGs) as a framework for Corporate Social Responsibility (CSR). *Sustainability*, *14*(3), 1222. DOI: 10.3390/su14031222

Sharma, R., Shahbaz, M., Kautish, P., & Vo, X. V. (2023). Diversified imports as catalysts for ecological footprint: Examining the BRICS experience. *Environment, Development and Sustainability*, *25*(4), 3153–3181. DOI: 10.1007/s10668-022-02177-x

Shaw, T. M. (2015). African agency? Africa, South Africa and the BRICS. *International Politics*, *52*(2), 255–268.

Shershneva, E. G., & Kondyukova, E. S. (2020). Green Banking as a Progressive Format of Financial Activity in Transition to Sustainable Economy. In S. D.B. (Ed.), *IOP Conference Series: Materials Science and Engineering* (Vol. 753, Issue 7). Institute of Physics Publishing. https://doi.org/DOI: 10.1088/1757-899X/753/7/072003

Shue, H. (2021). *The pivotal generation: Why we have a moral responsibility to slow climate change right now*. Princeton University Press.

Shusha, A. A. (2017). Does financial literacy moderate the relationship among demographic characteristics and financial risk tolerance? Evidence from Egypt, *Australasian Accounting. Business and Finance Journal*, *11*(3), 67–86. DOI: 10.14453/aabfj.v11i3.6

Siddeswara, N. (2020). Indian rural banking and finance: A study on progress and challenges. *International Journal of Applied Research*, *6*(3), 531–533.

Singha, R., & Yogesh, K. S. (2025a). Qualitative Instrumentation Field Tests and Expert Panel Reviews: A Focus on the Multidimensional Addiction Behaviour Scale (MABS) for Dissertation Research. In R. Throne (Ed.), *Qualitative Research Methods for Dissertation Research* (pp. 547-580). IGI Global Scientific Publishing. https://doi.org/DOI: 10.4018/979-8-3693-3069-2.ch020

Singha, R. (2024). Stress, Resilience, and Brain Performance. In Saluja, S., Kukreja, J., & Sharma, S. (Eds.), *Building Organizational Resilience With Neuroleadership* (pp. 14–29). IGI Global Scientific Publishing., DOI: 10.4018/979-8-3693-1785-3.ch002

Singha, R., & Kanna, S. Y. (2025). Neuroeconomic insights on addiction: Integrating the Multidimensional Addiction Behaviour Scale for treatment, prevention, and holistic wellbeing. In Reddy, K. (Ed.), *Behavioral economics and neuroeconomics of health and healthcare* (pp. 181–212). IGI Global., DOI: 10.4018/979-8-3693-6055-2.ch009

Singha, R., & Singha, S. (2023). Economic sustainability, mindfulness, and diversity in the age of artificial intelligence and machine learning. In *Machine Intelligence* (pp. 273–285). Taylor & Francis., https://www.taylorfrancis.com/chapters/edit/10.1201/9781003424550-15/economic-sustainability-mindfulness-diversity-age-artificial-intelligence-machine-learning-ranjit-singha-surjit-singha

Singha, R., & Singha, S. (2023b). The Role of Perception in Recruitment Processes. In Even, A., & Christiansen, B. (Eds.), *Enhancing Employee Engagement and Productivity in the Post-Pandemic Multigenerational Workforce* (pp. 275–296). IGI Global Scientific Publishing., DOI: 10.4018/978-1-6684-9172-0.ch014

Singha, R., & Singha, S. (2023c). Faith and culture in education: Fostering inclusive environments. In DeHart, J. (Ed.), *The Role of Faith and Religious Diversity in Educational Practices* (pp. 149–172). IGI Global., DOI: 10.4018/978-1-6684-9184-3.ch007

Singha, R., & Singha, S. (2024). Positive interventions at work: Enhancing employee wellbeing and organizational sustainability. In Baykal, E. (Ed.), *Fostering organizational sustainability with positive psychology* (pp. 151–179). IGI Global., DOI: 10.4018/979-8-3693-1524-8.ch007

Singha, R., & Singha, S. (2024a). Mental health treatment: Exploring the potential of augmented reality and virtual reality. In Hiran, K., Doshi, R., & Patel, M. (Eds.), *Applications of virtual and augmented reality for health and wellbeing* (pp. 91–110). IGI Global., DOI: 10.4018/979-8-3693-1123-3.ch006

Singha, R., & Singha, S. (2024b). Mindfulness-based interventions: Applications in Western and Indian psychology. In Sathiyaseelan, A., & Balasundaram, S. (Eds.), *Global applications of Indian psychology: Therapeutic and strategic models* (pp. 192–212). IGI Global., DOI: 10.4018/978-1-6684-9778-4.ch011

Singha, R., & Singha, S. (2024c). Educational innovation transforming higher education for workforce readiness. In Christiansen, B., & Even, A. (Eds.), *Advancing student employability through higher education* (pp. 37–55). IGI Global., DOI: 10.4018/979-8-3693-0517-1.ch003

Singha, S. (2024). Inclusive Responses to Diversity-Driven Populism. In Chacko Chennattuserry, J., Deshpande, M., & Hong, P. (Eds.), *Encyclopedia of New Populism and Responses in the 21st Century*. Springer., DOI: 10.1007/978-981-16-9859-0_446-1

Singha, S. (2024a). Unveiling Gender Dynamics in Digital Capitalism: Navigating the Path to Social Gender Equality. In Topçu, Ç. (Ed.), *Digital Capitalism in the New Media Era* (pp. 161–186). IGI Global Scientific Publishing., DOI: 10.4018/979-8-3693-1182-0.ch009

Singha, S. (2024b). Fostering a Culture of Sustainability Through Human Resources Practices. In Popescu, C., Martínez-Falcó, J., Marco-Lajara, B., Sánchez-García, E., & Millán-Tudela, L. (Eds.), *Building Sustainable Human Resources Management Practices for Businesses* (pp. 107–124). IGI Global Scientific Publishing., DOI: 10.4018/979-8-3693-1994-9.ch007

Singha, S. (2024d). Cultivating inclusive leadership: Navigating organizational culture in the digital era. In Darwish, D. (Ed.), *Effective technology for gender equity in business and organizations* (pp. 139–166). IGI Global., DOI: 10.4018/979-8-3693-3435-5.ch005

Singha, S. (2024e). Unveiling the synergy: Inclusive coaching practices in leadership. In Wefald, A. (Ed.), *Navigating the coaching and leadership landscape: Strategies and insights for success* (pp. 189–210). IGI Global., DOI: 10.4018/979-8-3693-5242-7.ch010

Singha, S., & Singha, R. (2023a). Understanding diversity: The power of differences. In Even, A., & Christiansen, B. (Eds.), *Enhancing employee engagement and productivity in the post-pandemic multigenerational workforce* (pp. 297–313). IGI Global., DOI: 10.4018/978-1-6684-9172-0.ch015

Singha, S., & Singha, R. (2024d). Cross-disciplinary collaborations and partnerships for sustainability education: Including community-based learning, industry partnerships, and international collaborations. In Goi, C. (Ed.), *Teaching and learning for a sustainable future: Innovative strategies and best practices* (pp. 17–37). IGI Global., DOI: 10.4018/978-1-6684-9859-0.ch002

Singha, S., Singha, R., & Ruben, V. M. (2023). Explorations of the links between multiculturalism and religious diversity. In DeHart, J. (Ed.), *The role of faith and religious diversity in educational practices* (pp. 120–148). IGI Global Scientific Publishing., DOI: 10.4018/978-1-6684-9184-3.ch006

Singha, S., & Sivarethinamohan, R. (2021). The role of women in the formation of organizational climates in various workspaces in Bengaluru, India. *Journal of International Women's Studies*, *22*(6), 13. https://vc.bridgew.edu/jiws/vol22/iss6/13

Singha, S., & Sivarethinamohan, R. (2022). Social inclusion, equality, leadership, and diversity to attain Sustainable Development Goal 5 in the Indian banking industry. *Journal of International Women's Studies*, *23*(5), 9. https://vc.bridgew.edu/jiws/vol23/iss5/9

Singha, S., & Sivarethinamohan, R. (2022a). Formation of positive organizational climate: Integration of Ubuntu diversity management in banks. *Journal of International Women's Studies*, *24*(4), 10. https://vc.bridgew.edu/jiws/vol24/iss4/10

Siri, R., Mondal, S. R., & Das, S. (2020). Hydropower: A renewable energy resource for sustainability in terms of climate change and environmental protection. *Alternative Energy Resources: The Way to a Sustainable Modern Society*, 93-113.

Sohag, K., Gainetdinova, A., & Mariev, O. (2023). Economic growth, institutional quality and deforestation: Evidence from Russia. *Forest Policy and Economics*, *150*, 102949.

Sohail, M. T., Ullah, S., & Majeed, M. T.. (2021). The shadow economy in South Asia: Dynamic effects on clean energy consumption and environmental pollution. *Environmental Science and Pollution Research International*, *28*, 29265–29275. DOI: 10.1007/s11356-021-12690-7

Solow, R. M. (1956). A Contribution to the theory of economic growth. *The Quarterly Journal of Economics*, *70*(1), 65–94. DOI: 10.5897/jeif2013.0518

Soni, N. (2024, December 2). *Domestic UPI frauds: Finance Ministry presented data in LokSabha*. CyberPeace Foundation. https://www.cyberpeace.org/resources/blogs/domestic-upi-frauds-finance-ministry-presented-data-in-loksabha

Soto, G. H., & Martinez-Cobas, X. (2024). Nuclear energy generation's impact on the CO2 emissions and ecological footprint among European Union countries. *Science of The Total Environment*, Volume 945, 173844, ISSN 0048-9697, DOI: <ALIGNMENT.qj></ALIGNMENT>10.1016/j.scitotenv.2024.173844

Statista. (2024, May 2). Official renewable energy capacity target in Algeria 2030, by energy source. https://www.statista.com/statistics/1282572/official-renewable-energy-capacity-target-in-algeria-by-energy-source/

Statista. (2025, March 21). *BRICS and G7 countries' share of the world's total gross domestic product (GDP) in purchasing power parity (PPP) from 2000 to 2024*. Statista Research Department. https://www.statista.com/statistics/1412425/gdp-ppp-share-world-gdp-g7-brics/

Statman, M. (1995). Behavioral finance versus standard finance, In *AIMR Conference Proceedings*, 7, 14-22, CFA Institute.

Steffen, W., Richardson, K., Rockström, J., Cornell, S. E., Fetzer, I., & Bennett, E. M.. (2015). Sustainability. Planetary boundaries: Guiding human development on a changing planet. *Science*, *347*(6223), 1259855. DOI: 10.1126/science.1259855

Stephen, M. D. (2012). Rising regional powers and international institutions: The foreign policy orientations of India, Brazil and South Africa. *Global Society*, *26*(3), 289–309.

Stern, N. (2007). The economics of climate change: the Stern review. cambridge University press.

Stern, D. I. (2004). The Rise and Fall of The Environmental Kuznets Curve. *World Development*, *32*(8), 1419–1439.

Stevens, J. (1996). Applied multivariate statistics for the social sciences, 3rd Edition. Mahwah, Lawrence Erlbaum, New Jersey.

Stiglitz, J. E. (2002). *Globalization and its discontents*. W. W. Norton & Company.

Stober, I., & Bucher, K. (2013). Geothermal energy. *Germany: Springer-Verlag Berlin Heidelberg*. doi, 10, 978-3.

Stuenkel, O. (2015). *The BRICS and the Future of Global Order*. Polity Press.

Suarez-Villa, L., & Hasnath, S. A. (1993). The effect of infrastructure on invention, İnnovation capacity and the dynamics of public construction investment. *Technological Forecasting and Social Change*, *44*(4), 333–358. DOI: 10.1016/0040-1625(93)90040-e

Sudolska, A., & Łapińska, J. (2020). Exploring determinants of innovation capability in manufacturing companies operating in Poland. *Sustainability (Switzerland)*, *12*(17), 1–20. DOI: 10.3390/su12177101

Sulaiman, E. K. (2012). An empirical analysis of financial risk tolerance and demographic features of individual investors, *2nd Annual International Conference on Accounting and Finance (AF 2012). Procedia Economics and Finance*, *2*, 109–115. DOI: 10.1016/S2212-5671(12)00070-6

Sulla, V., Zikhali, P., & Cuevas, P. F. (2022). *Inequality in Southern Africa: An assessment of the Southern African Customs Union*. World Bank Group. https://documents.worldbank.org/curated/en/099125303072236903

Sumaira, , Siddique, H. M. A. (2023). Industrialization, energy consumption, and environmental pollution: Evidence from South Asia. *Environmental Science and Pollution Research International*, *30*(2), 4094–4102. DOI: 10.1007/s11356-022-22317-0

Sung, J., & Hanna, S. D. (1996). Factors related to risk tolerance. *Financial Counseling and Planning*, *7*, 11–20.

Sunstein, C. R. (2025). *Climate justice: What rich nations owe the world—and the future*. The MIT Press., DOI: 10.7551/mitpress/15431.001.0001

Sutejo, B. S., Pranata, Y. K. N., & Mahadwartha, P. A. (2018). Demography factors, financial risk tolerance, and retail investors. *Advances in Social Science, Education and Humanities Research*, *186*, 80–83.

Swarajya Magazine. (2024, May 2). *India's income inequality eases in 2022–23, but wealth gap persists: Report*. https://swarajyamag.com/news-brief/indias-income-inequality-eases-in-2022-23-but-wealth-gap-persist-report

T.C. Enerji ve Tabii Kaynaklar Bakanlığı. (2025a). Kyoto Protokolü. https://enerji.gov.tr/evced-cevre-ve-iklim-kyoto-protokolu, Erişim Tarihi:16.04.2025.

T.C. Enerji ve Tabii Kaynaklar Bakanlığı. (2025b). Paris Anlaşması. https://enerji.gov.tr/evced-cevre-ve-iklim-paris-anlasmasi, Erişim Tarihi:16.04.2025.

Tabachnick, B. G., & Fidell, L. (2019). *Using multivariate statistics* (7th ed.). Pearson.

Taghvaee, V. M., Nodehi, M., & Saboori, B. (2022). Economic complexity and CO2 emissions in OECD countries: Sector-wise Environmental Kuznets Curve hypothesis. *Environmental Science and Pollution Research International, 29*, 80860–80870. DOI: 10.1007/s11356-022-21491-5

Takouleu, J. M. (2024, March 25). *Development of solar energy: A new turning point for Algeria.* Africa Energy Portal. https://africa-energy-portal.org/blogs/development-solar-energy-new-turning-point-algeria

Tanboğa, S. (2024). İklim Değişikliği ve Ekonomik Etkileri. Türkiye İhracatçılar Birliği (TİM).https://tim.org.tr/files/downloads/Mevzuat/Iklim_Degisikligi_ve_Ekonomik_Etkileri.pdf adresinden alındı. Erişim Tarihi: 08.03.2025.

Taşdöken, Ö., & Kahyaoğlu, H. (2022). Davranışsal makroekonomi çerçevesinde hane halkı borçluluk düzeyinin analizi. *Selçuk Üniversitesi Sosyal Bilimler Meslek Yüksekokulu Dergisi, 25*, 156–174. DOI: 10.29249/selcuksbmyd.1061507

Teevan, C., Medinilla, A., & Sergejeff, K. (2021). The Green Deal in EU foreign and development policy. ECDPM Briefing Note, 131.

Thakur, M. (2024). Cybersecurity threats and countermeasures in the digital age. *Journal of Applied Science and Education, 4*(1). Advance online publication. DOI: 10.54060/a2zjournals.jase.42

Thaler, R. (1985). Mental accounting and consumer choice. *Marketing Science, 4*(3), 199–214.

Thanki, H. (2015). Risk tolerance dependant on what? Demographics or personality type: Findings from an empirical research. *Journal of Marketing and Consumer Research, 6*, 48–56.

Thanki, H., & Baser, N. (2019). Interactive impact of demographic variables and personality type on risk tolerance. *Emerging Economy Studies, 5*(1), 42–54. DOI: 10.1177/2394901519825924

The Jerusalem Post. (2025, March 21). *Egypt signs agreement for wind power project in Gulf of Suez.* https://www.jpost.com/business-and-innovation/article-846992

Times of India. (2024, June 30). *Inequality declined between 2011–12 & 2022–23: Government data.* https://timesofindia.indiatimes.com/india/inequality-declined-between-2011-12-2022-23-government-data/articleshow/110826780.cms

Tingley, H. D. (2025). *The impact of economic shocks on financial risk tolerance using panel data analysis,* [Doctoral dissertation, Manchester Metropolitan University]. Manchester Metropolitan University's Research Repository (e-space).

Tomal, M. (2022). Testing for overall and cluster convergence of housing rents using robust methodology: Evidence from Polish provincial capitals. []. Springer Berlin Heidelberg. https://doi.org/10.1007/s00181-021-02080-w]. *Empirical Economics, 62*(4). Advance online publication.

Tooze, A. (2021). *Shutdown: How Covid shook the world's economy*. Viking.

Torras, M., & Boyce, J. K. (1998). Income, Inequality, and Pollution: A Reassessment of the Environmental Kuznets Curve. *Ecological Economics, 25*(2), 147–160.

Tsiantikoudis, S., Zafeiriou, E., Kyriakopoulos, G., & Arabatzis, G. (2019). Revising the Environmental Kuznets Curve for Deforestation: An Empirical Study for Bulgaria. *Sustainability, 11*(6), 4364. DOI: 10.3390/su11164364

Tsurumi, T., & Managi, S. (2010). Decomposition of The Environmental Kuznets Curve: Scale, Technique and Composition Effects. *Environmental Economics and Policy Studies, 11*(1-4), 19–36.

Tunio, F. H., Nabi, A. A., Memon, R. U. R., Fraz, T. R., & Haluza, D. (2025). Sustainability in High-Income Countries: Urbanization, Renewables, and Ecological Footprints. *Energies, 18*(7), 1599. DOI: 10.3390/en18071599

Türkeş, M. (2008). Küresel iklim değişikliği nedir? Temel kavramlar, nedenleri, gözlenen ve öngörülen değişiklikler. *İklim Değişikliği ve Çevre, 1*(1), 26-37.

Türkeş, M., & Kılıç, G. (2004). Avrupa birliği'nin iklim değişikliği politikaları ve önlemleri. *Çevre Bilim ve Teknoloji Teknik Dergisi,* 2, 35-52.

Türkeş, M. (2022). İklim diplomasisi ve iklim değişikliğinin ekonomi politiği. *Bilim ve Ütopya, 332*, 31–45.

Turnhout, E., Metze, T., Wyborn, C., Klenk, N., & Louder, E. (2020). The politics of co-production: Participation, power, and transformation. *Current Opinion in Environmental Sustainability, 42*, 15–21. DOI: 10.1016/j.cosust.2019.11.009

Ullah, M., Rashdi, U. S., & Shaikh, S. (2021). COVID-19 outbreak and risk tolerance of financial decision makers. *International Journal of Management, 12*(2), 433–440.

Ulucak, R., & Apergis, N. (2018). Does convergence really matter for the environment? An application based on club convergence and on the ecological footprint concept for the EU countries. *Environmental Science and Policy, 80*(June 2017), 21–27. DOI: 10.1016/j.envsci.2017.11.002

UN Climate Technology Centre & Network. (2025). About CTCN, 17.07.2025 tarihinde https://www.ctc-n.org/about-ctcn/partners-and-collaborators adresinden alınmıştır.

United Nations (UN). (1992). Unite Nations Framework Convention On Climate Change https://unfccc.int/resource/docs/convkp/conveng.pdf adresinden alındı. Erişim Tarihi: 08.03.2025.

United Nations Conference on Trade and Development (UNCTAD). (2024). *Economic Development in Africa Report 2024: Unlocking Africa's Trade Potential – Boosting Regional Markets and Reducing Risks.* https://unctad.org/publication/economic-development-africa-report-2024

United Nations Economic Commission for Africa (UNECA). (2024, December 5). *Unlocking Africa's trade potential with cutting-edge data tools.* https://www.uneca.org/stories/unlocking-africa%27s-trade-potential-with-cutting-edge-data-tools

Van de Venter, G. (2006). Financial planners' perceptions of risk tolerance. *2006 Financial Management Association's (FMA) Annual Conference*, 1-31, Salt Lake City, Utah, USA.

Van de Venter, G., Michayluk, D., & Davey, G. (2012). A longitudinal study of financial risk tolerance. *Journal of Economic Psychology*, *33*(4), 794–800. DOI: 10.1016/j.joep.2012.03.001

van Vuuren, D. P., Doelman, J. C., Schmidt Tagomori, I., Beusen, A. H. W., Cornell, S. E., & Röckstrom, J. (2025). Exploring pathways for world development within planetary boundaries. *Nature*, *641*, 910–916. DOI: 10.1038/s41586-025-08928-w

Vardy, M., Oppenheimer, M., Dubash, N. K., O'Reilly, J., & Jamieson, D. (2017). The Intergovernmental Panel on Climate Change: Challenges and opportunities. *Annual Review of Environment and Resources*, *42*, 55–75. DOI: 10.1146/annurev-environ-102016-061053

Varınca, K. B., & Gönüllü, M. T. (2006). Türkiye'de güneş enerjisi potansiyeli ve bu potansiyelin kullanım derecesi, yöntemi ve yaygınlığı üzerine bir araştırma. Ulusal güneş ve hidrojen enerjisi kongresi, 21, 23.

Venzke, I. (2025). Carr and the climate: Solidarity and sacrifice in international law. *London Review of International Law*, lraf004. https://doi.org/DOI: 10.1093/lril/lraf004

Veselica, R. (2019). The impact od digital ınnovation on natıonal competitiveness. In *The main directions in tax system'S reform in the Azerbaijan Republic* (p. 441). Issue March., https://www.researchgate.net/publication/341735109

Victor, D. G., Geels, F. W., & Sharpe, S. (2019). *Accelerating the low carbon transition.* The Case for Stronger, More Targeted and Coordinated International Action. Brookings Institution.

Vishwakarma, J. (2025, January 28). *UPI's share in India's digital payments jumps to 83%, RBI report says.* Indian Startup News. https://indianstartupnews.com/news/upi-share-in-indias-digital-payments-jumps-to-83-percent-rbi-report-says-8661582

Volk, A. A., Brazil, K. J., Franklin-Luther, P., Dane, A. V., & Vaillancourt, T. (2021). The influence of demographics and personality on COVID-19 coping in young adults. *Personality and Individual Differences, 168.* Advance online publication. DOI: 10.1016/j.paid.2020.110398 PMID: 32952250

Vukoszavlyev, S. (2019). The connenction between global innovation index and economic well-being indexes. *Applied Studies in Agribusiness and Commerce, 13*(3–4), 87–92. DOI: 10.19041/apstract/2019/3-4/11

Walker, S. E., Smith, E. A., Bennett, N., Bannister, E., Narayana, A., & Nuckols, T. (2024). Defining and conceptualizing equity and justice in climate adaptation. *Global Environmental Change, 87,* 102885. DOI: 10.1016/j.gloenvcha.2024.102885

Wallerstein, I. (2004). *World-systems analysis: An introduction.* Duke University Press.

Waluyo, E., & Terawaki, T. (2016). Environmental Kuznets Curve for Deforestation in Indonesia an ARDL Bounds Testing Approach. *Journal of Economic Cooperation an Development, 37*(3), 87–108.

Wang, H., & Hanna, S. (1997). Does risk tolerance decrease with age. *Financial Counseling and Planning, 8*(2), 27–31.

Wang, Q., Ge, Y., & Li, R. (2025). Does improving economic efficiency reduce ecological footprint? The role of financial development, renewable energy, and industrialization. *Energy & Environment, 36*(2), 729–755. DOI: 10.1177/0958305X231183914

Wang, S., He, Y., & Song, M. (2021). Global value chains, technological progress, and environmental pollution: Inequality towards developing countries. *Journal of Environmental Management, 277,* 110999. DOI: 10.1016/j.jenvman.2020.110999

Warsame, A., Mohamed, J., & Sarkodie, S. (2024). Natural disasters, deforestation, and emissions affect economic growth in Somalia. *Heliyon, 10,* 1–15. PMID: 38545204

Wasiuzzaman, S., & Edalat, S. (2016). Personality, risk tolerance and social network use: An exploratory study. *Managerial Finance, 42*(6), 536–552. DOI: 10.1108/MF-05-2015-0159

Watson, J., & McNaughton, M. (2007). Gender differences in risk aversion and expected retirement benefits. *Financial Analysts Journal, 63*(4), 52–62. DOI: 10.2469/faj.v63.n4.4749

Weber, M., Weber, E. U., & Nosić, A. (2013). Who takes risks when and why: Determinants of changes in investor risk taking. *Review of Finance, 17*(3), 847–883. DOI: 10.1093/rof/rfs024

Wei, J., Jiang, T., Ménager, P., Kim, D. G., & Dong, W. (2025). COP29: Progresses and challenges to global efforts on the climate crisis. *The Innovation*, *6*(1). PMID: 39872482

Weller, J. A., Levin, I. P., & Denburg, N. L. (2011). Trajectory of risky decision making for potential gains and losses from ages 5 to 85. *Journal of Behavioral Decision Making*, *24*(4), 331–344. DOI: 10.1002/bdm.690

Wen, Y., Haseeb, M., Safdar, N., Yasmin, F., Timsal, S., & Li, Z. (2022). Does Degree of Stringency Matter? Revisiting the Pollution Haven Hypothesis in BRICS Countries. *Frontiers in Environmental Science, 10*. Advance online publication. DOI: 10.3389/fenvs.2022.949007

World Bank Data. (2025a). World Bank Data: https://data.worldbank.org/indicator/NY.GDP.PCAP.CD retrieved from.

World Bank Data. (2025b). World Bank Data: https://data.worldbank.org/indicator/SP.POP.GROW retrieved from.

World Bank Data. (2025c). World Bank Data: https://data.worldbank.org/indicator/AG.LND.AGRI.ZS retrieved from.

World Bank Group. (2016). Digital Financial Inclusion. In the *World Bank*. https://www.worldbank.org/en/topic/financialinclusion/publication/digital-financial-inclusion

World Bank. (2025). Renewable energy consumption (% of total final energy consumption), 10.04.2025 tarihinde https://data.worldbank.org/indicator/EG.FEC.RNEW.ZS adresinden alınmıştır.

World Bank. (2025). *World Development Indicators*. Retrieved April 6, 2025, from https://databank.worldbank.org/source/world-development-indicators

World Bank. International Energy Agency (IEA), International Renewable Energy Agency (IRENA), United Nations Statistics Division (UNSD), & World Health Organization (WHO). (2024). *Tracking SDG 7: The energy progress report 2024* (English). World Bank Group. https://documents.worldbank.org/curated/en/099031225175211404

World Meteorology Organization. (2025). (WMO) Global Annual to Decadal Climate Update 2025-2029. https://wmo.int/sites/default/files/2025-05/WMO_GADCU_2025-2029_Final.pdf

Wu, L., Adebayo, T. S., Yue, X.-G., & Umut, A. (2023). The role of renewable energy consumption and financial development in environmental sustainability: Implications for the Nordic Countries. *International Journal of Sustainable Development and World Ecology, 30*(1), 21–36. DOI: 10.1080/13504509.2022.2115577

WWF. (2011). Yenilenebilir Enerji Geleceği ve Türkiye. WWF Raporu. http://awsassets.wwftr.panda.org/downloads/wwftr_yenilenebilirenerjigelecegive turkiye.pdf

Wylde, V., Prakash, E., Hewage, C., & Platts, J. (2023). Ethical challenges in the use of digital technologies: AI and big data. In *Advanced sciences and technologies for security applications* (pp. 33–58). https://doi.org/DOI: 10.1007/978-3-031-09691-4_3

Xiao, J. J., Alhabeeb, M. J., Hong, G. S., & Haynes, G. W. (2000). Risk tolerance of family business owners. *Consumer Interests Annual, 46*, 140–146.

Xin, G., Khan, H., & Ling, X. (2024). The impact of BRICS trade facilitation on China's import and export trade in agricultural products. *Frontiers in Sustainable Food Systems, 8*, 1397350. DOI: 10.3389/fsufs.2024.1397350

Yandle, B., Bhattarai, M., & Vijayaraghavan, M. (2004). Environmental Kuznets Curves: A Review of Findings, Methods and Policy Implications. *Research Studies (Pullman, Wash.), 2*, 1–16.

Yang, X. A. (2019). Theorizing the BRICS. In Xing, L. (Ed.), *The international political economy of the BRICS* (pp. 37–56). Routledge.

Yao, R., & Hanna, S. D. (2005). The effect of gender and marital status on financial risk tolerance. *Journal of Personal Finance, 4*(1), 66–85.

Yao, R., Hanna, S. D., & Lindamood, S. (2004). Changes in financial risk tolerance, 1983-2001. *Financial Services Review, 13*(4), 249–266.

Yao, Z., & Rabbani, A. G. (2021). Association between investment risk tolerance and portfolio risk: The role of confidence level. *Journal of Behavioral and Experimental Finance, 30*. Advance online publication. DOI: 10.1016/j.jbef.2021.100482

Yaşar, D. (2023). İklimler, Değişim Nedenleri ve Sonuçları M.E.Aydın, A.D.Şahin (Ed.) içinde, İklim Değişimi Çerçevesinde Su Kaynaklarının Mevcut Durumu ve Geleceği, *(s. 263-278) Türkiye Bilimler Akademisi.*

Yazıcıoğlu, Y., & Erdoğan, S. (2004). *SPSS uygulamalı bilimsel araştırma yöntemleri*. Detay Yayıncılık.

Ye, F. (2023). The New Development Bank and the structure of the multilateral development financial system. *Review of Development Economics, 27*(3), 1957–1972. DOI: 10.1111/rode.12995

Yıldırım, R., Ukelge, M., Sarac, E., & Oturakci, M. (2024). A novel approach for predicting global innovation index scores. *International Journal of Applied Management Science., 16*, 239–260. DOI: 10.1504/IJAMS.2024.140047

Yook, K. C., & Everett, R. (2003). Assessing risk tolerance: Questioning the questionnaire method. *Journal of Financial Planning, 16*(8), 48–55.

Yu, D., Wang, Z., & Nadeem, M. (2024). Assessing the predictive ability of information globalization under global value chains-environmental sustainability nexus in the BRICS economies: A nonparametric causality approach. *Natural Resources Forum*. https://doi.org/DOI: 10.1111/1477-8947.12500

Yüksel, I., & Kaygusuz, K. (2011). Renewable energy sources for clean and sustainable energy policies in Turkey. *Renewable & Sustainable Energy Reviews, 15*(8), 4132–4144.

Yurduseven, A., Şimşek, M., & Koca, G. (2024). *İklim Değişikliğinin Türkiye ve Avrupa Birliği Ülkeleri Açısından Değerlendirilmesi: CRITIC ve GIA Yöntemi. 10.* Uluslararası Ankara Bilimsel Araştırmalar Kongresi.

Yurttagüler, İ., & Kutlu, S. (2017). An Econometric Analysis of the Environmental Kuznets Curve: The Case of Turkey. *Alphanumeric Journal, 5*(1), 115–126.

Yu, T. H. K., Huarng, K. H., & Huang, D. H. (2021). Causal complexity analysis of the Global Innovation Index. *Journal of Business Research, 137*(August), 39–45. DOI: 10.1016/j.jbusres.2021.08.013

Zafeiriou, E., Kyriakopoulos, G., Andrea, V., & Arabatzis, G. (2023). Environmental Kuznets curve for deforestation in Eastern Europe: a panel cointegration analysis. *Environmental Kuznets curve for deforestation in Eastern Europe: a panel cointegration analysis, 85*, 9267-9287.

Zambrano-Monserrate, M., Carvajal-Lara, C., Urgilés-Sanchez, R., & Ruano, M. (2018). Deforestation as an indicator of environmental degradation: Analysis of five European countries. *Ecological Indicators, 90*, 1–8. DOI: 10.1016/j.ecolind.2018.02.049

Zecchini, S. (2020). Pitfalls in innovation policy making. *Journal of the International Council for Small Business, 1*(1), 36–41. DOI: 10.1080/26437015.2020.1714360

Zhang, R., Sun, K., Delgado, M. S., & Kumbhakar, S. C. (2012). Productivity in China's high technology industry: Regional heterogeneity and R & D. *Technological Forecasting and Social Change, 79*(1), 127–141. DOI: 10.1016/j.techfore.2011.08.005

Zhu, R., Xu, Q., Xiqiang, X., Sibt-e-Ali, M., Waqas, M., Ullah, I., & Anwar, A. (2024). Role of resources rent, research and development, and information and communication technologies on CO2 emissions in BRICS economies. *Resources Policy, 93*. Advance online publication. DOI: 10.1016/j.resourpol.2024.105072

Zimmermann, B., & Engelbrecht, S. (2024). Transforming work towards social-ecological sustainability: A capability perspective. *Transfer: European Review of Labour and Research*. Advance online publication. DOI: 10.1177/10242589241281014

About the Contributors

Oytun Meçik is a Professor at Eskişehir Osmangazi University, Department of Economics. Meçik completed his undergraduate education at Eskişehir Osmangazi University in 2008, his master's degree at Uşak University in 2010, and his doctorate in Economics at Anadolu University in 2014. He received the title of Associate Professor in Macroeconomics in 2017 and became a Professor in 2023. Meçik, who has conducted numerous studies in the fields of labor markets and social and economic networks, is currently researching social capital, education-job mismatches, the effects of digital transformation, and innovation economics. Meçik serves as editor and editorial board member in international journals and publishers. Meçik is a member of the Turkish Economic Association and the Regional Science Turkish National Committee.

***

Fatma Budun was born in Eskisehir. She graduated from Anadolu University's Public Administration department. She completed her master's degree in Economics at the Economics Department of the Social Sciences Institute at Eskisehir Osmangazi University and her PhD in the same department.

Lokman Dal is an independent researcher in Türkiye. His areas of work are Behavioral Finance, Business Administration, Leadership and Statistical Analysis. He has articles about financial risk tolerance, financial choices, servant leadership and ELECTRE method in field indexes and local book chapters.

Nuray Girginer works in the Numerical Methods of Department of Business Administration in Eskişehir Osmangazi University,. Her areas of work are numerical methods, quantitative decision making, statistical analysis, data analysis in social sciences, operations research, multi-criteria decision making techniques, etc.

Professor Girginer has numerous articles published in journals in SCI and field indexes, research projects and 4 scientific books .

Tuğba Koyuncu Çakmak, she received her bachelor's and master's degrees in economics. She completed her PhD in economics at Eskişehir Osmangazi University with a thesis consisting of three papers titled 'Three Essays on the Relationship between Unemployment, Employment and Environmental Pollution: Environmental Phillips Curve and Environmental Employment Curve Approaches'. Koyuncu Çakmak conducts econometric modelling research on sustainable economic growth, climate change, environmental pollution, employment and investment.

G. Mookambigai is a dedicated Ph.D. Scholar in the Department of Management Studies at Sathyabama Institute of Science and Technology (Deemed to be University), Chennai, India. Her broader areas of interest include CSR studies, organizational behavior, strategic management, and the role of CSR in fostering sustainable business practices. She is strongly committed to academic excellence and actively contributes to the scholarly community through research publications, conferences, and seminars. Ms. Mookambigai's work emphasizes interdisciplinary approaches, leveraging management principles to address key challenges in the banking and financial sectors.

R. Thamilselvan is a Professor in the Department of Management Studies at Sathyabama Institute of Science and Technology (Deemed to be University), Chennai, Tamil Nadu, India. With extensive academic and research experience, his area of specialization includes Accounting and Finance, with a strong focus on strategic financial management, corporate governance, and entrepreneurial finance. Dr. Thamilselvan has published widely in national and international journals, presented papers at reputed conferences, and actively guides research scholars. He is well-regarded for his industry-oriented teaching methods and dedication to nurturing future professionals in the field of management and finance.

Ayşenur Şakalak graduated from Selçuk University's economics department with a bachelor's, master's, and doctoral degree. Şakalak completed his master's thesis on "Charitable behaviours in the context of economic decisions and social preferences" and his doctoral thesis on "The relationship between economic growth and workers'income: The case of Turkey (1984-2017)". Şakalak worked as a research assistant at Tokat Gaziosmanpaşa University in 2019 and has been working as a lecturer at Selçuk University since 2020. Şakalak conducts research on environmental economics, behavioral economics, and institutional economics.

Mustafa Şeker successfully graduated from Bartın University with undergraduate and graduate degrees. He then successfully completed his PhD in Behavioral Economics at Bursa Uludag University. He worked as a project assistant during his PhD. He is currently working as an IOT specialist at the Besler Superfresh factory.

Öznur Taşdöken graduated from the Department of Economics, Faculty of Economics and Administrative Sciences at Dumlupınar University between 2007-2012. She completed her master's degree in economics at the Faculty of Economics, Department of Economics, Dokuz Eylül University, between 2013-2016, and successfully defended her doctoral dissertation in economics at the same university between 2017-2022, earning her Ph.D. Her research interests include economics, behavioural macroeconomics, data science, sustainable economics, and circular economy. She continues his academic studies. Since 2024, she has been working at the Antalya Chamber of Commerce and Industry in the Research and Trade Development Directorate. She has contributed to many national and international projects both in academic and business life. National projects are supported by TÜBİTAK and the Western Mediterranean Development Agency (BAKA). International projects are projects for the calls opened by the EU in different periods.

Hasan Umutlu graduated from Afyon Kocatepe University's Department of International Trade and Finance and completed his master's and doctoral programs in economics. He conducted a survey of economics academics in Turkey for his master's thesis titled "Economists between the state and the market: Opinions and attitudes of economists on the role of the state and the market" and his doctoral thesis titled "Transfer of economics education from theory to practice: The analysis of Turkiye". Umutlu currently continues his work as a research assistant at Düzce University. He continues his research in areas such as the environment, renewable energy, macroeconomics, and growth.

Index

A

B

C

D

E

F

G

I

K

M

P

R

S

T

W

www.ingramcontent.com/pod-product-compliance
Lightning Source LLC
LaVergne TN
LVHW060312031026
849161LV00035B/1446